PAROCHIALISM, COSMOPOLITANISM, AND THE FOUNDATIONS OF INTERNATIONAL LAW

This book examines the boundary between parochial and cosmopolitan justice. To what extent should international law recognize or support the political, historical, cultural, and economic differences among nations? Ten lawyers and philosophers from five continents consider whether certain states or persons deserve special treatment, exemptions, or heightened duties under international law. This volume draws the line between international law, national jurisdiction, and the private autonomy of persons.

M. N. S. Sellers is Regents Professor of the University System of Maryland and Director of the University of Baltimore Center for International and Comparative Law. He received his A.B. and J.D. degrees at Harvard University and was a Rhodes Scholar, Frank Knox Fellow, and T. H. Green Scholar at University and Wolfson Colleges, Oxford, where he completed his B.C.L. and doctorate. Professor Sellers has served as a visiting scholar at Georgetown University Law Center, the Lauterpacht Centre for International Law at Cambridge University, Erasmus University Rotterdam, the Hague Academy of International Law, and Bryn Mawr College. He is coeditor, with Elizabeth Andersen, of the Cambridge University Press book series ASIL Studies in International Legal Theory.

ASIL Studies in International Legal Theory

Series Editors

Elizabeth Andersen (ASIL)
Mortimer Sellers (University of Baltimore)

Editorial Board

Samantha Besson (Université de Fribourg)
Allen Buchanan (Duke University)
David Kennedy (Harvard University)
Jan Klabbers (University of Helsinki)
David Luban (Georgetown University)
Larry May (Vanderbilt University)
Mary Ellen O'Connell (University of Notre Dame)
Onuma Yasuaki (Meiji University)
Helen Stacy (Stanford University)
John Tasioulas (University College, London)
Fernando Tesón (Florida State University)

The purpose of the ASIL Studies in International Legal Theory is to clarify and improve the theoretical foundations of international law. Too often the progressive development and implementation of international law have foundered on confusion about first principles. This series will raise the level of public and scholarly discussion about the structure and purposes of the world legal order and how best to achieve global justice through law.

Volumes in the Series

International Criminal Law and Philosophy edited by **Larry May** and **Zachary Hoskins** (2010)
Customary International Law: A New Theory with Practical Applications by **Brian D. Lepard** (2010)
The New Global Law by **Rafael Domingo** (2010)
The Role of Ethics in International Law edited by **Donald Earl Childress III** (2011)
Global Justice and International Economic Law: Opportunities and Prospects edited by **Chios Carmody, Frank J. Garcia**, and **John Linarelli** (2011)
Parochialism, Cosmopolitanism, and the Foundations of International Law edited by **M. N. S. Sellers** (2012)

Parochialism, Cosmopolitanism, and the Foundations of International Law

M. N. S. SELLERS

University of Baltimore Center for International and Comparative Law

CAMBRIDGE
UNIVERSITY PRESS

CAMBRIDGE UNIVERSITY PRESS
Cambridge, New York, Melbourne, Madrid, Cape Town,
Singapore, São Paulo, Delhi, Tokyo, Mexico City

Cambridge University Press
32 Avenue of the Americas, New York, NY 10013-2473, USA

www.cambridge.org
Information on this title: www.cambridge.org/9780521518024

© Cambridge University Press 2012

First published 2012

Printed in the United States of America

A catalog record for this publication is available from the British Library.

Library of Congress Cataloging in Publication data

Parochialism, cosmopolitanism, and the foundations of international law
/ [edited by] M. N. S. Sellers.
    p.   cm. – (ASIL studies in international legal theory)
Includes bibliographical references and index.
ISBN 978-0-521-51802-4 (hardback)
1. Human rights.   2. International law.   3. Multiculturalism – Law and legislation.
I. Sellers, M. N. S. (Mortimer N. S.)   II. Title.   III. Series.
K3240.P373   2011
341.4′8–dc23   2011018857

ISBN 978-0-521-51802-4 Hardback

To Therese Sellers
first companion
December 29, 2010,
with love and admiration

Contents

Notes on Contributors

Armin von Bogdandy is Director at the Max Planck Institute for Comparative Public Law and International Law in Heidelberg.

Chios Carmody is Professor of Law at the University of Western Ontario.

Maxwell O. Chibundu is Professor of Law at the University of Maryland School of Law.

Sergio Dellavalle is Professor of Public Law and State Theory at the Faculty of Law of the University of Turin and Codirector of the Research Project "Paradigms of Public Order" at the Max Planck Institute for Comparative Public Law and International Law in Heidelberg.

James Griffin is White's Professor of Moral Philosophy Emeritus at the University of Oxford and a Fellow of Corpus Christi College.

Brian D. Lepard is Law Alumni Professor of Law at the University of Nebraska College of Law.

Ileana M. Porras is Professor of Law at the University of Miami.

M. N. S. Sellers is Regents Professor of the University System of Maryland and Director of the University of Baltimore Center for International and Comparative Law.

John Tasioulas is Quain Professor of Jurisprudence, Faculty of Laws, at University College London.

Preface

This book inaugurates the ASIL Studies in International Legal Theory, a book series dedicated to clarifying and improving the theoretical foundations of international law. Too often the progressive development and effective implementation of international law have foundered on confusion about first principles. This series seeks to raise the level of public and scholarly discussion about the structure and purposes of the world legal order and how best to achieve global justice through law.

The idea for this series grows out of the International Legal Theory Project of the American Society of International Law. Every year for the past decade, the ASIL has devoted special attention to a different aspect of international law, inviting scholars and practitioners to discuss the theoretical basis of such topics as customary international law, humanitarian law, and universal human rights. The society has published a special issue of the journal *International Legal Theory* each year, presenting the results of these conversations. The book series ASIL Studies in International Legal Theory replaces this annual publication with a series of monographs and edited volumes considering fundamental questions in the theory, justification, and progressive improvement of the doctrine, substance, and institutions of international law.

This series does not seek to settle all disputed questions in international law, but rather to improve the quality of the discussion. The field of international law has experienced a constant growth in importance over the past century, supported by vast public enthusiasm, with a strengthening influence over governments and international affairs. At the same time, the law has outrun its theoretical basis, which has led to confusion and rising frustration. This series responds to increasing public demand for greater justice, coherence, and theoretical sophistication in international affairs.

This first volume addresses the foundational question of parochialism in international law. Law by its very nature requires rules of general application, making the rule of law necessarily "cosmopolitan" when applied to international affairs. Yet circumstances differ vastly among the many peoples of the world. How then can there be a transcendent "international" law? This recurring question of generality and specificity in all human associations must reconcile liberty with law, independence with community, and the expression of treasured individuality with the realization of our common humanity.

The chapters collected in this volume grew out of a series of discussions held at Tillar House, the headquarters of the American Society of International Law, in Washington, D.C., under the auspices of the International Legal Theory Interest Group of the American Society of International Law. Leaders in this effort include Elizabeth Andersen and Charlotte Ku, present and past executive directors of the American Society of International Law; Lucy Reed, José Alvarez, James Carter, and Anne-Marie Slaughter, present and former presidents of the American Society of International Law; and present and past chairs of the International Legal Theory Interest Group of the American Society of International Law, Brian D. Lepard, Bryan Macpherson, Fernando Tesón, Onuma Yasuaki, Nicholas Onuf, and Joaquín Tacsan. Francesco Parisi deserves special thanks as founding editor of the ASIL publication *International Legal Theory*.

I would like to thank Laurie Schnitzer, Terican Gross, Netta Yochay, and Ian Foss for their work on this manuscript; Sheila Ward for her coordination of the meetings at Tillar House; and Finola O'Sullivan and John Berger for making Cambridge University Press the leading publisher in the field of international law. This book and this series would not exist without their encouragement. The American Society of International Law, the University of Baltimore Center for International and Comparative Law, the Lauterpacht Centre of Cambridge University, and Georgetown University Law Center gave me the practical and moral support that made this project possible. As always and for everything, I thank my wife Frances Stead Sellers and my daughter Cora Mary Stead Sellers, without whose comfort and inspiration my life and work would have no meaning.

Stanton Manor
December 29, 2010

1   Introduction

Mortimer Sellers

People are parochial in their commitments and beliefs, and rightly so. We live, for the most part, among our neighbors, in our own home places, with local landscapes, customs, climates, and conventions. Much that is sweetest in life is built among human societies, according to the happenstance of provincial circumstances. This social nature of humanity pulls us together, but it also draws us apart, as we construct vastly different cultural superstructures on the foundations of our shared human nature. For most of history, humanity has lived in small and tightly knit bands of at most two hundred persons. We are profoundly adapted to find community, justice, and altruism within these narrow social units, while viewing outsiders with suspicion and self-righteousness.[1] Peace, justice, and prosperity have advanced in the world as people have learned to expand their sense of sorority and fraternity to broader ranges of humanity, beyond their most immediate social affiliations.

When people view the whole world as one community, they become "cosmopolitans" or "citizens of the world" (as the word is usually translated), which might seem unreservedly desirable, were it not for the implication that citizenship is exclusive and that citizens of the world do not fully participate in the local societies to which they should belong. "Cosmopolitan" has often become a term of abuse in the hands of regional political leaders such as Joseph Stalin, who criticized "rootless cosmopolitans" as a threat to the integrity of the State.[2] More recent critics of globalization have attacked "cosmopolitan"

---

[1] For the implications of human evolution or international relations, see Bradley A. Thayer, *Darwin and International Relations: On the Evolutionary Origins of War and Ethnic Conflict* (Lexington, Kentucky, 2004); William R. Thompson, ed. *Evolutionary Interpretations of World Politics* (New York, 2001); Patrick James and David Goetze, eds. *Evolutionary Theory and Ethnic Conflict* (Santa Barbara, California, 2001).

[2] See, e.g., Erik van Ree, *The Political Thought of Joseph Stalin: A Study in Twentieth-Century Revolutionary Patriotism* (New York, 2002).

1

international law as a tool through which hegemonic powers exploit the weakness of less privileged regions and cultures.[3] Viewing the whole world as one community may not seem so desirable when political control of that community falls into the hands of a universal despot, ruling without regard to local circumstances or justice.[4]

The concept of justice not just within but also between states or peoples or other political communities is as old as humanity. Before proceeding to war, the Roman *fetiales* would slaughter a pig with the sacred flint, invoking Jupiter to strike them down unless their cause was just.[5] What distinguishes modern international law from its earlier counterparts is not the commitment to universal justice, which every nation shares, but its abstraction from any particular religious or cultural tradition. Hugo Grotius inaugurated a new era of international justice when he insisted that the fundamental principles of international law arise from human nature and would remain the same even if we were to concede (*etiamsi daremus*) that "which cannot be conceded without the utmost wickedness" – that there is no God.[6] The first comprehensive description of the fundamental requirements of international law began with the concept of a universal society of every human being,[7] resting on human nature, rather than any specific appeal to divine or other external authority.

The standard definition of international law as "those rules of conduct which reason deduces, as consonant to justice and common good, from the nature of the society existing among independent nations"[8] assumes both a universal standard ("reason") and the continued existence of parochial communities ("nations"). The question has always been how best to reconcile the two. Emer de Vattel advanced the accepted solution, which grounds the political independence ("sovereignty") of states on their existence as corporate "persons," deriving their legal rights from the individuals who associate to create them.[9]

---

[3] See, e.g., Richard Falk, Jacqueline Stevens, and Balakrishnan Rajagopal, eds. *International Law and the Third World: Reshaping Justice* (New York, 2008).

[4] See Immanuel Kant, *Perpetual Peace*, in *Kant's Political Writings*, ed. Hans Reiss; trans. H. B. Nisbet (Cambridge, 1970) at 113 on the dangers of universal monarchy and soulless despotism.

[5] Titus Livius, *Ab urbe condita*, I.24.8.

[6] Hugo Grotius, *De Iure Belli ac Pacis libri tres In quibus jus Naturae et Gentium item juris publici praecipua explicantur* (new edition, Amsterdam, 1646) at Prolegomena p. 5 (§11).

[7] *Ibid.* at §6 – Cf. Marcus Tullius Cicero, *De legibus*, I.vii.23.

[8] See James Madison, *An Examination of the British Doctrine which subjects to capture a Neutral Trade not open in a Time of Peace* (London, 1806), p. 41; Henry Wheaton, *Elements of International Law*, 8th ed. R. H. Dana (Boston, 1866), chapter I §14 (p. 20).

[9] Emmer. de Vattel, *Le Droit des Gens ou principes de la Loi Naturelle Appliqués á la conduite et aux affaires des Nations et des Souverains* (London, 1758), préface at pp. xiii–xiv, quoting Christian Wolff, *Jus Gentium Methodo scientifica pertractatum, in quo Jus Gentium naturale ab eo quod voluntarii, pactitii et consuetudinarii distinguitur* (Frankfurt and Leipzig, 1749).

This does not in itself settle the borders between the jurisdictions of international law, national law, and ordinary individual autonomy or self-direction,[10] which depend on the duties and rights of actual human beings.[11]

The challenge of reconciling parochialism with cosmopolitanism is thus inherent in the basic structure of international law. International law is universal and cosmopolitan with respect to those questions properly subject to its primary jurisdiction, but also exists in part to support the separate jurisdictions (the "freedom" and "independence") of individual citizens and states.[12] International law arises from the natural society of all humanity[13] – the "société universelle du Genre-humain"[14] – and specifically from our "cosmopolitan" obligations to this universal community,[15] yet as Vattel recognized at the dawn of the international modernity, the natural society of nations requires that the rights and independence of every state and separate community be taken into account.[16] This means, in many cases, tolerating injustice within states to maintain greater justice between them.[17] Just as every individual deserves a zone of privacy within which to make her or his own choices (and mistakes), so too every state deserves an area of self-determination, within which to construct its national identity.

The problem of parochialism in international law is similar in many ways to familiar questions of federalism, legal hierarchy, and subsidiarity in other national and transnational regimes.[18] At one extreme, strong nationalists deny that international law has any authority.[19] At the other extreme, some internationalists resist the possibility that local institutions should ever legislate or rule.[20] The first step in establishing any coherent theory of international law will be to determine the province of international jurisdiction, how this

---

[10] See *ibid.* at pp. xvii–xviii. [11] *Ibid.*, préliminaires §5, pp. 2–3.

[12] "Les Nations étant composées d'hommes naturellement libres et indépendans . . . les Nations, ou les Etats souverains, doivent être considerés comme autant de personnes libres." *Ibid.* at §4, p. 2.

[13] In addition to the references to the foregoing Cicero and Grotius, see Vattel, *Droit des Gens*, préliminaires §10, p. 6.

[14] *Ibid.* §11, p. 7. [15] *Ibid.* §12, p. 8.

[16] *Ibid.* §15, p. 9. [17] *Ibid.* §21, p. 12.

[18] The relationship of states within the United States of America to the federal government under the 10th Amendment to the U.S. Constitution or between member states of the European Union and the law of the Union itself, under Article 5(2) of the Treaty on European Union have both given rise to vast bibliographies.

[19] See, e.g., Jack L. Goldsmith and Eric A. Posner, *The Limits of International Law* (Oxford, 2005).

[20] See, e.g., *The International Post-War Settlement: Report by the National Executive Committee of the Labour Party to be presented at the annual conference to be held in London from May 29th to June 2nd, 1944* (London, 1944).

jurisdiction arises, and when, if ever, it trumps the rival jurisdiction of national or subnational institutions.

John Tasioulas initiates the discussion (Chapter 2) by raising the question of "legitimacy" in international law. Legitimacy in this context signifies the normative fact of being "justified" (rather than the empirical fact of being thought of as justified). International law and international institutions are "legitimate" (on this view) only to the extent that they actually enjoy a "right" to rule that "binds" their subjects with a duty of obedience. Put another way (in the vocabulary of Joseph Raz), legitimate directives impose content-independent and exclusionary reasons for action. Tasioulas observes that international law, like all law, claims to be legitimate in precisely this sense and then asks what would be needed to substantiate such assertions. Following Raz, Tasioulas suggests that international law enjoys legitimate authority when its subjects will better conform to reasons that apply to them by respecting the law's directives (and will conform less effectively when they do not). Legitimacy follows from general accuracy in conforming with applicable reasons. This "service" conception of legitimate authority concerns objectively valid goals. To be legitimate, international law must strengthen its subjects' conformity with reason, the ultimate purpose of all legitimate legal systems anywhere.

When legitimacy is understood in this way, it becomes clear that international law could be legitimate in some domains but not others. The test to be applied is whether *in fact* international law enhances conformity with the applicable objective reasons (or not). To be applicable at the international level, such reasons would have to obtain independently of individual or societal preferences and beliefs when these do not conform to objectively *true* judgments. Tasioulas understands the legitimate jurisdiction of international law to extend only so far as its grasp of applicable reasons transcends the abilities of more parochial authorities. Skeptics might challenge this assertion by denying that "true" ethical reasons ever apply to international affairs. Tasioulas responds that such an attitude of general skepticism would make it impossible to question *any* social practices, no matter how wicked. In fact, most seeming skeptics (to their credit) do hope for global justice and better societies. Their rhetoric contradicts their actual commitments.

The argument against the legitimacy of international law cannot, then, be that *no* legal or social arrangements are more legitimate than others but that international law in fact lacks the legitimacy that other systems possess. Tasioulas suggests that an "ethical pluralist" might salvage a quasi-skeptical position by embracing the positive value of maintaining rival and incommensurable legal or ethical regimes, but even then these separate societies, cultures, or states will need some overarching (cosmopolitan) perspective from which to adjudicate their disagreements. The argument must shift from attacking international law *as such* to challenging the scope of its jurisdiction by pushing for a more restricted or "minimalist" international legal system or by broadening the range of arguments through which the existing international rule of law is justified, to embrace the varied values that have resonance in the parallel but "incommensurable" ethical systems of rival societies. Tasioulas dismisses the facile dogma of value skepticism to support the softer benefits of "pluralism," constrained by a few ultimately cosmopolitan judgments about what is fundamentally right (or wrong) in international affairs.

Armin von Bogdandy and Sergio Dellavalle (Chapter 3) suggest that there are both "particularist" and "universalist" paradigms in international law. The universalist paradigm (which they ultimately prefer) seeks a "truly public" international order, encouraging societies to solve their conflicts by peaceful means through methods that advance their common interests. The particularist paradigm would confine public order (in this sense) within the borders of homogenous political communities. Dellavalle and von Bogdandy make explicit the unexamined "universalist" and "particularist" assumptions at the heart of international law that arose with modernity itself in the scholarship of European universities and insist on the necessary coherence and consistency that scholarly commentary brings to the practice of international law. Without a reasonable theory to support it, law loses its capacity to govern the behavior of citizens or states.

The incapacity of undertheorized law to govern human behavior becomes particularly apparent when (as in the case of the international legal system) the coercive mechanisms of public order are weak. Dellavalle and von Bogdandy praise the role of legal scholars on the International Law Commission and other public bodies in maintaining an overall account of the purpose and function of international law. Legitimacy and legality are both vitally important to a functioning public order, and neither is possible without the other. Legitimacy has natural-law connotations, but there will also be "positivist" elements in any lasting international order of peace. International law contains an increasing number of norms that bind states irrespective of their consent. These "public" laws need a strong theoretical basis to justify their transnational validity. Dellavalle and von Bogdandy identify the traditional European understanding of the nation-state as resting in part on a particularist paradigm, promoting the cultural solidarity of (separate) "peoples" and assuming that most human activity will be bounded by the nation-state's borders.

This separation between homogenous peoples has become much more difficult to maintain in the era of easy travel and communication. Globalization
has undermined the particularist paradigm of international law.

The increasing autonomy of international law and international organizations from the political preferences of individual nations may be the natural
consequence of globalization, but it threatens the self-determination of states.
This can be seen either as a valuable control on the unreasonable decisions
of the national political classes or the unjustified imposition of international
norms onto local societies. How one views international law as a universal
public order will depend to a large extent on whether the law makes local
institutions more just. Dellavalle and von Bogdandy see it as the task of contemporary scholarship to contribute to the creation of a more just international
order, supporting greater justice within as well as between states. The particularist paradigm tends to view states as necessarily in competition and therefore
at odds with each other. Dellavalle and von Bogdandy prefer to seek an inclusive order founded on transcendental principles of human interaction and
elaborated through dialogue between cultures.

The universalist paradigm of international law assumes that certain rights
and values are (or ought to be) shared by all individuals and all peoples. These
values include concern for other human beings (sociability) and respect for
reason (reasonableness), as applied to the problems of social cooperation.
Dellavalle and von Bogdandy identify these as two separate strands of the
universalist paradigm: respect for our common humanity on the one hand
and the application of our individual reason on the other. This idea of international law as the common law of a naturally sociable humanity implies
an "international community" of all human beings. The great challenge to
this conception of law is the evident fact that not all human beings actually
accept their connection with humanity as a whole. Contract theory offers one
very popular response to this dilemma by grounding law and ethics on the
self-interest of individuals rather than the common interests of the community. In the end, however, these two viewpoints are difficult to keep separate.
The real question is not how the community arises, but how far it should
extend: Can we accept a society expanded to embrace all human beings? If
not, international law loses legitimacy to control the activities of states.

Dellavalle and von Bogdandy cite the "cosmopolitan law" (*jus cosmopoliticum*) of Immanuel Kant as having first recognized not just (as others
had) the *civitas maxima* of international community but also the specific
rights of individuals in the international order. Global constitutionalism is
the latest instantiation of this search for global community through common
values and the common good. The international community views the state

as justified by its service to the human beings for whom it is responsible, and every state has a duty to provide specific services for the benefit of its citizens. Dellavalle and von Bogdandy cite Christian Tomuschat as a leading contemporary advocate of understanding international law in this way as ultimately an "individual-centered" (rather than a state-centered) system. At the same time (as Tomuschat understood), there can be no genuinely sustainable international legal order if national systems of government disintegrate. The international community collectively recognizes certain obligations as *erga omnes* and *jus cogens*. Dellavalle and von Bogdandy condition the legitimacy of states on respecting and implementing these fundamental obligations. The international order complements national legal orders as a further step in the process of civilization.

In an interdependent world, many decisions made by authorities in one polity substantially affect individuals living abroad. Dellavalle and von Bogdandy identify international law as a significant restraint on this often-negative consequence of globalization. Rather than advancing the hegemony of large and powerful states, international law may offer the most significant control over the self-interested impositions of some states onto others. Thus, a cosmopolitan or universalist conception of international law may be the best protection available for the parochial and particularist values so essential to human happiness. Cosmopolitanism supplies the necessary foundations for international law, but parochialism explains many of its most important purposes. Dellavalle and von Bogdandy reconcile universalism with particularism by understanding both in the light of global principles, applicable to all human beings. They propose that the next step should be a strengthening and deepening of international institutions to support a more just and equitable international public order, taking local interests more fully into account.

Ileana Porras (Chapter 4) examines the wide and often divergent set of meanings attributed to "cosmopolitanism" by students of international law and sets out to clarify the central and most useful senses of the term. Cosmopolitans begin by assuming a universal community of humanity in which each human being owes a duty of care to all the rest. This makes every other (smaller) human community contingent on respecting this basic duty to humanity as a whole. Local obligations can never fully displace the global community and the requirements it imposes on every human being. Porras does not suggest that states are morally irrelevant but that they cannot (for cosmopolitans) be politically absolute. Cosmopolitanism implies an attitude of engaged curiosity and tolerance in the face of cultural difference. For cosmopolitans, cultural differences are merely variations on the theme of humanity and should not be allowed further to separate us. Porras evaluates cosmopolitan conceptions of international law in the light of the liberal, pacifist, and commercial ideals with which they are so often associated.

Immanuel Kant has had a vast influence in advancing understanding of these related ideas, which Porras suggests have been imbedded in international law from the beginning. The contemporary turn to cosmopolitanism is in fact a return to origins, and the more intolerant forms of parochialism have always been somewhat at odds with the basic structure of international law. Classic liberal political theory developed in large part to justify the coercive capacity of the state, reconciling individual autonomy with collective decision making through the application of right reason to civil society. States exist (on this account) to serve the interests of *all* their citizens. Transposed to the international arena, this makes international law the servant of *all* states, and all the people who inhabit them. The sovereign state makes sense only in the company of other sovereign states, in the same way that the rights of the individual require the presence of other individuals to make sense. Both depend on finding an ordering principle that could serve to justify collective constraint, beyond mere force. For Kant, the ultimate goal of the international system is true or perpetual peace, which would enable the full (or at least a greater) development of human capacities.

Porras understands Kant's cosmopolitanism as offering his solution to the liberal problem of reconciling individual autonomy with collective decision making. The preexisting, permanent, and irreplaceable global community arises from the simple fact of coexistence. Humans desire the possibility of nonhostile encounters between strangers. International law is therefore a necessary aspiration of the human race. For Porras, as for Kant, cosmopolitan right is the end point toward which universal history must tend, for only through cosmopolitan right can humanity hope to create the required conditions for human flourishing. This cosmopolitan attitude makes peace possible and opens the door to commerce, which brings separated humanity back into relations of friendship. Because Earth is a finite space, human beings cannot disperse over an infinite area but must necessarily tolerate one another's company. Porras shows this doctrine of Vitoria, Grotius, and Kant to be at the basis of international legality. The duty of mutual hospitality leads to reciprocity and cross-cultural exchange.

New cosmopolitanists extend the theories of the early publicists by deepening the reach of international law. Commerce has vastly expanded the common interests of disparate peoples (as Grotius and Kant predicted it would), which makes the necessity and necessary scope of global justice much broader than it was before. Porras notes, however, that international law beyond the borders of republican liberal states raises all the problems of accountability, legitimacy, and enforcement that the nation-state first arose to address. The cosmopolitan assertion of a preexisting worldwide moral community seeks to solve this problem of legitimacy but seems to require the creation of stronger and more intrusive institutions of global governance. Porras worries that these may in turn weaken the present flawed but effective system of state-based rights. Liberal cosmopolitanism may undermine cosmopolitan liberalism if it saps the vitality of existing nation-states.

Most people think of human rights as being among the most cosmopolitan areas of law. James Griffin (Chapter 5) examines the basis of this assumption. If human rights are rights that we have simply by virtue of being human, then they share an essential element of the cosmopolitan perspective in their universality. That still leaves open the possibility of disagreement over the requisite sense of "human," or which aspects of humanity have relevance for understanding the nature of our rights. Griffin proposes that the best substantive explanation for the existence of human rights arises from the human capacity to imagine and define the possibility of a good life. This capacity allows for our "normative agency" or "personhood." Personhood in this sense must be protected not only through the principled recognition of its importance but also in the practical structure of society. So there are two grounds for human rights: personhood and practicalities. The existence of a right can be confirmed by showing, first, that it protects an essential feature of personhood, and, second, that its determinate content results from practical consideration of the nature of human society.

Personhood involves human interests that are not particular to any person or society, but also considerations of policy concerning how best to protect these interests in practice. This opens the door to culture, ethnicity, or other parochial considerations. Griffin suggests that many seeming differences between the ethical perceptions of different societies arise in reality from their different material conditions. Universal rights may apply differently in different circumstances. Autonomy, as protected by rights, and solidarity, which advances community, need not conflict and are both desirable. Human interests (a prudential value) imply human rights (a moral standard), but there may be a conventional element in applying this insight to particular societies. Griffin argues that the transition from prudence to morality progresses because a reasonable person who respects the prudential value (for example) of autonomy will also recognize the respect that is its due. This respect could take different forms in different circumstances. Such variations between societies do not reveal differences in the framework of basic evaluations but merely a highly constrained exercise in arational opting.

Griffin suggests that the primarily Western development of modern conceptions of international law and justice poses problems for the validity (for example) of universal human rights only to the extent that these Western-elaborated ideas are false or harmful or incomplete. Nothing prevents people in different societies from recognizing truths first comprehensively articulated by others. All societies mix the local with the global in varying degrees, with the global elements now often expanding because of the massive increase in global communication and commerce. The idea that an intersociety pluralism of conceptions of justice and the good is an ineradicable feature of international life makes little sense in the world as it exists today (if it ever did). The argument cannot be that deep-seated cultural differences are an inescapable element of international society but that they *ought* to be. If the local particularities of cultural tradition are desirable, then human rights and other cosmopolitan values might be better advanced by seeking out local counterparts for universal values and recognizing their importance. Griffin warns, however, that in doing so, we must not lose touch with the real and necessary structure of the universal rights themselves. Often it will be more effective to promote a universal vocabulary to support universal values.

Maxwell Chibundu (Chapter 6) examines the importance of parochial values in international law, both in the positive sense that they deserve respect and in the negative sense that more powerful nations may impose their own parochial conceptions of the law on other states through false claims of universality. Chibundu offers human rights as an example of an area of law in which the United States and other Western powers have imposed parochial viewpoints on the world, confusing local European traditions with the requirements of international justice. Yet the world continues to be divided into substantially self-regulating nation-states. Chibundu examines the particularism inherent in the liberal international order and suggests that modern cosmopolitan liberalism contains at its heart a fundamental contradiction between international human rights and the collective power of the state. The growing emphasis on universal human rights in international law has tended to delegitimize the state, whereas the valorization of the state as protector of its citizens (particularly after the World Trade Center attacks) has tended to minimize the equal application of supposedly universal rights.

Chibundu distinguishes "philosophical" from "legal" understandings of rights. Philosophers begin by examining human nature to see what it requires, whereas lawyers look for the "sources" of law. Lawyers (on this theory of the rule of law) should concentrate on the validity of claims that are redressable through governmental power. Legal discourse is less a statement of normativity than a description of existing human institutions. The *concept* of human rights as explained by philosophers may have a wide variety of practical *conceptions* in the practices of states. The dominant conception of human rights in contemporary international law recognized this in the Universal Declaration of Human Rights (UDHR) and other important expressions of the transnational consensus by presenting international human rights not as ends in themselves but as the means for achieving important international values, such as freedom, justice, and peace. Chibundu suggests that the Universal Declaration of Human Rights did not set out to promulgate legal rights, but rather to explain their purposes. The Declaration offers precepts, not rules. Legal rules are usually not universal, but specific, addressing the circumstances of a particular society.

Much of international law is best understood not as a set of categorical rules to be coercively enforced but as standards proposed for parochial implementation by states. Chibundu argues that by disrespecting states, human-rights-oriented international lawyers have weakened the main vehicle through which justice can be realized in practice. Most doctrines of contemporary international law arose in Europe in the shadow of specifically European circumstances. This makes the self-determination of nation-states particularly important in supporting the aspirations of formerly subject peoples. Chibundu identifies rights and other legal rules as creatures of the social institutions against which they are asserted. The dignity of the political community becomes just as important in this context as the ultimate treatment of the individual. Individuals can only actually enjoy freedom, justice, and peace in groups. They are subject to the power of existing nation-states, and it is from the governments of these states that they will receive any substantive protections that they actually enjoy.

Morally tinged claims of universal rights may mask completely unrelated factors of relative power and national interest. Chibundu warns that human rights and other international (and assertedly "cosmopolitan") rules are necessarily the products of the particularized histories and experiences of living societies. Under such circumstances, international law discourse may run the risk of forcing emerging nations into an alien pattern of thought. For the maturation of a society, the process of discovering, creating, interpreting, and applying rules is often as important as the rules themselves. Chibundu argues that rights should be realized through societies as they actually exist, without imposing some idealized globalization of the late-twentieth-century European consensus. Many supposedly universal values will prove on closer examination to be parochial, and many parochial values deserve greater respect from the international community because they reflect the actual needs and circumstances of existing societies.

Chios Carmody (Chapter 7) clarifies the nature of international law and universal human rights by considering the implications of international human obligations. Law remains part of a greater social process, which may itself be governed by universal rules but yields substantially different results in different parochial circumstances. The central problem is to identify the boundaries of communities within which rights discourse should take place. All rights are limited, but how this qualification is manifested will depend on socially situated obligations and other local elements of the legal system in question. Carmody suggests that communities constantly refine and redefine the legal relations that are the basis of their social arrangements. This leads to a necessary parochialism as communities measure the extent of local rights and obligations against their foundation in universal human rights and values.

Early modern students of international law, such as Samuel Pufendorf, well understood the necessary correlation between rights and obligations. Rights attributed to one person generally entail corresponding duties in others. These duties may apply to states, corporations, nongovernmental organizations, individuals, or others as required by the reach of their actual power or influence. Carmody points out that human rights necessarily imply an element of mutuality, limiting the (ab)use of rights when they begin to infringe on the rights of others. The law of international human rights therefore involves deciding what action is appropriate in a crowded legal landscape, which often requires some element of "balance." How this balance should be struck is a function of many culturally and contextually defined variables.

The concept of rights (for example) is a fairly late formulation in most legal cultures, which usually begin by defining the specific legal obligations of different members of society. If (as Carmody suggests) one central purpose of law is to maintain (or create) a harmonious society, then rights must be subject to public responsibilities, or they will weaken the social ties on which all communities ultimately depend. The reality of community therefore requires consideration of rights *and* obligations *together*. The exercise of individual autonomy must take into account the existence of a social responsibility toward those who will be detrimentally affected by what one does. This leads to different results in different communities. Carmody gives the example of modern slavery in West Africa, where successive attempts at legal emancipation have only worsened the practical status of slaves by undermining the social constraints that once protected them from abuse.

Carmody argues that even the most fundamental requirements of international law, such as the prohibition on slavery, will not be fully applicable to certain societies without deep-seated social change. Imposing international standards without modifying social attitudes would lead to chaos. At the same time, a general awareness of universal values may lead to gradual change. Even such strongly cosmopolitan doctrines as universal human rights will be parochial in their application, depending on the particular circumstances of particular peoples. Carmody concludes that the requirements of universal humanity must be identified and realized *within* preexisting communities. Law cannot be understood in the abstract, without reference to the communities in which it must actually exist.

Brian Lepard (Chapter 8) looks directly at one of the areas in which the practice of existing communities is most at variance with the requirements of international law. The freedom to change one's religion or belief, recognized by the UDHR in Article 18 and again in Article 18 of the International Covenant on Civil and Political Rights (ICCPR), has been undermined in many states by governments determined to protect their subjects against heresies and apostasy. The UDHR recognizes the importance of communities and their cultures (in Articles 27 and 29) to the full development of human personality, and this raises the possibility of conflict between community standards and religious belief. The ICCPR even contemplates limitations on the freedom publicly to *manifest* one's religious belief in the interests of public safety and the *fundamental* rights and safety of others.

How, then, to reconcile the freedom of religious belief with the community's desire to strengthen group cohesiveness through religion? Lepard finds a framework of "unity in diversity," already present in contemporary international law, that can help to provide the basis for a more elaborated theory of universal religious liberty. The ethical principle of unity in diversity begins with the presumption that all human beings are members of a single human family and owe each other a certain measure of concern and respect simply in virtue of their common humanity. At the same time, diversity of nationality, culture, opinion, and religion is to be cherished as enriching this one human family. Individuals have a right to associate with and take pride in their separate communities, which have certain rights of self-governance, in the context of a broader community of humankind.

Many provisions of contemporary international law, including the United Nations Charter and the UDHR, support this principle of unity in diversity. Lepard recalls "the inherent dignity" and "the equal and inalienable rights of all members of the human family," mentioned in Article 1 of the UDHR, which asserts that all human beings "should act toward one another in a spirit of brotherhood." This requires "tolerance and friendship among all nations, racial or religious groups" (Art. 26), and the ability for minorities "to enjoy their own culture, to profess or practice their own religion, or to use their own language" (Art. 27). Provisions such as these remind us of the social feelings that lead humans to seek unity with others, despite our superficial differences. The freedom of thought, religion or (more broadly) "moral choice" provides each human being with the ability to exercise "reason and conscience" in pursuit of the "spirit of brotherhood," as demanded by the UDHR in Article 1.

The requirements of fraternity and friendship imply an ethic of "open-minded consultation," engaging the views of others with seriousness and respect. Because religion or belief is so intimately linked with each person's identity as a moral agent, it must be freely chosen and accepted, according to each individual's conscience and personal search for spiritual truth. Thus, unity in diversity, freedom of moral choice, and open-minded consultation provide Lepard with a "background value system" through which to apply more traditional legal interpretive methodologies. Lepard concludes that because of its central role in the construction of individual and collective moral agency, the freedom to change one's religion or belief is absolute and should not be restricted in any circumstances. The fundamental ethical principle of open-minded consultation, if implemented, would reduce conflict and lead to reconciliation between nations and religious groups. Unity in diversity implies religious tolerance as a prerequisite for building a more peaceful and unified world.

Taken together, the insights of the first eight chapters of this volume confirm the importance both of parochial traditions and of cosmopolitan values in the theoretical foundations of international law. The concept of unity in diversity proposed by Lepard as the central value in the international legal order reflects both the universal standard of "reason" and the parochial reality of "nations" that has shaped international law from the beginning. If, as Tasioulas and Raz observe, nations are justified by their service to justice; if, as von Bogdandy and Dellavalle suggest, we need a "truly public" international order to better serve the interests of states; if Porras is right to argue that each of us owes a duty of care to the rest, then an international legal order will be necessary to protect the boundaries among state power, individual autonomy, and the jurisdiction of international law. Just as individual rights would not be safe without states to protect them, so states' rights will have no security in the absence of an international community to make them real.

The danger here is that international institutions will reach beyond the legitimate scope of their jurisdiction to oppress the very nations they were meant to protect. In the same way that the governments of states may abuse their authority to oppress their subjects, international law may become arbitrary or oppressive in the hands of thoughtless or self-interested cosmopolitans. Circumstances of total legal integrity will be difficult to achieve, but even when they prevail, some matters ought to be of primarily local concern. Different material conditions require different legal regimes. This is not necessarily (as James Griffin observed) a matter of real ethical difference but one of inevitable variation due to inescapable circumstances of time and place. Chibundu, Carmody, and Lepard's chapters each illustrate in different ways how parochial circumstances of history (Chibundu), social arrangements (Carmody), or religion (Lepard) require parochial recognition in the law.

That local affinities are important and worthy of protection has been a guiding principle of modern international law since its origins in the seventeenth and eighteenth centuries. International law should protect the liberty and independence of all states against the others, as national law should protect the liberty and independence of all persons against the rest. This makes the conflict between parochial and the cosmopolitan values in international law more apparent than real. Because nations are composed of persons who are by nature free and independent, nations or sovereign states also deserve recognition as free moral persons, worthy of our respect.[21] International law begins by assuming the natural society of all human beings, and therefore between all states and nations.[22] The purpose of this great society, and therefore of international law, is the happiness and advancement of all human beings, and of all nations, everywhere.[23]

Parochialism and cosmopolitanism are both essential elements at the foundation of international law and have been from the outset. International lawyers must articulate and better explain those rules of conduct that will best advance justice and the common good in the society of independent nations, as it actually exists. This requires in the first instance a much more detailed delimitation of the borders among the jurisdiction of international law, national law, and ordinary personal autonomy or self-direction. Which issues and which legal questions are best resolved by international institutions? Which policies and which legal controversies best belong to states? Which depend on the separate consciences of private individuals? Legal parochialism has a long history in the well-elaborated doctrines of federalism, subsidiarity, and civil and collective rights. Now lawyers must clarify the principles of international jurisdiction to better protect the parochial traditions that make life so varied, so interesting, and (when we are fortunate) so meaningful and profound.

---

[21] Vattel, *Droit de Gens*, at préliminaries, §4, p. 2.
[22] *Ibid.*, préliminaries §10, p. 6.   [23] *Ibid.*, préliminaries §12, p. 8.

2 Parochialism and the Legitimacy of International Law

John Tasioulas

Contemporary international law – including its institutional agents and mouthpieces, such as the United Nations, World Trade Organization, and International Court of Justice – asserts the "legitimacy" of its claim to govern an increasingly broad, diverse, and consequential array of activities within the global domain. However, this very domain manifests high levels of divergence in the cultural norms; patterns of economic and legal organization; religious, moral, and political creeds; and so on that are prevalent within and across its constituent states.[1] In light of these deep and ramifying differences, how can international legal norms and institutions avoid reflecting a partial or "parochial" perspective, with the result that their "legitimacy" is seriously imperiled? This chapter explores this rather vague, but prima facie genuinely disquieting, line of thought by considering two distinct, but readily confused, ways in which "parochialism" might undermine the legitimacy of international law. The first sees the challenge as arising from meta-ethical *skepticism* about ethical values in general; the second, by contrast, treats it as the upshot of the ethical doctrine of *pluralism*. The conclusion toward which this chapter steers is that skepticism, although more radically subversive in its implications for the legitimacy of international law, is not a promising way of articulating the anxiety about parochialism. By contrast, the less-frequently examined pluralist challenge poses a significant constraint on international law's legitimacy, albeit one that still leaves plenty of room for the legitimacy of a robust international legal order.

[1] This chapter draws, in both letter and spirit, on my contribution in *The Philosophy of International Law*. John Tasioulas "The Legitimacy of International Law," in *The Philosophy of International Law*, eds. Samantha Besson and John Tasioulas (Oxford: Oxford University Press, 2010).

I. WHAT IS LEGITIMACY?

What is "legitimacy"? According to a recent book-length study, the language of "legitimacy" has become "dominant and recurrent" in contemporary international relations, upstaging the language of legality, justice, and efficiency.[2] Perhaps somewhat cynically, one might suppose that its dominance at the level of international political rhetoric is not unconnected with its indeterminacy of sense, or at least with the lack of widespread agreement among international law practitioners on an univocal concept of legitimacy. Even if it is true that, as the author of the aforementioned study goes on to suggest, the concept remains "widely ignored in the academic discipline of international relations," the same cannot be said of contemporary legal and political philosophy, in which legitimacy has been the focus of sustained discussion by a number of influential writers. Without yet immersing ourselves in the intricacies of this work, there are two philosophical commonplaces about legitimacy that should orient our discussion from the outset.

The first is the distinction between legitimacy as a normative and as an empirical fact. On one reading, legitimacy refers to a normative fact, that is, that a given act, law, policy, or institution is, in some sense yet to be specified, *justified*. In other words, there are good reasons of a certain kind, although perhaps only defeasible reasons, that in some sense favor the act, law, policy, or institution. Contrast this with the *empirical* sense of legitimacy, which is best understood as parasitic on the normative sense. It is an empirical, but not normative, fact – a psychological or social fact – that a given act, law, policy, or institution is believed to be, or is treated as, normatively legitimate by a given individual or group. This is the familiar distinction between de jure and de facto legitimacy or authority, but it is one that is systematically overlooked by much contemporary work on "legitimacy" in international law. Insofar as I can discern, however, it is the empirical sense of legitimacy that predominates in those discussions, and this mainly for two reasons: on the one hand, a general reluctance to be seen to adopt a "value-laden" approach to theorizing, one that makes explicit normative claims; on the other hand, an overriding interest in the issue of *compliance* with international law and an associated tendency to focus on a proximate cause of compliance (i.e., the fact that a norm, among other things, is believed to be, or treated as, legitimate as opposed to the fact that it actually *is* legitimate as a matter of normative fact). This is not to deny, of course, that whether a law or legal institution enjoys normative legitimacy may depend in part on whether it is empirically

---

[2] Ian Clark, *Legitimacy in International Society* (Oxford: Oxford University Press, 2005), 1–2.

legitimate. For example, the fact that it is widely believed to be legitimate may render it more efficacious in securing the compliance of its putative subjects, and this superior "compliance pull" may be a consideration that has some bearing on its normative legitimacy. However, this is perfectly consistent with the conceptual distinction between normative and empirical legitimacy. The discussion in the rest of this chapter is concerned with legitimacy in the normative sense.

Second, we should clarify what kind of justification is in the offing in speaking of normative legitimacy. On the broadest reading, legitimacy is simply equivalent to "all things considered justification." So, an act, law, policy, etc. is legitimate in this sense provided, all things considered, there are undefeated reasons for performing it, imposing it, enacting it, and so on. It is legitimacy so understood that is frequently contrasted with legality, for example, and which figures in the once oft-heard contention that the 2003 U.S.-led invasion of Iraq was "legitimate" even if also strictly speaking "illegal." The idea seems to be that, all things considered, the military invasion was a justified act – an act of preemptive or preventative self-defence or else of prodemocratic regime change – despite contravening international law (and this is so whether or not the speaker regards the fact of its illegality as constituting in itself a genuine, albeit defeasible, reason against the war). Now, this all-things-considered sense of normative legitimacy is obviously the ultimate concern of practical reasoning. However, in this chapter, my topic is legitimacy as a standard of justification, and a source of reasons, that is one among many other standards that feed into judgments about what is all-things-considered justified.

One way of arriving at a conception of normative legitimacy that renders it one standard of assessment among others is by identifying the reasons that bear on normative legitimacy with a proper subset of the class of all practical reasons. A popular strategy along these lines, exemplified by Thomas Franck's *Fairness in International Law and Institutions*, is to link judgments of legitimacy to certain formal and procedural criteria. According to Franck, legitimacy is a complex standard of procedural fairness that governs the making, interpretation, and application of legal rules. The criteria it subsumes include determinacy of content, adherence to secondary rules concerning the creation, interpretation and application of the rules, and "treating like cases alike."[3] Given the ubiquity of judgments about "legitimacy" in the international context, there is an obvious rationale for associating them with

[3] Thomas M. Franck, *Fairness in International Law and Institutions* (Oxford: Oxford University Press, 1995), 30–46.

procedural and formal requirements of this kind, because the latter seemingly afford a standpoint of critical appraisal that is independent of many of the substantive ideological divisions between states.

Rather than take the notion of normative legitimacy to specify a limited domain of reasons, however, I construe it as a specific normative status. This status is aptly conveyed by the slogan that agents endowed with normative legitimacy enjoy "the right to rule," such that the exercise of this right "binds" their subjects by imposing duties of obedience. Can we say, more concretely, what the right to rule amounts to? I shall endorse the following answer, derived from the work of Joseph Raz: A has legitimate authority over B when A's directives are content-independent and exclusionary reasons for action for B. In other words, the directives are reasons by virtue of the fact that A issued them and not because of the content of any particular directive, and these reasons are not simply to be weighed along with other reasons that apply to B but, instead, have the normative effect of excluding at least some countervailing reasons.[4] Notice, however, that even if A has legitimate authority over B regarding a particular matter, B's duty to comply with A may be defeasible, such that, all things considered, B has compelling reasons to disobey A's directive.

Thus, whether international law and institutions possess legitimacy, in this sense, is a question conceptually distinct from the question of whether they accord with morality, or are economically efficient, or conduce to peaceful relations among states. Why focus on this particular understanding of legitimacy? First and foremost, because international law, as a species of the genus law, inherently lays claim to its own legitimacy.[5] Of course, some dispute that international law inherently lays claim to legitimacy because they reject the assumption that international law is really law. This sort of skepticism seems to me to rely either on an unacceptable conception of the general nature of law (e.g., as requiring the existence of a "sovereign") or a defective picture of international law (e.g., as lacking secondary rules of recognition). I shall not try to vindicate the fully fledged legal status of international law here. Note, however, that the fact that international law claims legitimacy does not entail that it actually possesses it; that it has it to the full extent of its claim; or that it is capable of possessing it under realistically attainable conditions. Nor, conversely, would its lack of legitimacy necessarily deprive it of its status as law. Instead, whether international law is, or can be, legitimate depends on

---

4 See Joseph Raz, Part I of *The Morality of Freedom* (Oxford: Oxford University Press, 1986); idem, "The Problem of Authority: Revisiting the Service Conception," *Minnesota Law Review* 90 (2006): 1003–44.

5 See Joseph Raz, "Authority, Law and Morality," in *Ethics in the Public Domain* (Oxford: Oxford University Press, 1994).

the conditions that must be met for the right to rule to obtain, and the extent to which international law, as it is or might be, satisfies those conditions.

Does it matter whether international law is legitimate? Certainly it is not the *only* thing that matters in assessing international law. It could have considerable value even if it lacked legitimacy – for example, it might be *instrumentally* valuable despite not binding those it purports to bind, by virtue of attaching reputational and other costs to undesirable behavior. Alternatively, it might acquire value by giving forceful *expression* to correct ethical standards irrespective of its instrumental efficacy in securing compliance with them. Still, the existence of a valuable but nonlegitimate legal order is not an ideal scenario, because a claim to authority is integral to international law's identity as a legal order.

II. THE STANDARD OF LEGITIMACY: CONSENT OR SERVICE?

What standard must be satisfied for international law to be legitimate? In other words, what are the conditions that must obtain for international law's claim to normative legitimacy to be valid? Perhaps the dominant view of legitimacy among international lawyers can be summed up in one magic word: *consent*. International law is legitimate only to the extent that the states it purports to bind have previously consented to the relevant law or to the lawmaking procedure through which it came into being. Similarly, international institutions are legitimate only to the extent that the states they purport to bind have consented to being governed by them. Moreover, by resolutely locating the mainspring of legitimacy in the will of international law's subjects, the consent theory seems to offer a promising response to the anxiety about parochialism. We needn't worry so much that the prescriptions of international law and institutions one-sidedly reflect the interests or values of only some members of international society, for example, those of Western or wealthy states, because they are not binding on any state except through the consent of the latter.

This is not the place to explain in detail why I believe this theory is irredeemably flawed. Two broad observations will have to suffice. The first is that those who adhere to the consent theory seldom betray any appreciation of its potentially subversive consequences. If international law is grounded in the consent of states, then vast swathes of international law, including some quite central norms, are of doubtful legitimacy. Norms of customary international law, for example, would not bind those states that did not consent to them because they had no opportunity to do so as they did not exist at the time the relevant norms crystallized. Meanwhile, the category of customary *jus cogens* norms would be comprehensively debunked, because there are no obligations that apply to states independently of their consent. Even that supposed bastion of consent theory, treaty law, does not emerge unscathed. Quite apart from the reservations that eviscerate many states' acceptance of treaty obligations, there is the obvious fact that a state's entry into various treaties is often dubiously voluntary, being essentially a capitulation to the economic or other pressure exerted by more powerful states. Finally, the phenomenon of "bureaucratic distance" – the chasm that can open up between what states sign up to in establishing international legal institutions and the actual day-to-day functioning of those institutions – undermines the claim that states have genuinely consented to the wide-ranging and intrusive forms of governance in which those institutions engage.[6] Now, defenders of consent theory might be undeterred by these concerns. Their aim, after all, is to offer a compelling standard of legitimacy; whether international law fares well by it is a different matter. A certain type of consent theorist might even relish drawing attention to international law's defects in point of legitimacy, drawing unflattering comparisons with the legitimacy enjoyed by the laws of democratically elected governments. However, most consent theorists, not being skeptics about the legitimacy of international law, will not find this die-hard approach especially attractive.

The second broad observation is that, quite apart from its subversive implications, the consent theory of the legitimacy of international law seems inherently flawed. To begin with, most of its proponents are oblivious to the irony of grounding the legitimacy of international law in the consent of states, when many states are controlled by oppressive and undemocratic governments that do not themselves enjoy domestic legitimacy on even the most lenient consent-based standard. Of course, we could imagine a consent theorist insisting that the only consent that counts for the legitimacy of international law is that of states whose governments are suitably representative of the interests and preferences of their subjects. However, this seems to deprive us of an explanation for the legitimacy of international law in cases in which, arguably, it is most required, such as to bind oppressive and undemocratic regimes. Leaving this point aside, there is still the deeper question of why consent should be thought the ultimate basis for legitimate authority. In the domestic case, do we really need to strain to find some sense in which murderers or rapists have consented to the laws prohibiting their crimes before we can judge those laws to be binding on them? Conversely, would the fact that a sufficiently benighted populace consented to rule by a government that pursued highly discriminatory policies against women or ethnic minorities, for example, generate even a *pro tanto*

---

[6] All these points are well made by Allen Buchanan, "The Legitimacy of International Law," in *The Philosophy of International Law.*

obligation on them to obey its offensive legislation? Consent seems to be neither a generally necessary nor sufficient condition for legitimacy. This is not to deny that consent can sometimes generate obligations, including obligations of obedience, but only under the right conditions, and it is those conditions that need to be articulated by a general standard of legitimacy. In my view, the most compelling version of that standard allows for the possibility of legitimate authority even in cases in which the subjects have not consented to being ruled by the would-be authority. Moreover, the conditions under which consent does generate obligations of obedience will typically be those in which there is already an obligation of obedience independent of consent.[7]

What is this other general standard of legitimacy? Following Joseph Raz, the leading contemporary exponent of a classical tradition of thought about legitimate political authority, the origins of which can be traced back to Aristotle and Aquinas, I endorse the claim that the Normal Justification Condition (NJC) is typically a sufficient condition for legitimate authority both domestically and internationally:

> NJC: *A* has legitimate authority over *B* if the latter would better conform with reasons that apply to him if he intends to be guided by *A*'s directives than if he does not.[8]

Thus, an authority is legitimate when its putative subjects would likely better conform with the reasons that apply to them by treating the putative authority's directives as content-independent and exclusionary reasons for action than if they acted on their own assessment of the balance of reasons. This is aptly dubbed a "service conception" of legitimate authority, but the adjective should not mislead us into supposing that what confers legitimacy on an authority is the fact that it assists its subjects' fulfillment of their subjectively given preferences or goals. Instead, the reasons in question are ultimately objective: they concern what the subjects' goals should in fact be, not what they are, and what they should be is a matter about which our judgments admit of plain and simple truth. Moreover, these objective reasons are highly diverse, embracing not only reasons of self-interest but crucially also moral reasons.

There is a diversity of ways in which international law might satisfy the NJC. Classically, a powerful agent can help resolve problems of cooperation and

---

[7] See Raz, *The Morality of Freedom*, 88–94. For compelling arguments to the effect that consent is neither a necessary nor a sufficient general condition for the legitimacy of international law, see Allen Buchanan, *Justice, Legitimacy and Self-Determination: Moral Foundations for International Law* (Oxford: Oxford University Press, 2004); *idem*, "The Legitimacy of International Law."

[8] Raz, "The Problem of Authority," 1014.

coordination by laying down standards that its putative subjects have reason to comply with because, inter alia, it is likely to be generally obeyed. All states face problems – such as disease, economic instability, environmental degradation, the proliferation of weapons of mass destruction, and refugee movements – that cannot be adequately addressed by individual states acting alone but only through a framework for cooperation and coordination. International law can provide such a framework, largely by virtue of the propensity of states to obey it. To maintain this source of legitimacy, it must not stray too far from implementing values that resonate widely with its would-be subjects. Of course, international law conspicuously lacks generally effective enforcement mechanisms in dealing with recalcitrant states. Although formal mechanisms exist – ranging from military enforcement measures under Chapter VII of the UN Charter to the power of the UN High Commissioner for Human Rights to criticize states for serious human rights violations – they often lie dormant because of lack of political will, or else are deployed ineffectively or selectively. What matters for legitimacy, however, is enhanced conformity with reason than would otherwise be the case, not perfect conformity. Moreover, the pressure to conform need not be channeled exclusively through formal sanctions, as is shown by the way respected NGOs such as Amnesty International invoke public international law to influence state behavior, often by shaping public opinion.

This is just one way in which the NJC might be satisfied. Other possibilities include the cognitive advantages of taking international law as a guide to conduct (e.g., the claim that customary international law is a distillation of the time-tested collective wisdom of states, fruitfully drawing on their divergent perspectives and experience in resolving common problems). Or the way in which it cures volitional defects (e.g., by blocking the tendency of states to capitulate to internal pressures to act in ways that transgress basic norms of justice). Or by conferring certain decision-procedural benefits on its subjects (e.g., all states have reasons to promote peace, but efforts to do so unilaterally, for example, by a superpower pursuing a policy of prodemocratic regime change, risk being counterproductive, compared with conforming to the international law on the use of force).[9] Allen Buchanan recently mounted an important defense of the legitimacy of international human rights law on

---

[9] For a general discussion of the ways in which the NJC might be met, see Raz, *The Morality of Freedom*, 75f. For elaboration regarding international law, see John Tasioulas, "The Legitimacy of International Law." States, of course, are not the only subjects of international law, but they are for good reasons its primary subjects, and at the risk of some distortion, I focus on states rather than those other subjects (e.g., international organizations, peoples, multinational corporations, NGOs, individuals, etc.).

the basis of its epistemic role in enabling us to identify genuine moral human rights.[10] Although there is much of value in Buchanan's argument, I think it is undermined by a failure to heed the distinction between *practical* and *theoretical* authority. Epistemic superiority by itself can only confer theoretical authority, that is, it can make someone a source of content-independent reasons for belief regarding a given subject matter. If international human rights law is to enjoy *practical* authority in virtue of its epistemic advantages – that is, if it is to generate content-independent reasons for *action* – then these advantages must be appropriately bound up with *other* qualities (e.g., relating to efficacy in securing coordination or curing volitional defects, etc.) such that one is more likely to conform with reason if one took that law as practically binding.

Of course, skeptics about the legitimacy of international law will protest at many of the preceding claims. Arguably, however, the question of real interest is not whether international law possesses *any* legitimacy, even in such workaday domains as international telecommunications or postal services, but the *extent* of its legitimate authority. On the service conception, the scope of legitimacy is prone to "domain fragmentation," so that a legal system's claims of legitimacy are justified in some domains but not in others. This permits us to judge that some international law regimes – for example, the UN Charter and corresponding customary norms governing the use of force – are legitimate even if other branches of international law, such as the doctrines and institutions animated by a Procrustean free market ideology or by hopelessly vague and endlessly proliferating claims about "human rights," are not. Making such judgments is no easy task, with the result that we may often be uncertain whether a given segment of international law satisfies the NJC; by contrast, consent-based or democratic standards of legitimacy seem to promise greater certainty. Rather than take this as an objection to the service conception, however, one might regard it as faithfully reflecting our complex epistemic situation.

Now, a familiar challenge to the legitimacy of international law is that it imposes "parochial" values on people and societies that do not share them. Some "multicultural" critics see international law as a manifestation of Western cultural "imperialism"; for feminists, it embodies such "patriarchal" values as autonomy, rights, and justice at the expense of the quintessentially feminine ethics of "care"; neoconservatives decry the influence on international law of bureaucratic and pacifist European traditions of governance;

---

[10] See A. Buchanan, *Human Rights, Legitimacy, and the Use of Force* (Oxford: Oxford University Press, 2010), ch. 4.

and for the antiglobalization movement, it is a tool in the capitalist market's quest for worldwide dominance. All these claims can be articulated under the aegis of the service conception. According to the NJC, legitimacy is secured by enhancing conformity with *objective* reasons – reasons that obtain independently of individual or societal preferences and beliefs, and regarding the existence and content of which it is possible to arrive at *true* judgments. In their different ways, the complaints about parochialism deny that international law facilitates conformity with such reasons, as opposed to the counterfeit "reasons" asserted by certain dominant groups, no doubt in furtherance of their own self-serving agendas. Henceforth, I refer to the first, "Western imperialist" version of the objection, and to human rights morality and law as its target.

The obvious initial response to the challenge of parochialism is to undertake the taxing work of deliberating about whether, in any given domain, objective reasons are best fulfilled through obedience to international law. There are two large mistakes to avoid when engaging in such inquiries. The first is the genetic fallacy, according to which the localized historical origin of ethical notions by itself taints their claim to objective standing; conversely, we should not imagine that worldwide adherence to certain values would in itself show that they are objectively correct. Even granting the contestable claim that the idea of human rights has an exclusively Western pedigree, this is not incompatible with its containing objective truths that bear on all human beings, any more than the European origin of the theory of relativity renders non-Europeans rationally impervious to its claim to truth. Of course, we should guard against the danger that these ideas might embody an etiolated view of the layout of reason, especially given the ignorance, arrogance, and downright malevolence that Westerners have historically displayed toward other cultures. Nonetheless, its tainted historical origins cannot preempt the answer to the question of whether international law informed by human rights morality here and now satisfies the NJC.

The other error is that objective reasons dictate uniform outcomes because, simply by virtue of their objectivity, they are inherently insensitive to variation in circumstances. Objectivity does not entail the straightjacket of prescriptive invariance: contingent, nonnormative circumstances may objectively alter cases, so that what counts as fidelity to the same values, reasons, and norms is a dynamic matter, varying from case to case. Hence, the practical import of the reasons we have to respect human rights will vary according to such contingent facts as a society's level of economic development, technological capacities, and even its climate. One implication of this environmental relativity for human rights law is that the reasons to respect and promote human rights do not necessarily single out one specific institutional arrangement for doing so, such as democratic elections, free markets, or U.S.-style judicial review, as required in all societies. Another is that once appropriate institutions are established, they need leeway to interpret and implement human rights in light of the relevant societal context (something recognized by the legal doctrine of "margin of appreciation").

The anticipated reply – that we have grossly underestimated the force of the parochialism objection – will come in at least two significantly different versions, one based on ethical skepticism, the other based on ethical pluralism I consider each in turn in the following two sections.

III. PAROCHIALISM (1): SKEPTICISM

The skeptical version involves a blanket rejection of the objectivity of (ethical) reason: the NJC cannot be satisfied because there are no objective (ethical) reasons for action. Let me focus specifically on the targeting of ethical reason. Ethical skepticism of this sort is a deeply entrenched belief – indeed, because it is so often uncritically held, it may be more accurately called a dogma – in contemporary thought about international law. It is a supposed platitude that unites not only theorists as otherwise apparently diverse as realists in international relations, postmodern feminists, "critical theorists," and liberal cosmopolitans but even the authors of sober black-letter tomes who otherwise display few, if any, pretensions to theory. Consider, for example, the following passage from a recent volume coauthored by two leading British international lawyers:

> For the New Haven school the over-riding and determinative value [of international law] is the promotion of human dignity. While this is presented as an objective standard and the process as scientific, in reality in a world of deeply held diverse ideologies, religious beliefs and cultural practices, such values are inevitably subjective. Too often, by adopting this approach the Yale School has been found to favour law that is in accordance with US policy-making.[11]

Compare the following statement by a prominent European theorist of international law:

> The universal character of "human rights" is therefore a rationalistic postulate not only without substantiation in the theoretical sphere but also historically contested by cultures different from western culture . . . [T]he risk is thus

---

[11] Alan Boyle and Christine Chinkin, *The Making of International Law* (Oxford: Oxford University Press, 2007), 13.

very great that the cosmopolitan project implicit in the western doctrine and policy of human rights is in actual fact operating as – and is perceived as – an aspect of that process of the "westernization of the world" which is currently overrunning the technologically and economically weaker cultures, depriving them of their identity and dignity.[12]

Both passages exemplify a single pattern of thought. First a supposed value underlying international law's claims of legitimacy is identified ("human dignity," "human rights"). On the basis of what looks like a general metaethical stance of skepticism, it is asserted that such a value is merely "subjective." The conclusion is drawn that international law's legitimacy cannot be grounded in this value; instead, the attempt to do so, in a heterogeneous world, amounts to nothing more than the unjustified imposition of the parochial agendas of the powerful ("U.S. policy making," the " Westernization of the world," etc.) on societies that do not subscribe to them.

The first thing that should strike us about this line of thought is that, a few honorable exceptions aside, the idea that skepticism about the objectivity of ethics is a highly controversial thesis in metaethics and not a platitude, one in need of sustained articulation and defense, is barely registered. The next, even more worrying, thing worth noticing is that this line of argument teeters on the brink of self-contradiction. On the one hand, critics of this stamp seem committed to the nonobjectivity of ethical thought in general. On the other hand, they themselves make ethical judgments that they ostensibly treat as well founded, hence as "superior" to rival views. These include, for example, judgments to the effect that the Western policy of human rights is wrongly depriving non-Western cultures of their "identity and dignity" (Zolo) or that a legitimate international law is one based on the consent of its subjects (Boyle and Chinkin). Now, there are ways that such writers can be rescued from the charge of self-contradiction. One is by charitably disregarding their official endorsement of a general ethical skepticism, treating them instead as proponents of a doctrine of ethical pluralism (see Section IV). However, there is also a way to salvage the coherence of their arguments without dropping the commitment to general ethical skepticism. Instead of interpreting them as attempting to draw an ethical conclusion from an argument that includes a generalized ethical skepticism as a premise, they can be seen as engaged in an *ad hominem* attack on attempts to ground the legitimacy of international

---

[12] Danilo Zolo, *Cosmopolis: Prospects for World Government* (Cambridge: Polity Press, 1997), 118–19. Elsewhere, Zolo makes it clear that he aligns himself with "the entire tradition of ethical non-cognitivism, from Hume . . . to Rorty" and invokes that tradition as a key plank in his rejection of universalism. *Ibid.*, 59.

law in certain values by questioning the claimed "objectivity" of those values on the basis of a general ethical skepticism. Even if they can be exonerated of the charge of incoherence in this way, their rejection of ethical objectivity nonetheless remains deeply problematic. This is because it apparently rules out the possibility of radical, non-question-begging criticism of social practices, no matter how seemingly wicked.[13] This is a consequence of general ethical skepticism that has not exercised many of its proponents in international law and legal theory, including self-styled "critical theorists," nearly as much as it should.[14]

It is a testament to the powerful grip of this skeptical orthodoxy that a number of prominent writers try to evade skepticism's apparently corrosive implications for international law's legitimacy without taking a stand on the issue of ethical objectivity. One such attempt is the argument from modernity, which goes roughly as follows: (i) commitment to the values that underlie human rights – for example, individual autonomy – is ultimately the product not of any specific cultural ethos, but of the "independent variables" that define the conditions of modernity – such as industrialization, urbanization, growth in scientific and technological understanding; (ii) these conditions are pervasive and inescapable features of the modern world, exerting a steady liberalizing influence on both Western and non-Western societies; therefore, (iii) those societies that do not currently display a notable allegiance to human rights will eventually come to do so.[15] This argument has the merit of reminding us that cultures are not static and self-enclosed, but constantly evolving, partly as a result of interactions with other cultures. However, it fails to neutralize the skeptical challenge. First, its empirical premises are highly contestable: why should we subscribe to the vulgar Marxist thesis, seemingly implicit in (i), that value commitments are merely by-products of underlying socioeconomic forces? Even if we grant it, it is hardly obvious that the "inexorable forces of economics, technology and communications"[16] reliably work in favor of belief in personal freedom and human rights, as per (ii). Consider the plausible rival

[13] See John Tasioulas, "Consequences of Ethical Relativism," *European Journal of Philosophy* 6 (1998): 172–202.
[14] Martha Nussbaum has powerfully expressed similar concerns about the debilitating outcome of feminist legal theorists' entanglement with the forms of skepticism about reason made fashionable by postmodernist theory; see Martha C. Nussbaum, *Sex and Social Justice* (Oxford: Oxford University Press, 2000).
[15] See Thomas M. Franck, "Is Personal Freedom a Western Value?" *American Journal of International Law* 91 (1997): 593. Cf. J. Habermas, "Remarks on Legitimation through Human Rights," *The Postnational Constellation: Political Essays* (Cambridge: Polity Press, 2001), 121. For a more detailed critique of the argument from modernity, see John Tasioulas, "International Law and the Limits of Fairness," *European Journal of International Law* 13 (2002): 1000–44.
[16] Franck, "Is Personal Freedom a Western Value?," 624.

hypothesis that by fraying traditional identities and communal bonds, modernity provokes an illiberal backlash in the form of authoritarian government and religious fundamentalism. Even bracketing these empirical reservations, the argument fails because its conclusion shows only that history is "on the side" of human rights, not that there is any compelling *reason* to endorse their victory, inexorable or not. It is the absence of any such reason that animates the skeptic about human rights.

An alternative evasive strategy, famously employed by John Rawls, avoids this defect by appealing not simply to conditions of modernity, but to the *values* implicit in a liberal democratic culture. Yet it aims to defuse the charge of Western parochialism while strenuously prescinding from any commitment to the "objectivity" of those values, in any sense of that term debated by philosophers. How does Rawls square this circle? Although his Law of Peoples is an "extension" of a liberal conception of justice to the regulation of a Society of Peoples, it is "not necessarily" "ethnocentric or merely western" – in Rawls's cautious formulation – because its *content* can be affirmed for their own divergent moral reasons by nonliberal societies.[17] This is because the Law of Peoples does not simply project onto the global level the requirements of justice applicable within a liberal state. For example, its schedule of human rights is only a subset of the full array of liberal constitutional rights, omitting rights to free speech, equal religious liberty, an adequate standard of living, among others.[18] Yet this argument fails to address the parochialism objection in just the situation in which an answer is most needed: when the objection is advanced by nonliberal and nondecent states that, as a result of persistent and grave violations of the human rights of their own members, are rendered vulnerable by the Law of Peoples to military intervention by well-ordered societies.[19] Moreover, even decent peoples – the sole category of nonliberal society that can accept the Law of Peoples for moral reasons – might understandably baulk at being designated objects of "toleration" under its principles, to be protected from forcible intervention only because they are "not fully unreasonable,"[20] when the operative criterion of reasonableness ultimately derives, by way of apparently little more than stipulation, from a liberal democratic outlook they do not share. Finally, this is not yet to raise the question whether liberal societies can accept the Law of Peoples in the absence of a justified belief that the aspects of liberal democratic culture from which it derives can be given an objective vindication. In short, Rawls's strategy is more a capitulation to parochialism than its successful avoidance.

[17] John Rawls, *The Law of Peoples* (Cambridge, MA: Harvard University Press, 1999), 121.
[18] *Ibid.*, 68, 78–79.   [19] *Ibid.*, 90.
[20] *Ibid.*, 74.

Richard Rorty has urged Rawlsians to respond to such objections by biting the bullet of cultural imperialism. They should frankly embrace a "liberal ethnocentrism" by maintaining their commitment to the global spread of Enlightenment *values* while jettisoning the Enlightenment *philosophical* aspiration of giving those values an objective grounding.[21] Yet this beguiling maneuver fails to grasp that the claim to objectivity is internal to ethical thought, not a dispensable or outmoded philosophical add-on, partly because Rorty presupposes an outlandish, and certainly noncompulsory, interpretation of what objectivity is.[22] One way in which Rorty's interpretation of objectivity is distorted is that he sees it as incorporating the belief that "objective" values are destined to be historically triumphant. Following Nietzsche, Rorty regards this historicist belief as a manifestation of the resentment of the weak toward "the strong." This resentment is so great that it conjures up a "noncontingent and powerful ally" – "if not a vengeful God, then a vengeful aroused proletariat, or, at least, a vengeful superego, or, at the very least, the offended majesty of Kant's tribunal of pure practical reason" – that will enforce those values or hurt those who transgress them.[23] Against this fantasy, Rorty insists that the historical fate of liberal values is a contingent matter: "it *just happened* that rule in Europe passed into the hands of people who pitied the humiliated and dreamed of human equality, and . . . it may *just happen* that the world will wind up being ruled by people who lack any such sentiments or ideals."[24]

Now, the obvious response is that two distinct senses of contingency are conflated here: contingency as antiobjectivity and contingency as antinecessity. In denying contingency as antiobjectivity, the objectivist is not committed to the historicist claim that objective values will inevitably triumph in history. His view is perfectly compatible with the possibility, or inevitability, that power will be concentrated in the hands of those who repudiate sound ethical values, or even that the great mass of people will cease to believe in or adhere to such values. This despite the fact that a number of objectivist ethical outlooks – such as Christianity, Enlightenment progressivism, and Hegelianism – have combined objectivism and historicism. Instead, the objectivist is committed

[21] Richard Rorty, "Justice as a Larger Loyalty," in *Cosmopolitics: Thinking and Feeling Beyond the Nation*, eds. P. Cheah and B. Robbins (Minneapolis University of Minnesota Press, 1998), 56.

[22] See John Tasioulas, "The Legal Relevance of Ethical Objectivity," *American Journal of Jurisprudence* 47 (2002): 211–54.

[23] Richard Rorty, "Human Rights, Rationality, and Sentimentality," in *On Human Rights: The Oxford Amnesty Lectures 1993*, eds. S. Shute and S. L. Hurley (New York: Basic Books, 1994), 130.

[24] Richard Rorty, *Contingency, Irony, Solidarity* (Cambridge: Cambridge University Press, 1989), 184–85.

to the claim that if sound ethical beliefs do triumph, a potential kind of explanation of why they did so invokes the truth of those very beliefs.[25] Call this a "vindicatory" explanation. To this extent, the objectivist will dispute Rorty's thesis that all we can say is that it "just happened" that those values were converged upon. However, this does not imply their objectivity guarantees people will come to believe or act on correct values. Historicism is no more implied by the thesis of ethical objectivity than it is, contra the argument from modernity, capable of putting it in abeyance. The objectivist affirms only the *possibility* of vindicatory explanations, and he or she would be wise to pair this metaphysical claim with advocacy of intercultural dialogue, conducted in an inclusive and fallibilist spirit, as a vital epistemic conduit to the truth.

Even when disentangled from the historicist dogma, one might remain skeptical about the prospects for vindicatory explanations of ethical beliefs. Bernard Williams, for example, challenges the idea that the emergence of belief in human dignity and human rights (what, in misleading shorthand, we might refer to as "liberalism") can be given such an explanation:

> If we consider how these forms of argument came to prevail, we can indeed see them as having won, but not necessarily as having won an argument. For liberal ideas to have won an argument, the representatives of the *ancien regime* would have had to have shared with the nascent liberals a conception of something that the argument was about, and not just in the obvious sense that it was about the way to live or the way to order society. They would have had to agree that there was some aim, of reason or freedom or whatever, which liberal ideas served better or of which they were a better expression, and there is not much reason, with a change as radical as this, to think that they did agree about this, at least until late in the process. If in this sense the liberals did not win an argument, then the explanations of how liberalism came to prevail – that is to say, among other things, how these came to be our ideas – are not vindicatory.[26]

---

[25] For a compelling defence of ethical objectivity so understood, see David Wiggins, *Ethics: Twelve Lectures on the Philosophy of Morality* (London: Penguin, 2006), 359*f*. For Rorty's denial that we can adequately distinguish such purportedly vindicatory explanations from nonexplanatory *celebrations* of the same historical phenomena, and his endorsement of causal explanations of modernity from the point of view of "a bluff economic historian," see Richard Rorty, "Comment on Pippin," *European Journal of Philosophy* 7 (1999): 213–16.

[26] Bernard Williams, *Philosophy as a Humanistic Discipline* (Princeton: Princeton University Press, 2006), 190–1. Williams' gloss on vindicatory explanation (which we need not contest) is one that satisfies the following condition: "the later theory, or (more generally) outlook, makes sense of itself, and of the earlier outlook, and of the transition from the earlier to the later, in such terms that both parties (the holders of the earlier outlook, and the holders of the later) have reason to recognize the transition as an improvement," *ibid.*, 189.

Williams goes on to argue controversially that the unavailability of a vindicatory explanation of liberalism should not undermine our commitment to it; but leaving that issue aside, I want to challenge his insistence on its unavailability.

That insistence reflects his assumption that vindicatory explanations pivot on the possibility of faithfully reconstructing an argument between contending ethical views in which the parties share a fairly determinate conception of the criteria that govern its resolution. However, this assumption seems gratuitously restrictive to me. To begin with, from Williams's own perspective it threatens to prove too much. He wishes to contrast beliefs in natural science with those in ethics precisely with respect to the availability of vindicatory explanations; science, unlike ethics, can aspire to deliver objective truths because we may reasonably hope to give vindicatory explanations of convergence in scientific belief. However, if we consider revolutionary shifts in scientific worldviews, it is questionable that they satisfy Williams's demanding criterion. How credible is it, for example, that Galileo really won an "argument" – with mutually agreed-on *ex ante* criteria of success – for example, criteria regarding what counts as an adequate "explanation" of astronomical phenomena – against Cardinal Bellarmine?[27] Nor is this merely an ad hominem point, because the failure to accommodate paradigmatic instances of progress in natural science counts heavily against any interpretation of objectivity.

However, the more important objection is just the direct one that his assumption does not have a credible claim to be accepted as setting a necessary condition for any successful vindicatory explanation. What is ultimately at stake in offering such an explanation is whether the transition to a new set of beliefs can best be explained as intellectual progress, as an improved fit between what we believe and the way the world is independently of our beliefs. This is first and foremost a matter of coming to see the world aright, not of winning an argument, even if only an argument with oneself, conducted according to preestablished rules. Indeed, the transition to an improved understanding of the matter in question might, in part, involve a realization that the way in which the issue had hitherto been framed (not only by those with different views, but also by oneself) was in some ways deeply flawed. In the case in which a vindicatory explanation does involve a disagreement between contending outlooks, the imperfections of the defeated outlook cannot be so egregious as to compromise the sense that the new beliefs constitute an improved understanding

---

[27] Essentially the same point is made by Hilary Putnam in criticizing Williams's philosophy of science as "naive": "if quantum mechanics 'explains' phenomena, it does so in a sense of 'explain' that would have been as alien to the ways of thinking of a classical physicist as talk of 'the rights of man' would have been to someone living in the *ancien regime*." Hillary Putnam, *Ethics without Ontology* (Cambridge, MA: Harvard University Press, 2004), p. 150, n. 22.

of what is recognizably the same subject matter: it is because Bellarmine and Galileo, and Filmer and Locke, were in some suitably robust sense disagreeing about a shared subject matter that we can regard the views of one as an improvement on those of the other. Compliance with the standard imposed by Williams has not, however, been remotely shown to embody a necessary condition for not "changing the subject" in this way.

IV. PAROCHIALISM (2): PLURALISM

Does it follow from the argument in the preceding section that all the many and varied critiques of international law's "parochialism," "ethnocentrism," "bias," "lack of inclusiveness," and so on that have struck a responsive chord with so many of their readers are, if not strictly speaking self-defeating, at least highly tendentious? Yes and no. Insofar as these critiques are interpreted – as many of them are presented by their authors – as based on a general endorsement of a skeptical or nonobjectivist view of ethical thought, then I think that discouraging conclusion does probably follow. However, if we exercise a little interpretative charity, we need not construe them in this way, even if this contradicts the advertised self-understanding of their proponents. Instead, we may treat the invocation of skepticism about the objectivity of ethical thought as an unfortunate, as well as typically unclarified and undefended, piece of theoretical overkill on the part of writers whose chief preoccupations are not at all *metaethical* but, as their often highly charged condemnatory language betrays, intensely ethical. My suggestion is that the ethical doctrine that may often be charitably taken to underlie critiques of international law's parochialism is some inchoately grasped form of *ethical pluralism*.

Ethical pluralism, as I understand it, has no truck with metaethical doctrines like skepticism or relativism; instead, it is itself an ethical doctrine, one that presents itself as objectively correct. It is an amalgam of the following claims: (i) there are many irreducibly distinct ethical values; (ii) these values can come into conflict in particular situations; (iii) some of these conflicts are incommensurable in that responses to them are not subject to a complete ranking – that is, they cannot all be ranked as better or worse than each other, nor as equally good; and (iv) at the level of individual and collective forms of life, there are many different and conflicting ways of responding to these values that also are not subject to a complete ranking. An implication of (iv) is that the idea of the single best way of individual or collective life, even given "ideal" conditions, is a chimera. Ethical pluralism, so understood, has been propounded by a variety of philosophers in recent years, including Isaiah Berlin, Hilary Putnam, Joseph Raz, and Susan Wolf, all of whom combine it with a commitment to ethical objectivity. Nevertheless, it is true that the most prominent philosophical advocates of ethical objectivity throughout history have tended to subscribe to some form of ethical monism, in the sense that they would have disputed one or more of the theses (i) through (iv), especially (iii) and (iv). Yet although this historical fact may help explain why the thesis of ethical objectivity is often thought to imply a rejection of pluralism, no such implication follows from the logic of the situation. The objectivity of ethical thought is a distinct matter from the issue of whether ethics is pluralistic in character.

If ethical pluralism is true, the question arises as to whether particular norms of public international law, even if they exemplify an in principle eligible ordering of the relevant values, represent only one such ordering among others. If this possibility is realized, then societies subject to purportedly universally binding international laws that reflect orderings they do not endorse might properly complain that those norms unjustifiably impose an alien, usually "Western," perspective on them at the expense of no less valuable forms of life sustained by their own cultures. They need not deny that, abstractly considered, there are objective and undefeated reasons for adopting the Western outlook. All they need to establish is that the situation is symmetrical with respect to their own outlook and that, because this outlook is already theirs, they have a decisive (or at least an undefeated) reason to adhere to their own ethical tradition without being subject to countervailing international legal norms.

To the extent that international human rights law (to keep with our original focus) purports to reflect background moral norms of human rights, the worry is that the latter lack the requisite universally binding character necessary to confer legitimacy on the former. If so, international human rights law is a mechanism through which non-Western societies are illegitimately pressured into refashioning themselves along Western lines. However, can anyone credibly deny that a right to be free from torture is possessed by all humans and should be respected by all societies? Of course not, but other putative norms of human rights morality might be less easily defended against the pluralist challenge. It is in relation to this pluralist concern, and not simply that of environmental relativity, that we may interpret David Wiggins's suggestive distinction between "true internationalism" and the ambitious "global ethic" that inspires much of the contemporary human rights culture.[28] The latter endeavors to lay down a mass of highly general principles that apply to all societies,

---

[28] Wiggins, *Ethics*, 355–56.

such as those contained in the UN Millennial Development Goals, principles that aim to generate solutions to all the major problems confronting those societies. The former, in a pluralistic spirit, seeks to arrive at international norms by starting out from the identification and critical elaboration of ideas that members of different societies find they can really share – the qualification "really," presumably, underscores an objectivist constraint. Insofar as this process has a legal-political upshot, Wiggins believes it is best exemplified by instruments that express the "universally valid proscription of specific evil" – such as torture, genocide, imprisonment without charge, and forced labor. Like Rawls's argument, this suggests a briefer list of human rights compared with that which currently finds favor in international legal doctrine, yet without problematically sidelining the aspiration to objectivity.

Now, of course, one might dispute Wiggins's minimalist conclusion even within a pluralist framework. For example, it is not obvious why the eradication of extreme poverty, and a human right to be free from it, does not count as a universally valid proscription of specific evil to which all societies have decisive reason to adhere. Certainly, such a right is vulnerable to disastrously self-serving forms of interpretation and implementation on the part of powerful states, international institutions, NGOs, and multinational corporations, but the same is true of the universally valid prohibitions endorsed by Wiggins. Still, the key point for present purposes is not where precisely to draw the line between universal norms and objective norms with a narrower scope of application, but that pluralism indicates that this line will need to be drawn somewhere. Thus, a pluralist who is sanguine about basic socioeconomic human rights might wonder whether supposed human rights to equal religious liberty or nondiscrimination on the grounds of sex or sexual orientation do not presuppose orderings of values that, although in principle eligible, are certainly not demanded of all societies. To take another example, perhaps Tzvetan Todorov is correct in arguing the high value European societies reasonably place on individual autonomy, and therefore on the capacity of the perpetrator of even the most heinous wrongdoing to atone, justifies the prohibition of the death penalty, as in Article 1 of Protocol No. 6 to the Convention for the Protection of Human Rights and Fundamental Freedoms.[29] It is a further question, however, whether the only eligible orderings of the relevant values justify the same conclusion, with the result that the right, to life must be interpreted by all societies as incompatible with capital punishment.

---

[29] Tzvetan Todorov, *The New World Disorder: Reflections of a European* (Cambridge, U.K.: Polity Press, 2005), 68. Note that the protocol's prohibition does not extend to times of war.

Moreover, with respect to some of these rights, it is not even clear whether Western societies have unequivocally committed themselves to the requisite orderings of values, as is suggested by ongoing and divisive disputes about gender equality, gay rights, and the death penalty in those societies.

The implications of pluralism for international human rights law are not confined to which supposed human rights genuinely count as such in morality. Although no one is likely to deny the existence of a human right against torture, pluralism allows for the existence of a diversity of acceptable ways of justifying such a right. If this possibility is realized, we should resist automatically locking the official justification of the legal human right against torture into the ordering of values represented by just one justification.[30] This lets us put a benign gloss on Jacques Maritain's notorious quip that the drafters of the Universal Declaration of Human Rights "agree[d] about the rights, but on condition no one asks us why." If there are incommensurable pathways to the same schedule of human rights, then it is not the case that one of them is superior to all the others. There is no compulsion, therefore, to disagree at the level of underlying justifications. Here pluralism rides to the assistance of international law's legitimacy because it liberates us from the constraining assumption, which has dominated the philosophical discourse of human rights, that there is a single correct grounding of those rights.

Now, it seems to me a limitation of the moral theory of human rights developed in James Griffin's recent fine book that it does not take full advantage of the potential for such a pluralistic grounding of human rights.[31] Griffin construes human rights as grounded in a restricted subset of universal human interests, which he calls the goods of personhood or normative agency; these are autonomy (being able to choose one's conception of a worthwhile life), liberty (being free from external interference to pursue one's choices), and the minimum material provision necessary for meaningful autonomy and liberty. This restriction on human rights–generative interests strikes me as problematic for a variety reasons. For example, I find it deeply counterintuitive that the

---

[30] For an instructive comparison of Western/liberal and Buddhist justifications of that right, appealing, respectively, to autonomy and the noninfliction of suffering, see Charles Taylor, "Conditions for an Unforced Consensus on Human Rights," in *The East Asian Challenge for Human Rights*, eds. J. R. Bauer and D. A. Bell (Cambridge: Cambridge University Press, 1999).

[31] Griffin considers various formulations of the "parochialism" challenge to the morality of human rights – in terms of ethical relativism, the need for de facto cross-cultural convergence and the value of toleration within a Rawlsian framework. Unfortunately, he does not explicitly consider the bearing of an objectivist doctrine of ethical pluralism, which is what I am pressing in this section. James Griffin, chapter 7 of *On Human Rights* (Oxford: Oxford University Press, 2008).

severe pain inflicted by torture should be barred from directly contributing to the grounding of the human right against torture. Instead, appealing to our interest in avoiding severe pain, as well as our interests in autonomy and liberty, and no doubt other universal interests besides, seems to furnish a more intuitively compelling justification of that right. The problem with Griffin's theory that I wish to highlight here, however, is the way in which it needlessly renders human rights morality vulnerable to the objection that, by operating exclusively within the framework of personhood, it reflects a distinctively "Western" or "Enlightenment" outlook that constitutes only one ordering of values among others. Construing human rights as grounded in a plurality of universal human interests beyond the three appealed to by Griffin, such as achievement, knowledge, friendship, play, and the avoidance of pain, we enhance the prospects that there may be a diversity of justificatory routes to the selfsame schedule of human rights. The point I am making here does not primarily bear on the pragmatic concern regarding which story about human rights would be most efficacious in inducing non-Western cultures to acknowledge and comply with them; rather, it is based on the thought that some existing or potential cultural variation may reflect the objective truth of ethical pluralism, and that human rights morality should be appropriately responsive to that truth if its claim to bind all cultures is to be justified.[32]

Having recognized a plurality of justificatory routes to the same human right, we should also allow that there may be diverse ways of specifying the content of that right, and of trading it off against countervailing considerations in cases of conflict, that are also not subject to a complete ranking. Again, international law will be impaired in its legitimacy to the extent that it is not appropriately responsive to such diversity. None of this is to suggest, however, that accommodating pluralism to the fullest extent is everywhere a necessary condition of international law's legitimacy. Often there are reasons that tell against such an approach. For example, the desirability of coordination on the basis of highly determinate legal norms in certain areas may make it all-things-considered acceptable to privilege one ordering of values in interpreting those norms over alternative eligible orderings favored by other societies. My contention is only that (i) value pluralism has a significant, but hitherto insufficiently appreciated, bearing on the satisfaction of the NJC by international law, and (ii) many of the critiques of the legitimacy of international law on the grounds of its supposed "parochialism" are best seen as giving expression to a pluralistic, rather than a skeptical, vision of morality.

---

[32] For a general discussion of Griffin's theory of human rights, see John Tasioulas, "Taking Rights out of Human Rights," *Ethics* 120 (2010): 647–678.

Notice, however, that embracing thesis (ii) comes at a price for those critics of international law's "parochialism" who formerly appealed to ethical skepticism. A shift in stance to a position reflecting ethical pluralism requires that they explicitly engage in *ethical* argument, showing that eligible orderings of values are being unjustifiably excluded by existing international legal norms. This way of proceeding is, of course, significantly more challenging – but also more rewarding – than unhelpful hand-waving about the "subjectivity" or "relativity" of values.

v. CONCLUSION

I have explored only two ways in which the legitimacy of international law might be impugned on the basis of its supposed "parochialism." There are, of course, many other ways of formulating that challenge. Two alternative formulations are worth mentioning in closing. The first is the claim of *exceptionalism*. According to this, some or all international laws enjoy legitimacy with respect to *most*, but not *all*, of their putative subjects. The service conception of authority admits this possibility, because whether the NJC is fulfilled is a relational matter that can vary from one subject to another. So, for example, it might be argued that given special characteristics of the United States – its status as the sole remaining superpower combined with its commitment to the promotion of democracy and human rights, and so on – it is not bound by international legal norms prohibiting the preventative or preemptive use of force that quite properly bind other states that do not possess these characteristics. Of course, the exceptionalist argument is not restricted to carving out a sphere of autonomous action for the powerful; under its auspices one might also argue that key norms of the international legal economic order, for example, do not bind the most impoverished states because they are not best able to conform to the reasons that apply to them by taking those norms as authoritative. A second, perhaps rather more plausible, line of argument appeals to the value of *freedom* (or, in a more familiar phrase in this context, sovereignty) for the collectivities – primarily states – over which international law asserts the legitimacy of its rule. This resonates with those critiques of the legitimacy of international law that claim it sometimes intrudes on domains in which states should be free to reach their own decisions. So, the thought here is that among the reasons that apply to states are the reasons they have to reach decisions for themselves unconstrained by demands of international law, even if (within limits) their conduct is as a result less likely to comply with the *other* reasons that apply to them than if they had proceeded on the basis that they were subject to the authority of international law on the matter.[33]

The NJC, I believe, provides an illuminating framework within which to elaborate and assess the challenges to the legitimacy of international law, including the multifarious challenges that fall under the heading of "parochialism." However, adopting that framework means abandoning the facile dogma of value skepticism invoked by so many theorists of international law, from one end of the political spectrum to the other. I am convinced this would be no bad thing.

[33] Both of these lines of argument are explored in somewhat greater detail in Tasioulas, "The Legitimacy of International Law" note 1.

3   Parochialism, Cosmopolitanism, and the Paradigms of International Law

Armin von Bogdandy and Sergio Dellavalle

I. OBJECTIVES OF THE INQUIRY AND ITS PLACE IN LEGAL SCHOLARSHIP

A. *Paradigms of International Law*

An international lawyer, when publishing, deciding or advising about the law, should be cognizant of the possible theoretical foundations of his or her position as well as of those of opposing views, not least because such awareness can help to develop legal solutions that all parties can live with. Theories about the nature and the finality of international law arise within the framework of their fundamental conceptual preconditions – their underlying "paradigms" or assumptions about the world. Understanding these paradigms should provide a better framework for reconciling the diverse and contrasting positions within international legal scholarship. Greater conceptual clarity about the underlying paradigms will also support intercultural dialogue on international law. International legal scholarship should not be limited to debate about the best interpretation of a given norm in a given situation. It should also extend to a broader discourse about the varied conceptions of legal order that have developed in different legal cultures throughout the world.

Parsimony is an essential element of a good scientific inquiry. This chapter situates the impressive variety of visions of international law that have been formulated during its long history – and therefore also the *parochial* and the *cosmopolitan* understanding of human rights – within the framework of its two traditionally competing paradigms: particularism and universalism.[1] By paradigm, we mean the fundamental conceptual preconditions on the basis

---

[1] Our paradigms echo the old dichotomy of *realism* and *idealism*. However, we consider the terms *realism* and *idealism* and the respective conceptual reconstruction as unfortunate; see in detail, sect. III.B, *infra*.

of which theories are developed.[2] By theory, we understand a conceptual construction that explains phenomena and provides orientation. The paradigm of particularism forms the basis of all theories of international law that assert that true public order is only possible within the framework of a limited community. Hence, it is strictly related, albeit not identical, to the parochial approach to the human rights question as the theory that asserts that rights and values are deeply and inseparably rooted in the cultural soil of a specific tradition. If one accepts the particularistic claim, then the order that international law provides is substantially different from the order that can be accomplished within the single polity. In fact, from the particularistic point of view, international order would be better described as a containment of disorder. In contrast, the paradigm of universalism underlies all positions asserting that a truly public order on a global scale is possible at all. Once again, the closeness to the concept of cosmopolitanism is evident – and, once again, they are not precisely the same.

By *truly public order*, we understand a situation in which common rules ensure that human interaction remains peaceful. There will always be conflict, but conflicts are channeled by procedures that succeed in suppressing unilateral violence. It is important to stress that the concept of public order does not imply the absence of conflict. Attempting to ban conflict would be unrealistic and even undesirable because it would remove an important tool for adapting institutions and policies to social change. Rather, order should be understood as a situation in which a society succeeds in resolving conflicts through peaceful methods. Moreover, in times in which international collective action is necessary to maintain peace and improve human well-being, the concept of public order also includes institutions, procedures, and instruments for the fulfillment of collective aims at the international level.

Such an order would have to be a developed form of international law with features similar to those already familiar in domestic public law. In other words, a truly public order would require a *public* international law with an emphasis on the *public* component, similar to the *Ius Publicum* of the continental European tradition.[3] This *Ius Publicum* implies the existence of a legal framework for the exercise of any kind of power. For that reason public law is more than just an administrative law that serves politics as an instrument. *Ius Publicum* must also be more than a framework for politics. Public law should provide instruments for the realization of common interests. This

[2] This definition of paradigm is closely related, although not identical, to the definition proposed by Thomas Kuhn, *The Structure of Scientific Revolutions* (Chicago: Chicago U. P., 1963).

[3] M. Stolleis, *Nationalität und Internationalität. Rechtsvergleichung im öffentlichen Recht des 19. Jahrhunderts* (Stuttgart: Franz Steiner Verlag, 1998).

truly public international law has an important administrative dimension. As a structure and an instrument for the realization of public goods and interests, public international law in this sense would be more than a law of coexistence, more than a law of coordination, and more than a law of cooperation. *Public* international order and *public* international law would not, however, necessarily need to encompass international institutions that control instruments for coercive action, such as the police or military personnel. The example of the European Union proves that international *public* law and international *public* order are feasible even without granting transnational institutions the competence to use coercion. In the global context, the advancement of this project of truly public international order and law hinges to a large extent on the fate of international criminal law. If the regulatory project of the Rome Statute of the International Criminal Court[4] succeeds, an important element of global order will be in place without creating any global institution that resembles a state.

Particularism and universalism have been the dominant paradigms of international law scholarship for centuries and remain powerful conceptual tools, providing orientation to those working theoretically or practically in the field. Embracing one or the other paradigm gives rise to greatly varying understandings and interpretations of international rules and principles. Practical examples of such difference of interpretation include the construction of Article 2, Para. 4 United Nations Charter (UNC) or Article 51 UNC, and the understanding of the competences and responsibilities of the UN Security Council. Similar differences arise concerning the interpretation of international human rights instruments and of the competences of international courts and tribunals.

Nevertheless, our reduction of the conceptual premises of international law to only two paradigms must be qualified in two ways. First, particularism and universalism focus on the possible range of a truly public order. They respond to the question how far truly public order can or should reach. Should order confined within borders of the homogeneous political community (particularism), or does it potentially include all societies and human beings (universalism)? The two paradigms can succeed in mapping the competing theories of international law because at their core they contain a conceptual element that advances a more or less explicit statement about the feasible extension of public order. However, if we go beyond questioning the range of order and also include considerations of structure, the general paradigms of particularism and universalism might need some elaboration. This will remain marginal

---

[4] Rome Statute of the International Criminal Court, 2187 U.N.T.S. 38544 (July 17, 1998).

in the present analysis but could become more central in a further inquiry centered on the conceptual foundations of a general theory of public law and order. Second, although we claim that particularistic or universalistic attitudes explain the views of international lawyers, both in theory and practice, there have been some indications that this traditionally rigid dichotomy may be slipping. Once we have specified the reasons favoring our preference for the universalistic paradigm, we will suggest that the best form of universalism will also take particularism into account to some extent. In other words, as regards the approach to human rights, the cosmopolitan view cannot effectively stand without being related to an enlightened form of parochialism.

The analysis develops as follows: first one must understand the role of theory in international legal scholarship. In many countries, legal scholarship is overwhelmingly viewed as being an entirely practical affair without reference to its theoretical foundations. Second, we consider the legitimacy of today's international law given its deep encroachments on political self-determination (section II). The idea is that scholars as well as students will find the study of the two paradigms more interesting if they see their relevance for an important current debate. The third section of this chapter presents the paradigm of particularism as well as the related parochial understanding of values and rights in more detail. The fourth section presents the paradigm of universalism and the cosmopolitan approach to human rights. In conclusion, we suggest how these paradigms inform concrete interpretations, but also indicate how legal scholarship as a practical science can overcome theoretical cleavages (section V).

B. International Legal Scholarship: Tasks, Methods, and the Role of Theory

The role of theory in legal scholarship is disputed. Some scholars question the usefulness of theory for legal scholarship and portray theories as abstract, little connected with the positive law and of little use, even detrimental, to the tasks of the legal scholar.[5]

1. Practical Legal Scholarship and Conceptual Thought
A first dimension of legal scholarship is the description and teaching of international law. This practical dimension has played a crucial role since the inception of legal scholarship in the High Middle Ages as a core element

---

[5] We begin our discussion of theory by reviewing the German tradition.

of the European university. A university was usually composed of four faculties: theology, law, medicine, and philosophy, with "philosophy" extending to
all the sciences. Legal scholarship was institutionalized in the process of the
formation of the territorial organizations, which later became the European
states. Law has played an important role in the development of European
institutions since the High Middle Ages, as other normative orders of general
application gradually lost strength. This very high value placed on law became
a striking characteristic of European society.

Scholarship assumed the role of describing and teaching the law. In perhaps
no other academic activity are research and education so closely connected
as they are in legal science. In this respect, the establishment of public law
as a separate discipline in seventeenth-century Germany is telling. Public law
consisted of the identification of a scientific object within the set of positive
norms, the identification of a specific scientific purpose in the formulation
of structures and leading principles, and, on this basis, the orientation toward
academic instruction, institutionally anchored in the universities.[6] These have
been and remain the standard bases on which the scientific nature of the discipline rests. Thanks to this orientation, the development of adequate material for instruction and documentation constitutes one of the central tasks of
research in legal science: across Europe, practice-oriented genres of scientific
literature – the leading treatises and textbooks, both the academic and the
practitioner's handbooks or encyclopaedias, or the commentaries tailored to
practice – receive significantly more scholarly attention than in most of the
other sciences. International public law has been integral part of this, in particular within the Holy Roman Empire. The public law of the empire was a body
of law assembled from diverse components, including its own particular laws,
the rights of the territories, and a set of norms that would now be conceived of
as international.[7]

Such documentary activity remains an important element of international
legal scholarship, not least because it provides for the memory of the social
system in general and the legal system in particular. Accordingly, a good
description of an international treaty is and remains a worthwhile and difficult
scholarly aim. One cannot simply list the provisions; the scholar needs to give
them order, to provide some context, to explain what was controversial in
the negotiations and why certain solutions were adopted. A similar scholarly

---

[6] A. v. Bogdandy, *Handbuch Ius Publicum Europaeum 2: Offene Staatlichkeit – Wissenschaft
vom Verfassungsrecht*, eds. Bogdandy, Villalón, and Huber (Heidelberg: C. F. Müller Verlag,
2007), §27 Deutschland, pp. 436–491, sidenote 1.
[7] For more detail, see Stolleis, *supra* note 3, at 20 *et seq.*

exercise might be to bring all relevant statements on the legality of an international incident, such as the wars in Kosovo or Iraq, into a meaningful whole to describe the pertinent *opinio iuris*. Another object of reporting is the decisions of important courts and tribunals. To present a decision by the International Court of Justice (ICJ) as a meaningful and coherent text is a challenging task – not least because of its internal procedure, which calls every judge to write an opinion without knowing the position of the other judges, but also because they often hold differing ideas about the nature of international order. Already in this type of research, theories can play a role: opinions and ideas are easier to grasp if they are linked to theories – in our case, general conceptual constructions about the proper role of international law.

Certainly, the role of the legal scholar in most academic systems today goes beyond documentation. A further important activity is to make suggestions for resolving disputes. For many lawyers, law acquires its full reality only once it is applied to a conflict. Here Western cultures and other cultures may differ. Conflict may be less troubling to European lawyers. Some ascribe progress to conflict, and there are even theories that explain social order through the existence of conflict and its successful resolution.[8] Conflict is not seen as something to avoid but as something to be processed in search of a constructive solution. That is where the role of law comes in, and legal scholarship has its role to play. Lawyers translate the divergent interests into legal positions, thereby preparing them to be resolved through a legal process. Moreover, the norms that govern a conflict are often not very clear in determining which side should prevail. This vagueness is particularly prevalent in international law for many reasons, such as multilingualism, different legal traditions, the lack of a compulsory jurisprudence and the decision making at diplomatic conferences or governmental bodies in contrast to domestic parliamentary process. Article 2 Para. 4 and Article 51 of the UNC provide excellent examples of this indecisiveness.[9] To what extend should one interpret the provisions on the use of force in international relations in a way that constrains intervention? What was legal or illegal during the Kosovo war in the former Yugoslavia? Here, the role of legal scholarship as a practical science is to submit proposals for interpreting a norm in a specific conflict, or to evaluate a given interpretation,

---

[8] R. Dahrendorf, *Der moderne soziale Konflikt* (Wiesbaden: VS für Sozialwissenschaften, 1992), 50, 282 *et seq.*; G. Frankenberg and Tocquevilles Frage, "Zur Rolle der Verfassung im Prozeß der Integration," in *Bundesverfassungsgericht und gesellschaftlicher Grundkonsens*, eds. Schuppert and Bumke (Baden-Baden: Namos, 2000), 31, 44, *et seq.*

[9] See, e.g., *Military and Paramilitary Activities in and against Nicaragua (Nicar. v. U.S.)*, Merits, June 27, 1986, ICJ Reports 11, paras. 191–95; *Oil Platforms (Iran v. U.S.)*, Nov. 6, 2003, ICJ Reports 161, paras. 46–64.

advanced by a government or by the ICJ. When the law is vague, who decides the ambiguity? Certainly, any interpretation has to operate according to the standards laid down in Articles 31 and 32 of the Vienna Convention on the Law of Treaties (VCLT), but they hardly ever provide a clear result. Thus, fundamental ideas about the nature and finality of the international order often play an important, informing role when it comes to interpreting the law, and theories develop these understandings and clarify their bases and implications. Note, however, that in most cases, a theory cannot provide the "right solution" to a case. Theory helps to clarify premises and the force of arguments as well as to check their consistency.

Legal scholarship as a practical science has a further role to play with respect to law as a policy instrument. This is an aspect often little developed in legal education. If addressed, it is usually presented in the context of a teleological or purposive interpretation. It requires a norm to be interpreted in such a way that its objectives may be realized. Article 2 Paras. 4 and Article 51 of the UNC may serve as an example. The objective is international peace. What kind of interpretation best serves this objective? An interpretation within the universalistic paradigm will strive to curtail any unilateral form of military action and to strengthen international bodies, of which an interpretation within the particularistic paradigm will be more skeptical. When it comes to teleological interpretation, theories about the conceptual premises of the international order, the role of hegemony, and the potential of international courts and tribunals will all play a role in fleshing out the various possibilities. Consequentialist reasoning, which is an important aspect of teleological or purposive interpretation, is more convincing if it is founded on sound theory. Legal scholarship that proposes or evaluates such interpretation is more convincing if it takes relevant theories into account.

The policy function of legal scholarship is not limited to interpretation. The legal scholar is often called on to give advice within the legislative process. In many international treaty negotiations, legal scholars play an important role, and the United Nations' International Law Commission, which helps the General Assembly in the progressive development of international law under Article 13 of the Charter, counts many academics among its members. The policy advice function is important for legal scholarship's public role and recognition. In our complex world, good legal advice within the political process should be able to explain itself in more conceptual (which is to say theoretical) terms. Any legal scholar who advises on important issues of international law should be able to situate his or her advice in an overall account of what international order is about.

Legal scholars consider issues of legality, debating whether certain behavior or an act conforms to the law. Next to the question of legality, and in an uneasy relationship with it, sits the question of legitimacy, which discusses whether there are "good grounds" or "good reasons" for certain behavior or an act – whether they are "acceptable." Certainly, the thrust of modern European legal development has been to seek a situation where the legality of certain behavior or an act also settles the issue of legitimacy; this is one of the primary aims of liberal and democratic constitutions. Yet the issue of legitimacy continues to have a life of its own, in particular with respect to international law. The war against Yugoslavia, for example, which sought to prevent human rights violations, may have been illegal but legitimate. With respect to the war of the United States intervention against Iraq, all conceivable positions have been held: that it was legal and legitimate, illegal but legitimate, legal but illegitimate, and illegal and illegitimate. Today many legal scholars see the issue of legitimacy as being equally important as that of legality,[10] and the public institutions usually expect legal scholars to have an informed standpoint in this question. Yet any convincing argument about the "acceptability" requires some conceptual premises that lie outside the law and will usually be (in the case of international law) congruent either with the universalistic or with the particularistic paradigm.

2. Theoretical Legal Scholarship

The argument has been made here that theoretical, conceptual thought is important for legal scholarship as a practical science. In this respect, legal scholarship is not so much a producer of theory as a consumer. However, conceptual construction is also an important part of legal scholarship. The relevant production can be divided into two fields: doctrinal constructions, which are conceived to be "inherent" in the law, providing arguments to be immediately used in legal discourse, and other conceptual constructions, which are "external," being of a sociological, politological, or philosophical nature.

In continental Europe, conceptual thinking in legal scholarship usually takes a doctrinal form that is conceived to be "internal" to the legal order; this understanding also informs Article 38 para. 1, section c of the ICJ Statute.[11] This stream of scholarship is often described as "positivist," but a better

---

[10] See Wolfrum and Röben (eds.), *Legitimacy in International Law* (Berlin: Springer, 2008).

[11] A. Pellet, "Art. 38," in *The Statue of the International Court of Justice. A Commentary*, eds. Zimmermann, Tomuschat, and Oellers-Frahm (Oxford: Oxford U. P., 2006), pp. 677–792, paras. 245–64.

denomination is "doctrinal constructivism." Conceptual thinking in the form
of doctrinal constructivism goes beyond oversight of the body of positive law
and guidance for interpreting a norm in case of conflict. Its agenda aims
primarily at a structuring of the law using autonomous concepts, concepts
developed by legal scholars following the legal-conceptual (*begriffsjuristisch*)
stream of the historical school of law. To accomplish such a structuring, law is
detached from social reality and tied to legal instruments that flow from sources
of law. From this foundation, the positive material is transcended, not by way
of political, historical, or philosophical reflection, but through structure-giving
concepts such as *state, sovereignty, treaty, peremptory norms*, or *monism* and
dualism. Even though many of these concepts, in retrospect, clearly have *natural law* connotations,[12] they are conceived of as *specifically legal* and, thus,
autonomous. As a consequence, they fall under the exclusive competence
of legal science. The highest scientific goal is to present, or rather to recon-
struct and represent law as complexes of systematically coordinated concepts.
The key scientific competencies thus become abstraction, the development
of concepts, and the corresponding arrangement of the legal material.[13] In
crafting such concepts, legal scholarship creates for itself an autonomous area
of discourse and argumentation, a sort of middle level between natural law,
which is primarily within the competence of philosophy and theology, and
the concrete provisions of positive law, which are in the direct grasp of politics
and the courts. The functional legitimization of the discipline flows from its
specific competence over these concepts and the consequent structuring of the
legal material. Such activity might provide legitimization under the premise
that only a conceptually permeated body of law represents a rationalized and
thereby rational body of law.[14] Without doubt, the way a "legal system" is understood has changed over the past century. At its beginning, a system tended to be
crypto-idealistically understood as inherent in the law, whereas today systems
are more often seen as conceptual instruments for ordering and managing
the law. Similarly, the understanding of what a system can accomplish in the
law has changed; scholars are usually more sceptical today than they were

---

[12] On the philosophical background of this scholarly agenda, see J. Rückert, *Idealismus,
Jurisprudenz und Politik bei Friedrich Carl von Savigny* (Ebelsbach: Rolf Gremer, 1984),
232 *et seq.*

[13] Not every scholarly contribution presents a great doctrinal design. Much more common is a
type of scholarship that, as a sort of "upkeep" and "tending" of international law, systematizes
new legal developments within the established scholarly schemes – that is, doctrine – and,
in doing so, contributes to the preservation of the systemic nature of the law and the legal
relevance of the great "teachings."

[14] For a classic on this topic, see M. Weber, *Wirtschaft und Gesellschaft*, 5th ed. (Tübingen: JCB
Mohr, 1972), 825 *et seq.*

one hundred years ago. Yet this does not diminish the system-orientation of scholarship as such, at least on the European continent.[15] The autonomy of such doctrinal constructions is, however, not total. In particular, the founding concepts and thereby the differing constructions can be better grasped if they are fitted within our leading paradigms. A doctrinal construction centered on "sovereignty" or "nonintervention" sits squarely within the particularistic paradigm, whereas one centered on "universal human rights" and an "emergent international constitutional order enshrined in the UN Charter" fits the universalistic model.

Although doctrinal constructivism is an important element of theoretical legal scholarship, it does not exhaust scholarship's theoretical aspirations. Of particular importance is the scholarly attempt to "integrate reality" and to reflect on its foundations. This brings legal scholarship into exchange and competition with other disciplines that also strive to analyze and interpret social reality. In contrast to the success of the agenda of the "positivist legal method," the "integration of reality" and theoretical reflection fail to conjoin into a common disciplinary platform, because (unlike the doctrinal sphere) the relevant insights are often incommensurate. The discipline encompasses contributions that can only be understood as essayistic speculation but also contributions that draw on established theories from the humanities or social sciences and adapt their thought to usages within the legal discourse or the quantitative methods of empirical social sciences. Legal scholarship shares many interests with other sciences: for instance, the questions of how to understand sovereignty or how to conceive the legitimacy of international order. Scholars debate whether international law is a system based on universal values shared by everyone or an instrument of American or Western hegemony, whether it is a common law of mankind or of a global civil society, a managerial instrument for functional elites or an instrument for the coordination of state interests, and, above all, whether a lasting international order of peace is feasible and how can it be achieved.

Often, it is this sort of scholarly output that is best received in the other sciences and even by the wider public. The fact that such works are well received shows the resilience and persistence of the Western tradition in comprehending both the political and social spheres in legal categories, notwithstanding powerful competition especially from the economic, social, and historical sciences. Some theories, which form part of these expansions to legal scholarship

[15] *Cf.* D. Kennedy, "The Disciplines of International Law and Policy," *Leiden J. of Intl. L.*, 12 (1999): 9–133; M. Koskenniemi, *The Gentle Civilizer of Nations* (Cambridge, Cambridge U. P., 2001).

and its interpretive arsenal, have experienced broad resonance in the process of societal self-comprehension; we discuss some of them later. Our claim so far is simply that our two paradigms lead a to better grasp of this theoretical landscape.

Thus, we have seen that legal scholarship comes in different variants with distinct theoretical baggage. Each mode has its function and specific rationality, and the importance of the various modes varies considerably between the various scientific communities. For all modes, however, it is useful to search for theoretical foundations, not to find the solution for a practical problem, but rather to proceed in a reflective and scientific spirit.

ii. UNIVERSALISM, PARTICULARISM, AND THE LEGITIMACY OF PUBLIC INTERNATIONAL LAW

The two main strands of occidental thinking about international law and their opposing outlooks become apparent in the current debate about the legitimacy of international law within the process of globalization. From a non-Western perspective, the most serious deficit of legitimacy in international law may be its Western origin and perhaps its Western bias.[16] This, however, is not the main legitimacy issue discussed among Western scholars. Here, the main challenge comes from those who argue, mainly under the particularistic paradigm and specifically from the parochialist point of view, that the growth of international law in the era of globalization threatens one of the main achievements of Western civilization: liberal democracy. They are opposed by those who claim, mostly under the universalistic paradigm and from the cosmopolitan point of view, that international law leads to a new and promising world. Before exploring the two paradigms of particularism and universalism in more detail in sections III and IV, this section presents them in the context of this debate.

Reviewing a range of well-known scholarly arguments will reveal their underlying conceptions of the further development of international law. This discussion proceeds in three steps. The first step better defines the problem and the core concepts, such as globalization, legitimacy, and democracy. The second step presents important conceptions relating to the impact of globalization on the reality of democracy in a world organized around statehood.

---

[16] *Cf.* B. S. Chimni, "The Past, Present and Future of International Law. A Critical Third World Approach," *Melbourne J. of Intl. L.* 8 (2007): 499–515; M. Mutua, *Human Rights: A Political and Cultural Critique* (Philadelphia: U. Pa. P., 2002).

The third step submits conceptions for the protection and development of democracy in the process of globalization and relates them to conceptions on the future development of international law.

A. Defining the Problem

1. The Growing "Publicness" of Public International Law and Its Nonparliamentary Nature

The legitimacy problem of international law is closely linked to its growing "publicness." The term *public* carries many meanings. In this context, the most important is that international law contains an increasing number of norms that bind states irrespective of their consent. Important examples include Security Council resolutions under Chapter VII; the development of international treaties through independent international bodies such as the dispute settlement institutions of the WTO or the human rights bodies; other activities of international institutions that often succeed in framing important policy fields, such as the OECD Pisa policy with respect to primary and secondary education; or the development of international customary law irrespective of the concrete consent of a concerned state.

One can even understand the ever-denser layer of international treaties as a danger to the democratic principle. With respect to the democratic principle, legislation through international treaties is problematic from a static perspective, and even more so in a dynamic one. From the static perspective, the drawback can be found in the fact that although national (and consequently often democratic[17]) sovereignty is formally respected, the content of the rules is determined in intergovernmental negotiations according to traditional diplomatic procedures. An open public discourse that can influence the rules, an essential element for democratic legitimacy according to most theories, is severely limited. The autonomy of the bureaucratic-governmental elites is far greater than it is in the national political process. Although this is a general feature of international relations it is particularly so in international trade relations: the GATT 1947 and WTO have so far been among the most secretive. This secrecy is viewed as an instrument that strengthens national negotiators who are in favor of trade liberalization.[18] Furthermore, with the

---

[17] The argument applies to the extent that states' internal structures can be considered democratic. The problem with respect to citizens living under autocratic rule requires a separate investigation.

[18] J. Goldstein and L. Martin, "Legalization, Trade Liberalization, and Domestic Politics," *Intl. Orgs.* 54 (2000): 603, 612.

possible exception of the United States Congress, national parliaments show
a far greater deference to governmental proposals if they concern international treaties rather than autonomous domestic legislation. As the discussion
on the role of national parliaments in the EU legislative process has clearly
revealed, there is little hope of improving the input of national parliaments
into transnational rule-making during negotiations.[19]

The democratic problem grows even worse when viewed in a dynamic perspective. In modern times, *law* has often been understood to be synonymous
with *positive law*.[20] The main feature of the positivity of law is the legislature's
grasp of and responsibility for the law:[21] the law is posited by a legislature or
is at least – in case of the common law or other judge-made law – subject to
the legislature's competence to intervene at any given moment, amending or
derogating a rule that an autonomous adjudicative process has developed.[22]
This positivity of the law is an important aspect of the democratic sovereignty
of a polity: in democratic societies, the majority, usually conceived as a unitary
subject organized through the elected government, can at any moment intervene in the body of law and change it.[23] Under constitutional systems, most
social issues are subject to rules that can be enacted by a simple majority or
through delegated legislation. The possibility of fast intervention is a leading
principle in framing the respective rule-making competences.[24]

International law undermines the positivity of law in this sense. Once
a treaty is set up, the political grasp on its rules is severely restricted – not
normatively, but in all practical terms. Although international legislation
respects the democratic principle insofar as treaties are negotiated and
concluded mostly by democratically elected governments, treaties totally

---

[19] P. Norton, "National Parliaments and the European Union: Where to from Here," in *Lawmaking in the European Union*, eds. Craig and Harlow (1998), 209; D. Judge, "The Failure of
National Parliaments?" *West European Politics* 18 (1995): 79.

[20] G. W. F. Hegel, *Grundlinien der Philosophie des Rechts* (Berlin: Akademie Verlag, 1970),
§ 3.

[21] E. W. Böckenförde, "Demokratie als Verfassungsprinzip," in *Staat, Verfassung, Demokratie*,
ed. E. W. Böckenförde (Frankfort am Main: Suhrkamp, 1991), 289, 322.

[22] For the specific situation in common law countries, see P. Atiyah and R. Summers, *Form and
Substance in Anglo-American Law* (Oxford: Clarendon P., 1991), 141 *et seq.*

[23] A. v. Bogdandy, *Gubernative Rechtsetzung* (Tübingen: Mohr Siebeck, 2000), 35 *et seq.* The
guarantee of an efficient legislature is a leitmotif of many constitutional developments in the
past fifty years.

[24] In detail, M. Hilf and M. Reuß, "Verfassungsfragen lebensmittelrechtlicher Normierung,"
Zeitschrift für das gesamte Lebensmittelrecht 289 (1997): 290 *et seq.*; R. Schmidt, "Staatliche
Verantwortung für die Wirtschaft," in *Handbuch des Staatsrechts des Bundesrepublik Deutsch-
land*, vol. III, eds. Isensee and Kirchhof (Heidelberg: C. F. Müller, 1988), § 83; on the economic
constitution in Germany and the European Union, see D. Gerber, *Law and Competition in
Twentieth Century Europe* (Oxford: Oxford U. P., 1998), 232 *et seq.*

modify the relationship between law and politics. By ratifying an international treaty, a current majority in a polity puts its decision largely outside the reach of any new majority.[25] This restriction is particularly important in the cases such as the WTO or bilateral investment treaties because in such cases "corrective" political influence (i.e., noncompliance) becomes difficult because of the obligatory WTO or International Centre for Settlement of Investment Disputes (ICSID) adjudication. Certainly, the democratic autonomy of the new majority is preserved to some extent through the right of withdrawal, as, for example, through Article XV of the WTO. However, this right supports the democratic legitimacy of the WTO only as much as the individual's right to emigrate does the democratic legitimacy of a state.[26] It can hardly be considered as sufficient as it is not a realistic option.

This limitation of democratic self-governance might seem to be the inevitable result of a system of treaty-based international cooperation. Some might argue that the problem is intrinsic to international law. Yet necessity and inevitability are poor normative grounds because they collide with the principle of freedom. Much of contemporary international law goes beyond simple international relations and seeks to establish a "comprehensive blueprint for social life"[27] that will have an impact on democratic self-government far beyond traditional international rules.

Much of the development of international law since the eighteenth century has been built on private law concepts, mostly derived from contract law. As the Permanent Court of International Justice (PCIJ) famously declared in its *Lotus* decision: "International law governs the relations between independent States. The rules binding upon States emanate from their own free will as expressed in conventions or by usages . . . in order to regulate the relations between these co-existing independent communities or with a view to the achievement of common aims. Restrictions upon the independence of States cannot therefore be presumed."[28] Because states are conceived by classical international law as if they were individuals, the will of a government came to be equated with the will of all citizens. In this light there is no legitimacy

---

[25] K. Abbott and D. Snidal, "Hard and Soft Law in International Governance," *Intl. Org.* 54 (2000): 421, 439; J. Goldstein et al., "Introduction: Legalization and World Politics," *Intl. Org.* 54 (2000): 385, consider this a common political strategy.

[26] See *Universal Declaration of Human Rights* (1948), Art. 13, Para. 2; *International Covenant on Civil and Political Rights* (1966), Art. 12, Para. 2; Protocol No. 4 of the *European Convention on Human Rights*, Art. 2, Para. 2; see P. Weis and A. Zimmermann, "Emigration," in *Encyclopedia of Public International Law*, vol. II, ed. Bernhardt (Amsterdam: North Holland, 1995), 74.

[27] C. Tomuschat, "International Law: Ensuring the Survival of Mankind on the Eve of a New Century," in *Recueil des Cours*, vol. 281 (Leiden: Martinus Nijhoff, 2001), 13–438, 63.

[28] *The Case of the S.S. Lotus* (Fr. v. Tur.), P.C.I.J., Ser. A, No. 10, 1927.

problem in international law, according to the Roman dictum *volenti non fit iniuria*. Today, however, these premises crumble; therefore, the issue of legitimacy comes to the fore.

Thus, many international norms severely limit the freedom of a political community to organize itself. Why should such limitations be accepted? Once this might have been discussed in terms of the morality of international law.[29] More recently the debate has turned sociological, and *legitimacy* became the core notion. Legitimacy in this context refers to all good grounds for accepting the curtailment of freedom in a specific historic setting. Our contemporary setting is defined for many by *globalization*.

2. Globalization

"Globalization" and related terms[30] comprise a disparate set of ideas, the common thread of which is the weakened influence of the traditional nation-state, at least in its European variant. This transformation affects the legitimacy of the law because the nation-state has so far formed the only framework for democracy's successful realization.

The traditional European understanding of the nation-state is mostly based on the particularistic paradigm – in particular, on the assumption of a fundamental congruence between a people integrated by strong economic, cultural, and historic bonds and its state, the main task of which is to organize and develop this nation. The nation-state, visualized through borders, colored areas on maps, symbols, buildings, and persons, provides the all-encompassing unity in which human life finds its place and sense.[31] In the traditional understanding, the nation-state is seen as the highest form of realization of a people bound in solidarity. It is the source of all law and the foundation and framework of the national economy. Only through the nation-state can the national language, literature, system of science and arts, and culture in general realize their full potential. The space in which most human activity occurs is thought to be defined by a nation-state's borders. A further constitutive element is the supremacy of state politics over all other societal spheres. All of these spheres are subject to political intervention.

---

[29] As used, for example, in E. H. Carr, *The Twenty Years' Crisis, 1919–1930: An Introduction to the Study of International Relations* (New York: Harper Perennial, 1940).

[30] M. Albert, "On Boundaries, Territory and Postmodernity," *Geopolitics* 3 (1998): 53; K. D. Wolf, "Die Grenzen der Entgrenzung," in *Regieren in entgrenzten Räumen*, ed. Kohler-Koch (Wisenbaden: VS Verlag für Sozialwissenschaften, 1998), 77, 81 *et seq.*; T. Cottier, "A theory of direct effect in global law?" in *Liber Amicorum Claus-Dieter Ehlermann*, eds. A. v. Bogdandy et al. (2002), 99; E. Stein, "International Integration and Democracy: No Love at First Sight," *Am. J. Intl. L.* 95 (2001): 489.

[31] F. Meinecke, *Weltbürgertum und Nationalstaat*, 2nd ed. (München: R. Oldenbourg, 1911), 7.

This understanding of the nation-state finds its legal basis in the traditional concept of sovereignty. Under international law, sovereignty protects the state against foreign interference.[32] Under municipal law sovereignty expresses the state's supreme power and therefore its supremacy over all other societal spheres.[33] Under a democratic constitution, *popular* sovereignty is nothing but the realization of democracy on which the legitimacy of all public power rests.[34] On this basis, the symbiosis of the nation-state and democracy was formed. This remains the dominant conception of democracy today.[35]

The term *globalization* indicates developments which might undermine this symbiosis.[36] The common ground between the different understandings of globalization is the observation that there has been a massive global increase in interaction between the same spheres of different nations, especially since the beginning of the 1990s. Globalization goes beyond the phenomenon of the interdependence of states because it is said to lead to a partial fusion of once separate national realms, in particular the fusion of national economies into a single world economy. However, hardly anyone argues that globalization in its present form entails a development toward a fully borderless world.[37] If state borders become less important or easier to overcome in some respects and for some individuals, there is little evidence to suggest that they will ultimately become obsolete for everybody.

---

[32] Most visible in the PCIJ's *Lotus* decision, *supra* note 28.

[33] A. Randelzhofer, "Staatsgewalt und Souveränität," in *Handbuch des Staatsrechts*, vol. I, eds. Isensee and Kirchhof (Berlin: C.F. Müller, 1995), § 15, para. 25 *et seq.*, 35 *et seq*; C. Möllers, *Staat als Argument* (München, C.H. Beck Verlag, 2001) 291 *et seq.*

[34] H. Heller, "Die Souveränität. Ein Beitrag zur Theorie des Staats- und Völkerrechts," in *Gesammelte Schriften*, vol. 2 (Tübingen: Mohn Siebeck Verlag, 1971) 31 *et seq.*

[35] U. Volkmann, "Setzt Demokratie den Staat voraus?" *Archiv für öffentliches Recht* 127 (2002): 575, 577, 582; M. G. Schmidt, *Demokratietheorien* (Wisenbaden: VS Verlag für Sozialwissenschaften, 1995), 13.

[36] For more detail, see the report of the German Federal Parliament's (Bundestag) committee on "Globalization of the World Economy – Challenges and Strategies," Enquête Commission, *Globalisierung der Weltwirtschaft – Herausforderungen und Antworten*, Final Report, BT-Drucks. 14/9200, 49 *et seq.*; ibid. *Summary of the Final Report* (June 24 2002), at http://www.bundestag.de/gremien/welt/sb_glob_kurz.pdf; M. Ferrarese, *Le istituzioni della globalizzazione* (Bologna: Il Mulino, 2000), 11 *et seq.*; S. Hobe, "Die Zukunft des Völkerrechts im Zeitalter der Globalisierung," *Archiv für Völkerrecht* 37 (2000): 253; K. Dicke, "Erscheinungsformen und Wirkungen von Globalisierung in Struktur und Recht des internationalen Systems," *Berichte der Deutschen Gesellschaft für Völkerrecht* 39 (2000): 13; most influential are numerous books published in U. Beck's series "Edition Zweite Moderne" from 1997, in particular U. Beck, *Was ist Globalisierung?*, 3rd ed. (Berlin: Suhrkamp Verlag, 1999), 48 *et seq.*

[37] C. Möllers, "Globalisierte Jurisprudenz," *Archiv für Rechts- und Sozialphilosophie Beiheft* 79 (2001): 41, 46 *et seq.*

The term globalization was critical of the effects of the growth in global markets. However, the term made its way into the parlance of free-traders and gained favor in business circles to describe diverse forms of global contraction and the phenomenon of "debordering."

Global contraction and the decrease in the importance of borders are often be ascribed to changes in communications and transport technologies, a development already identified by *Karl Marx* and *Friedrich Engels*.[38] The multifaceted developments brought together under the term globalization are not, however, simply the result of a quasi-natural evolution of technical invention. They are also the fruit of conscious political decisions that have contributed to the dismantling of various borders. The recent opening of China is an excellent example for a political decision to embrace globalization.

Strengthened transnational bonds and partial fusions have led to a "denationalization," which is manifest in multiple phenomena.[39] An increasing number of persons have daily contact with individuals outside their nation; numerous persons migrate outside their original cultural spheres in search of a better life; national economies are increasingly becoming bound to a global economy; national cultures are placed in a context of a globally operating entertainment industry; and in numerous academic fields, a career depends on being published in a handful of international journals. At the same time, *globalization* indicates new dangers that are not confined to a distinct territory. Such dangers extend from climate change to financial crises to globally operating criminal and terrorist groups.

Finally, *globalization* stands for the proliferation of international organizations and the expansion of international law, which, depending on the conception, promote globalization, simply institutionalize it, or try to shape a globalized world for the benefit of the public welfare. The increasing autonomy of international law and international organizations from the political preferences of individual states is viewed by some as a prerequisite of a system of international law that meets the challenges of globalization.[40] National law, once considered the expression of the will of a people, accordingly implements ever more international rules resulting from an international process that is

---

[38] K. Marx and F. Engels, "Das Kommunistische Manifest," in *Das Manifest der kommunistischen Partei*, 2nd ed. (März: Reclam Verlag, 1980), at 47.

[39] M. Zürn, *Regieren jenseits des Nationalstaats* (Berlin: Suhrkamp Verlag, 1998), 65 *et seq.*: "De-nationalisation."

[40] *Cf.* C. Tietje, "Die Staatsrechtslehre und die Veränderung ihres Gegenstandes," *Deutsches Verwaltungsblatt* 118 (2003): 17, 1081, 1087.

necessarily different from processes under domestic constitutions.[41] National law is thereby denationalized. Thus, national politics come to be bound by a multiplicity of legal and factual constraints originating from outside the nation-state. To the extent that national politics reflect democratic processes, globalization and democracy clash.

3. Legitimacy – in Particular, Democratic Legitimacy

Legitimacy refers to grounds for accepting the law, and in this case whether international law may merit acceptance and obedience.[42] Many grounds can be adduced. Many base the legitimacy of international law on the effective protection of common goods and interests. In the international sphere, the maintenance of peace or the protection of the environment is of particular importance in this respect.[43] When public law provides for order, individual security, economic growth, and individual well-being, it builds a form of legitimacy that today is often termed as output legitimacy. A second category of legitimacy arises when public law respects and protects the fundamental interests of the individual – in particular, those expressed in human rights and due process of law. The third category is democratic legitimacy, also called input legitimacy.

To some it once seemed that the fall of the Berlin Wall and the dissolution of the Soviet bloc settled all fundamental issues concerning the principle of democracy with respect to the organization of public power.[44] Western scholars often assume that there is an almost universal and increasingly legally based consensus regarding the *necessary* requirements of democracy. International

---

[41] D. Thürer, "Völkerrecht und Landesrecht – Thesen zu einer theoretischen Problemumschreibung," *Schweizerische Zeitschrift für Int. und Europäisches Recht* 9 (1999): 217; Tietje *supra* note 40, at 1093, see "domestic and international law as a functional unity."

[42] Regarding this general discussion see Wolfrum and Röben, *supra* note 10; D. Bodansky, "The Legitimacy of International Governance: A Coming Challenge for International Environmental Law," *American Journal of International Law* 93 (1999): 596; P. T. Stoll, *Globalisierung und Legitimation* (Göttinger inaugural lecture), (available at: http://www.cege.wiso.uni-goettingen. de/Veranstaltungen/antrittsvorlstoll.pdf); *cf.* S. Kadelbach, *Zwingendes Völkerrecht* (Berlin: Duncker & Humbolt, 1992), 130 *et seq.*

[43] S. Cassese, "Lo spazio giuridico globale," 52 *Rivista Trimestrale di Diritto Pubblico* 52 (2002): 323, 331 *et seq.*; in detail M. Kumm, "The Legitimacy of International Law," *Eur. J. Intl. L.* 15 (2004): 907; The issue of the legitimacy of international law addresses the rational grounds why international law may merit obedience: D. Bodansky. "The Legitimacy of International Governance: A Coming Challenge for International Environmental Law," *Am. J. Intl. L.* 93 (1999): 3, 596 *et seq.*

[44] The most visible expression of this belief is F. Fukuyama, *The End of History and the Last Man* (New York: Harper Perennial, 1992), 133 *et seq.*

law,[45] comparative law,[46] as well as political and constitutional theory[47] all seem to agree on the required elements and among them that governmental personnel must ultimately derive their power from citizen-based elections that are general, equal, free, and periodic. Moreover, all public power should be exercised in accordance with the rule of law and must be restricted through the guaranteed possibility of a periodic changes in officeholders.[48]

This consensus with respect to the requirements of democracy has not, however, lead to a consensus on theory and premises. One still has to distinguish an understanding of democracy that takes as its starting point the people as a macrosubject (the holistic concept of democracy, often linked to particularism and parochialism) from one that designates affected individuals as its point of reference (the individual, civil, or fundamental rights concept of democracy, including the deliberative theory of democracy, often linked to universalism and cosmopolitanism). It is likewise not decided whether democracy is concerned with the self-determination of a people or of affected individuals (the emphatic or emancipatory conception of democracy) or whether it simply requires effective control over those who govern (the skeptical understanding of democracy).[49] Democracy remains an essentially contested concept.

---

[45] Groundbreaking: T. Franck, "The Emerging Right to Democratic Governance," *Am. J. Intl. L.* 86 (1992): 46; G. Dahm, J. Delbrück, and R. Wolfrum, *Völkerrecht* (Stuttgart: W. Hohlhammer Verlag, 2002), 14 *et seq.*; J. A. Frowein, "Konstitutionalisierung des Völkerrechts," *Berichte der Deutschen Gesellschaft für Völkerrecht* 39 (2000): 427, 431 *et seq.*; see also M. Nowak, *U.N. Covenant on Civil and Political Rights – CCPR Commentary* (Kehl-am-Rein: Engel, 1993), 435 *et seq.*; for a critique see M. Koskenniemi, "Whose Intolerance, Which Democracy?" in *Democratic Governance and International Law*, eds. Fox and Roth (Cambridge: Cambridge U. P., 2000), 436; B. Roth, "Evaluating Democratic Progress," in *Democratic Governance and International Law*, eds. Fox and Roth (Cambridge: Cambridge U. P., 2000), 493.

[46] N. Dorsen et al., *Comparative Constitutionalism* (Saint Paul, MN: West Group, 2003), 1267 *et seq.*; C. Grewe and H. Ruiz Fabri, *Droits constitutionnels européens* (Paris: Presses Universitaires France, 1995), 223 *et seq.*

[47] Schmidt, *supra* note 35, at 17; G. Sartori, *Demokratietheorie* (Darmstadt: Wissenschaftliche Buchgesellschaft, 1992), 33, 40.

[48] "Democratic government is based on the will of the people, expressed regularly through free and fair elections. Democracy has at its foundation respect for the human person and the rule of law. Democracy is the best safeguard of freedom of expression, tolerance of all groups of society, and equality of opportunity for each person. Democracy, with its representative pluralist character, entails accountability to the electorate, the obligation of public authorities to comply with the law and justice administered impartially. No one will be above the law." *Charter of Paris for a New Europe*, 30 I.L.M. 190, 194 (1991).

[49] For a convincing reconstruction from the perspective of the German constitutional scholarship, see Volkmann, *supra* note 35, at 582 *et seq.*; other reconstructions by P. Mastronardi, "Demokratietheoretische Modelle – praktisch genutzt," *Aktuelle Juristische Praxis* 7 (1998): 4, 383; Schmidt, *supra* note 35, at 115 *et seq.*

These different conceptions of democracy lead to different results on some issues in the municipal realm, such as granting electoral rights to resident foreigners, allowing citizen participation in administrative procedures, or employee involvement in public or private organizations' decision making. These divergences do not, however, affect or endanger the solid consensus on the institutions and procedures required for the realization of democracy within a state.

Such a consensus does not extend to the issue of how globalization affects the realization of democracy and how it can be maintained in the process of globalization. In both regards the differing conceptions of democracy result in conflicting diagnoses or proposals, none of which command any larger support. Thus the theoretical discussion of democracy acquires its greatest relevance on the transnational level.[50]

B. *Effects of Globalization on States and Their Resources of Legitimacy*

1. Globalization as a Threat to National Self-Determination

Most academic treatments of the relationship between globalization and democracy have a diagnostic character. More often than not, they come to the conclusion that globalization endangers democracy in its current form. That endangerment is usually considered to arise "behind the scenes." Unlike the danger to democracy posed by authoritarian governments, globalization does not intervene directly in the democratic decision-making process. More specifically, three theoretical positions appear to be of particular importance.[51]

The first position considers the developments subsumed under the term *globalization* as an expansion of U.S.-American interests and lifestyles. Accordingly, globalization (understood in this way) is little more than another term for American hegemony.[52] In this version, globalization means the economic triumph of *American* neoliberalism, which primarily benefits *American* enterprises, the cultural dominance of the *American* entertainment industry, which

---

[50] The debate in the European Union shows that such a discussion can lead to convincing results. Following an intensive and sharp, and sometimes apparently uncompromising, debate, the model of dual legitimation has become a widely agreed-on solution. The main focal point is a dual form of representation, through representatives of the peoples as macrosubjects (Council, European Council) on the one hand, and through representatives of the individual Union citizens (European Parliament) on the other.

[51] For an overview, see E. Altvater and B. Mahnkopf, *Grenzen der Globalisierung. Ökonomie, Ökologie und Politik in der Weltgesellschaft*, 4th ed. (Münster: Westfälisches Dampfboot, 1999), 542 *et seq.*

[52] U. Mattei, "A Theory of Imperial Law," *Ind. J. of Global L. Stud.* 10 (2003): 1, 383; S. Sur, "The State between Fragmentation and Globalization," *Eur. J. Intl. L.* 8 (1997): 421, 433.

transforms social patterns in other nations, or the leading academic role of *American* universities. All of this is seen to occur in a framework of historically unprecedented *American* political and military supremacy. Central international institutions, especially the International Monetary Fund, the World Bank, and the WTO – and to a lesser extent the United Nations – are considered agents of this development.[53]

This threatening scenario is based mainly on understandings of democracy that view self-determination as the be-all and end-all of democracy, whether they rest on a holistic tradition concerned with the self-determination of a people or on a fundamental rights tradition concerned with the self-determination and self-realization of individuals. Accordingly, globalization endangers democracy because it builds pressure to assimilate and leads to heteronomy, as a result of which the national democratic process is no longer free to shape the nation's life. This criticism of globalization is found in various – otherwise contrasting – theoretical and ideological camps. It is present within both the conservative criticism of mass culture (*Kulturkritik*) and the emancipatory conceptions of democracy. It is important to stress that according to this understanding, globalization does not necessarily lead to a weakening of state institutions. Few proponents of this position doubt that globalization is driven by the political power of the United States.

A second critical position views globalization as capitalism's attempt to increase profits, to conquer markets, and – in the Western welfare states – to reduce profit-restricting social achievements.[54] The danger for democracy lies, with regard to the Western democracies, above all in the undermining of the democratic balance attained between the opposing class interests. This position is mainly based on an emancipatory understanding of democracy, which is most prominent in European social democratic parties,[55] but it can also be of a Marxist-Leninist provenance. Representatives from developing nations often consider globalization as an extension of colonial economic dependency for the benefit of Western businesses and states.[56] This version by

---

[53] N. Krisch, "Weak as a Constraint, Strong as a Tool? The Place of International Law in U.S. Foreign Policy," in *Unilateralism and U.S. Foreign Policy*, eds. Malone and Khong (Boulder, CO: Lynne Reiner, 2003), 41; R. Rilling, "'American Empire' als Wille und Vorstellung. Die neue große Strategie der Regierung Bush," *R.L.S.-Standpunkte* 5 (2003): 1.

[54] Altvater and Mahnkopf, *supra* note 51, at 562 *et seq.*; Beck, *supra* note 36, at 14; H. P. Martin and H. Schumann, *Die Globalisierungsfalle. Der Angriff auf Demokratie und Wohlstand* (Hamburg: Rowholt Tb., 1996), 193 *et seq.*

[55] In more detail, Schmidt, *supra* note 35, at 159 *et seq.*

[56] A. Anghie, "Time Present and Time Past: Globalization, International Financial Institutions, and the Third World," *N.Y.U. J. of Intl. L. & Pol.* 32 (1999–2000): 243, particularly 246 *et seq.*, 275 *et seq.*; a helpful overview of the multilayered discussion is provided by B. S. Chimni, "Towards a Radical Third World Approach to Contemporary International Law," *Intl. Center for Comp. L. & Pol. Rev.* 5 (2002): 16, 21 *et seq.*

no means proclaims the decline of the state, which is viewed instead as the most important agent for the implementation of particular interests.

The third position lacks the immediate critical impetus of the other two. It focuses rather on the fundamental weakening of national institutions' power to shape a nation's life resulting from the increased strength of transnationally operating groups of individuals and organizations – in particular, economic actors, but also criminal organizations. These groups are seen to have moved from the national into the international realm and as having emancipated themselves – at least partially – from the political supremacy of state institutions.[57] This position views globalization much more as a spontaneous evolutionary development than do the first two.[58]

Political attempts by state institutions to counter the negative aspects of globalization are judged ambivalently in this understanding. Accordingly, as opposed to the first two versions, international law and in particular international economic law are not construed as the driving forces of globalization; rather they are seen as capable of promoting global welfare. Nevertheless, the international mechanisms that aim through law to order the spontaneous process of globalization, including those of global governance,[59] may come under criticism because of their detrimental effect on democracy. This viewpoint questions the absence of democratic control, the lack of transparency and responsiveness, the technocratic character of collective decision making, and the difficulty of changing established rules.[60]

This understanding is further developed by various theoretical schools.[61] The system theory, as elaborated by *Niklas Luhmann*, sharpens the critique

---

[57] J. T. Mathews, "Power Shift," 76 *Foreign Affairs* (1997): 1, 50 *et seq.*; N. Luhmann, Der Staat des politischen Systems, in *Perspektiven der Weltgesellschaft*, ed. Beck (Berlin: Shurkamp, 1998), at 375; Zumbansen, "Die vergangene Zukunft des Völkerrechts," *Kritische Justiz* 34 (2001): 46, 59 *et seq.*

[58] Enquête Commission, *supra* note 36, at 56.

[59] Commission on Global Governance, "On Global Governance," in *Our Global Neighbourhood: Report of the Commission on Global Governance* (Oxford: Oxford U. P., 1995), 253 *et seq.*; D. Messner and F. Nuscheler, "Global Governance. Organisationselemente und Säulen einer Weltordnungspolitik," in *Weltkonferenzen und Weltberichte. Ein Wegweiser durch die internationale Diskussion*, eds. Messner and Nuscheler (Bonn: Dietz Verlag J. H. W. Nachf, 1996), 12, 21.

[60] Considerations of this kind focus on the WTO: S. Charnovitz, "WTO Cosmopolitics," 34 N.Y.U. J. Intl. L. & Pol. (2002): 299 *et seq.*; M. Krajewski, *Verfassungsperspektiven und Legitimation des Rechts der Welthandelsorganisation* (Berlin: Duncker & Humblot, 2001), 217 *et seq.*; M. Hilf and B. Eggers, Der WTO-Panelbericht im EG/USA-Hormonstreit, Europäische Zeitschrift für Wirtschaftsrecht 8 (1997): 559; generally J. Crawford, *Democracy and International Law*, British Yearbook Intl. L. 64 (1994): 113 *et seq.*

[61] Powerful and influential C. Schmitt, *Der Begriff des Politischen*, 2nd ed. (Berlin: Duncker & Humblot, 1963), 10 of the foreword: "Die Epoche der Staatlichkeit geht nun zu Ende" ("The era of statehood is coming to an end").

considerably. According to Luhmann the most important sectors of national societies have already been fully globalized, and a global society with a global political system (the "international community") has been formed. However, neither the global nor the national political systems, which subsist as partial systems, are considered to enjoy supremacy over other societal spheres.[62] The demise of the supremacy of politics is a key assertion of this theoretical camp with profound consequences for democracy.

This dramatic diagnosis of the fundamental weakening of traditional democratic institutions is by no means limited to Luhmann. Some international relations theorists assert the existence of an integrated (or "debordered") world in which the nation-state will become increasingly irrelevant.[63] On the basis of a number of sociological studies, the majority opinion of the German Parliament's Enquête Commission on globalization similarly concluded that globalization causes a substantial erosion of democratic decision making in national institutions.[64]

2. Globalization as an Instrument of Democratization

These bleak visions contrast with optimistic accounts. There is by no means a consensus that globalization weakens the realization of the democratic principle. Rather, some see a close interaction between globalization and democratization, which increases the legitimacy of states. In this respect, it is helpful to distinguish between on the viewpoint that focuses on economic development and one more interested in the further development of international law.

The first school of thought, to which the periodical *The Economist* and the minority of the German Parliament's Enquête Commission belong, emphasizes the positive democratic effects of free trade and communicative freedoms.[65] This approach stresses the link between global free trade and prosperity on the one hand and prosperity and democracy on the other.[66] Political

---

[62] N. Luhmann, *Die Weltgesellschaft*, 57 A.R.S.P. (1971): 1, 27 *et seq.*; ibid., *Die Gesellschaft der Gesellschaft* (Berlin: Shurkamp, 1997), 145 *et seq.*; ibid., "Der Staat des politischen Systems," in *Perspektiven der Weltgesellschaft*, ed. Beck (Berlin: Shurkamp, 1998), 376 *et seq.*; G. Teubner, "Globale Bukowina: Zur Emergenz eines transnationalen Rechtspluralismus," *Rechtshistorisches J.* 15 (1996): 255 *et seq.*

[63] Forschungsgruppe Weltgesellschaft, "Weltgesellschaft: Identifizierung eines 'Phantoms'" Politische Vierteljahresschrift 37 (1996): 5, 12.

[64] Enquête Commission, *supra* note 36, at 56.

[65] Enquête Commission, *supra* note 36, at 461 *et seq.* (minority vote).

[66] Regarding the correlation between trade and wealth, see P. Chow, "Causality between Export Growth and Industrial Development," *J. Dev. Econ.* 26 (1987): 55 *et seq.*; A. Harrison, "Openness and Growth: A Time-Series, Cross Country Analysis for Developing Countries," *J. of Dev. Econ.*

self-determination plays a lesser role in this liberal tradition of the democratic theory, which values democracy primarily for its efficacy in ensuring the control and responsiveness of politicians and bureaucrats.

Against this background, a limitation on the reach of national political activity due to the pressures of globalization is not considered as fundamentally negative or hostile to democracy. Rather, these pressures are seen as tending to limit the scope for unreasonable decisions of the political classes that damage the interests of the majority by consumers.[67] Moreover, democracy and fundamental rights are strengthened through global publicity and the influence of global media, which loosen the grasp of authoritarian regimes on individuals.

Another school of thought, more interested in law than economics, reaches remarkably similar conclusions. This school embraces the universalistic paradigm, encouraging an increasingly stringent and dense set of international rules that bind national governments.[68] This presupposes a deepening ethical dimension of international law, the law's expansion and more effective enforcement, and a partial emancipation from the will of the individual state.[69] All these developments responded to the challenges of a globalized world. The core institutions of international law are seen as increasingly effective instruments for controlling dictatorial regimes and promoting democratic

---

48 (1996): 419 *et seq.*; A. J. Frankel and D. Romer, "Does Trade Cause Growth?" *Am. Econ. Rev.* 89 (1999): 379 *et seq.*; A. D. Irwin and M. Tervio, "Does Trade Raise Income? Evidence from the Twentieth Century," *J. of Intl. Econ.* 57 (2002): 1 *et seq.*; Regarding the correlation between wealth and democracy J. Helliwell, "Empirical Linkages between Democracy and Economic Growth," *British J. Pol. Sci.* 24 (1994): 225 *et seq.*; R. J. Barro, "Determinants of Democracy," *J. Pol. Econ.* 107 (1999): 158 *et seq.*; D. Acemoglu and J. A. Robinson, "Why Did the West Extend the Franchise? Democracy, Inequality and Growth in Historical Perspective," *Quart. J. Econ.* 115 (2000): 1167 *et seq.*

67 W. Meng, "Gedanken zur Frage unmittelbarer Anwendung von WTO-Recht in der EG," in *Recht zwischen Umbruch und Bewahrung: Völkerrecht, Europarecht, Staatsrecht. Festschrift Für Rudolf Bernhardt*, eds. U. Beyerlin et al. (Berlin: Springer, 1995), 1063, 1080 *et seq.*

68 This school of thought is particularly strong in the German-speaking scholarship, Frowein, *supra* note 45, at 440 *et seq.*; C. Tomuschat, "International Law as the Constitution of Mankind," in *International Law on the Eve of the Twenty-First Century: A View from the International Law Commission* (New York: United Nations Publications, 1997): 37 *et seq.*; R. Uerpmann, "Internationales Verfassungsrecht," *JuristenZeitung* 56 (2001): 565, 566 *et seq.*; T. Cottier and M. Hertig, "The Prospects of 21st Century Constitutionalism," *Max Planck Yearbook U.N. L.* 7 (2003): 261; see also P.-M. Dupuy, "The Constitutional Dimension of the Charter of the United Nations Revisited," *Max Planck Yearbook U.N. L.* 1 (1997): 1 *et seq.*

69 H. Mosler, "The International Society as a Legal Community," *R.d.C.* 140 (1974): 1, 31 *et seq.*; Tomuschat *supra* note 27, 72 *et seq.*; B. Fassbender, "Der Schutz der Menschenrechte als zentraler Inhalt des völkerrechtlichen Gemeinwohls," *Europäische Grundrechte-Zeitschrift* 30 (2003): 1, 2 *et seq.*

forms of government.[70] Globalization seen in this light becomes the impetus
for strengthened domestic democratic institutions.[71]

C. Strategies to Respond to the Challenge

Those who wish to strengthen the legitimacy of international law may pursue any one of a number of strategies. One approach might seek to improve
the problem-solving capacity of international law in general and international
institutions in particular in the hope that more efficiency and effectiveness
will improve output legitimacy. A second strategy is centered on human rights,
seeking to impose such rights against states, but also against rights-endangering
institutions such as the UN Security Council or the World Bank. International
law gains legitimacy by protecting fundamental human interests and universal values. Conceptually the most difficult question remains how to uphold
democratic legitimacy in this context.[72]

---

[70] Franck, "The Emerging Right to Democratic Governance," *Am. J. Intl. L.* 86 (1992): 46, 47 *et
seq.*; Stein, *supra* note 2, 533 *et seq.*; M. Beutz, "Functional Democracy: Responding to failures
of accountability," *Harv. J. Intl. L* 44 (2003): 387, 391 *et seq.*

[71] Culminating in the right to intervention: early on O. Schachter, "The Legality of Pro-
Democratic Invasion," *Am. J. Intl. L.* 78 (1984): 645, 649 *et seq.*; M. Halberstam, "The Copen-
hagen Document: Intervention in Support of Democracy," *Harv. J. Intl. L.* 34 (1993): 163,
175; F. Tesón, *A Philosophy of International Law* (Boulder, CO: Westview P., 1998), 55, 57;
critical M. Koskenniemi, "Die Polizei im Tempel," in *Einmischung Erwünscht? Menschenrechte und Bewaffnete*, ed. H. Brunkhorst (Frankfurt am Main: Fischer, 1998), 63, 64 *et seq.*
For the position that international law is strengthened through the process of globalization, see
M. List and B. Zangl, "Verrechtlichung internationaler Politik," in *Die neuen internationalen
Beziehungen*, eds. G. Hellmann, K. Wolf, and M. Zürn (Baden-Baden: Nomos, 2003), 387
et seq.

[72] Most academic contributions regarding the protection and development of democracy in the
process of globalization have not yet been developed into detailed models. Rather, they exist in
a preliminary stage involving the testing of ideas on a new and by no means fully understood
phenomenon. In particular, international legal scholarship in continental Europe does not
yet focus on the democratic legitimacy of international law and international organizations.
The close connection between U.S. international legal scholarship and the discipline of
international relations leads to a more intensive perception; for a useful compilation, see G.
Fox/B. Roth (eds.), *Democratic Governance and International Law* (Cambrdige: Cambridge
U. P., 2000); the contributions in Alfred C. Aman Jr., "Globalization and Governance: The
Prospects for Democracy," *Ind. J. Global L. Stud.* 10 (2003): 1. Yet the subject is also considered
by American scholars to be in an embryonic phase, C. Ku and H. Jacobson, "Broaching the
Issues," in *Democratic Accountability and the Use of Force in International Law*, eds. C. Ku and
H. Jacobson (Cambridge: Cambridge U. P., 2003), 3, 8. In continental European journals, there
have been relatively few recent contributions that have focused on this subject. The United
Kingdom is situated, like most, halfway between the European and American positions. The
European Journal of International Law does not differ in this respect, with contributions from
S. Wheatley, "Democracy in International Law: A European Perspective," *Intl. Comp. L.* 51
(2002): 225, 227 *et seq.*; *ibid.*, "Deliberative Democracy and Minorities," *Eur. J. Intl. L.* 14 (2003):

The principle of democracy arises most often: first, as an international legal requirement regarding national systems of government and, second, in connection with parliamentary control of foreign policy.[73] This section considers the conceptual foundations of both views of democracy, in relation to the particularistic and the universalistic paradigms.

1. The Particularistic-Parochial Response: State Sovereignty as the Leading Principle

One approach to safeguarding democracy within the process of globalization follows the particularistic paradigm, claiming that democracy can only be successfully realized within the borders of a nation-state.[74] This approach is substantiated by the parochial understanding of the origin of rights and values, which are essentially situated within a specific cultural and historic tradition. The primary concern there would be the protection of and a return to the political supremacy of national democratic institutions – in other words, the protection of state sovereignty against outside interference. As a result, this approach resists the transnationalization of societal spheres and the autonomization of international political decision making and international lawmaking.[75]

The particularistic-parochial approach may seek to slow down or even reject globalization as a threat to democracy. As Ernst-Wolfgang Böckenförde, perhaps the most eminent living German *Staatsrechtslehrer*, puts it: "If statehood [and therefore democracy] is to be preserved, then a counter-thrust against

507; Sur, "The State between Fragmentation and Globalization," *Eur. J. Intl. L.* 8 (1997): 421; S. Marks, "The End of History? Reflections on Some International Legal Theses," *Eur. J. Intl. L.* 8 (1997): 449.

[73] A. Randelzhofer, "Zum behaupteten Demokratiedefizit der Europäischen Gemeinschaft," in *Der Staatenverbund der Europäischen*, eds. P. Hommelhoff and P. Kirchhof (Heidelberg: C. F. Müller, 1994): 39, 40 *et seq.*; it is difficult to find more detailed discussions in general textbooks, *cf.* K. Doehring, *Völkerrecht* (Heidelberg: C. F. Müller, 1999), paras. 117, 239, and 990; K. Ipsen, *Völkerrecht*, 4th ed. (München: Beck Juristischer Verlag, 1999), 374 *et seq.*; P. Kunig, "Völkerrecht und staatliches Recht," in *Übungen im Völkerrecht*, 2nd ed., ed. W. Graf Vitzthum (Berlin: de Gruyter, 2001), 87, 93 *et seq.*; M. Shaw, *International Law*, 4th ed. (Cambridge: Cambridge U. P., 1997), 177 *et seq.*; P. Daillier and A. Pellet, *Droit International Public*, 6th ed. (Paris: LGDJ, 1999), 427 *et seq.*; B. Conforti, *Diritto Internazionale*, 5th ed. (Milan: Editoriale Scientifica, 1997), 191 *et seq.*; J. González Campos et al., *Curso de Derecho Internacional Público* (New York: Civitas, 2002), 432 *et seq.*

[74] J. Isensee, "Abschied der Demokratie vom Demos," in *Festschrift für Paul Mikat*, eds. D. Schwab et al. (Berlin: Dunker & Humblot, 1989), 705.

[75] E. W. Böckenförde, "Die Zukunft politischer Autonomie," in *Staat, Nation, Europa* (Berlin: Suhrkamp, 1999), 103, 124 *et seq.*; similar to Hillgruber, "Souveränität – Verteidigung eines Rechtsbegriffs," 57 *JuristenZeitung* (2002): 1072; J. Isensee, "Die alte Frage nach der Rechtfertigung des Staates," *JuristenZeitung* 54 (1999): 6, 265, *et seq.*; P. Kahn, "American Hegemony and International Law," *Chicago J. Intl. L.* 1 (2000): 1, 3, *et seq.*; J. Rubenfeld, "The Two World Orders," in *American and European Constitutionalism*, ed. G. Nolte (2005): 280–96.

the globalization process appears necessary in the form of a struggle for the re-establishment of the supremacy of politics in a governable space."[76] To counter transnational interdependence detrimental to democracy, the development of international law must, in this view, also be slowed down or even rejected. This is especially true in so far as it supports transnational interdependence or affects spheres in which lawmaking and political decision making require maximum legitimation, particularly with regard to the redistribution of resources, security, or national identity. From this perspective, the growth of transnational interdependence makes parliamentary control of foreign policy seem insufficient to protect democracy. In the absence of a global demos, international law lacks the necessary sources of legitimacy. This viewpoint questions globalization as a path for increasing societal wealth and individual freedom and accords the principle of democracy fundamental primacy.

Translated into the categories of international law, this understanding corresponds to a position that considers mere coordination[77] – rather than cooperation or even integration – as the appropriate task and gestalt for international law.[78] Accordingly, the concept of sovereignty, viewed as maximum state autonomy, becomes the guiding paradigm for the development of international law. The international system should therefore aim at sovereign equality and not at the democratization of the international system. In other words: the principle of democracy translates in the international realm into the principle of sovereign equality.

Another approach would allow for state cooperation beyond mere coordination, but on an informal basis. This position is not opposed to cooperation as such, but considers the processes of international legalization and autonomous international legislation to be problematic under the democratic principle.[79] Because cooperation affects democratic self-determination more than simple coordination would, it should be kept more seriously outside the ambit of

---

[76] Böckenförde, *supra* note 21, at 123; also D. Schindler, "Völkerrecht und Demokratie," in *Liber Amicorum Professor Seidl-Hohenveldern*, eds. G. Hafner, et al. (Alphen aan den Rijn: Kluwer Law International, 1998), 611, 618, asserts a tension impossible to overcome.

[77] Similarly, W. Friedmann, *The Changing Structure of International Law* (New York: Columbia U. P., 1964), 60 *et seq.*

[78] P. Weil, "Vers une normativité relative en droit international?" *Revue Générale de Droit International Public* 86 (1980): 5, 44, *et seq.* This sceptical position can be confined to individual areas, as one of the current author's proposal of model of "coordinated interdependence" for the interpretation and development of WTO law: A. v. Bogdandy, "Law and Politics in the WTO. Strategies to Cope with a Deficient Relationship," *Max Planck Yearbook U.N. L.* 6 (2002): 609, 612, 653 *et seq.*

[79] J. Goldstein et al., "Introduction: Legalization and World Politics," *Intl. Org.* 54 (2000): 385 *et seq.*

formal and binding international law. This would allow national politicians to retain control, and to be able to change their commitments, when national democratic processes require it. Technocrats could then guide international institutions, without wielding ultimate legal control.[80] The G8, OECD and similar institutions operating without legally binding instruments but in informal cooperation with national administrations can then serve as supporters of international democracy by promoting international cooperation responsive to the democratic principle.[81]

Certain forms of unilateralism provide a third viewpoint that would also support the primacy of national sovereignty, while allowing states to enjoy the benefits of globalization.[82] United States authors often take this approach, which also appears in European thinking.[83] A democratic justification of unilateral policy can easily be given. According to a widespread – although not uncontested – understanding, the principle of democracy under a given constitution applies *only* to the relationship between those to whom the constitution grants power and the citizenry of that state. The effects of domestic law and policy on foreigners or other peoples consequently lie outside the ambit of this principle.[84]

In this understanding, if globalization is considered desirable or inevitable, it should be shaped, when possible, according to preferences and decisions found in the national democratic process. The implementation of national interests vis-à-vis the interests of other states and foreigners can accordingly be construed as the realization of the democratic principle of the legally relevant constitution – that is, the constitution that grants power to the national

[80] G. Junne, "Theorien über Konflikte und Kooperation zwischen kapitalistischen Industrieländern," in *Theorien der Internationalen Beziehungen*, ed. V. Rittberger, Supp. 21 (Opladen: Westdeutscher, 1990), 353, 364 *et seq.*; A.-M. Slaughter, "The Real New World Order," *Foreign Affairs* 76 (1997): 183, 184 *et seq.*; also published as *ibid.*, "Government Networks: The Heart of the Liberal Democratic Order," *supra* note 45, at 199; R. Stewart, "Administrative Law in the Twenty-First Century," N.Y.U. L. Rev. 78 (2003): 437, 455, *et seq.*

[81] See the contributions in the collected volumes: J. Kirton and G. von Furstenberg (eds.), *New Directions in Global Economic Governance* (Surrey, UK: Ashgate, 2001); J. Kirton et al. (eds.), *Guiding Global Order* (Surrey, UK: Ashgate, 2001); P. Hanjal, *The G7/G8 System – Evolution, Role and Documentation* (Surrey, UK: Ashgate, 1999).

[82] For the basis of a singular American status in international law: M. Reisman, "Assessing Claims to Revise the Laws of War," Am. J. Intl. L. 97 (2003): 82 *et seq.*, 90; as an expression of democratic constitutionality: Kahn, *supra* note 75, at 10 *et seq.*, 18; Rubenfeld, *supra* note 75; an extensive account of the conceptional background by E. Afsah, "Creed, Cabal or Conspiracy – The Origins of the Current Neo-Conservative Revolution in US Strategic Thinking," *German L. J.* 4 (2003): 901 *et seq.*

[83] R. Cooper, *The Breaking of Nations. Order and Chaos in the Twenty-first Century* (London: Grove Atlantic, 2003), 83 *et seq.*

[84] Kahn, *supra* note 75, at 8.

government in question. Seen in this light and constitutionally speaking, *only* (for example) the U.S. president's responsibility toward the American people is legally relevant, and enforcing American national security against Afghanistan or Iraq contains a democratic dimension.[85] To be sure, not all scholars who construe democracy on this theoretical basis advocate unilateralism. There is room for different approaches if further considerations and principles are given more weight, such as peace,[86] international cooperation, or respect for international law.[87] It is, however, important to see that international obligations almost by necessity lead to a constriction of democracy under this understanding.

2. The Universalistic-Cosmopolitan Responses: Universal Law versus State-Centered Integration

The starkest contrast to these particularistic-parochial approaches appears in the attitudes of those who advocate a universalistic-cosmopolitan law that they consider to be the ultimate normative objective of modernity. Such law should, they argue, be the foundation and expression of a democratic global federation or cosmopolitan democracy. The nation-state on this theory would be no more than an intermediate stage in the institutional evolution of public power. This understanding rests on a long tradition that has left its marks on international law scholarship,[88] as well as on political thinking in general.[89] Its main premise is that only a democratic world federation can lay down law that shapes globalization according to the needs of humanity. The international political level must itself operate democratically to satisfy the democratic

[85] See the National Security Strategy of the United States: "In the war against global terrorism, we will never forget that we are ultimately fighting for our democratic values and way of life." White House, *The National Security Strategy of the United States of America*, September 2002, III, at http://georgewbush-whitehouse.archives.gov/nsc/nss/2002/nss.pdf. In this sense, one can also point to the Reform Treaty amending the Treaty of the European Union Article 2 to read in para. 5: "In its relations with the wider world the Union shall uphold and promote its values and interests." Treaty of Lisbon amending the Treaty on European Union and the Treaty establishing the European Community, O.J. C 306/1 (2007).

[86] L. Chieffi, *Il valore costituzionale della pace* (Napoli: Liguori, 1990).

[87] For example, the German Federal Constitutional Court (BVerfG), BVerfGE 89, 155, 185, *et seq.*

[88] G. Schelle, *Le Pacte des nations et sa liaison avec le traité de paix* (Paris, 1919), 101 *et seq.*, 105 *et seq.*; *ibid.*, *Précis de Droits des Gens* 1 (1932): 188 *et seq.*; W. Schücking, "Die Organisation der Welt," in *Festschrift für Paul Laband*, ed. W. van Calker (1908), 533 *et seq.* Kelsen, the most significant representative of monism in international law, remains cautious – to some extent, even skeptical. See H. Kelsen, *Peace through Law* (Chapel Hill: U. of N.C. P., 1944), 9 *et seq.*

[89] See, e. g., E. Jünger, *Der Weltstaat. Organismus und Organisation* (Stuttgart: Ernst Klett, 1960).

principle.[90] This proposition usually stems from a fundamental rights understanding of democracy,[91] which focuses mostly on self-determination. Only
such an emphatic understanding of democracy is capable of demanding a
world federation, something that many consider to be utopian.[92]

Yet the demand for a democratic world federation can legally be construed
from the principle of democracy set out in national constitutions. If the principle is understood as requiring individual self-determination, then there is a
structural democratic deficit in the age of globalization. Many state measures
have an impact on individuals in other states. However, these persons, as noncitizens, have almost no way of asserting their interests and preferences within
the democratic process of the regulating state. Against this background, participation in global democratic institutions may overcome democratic deficits
in national decision-making processes. Thus, the principle of democracy in
the constitutions of many states can be construed as aiming toward an almost
Hegelian overcoming (*Aufhebung*) of traditional statehood.

Most recent publications on international law that envisage a world federation devote little space to the democratic principle.[93] Research in other
disciplines has been much more prolific in this regard.[94] The key for democratization of the international realm is often considered to be a global institution
of a parliamentarian nature. Such an institution would catalyze global democratic processes and the formation of a global public.[95] It is not uncommon

---

[90] D. Archibugi, "Principi di democrazia cosmopolita," in *Diritti Umani e Democrazia Cosmopolita*, eds. D. Archibugi and D. Bettham (Milano: Feltrinelli, 1998), 66, 90, *et seq*. Some
scholars consider national elections as hardly capable of legitimizing important governmental
decisions on the international plane; *cf.* H. Brunkhorst, *Solidarität. Von der Bürgerfreundschaft
zur globalen Rechtsgenossenschaft* (Berlin: Suhrkamp, 2002), 20.

[91] F. Müller, *Demokratie zwischen Staatsrecht und Weltrecht* (Berlin: Nuncker and Humbolt,
2003), 11 *et seq*.; J. Habermas, *Faktizität und Geltung* (Berlin: Suhrkamp, 1992), 532 *et seq*.,
passim; C. Offe and U. K. Preuß, "Democratic Institutions and Moral Resources," in *Political
Theory Today*, ed. D. Held (Stanford, CA: Stanford U. P., 1991), 143 *et seq*.

[92] Presented as an outright ethical obligation by O. Höffe, *Demokratie im Zeitalter der Globalisierung*, 2nd ed. (München: C. H. Beck'sche, 2002), 267.

[93] *Cf.* B. Fassbender, "The U.N. Charter as a Constitution," *Columbia J. T. L.* 36 (1998): 574
et seq.; *ibid.*, "UN Security Council Reform and the Right of Veto. A Constitutional Perspective," *Columbia J. T. L.* 36 (1998): 301 *et seq*.; S. Hobe, *supra* note 36, at 281; J. Delbrück,
"Wirksameres Völkerrecht oder neues 'Weltinnenrecht'," in *Die Konstitution des Friedens als
Rechtsordnung* (Berlin: Duncker and Humblot, 1996), 318 *et seq*.; but see also his more recent
piece, *ibid.*, "Exercising Public Authority Beyond the State," *Indiana J. of Global Legal Stud.*
10 (2003): 1, 29, 37 *et seq*.

[94] The theoretical breadth of approaches is evident when comparing O. Höffe's Kantian book
Demokratie im Zeitalter der Globalisierung, *supra* note 92, with the Hegelian approach taken
by H. Brunkhorst, *Solidarität*, *supra* note 90, at 110, 184.

[95] With concrete proposals Archibugi, *supra* note 90, 98 *et seq*., 109; also D. Held, *Democracy
and the Global Order* (Stanford, CA: Stanford U. P., 1995), 278 *et seq*.; *ibid.*, "Kosmopolitische

for the European Union to be viewed as an example of such a development.[96] The constitutions of the established democratic nation-states are sometimes also conceived as models for a new global order. Some authors suggest that this needs to be a new, but little-defined, set of institutions to anchor democracy on the world plane.[97] Within such models, existing representative organs are often accorded only a subordinate role.

Be that as it may, cosmopolitans view lawmaking under contemporary international law as unsatisfactory and in need of a far more solid democratic basis. Many scholars place much emphasis on transnationally operating nongovernmental organizations, which they construe as offering a possible nucleus for a future democratic global public capable of animating global democratic institutions.[98]

The other strand of thinking under the universalistic paradigm advocates intense cooperation among democratic nation-states and focuses accordingly on the international law of cooperation. The key belief is that the democratic nation-state is and remains the essential framework for the realization of the democratic principle as well as the pivotal point of the international system. The nation-state is viewed as capable of thoroughly mastering the challenge of globalization in close cooperation (including partial integration) with other states and with the aid of international organizations.[99] In the course of globalization, the nation-state has been weakened and fragmented. Nevertheless, the two core premises of a well-functioning democracy within a nation-state are considered to remain intact:[100] national elections and parliamentary institutions continue to convey a sufficient amount of democratic legitimacy and the state retains the capacity to enforce its will throughout the national society.

Under German constitutional law, the "openness" of Germany toward international legal regimes of a cooperative nature is constitutionally required.[101]

Demokratie und Weltordnung. Eine neue Tagesordnung," in *Frieden durch Recht*, eds. M. Lutz-Bachmann and J. Bohman (Berlin: Surhkamp, 1996), 220 *et seq.*, 232.

[96] Early on J. Monnet, *Memoires* (New York: Doubleday and Co., 1976), 617; also E. U. Petersmann, "The Transformation of the World Trading System through the 1994 Agreement Establishing the World Trade Organization," *Eur. J. Intl. L.* 6 (1995): 161, 221.

[97] Müller, *supra* note 91, at 143.

[98] Brunkhorst, *supra* note 71, at 209 *et seq.*; Müller, *supra* note 91, at 139.

[99] As a form of "global governance," *cf.* Enquête Commission – Summary, *supra* note, 36, at 76 *et seq.*; K. König, "Governance als Steuerungskonzept," in *Governance als entwicklungs und transformationspolitisches Konzept*, eds. K. König et al. (Berlin: Duncker & Humbolt, 2002), 9 *et seq.*

[100] C. Walter, "Constitutionalizing (Inter)national Governance," *German Yearbook Intl. L.* 44 (2001): 170 *et seq.*

[101] According to the preamble, the Basic Law is "moved by the purpose to serve world peace as an equal part of a unified Europe"; in detail, H. Mosler, "Die Übertragung von Hoheitsgewalt,"

The same is true for the European Union.[102] Such openness can be deduced from the constitutional principle of democracy. The argument runs in much the same way as the one already presented with respect to cosmopolitan democracy. The deduction is based on a fundamental rights understanding of democracy that not only includes citizens, but requires – to minimize heteronomy – that the preferences and interests of affected foreigners be taken into account.[103] Thus, international law acquires its own specific democratic significance, unavailable to domestic law, because international law is the standard instrument for giving foreigners a voice in national lawmaking.[104]

This school of thought distinguishes itself from the viewpoint more focused on state sovereignty because it does not understand openness toward international law and international policy as a disadvantage for democracy. On the contrary, according to this vision, such openness realizes a democratic potential that the closed or hegemonic state cannot attain. Loss of national self-determination is compensated for by greater transnational participation.

Some cosmopolitans view global democratic institutions as impractible legal and political projects and normatively problematic. For example, Kant's essay "Perpetual Peace" views a world federation as potentially despotic.[105] This school of thought attracts the support of most international legal scholars. Within it, two positions for determining the appropriate forum for cooperation can be distinguished: the unitarian model of legitimation and the pluralist model of legitimation.

Under the first model, the democratic principle can be institutionally realized *only* through the choices of the electorate. Public acts achieve a democratic quality only when they are either enacted (exceptionally) by the citizenry as such (through referenda) or can be traced back to the decisions of elected

---

in *Handbuch des Staatsrechts der Bundesrepublik Deutschland*, vol. VII, eds. J. Isensee and P. Kirchhof (Heidelberg: C. F. Müller, 1992), § 175, para. 14; Tietje, *supra* note 40, at 1087.

[102] Consolidated Versions of the Treaty on European Union and the Treaty Establishing the European Community, O.J. C 321E/1, art. 11 EU Treaty; even more forcefully, the Lisbon Reform Treaty inserting the new Article 10a on the Union's external action, *supra* note 85.

[103] S. Langer, *Grundlagen einer internationalen Wirtschaftsverfassung* (München: Beck, 1995), 23 *et seq.*, 51; for an appropriate understanding of the concept of sovereignty, see *Völkerrecht*, *supra* note 45, at 218 *et seq.*; R. Wahl, *Verfassungsstaat, Europäisierung, Internationalisierug* (Berlin: Suhrkamp, 2003), 17. This notion is also expressed in BVerfGE 83, 37, 52.

[104] Some reports of the WTO's Appellate Body seem to be inspired by this understanding; WTO Appellate Body Report, *Standards for Reformulated and Conventional Gasoline*, AB-1996–1, WT/DS2/AB/R (April 29, 1996); *United States – Import Prohibition of Certain Shrimp and Shrimp Products, Recourse to Article 21.5 of the DSU by Malaysia* AB-2001–4, WT/DS58/AB/R (November 21, 2001).

[105] I. Kant, "Zum ewigen Frieden," in *Kleinere Schriften zur Geschichtsphilosophie, Ethik und Politik*, ed. K. Vorländer (Hamburg: Meiner, 1964), 115, 147.

bodies ("chain of democratic legitimation").[106] According to this understanding, the democratic legitimacy of international law can be improved by better parliamentary control of the executive,[107] the establishment of international institutions of a parliamentary nature,[108] or referenda.

The involvement of those affected or other civil actors in decision-making processes does not satisfy the democratic standards of the unitarian model. Rather, it sees the democratic principle as shedding negative light on such participatory procedures, because they represent a potential threat to the democratic "chain of legitimation." This point distinguishes unitarian democracy from the pluralist model described later: civil participation – in particular, that of NGOs – cannot strengthen the democratic credentials of international law or international politics. Unitarian democrats would say that no such procedures comply with the core requirements of the democratic principle, above all the requirement of democratic equality.[109]

Consequently, unitarian democrats would suggest that democratic openness to the interests of citizens of other states must be carried out procedurally through governmental cooperation as well as through international bodies that are essentially controlled by national governments. Thus, the executive and technocratic character of international political processes is not viewed within this framework as being problematic. Moreover, further international legalization and a cautious development of international organizations toward more autonomy ("the constitutionalisation of international law"[110]) do not raise concerns. The basic premise of this position is that additional international

---

[106] The "chain of legitimation" is a core concept of German constitutional law; see E.-W. Böckenförde, "Mittelbare/repräsentative Demokratie als eigentliche Form der Demokratie," in *Festschrift für Kurt Eichenberger*, ed. G. Müller (Basel: Beburtstag, 1982), 301 *et seq.*, 315; this has been important in numerous decisions of the Federal Constitutional Court; see most recently BVerfG, Az.: 2 BvL 5/98 5. December 2002, note 156, further references concerning earlier decisions (available at: http://www.bundesverfassungsgericht.de/cgi-bin/link.pl?entscheidungen).

[107] *Cf.* R. Wolfrum, "Kontrolle der auswärtigen Gewalt," *Veröffentlichungen der Vereinigung der Deutschen Staatsrechtslehrer* 56 (1997): 38 *et seq.*, 45 *et seq.*, 61 *et seq.*; aslo K. Hailbronner, "Kontrolle der auswärtigen Gewalt," *Veröffentlichungen der Vereinigung der Deutschen Staatsrechtslehrer* 56 (1997): 7 *et seq.*

[108] S. Kadelbach, "Die parlamentarische Kontrolle des Regierungshandelns bei der Beschlußfassung in internationalen Organisationen," in *Neuere Probleme der parlamentarischen Legitimation im Bereich der auswärtigen Gewalt*, ed. R. Geiger (Baden-Baden: Nomos, 2003): 41, 53, 56 *et seq.*; for an overview of the relevant international practice H. Schermers and N. Blokker, *International Institutional Law*, 3rd ed. (Cambridge: Cambridge U. P., 1995), § 558 *et seq.*; H. Lindemann, "Parliamentary Assemblies, International," in *Encyclopedia of Public International Law*, vol. 3, ed. R. Bernhardt (1997), 892–98; C. Walter, "Parliamentary Assemblies, International, Addendum," in *Encyclopedia of Public International Law*, vol. 3, ed. R. Bernhardt (1996), 898–904.

[109] Stoll, *supra* note 42, at V.A.4.b, VII.   [110] Uerpmann, *supra* note 68, at 565 *et seq.*

legalization and more autonomous international lawmaking are required to cope with the challenge of globalization. Accordingly, limitations on national democracy do not constitute the main legitimation problem of international law. This understanding can be summarized as follows: although there cannot yet be a democratic world federation, there can be a world of closely and successfully cooperating democracies; it is the task of contemporary scholarship to contribute to realizing this objective.[111]

In contrast, the second, pluralist position holds that the international law of cooperation can substantially increase the democratic legitimacy of international law if new forms of civic participation are adopted. Such forms, going beyond elections and referenda, are possible avenues for the realization of the democratic principle and adequate responses to the detachment of international processes from national parliamentary control.[112] The underlying premise is that enabling the participation of NGOs, as exponents of international civil society, represents a prime strategy to further the democratic principle on the international plane.[113] Such views usually reflect a fundamental rights understanding of democracy focused on the opportunity for participation of the individual, but sometimes also neocorporative theories of democracy.[114]

The central institutional issue for the pluralist approach to democratic legitimacy concerns the development of decision-making systems in such a way that civil actors can participate in international procedures and ultimately in international lawmaking, conveying social interests, preferences, and values. This position emphasizes the need for transparency in international politics,

---

[111] This also appears as the vision of J. Habermas, "Hat die Konstitutionalisierung des Völkerrechts noch eine Chance," in *Der gespaltene Westen* (Berlin: Suhrkamp, 2004), 113, 134, *et seq.*, 137 *et seq.*; J. Habermas, *The Divided West* (Cambridge: Polity, 2006), 115 *et seq.*

[112] Of particular interest in recent years has been civil actors' access to the WTO Dispute Settlement mechanism: P. Mavroidis, "Amicus Curiae Briefs before the WTO: Much Ado about Nothing," in *Liber Amicorum Claus-Dieter Ehlermann, supra* note 30, at 317 *et seq.*; D. Steger, "Amicus Curiae: Participant or Friend? The WTO and NAFTA Experience," in *Liber Amicorum Claus-Dieter Ehlermann, supra* note 30, at 419 *et seq.*; H. Ascensio, "L'amicus curiae devant les juridictions internationales," *Révue Générale de Droit International* 105 (2001): 897 *et seq.*

[113] *Enquête Commission, supra* note 36, at 439 *et seq.*; B.-O. Bryde, "Konstitutionalisierung des Völkerrechts und Internationalisierung des Verfassungsrechts," *Der Staat* 42 (2003): 1, 8 *et seq.*; R. Khan, "The Anti-Globalization Protests: Side-Show of Global Governance, or Law-Making on the Streets?," *Zeitschrift für ausländisches öffentliches Recht und Völkerrecht (Heidelberg J. Intl. L.)* 61 (2001): 323; Charnovitz, *supra* note 113, at 299; I. B. Boutros-Ghali, *An Agenda for Democratization* (New York: United Nations Publications, 1997), 34 *et seq.*

[114] This latter understanding informs the EU Commission's White Paper on European Governance, see COM(2001) 428 Final (July 27, 2001) (available at: http://eur-lex.europa.eu/LexUriServ/site/en/com/2001/com2001_0428en01.pdf).

seeing openness as indispensable for effective democratic development in the nascent transnational civil society.

D. New Approaches

The preceding understandings rest on the premise of the supremacy of politics over other societal spheres. However, numerous scholars posit the decline of this supremacy, leading to a new disorder through overwhelming differentiation and fragmentation. Some even go so far as to claim that the world is returning to a situation last seen in the Middle Ages.[115] The supremacy of the nation-state over other societal spheres is said to have become substantially eroded, leading to the inability of the state to organize society effectively. Any conception that envisages the realization of democracy through the supremacy of politics would thus be futile and hopeless in the era of globalization.

With reference to the future of democracy, most advocates of this vision agree that democracy organized through state procedures has lost much of its meaning. Accordingly, the political apathy of many citizens appears intuitively comprehensible. Some even diagnose – by no means joyously – the end of democracy.[116] Public law scholarship cannot shrug off such a diagnosis. Should it prove convincing, a fundamental reorientation of constitutional scholarship and practice would be advisable, requiring, for example, the horizontal application of fundamental rights to protect individuals from infringements by other private actors.[117] For constitutional law to realize its basic principles throughout the entire society,[118] new legal institutions would have to be conceived and established.

Notwithstanding the supposed demise of the supremacy of politics, there are also proposals for maintaining democracy in this new setting. They can

---

[115] Hedley Bull, *The Anarchical Society. A Study of Order in World Politics* (London: The Macmillan Press, 1977), 254 *et seq.*; Paolo Grossi, "Unità giuridica europea: un medioevo prossimo futuro?" *Quaderni fiorentini per la storia del pensiero giuridico moderno*, 31/1 (2002): 39; Dimitri D'Andrea, "Oltre la sovranità. Lo spazio politico europeo tra post-modernità e nuovo medioevo" *Quaderni fiorentini per la storia del pensiero giuridico moderno*, 31/1 (2002): 77.

[116] J.-M. Guéhenno, *Das Ende der Demokratie* (München: Deutscher Taschenbuch, 1994), 13 *et seq.*, 162, and passim; similarly "Die Zukunft politischer Autonomie," *supra* note 75, at 116; R. Dahl, "Can International Organizations Be Democratic?" in *Democracy's Edges*, eds. I. Shapiro and C. Hacker-Cordón (Cambridge: Cambridge U. P., 1999), 19 *et seq.*

[117] D. Thürer, "Modernes Völkerrecht: Ein System im Wandel und Wachstum – Gerechtigkeitsgedanke als Kraft der Veränderung?" *Zeitschrift für ausländisches öffentliches Recht und Völkerrecht* 60 (2000): 557, 587 *et seq.*; G. Teubner, "Globale Zivilverfassungen: Alternativen zur staatszentrierten Verfassungstheorie," *Zeitschrift für ausländisches öffentliches Recht und Völkerrecht* 63 (2003): 1, 4 *et seq.*; Guéhenno, *supra* note 116, at 14.

[118] This is a core concern of European public law scholarship.

best be described as aiming to limit the power of powerful actors. Gunther Teubner asserts the formation of a new system of the separation of powers provided by separate and competing social systems. These systems in turn are seen as responding to the democratic principle through the formation of "dualistic social constitutions." Any such system is divided into a spontaneous sphere that allows for the participation of individuals and an organizational sphere that checks the other systems.[119] It is also argued that democracy might be maintained through another radically innovative avenue, such as basing new law less on the decisions of public bodies than on spontaneous developments in international society. The prime example of such development is the alleged emergence of legal norms as a result of the arousal of international society in response to specific situations.[120]

Positions in the "governance" debate arrive at similar conclusions to the extent that consensual forms for the development and implementation of policy are considered to be appropriate responses to the challenges of globalization. Given the largely fragmented international system, the consensus of large businesses, NGOs, and further important actors is deemed necessary and adequate.[121] Such approaches are based mostly on models of associative democracy,[122] in which democracy is realized through consultation between the representatives of collective interests.

As interesting as many of these new approaches may be, they must be interpreted in the light of the paradigms that inform Western international scholarship as a collective exercise.[123] Particularism and universalism still supply the main conceptual framework of international lawyers. They will now be presented in more detail.

---

[119] G. Teubner, "Privatregimes: Neo-spontanes Recht und duale Sozialverfassung in der Weltgesellschaft," in *Festschrift für Spiros Simitis*, ed. D. Simon (Baden-Baden: Nomos, 2000), 437, 447 *et seq.*; "Globale Zivilverfassungen," *supra* note 117, at 25 *et seq.*

[120] "Globale Bukowina," *supra* note 117, at 255; A. Fischer-Lescano, "Globalverfassung: Verfassung der Weltgesellschaft," A.R.S.P. 88 (2002): 349, 356 *et seq.*; see also M. Reisman, "A Critique of International Treaty Making," in *The Development of International Law in Treaty Making*, ed. R. Wolfrum (New York: Springer, 2004).

[121] *Our Global Neighbourhood: Report of the Commission on Global Governance*, *supra* note 59, 253 *et seq.*

[122] P. Schmitter, "Interest, Association, and Intermediation in a Reformed Post-Liberal Democracy," in *Staat und Verbände*, ed. W. Streeck (Wiesbaden: VS für Sozialwissenschaften, 1994), 161; A. Martinelli, "Governance globale e responsabilità democratica," in *L'Italia e la politica internazionale*, eds. F. Bruni and N. Ronzitti (Bologna: Il Mulino, 2001), 47, 51 *et seq.*

[123] In detail D. Kennedy, *supra* note 15.

III. PARTICULARISM: THE IMPOSSIBILITY OF GLOBAL ORDER

A. *The Core of the Paradigm*

The particularistic paradigm has had enormous influence on the history of international law. Particularism was already present in the Greek roots of occidental political thinking. All theories in the particularistic paradigm share two basic assumptions. The first sees order as possible only within the specific polity; it cannot extend to humankind as a whole. The second assumption asserts that a polity is only viable if its internal cohesion depends on something that is exclusively shared by all members of the group, that is, if it is in some ways parochial. Indeed, in this paradigm – that is, in this certain way of understanding social order in general, and international law specifically – is also the origin of the parochial understanding of human rights, collocating them as a product of the "particular" historic and cultural conditions of a social and political community. As a consequence of these assumptions, polities are conceived of as being in perpetual competition, or even conflict, with each other. The competition for scarce resources in a world without any universally shared public order has a tendency to strengthen each polity's internal separate ties. This second dimension of *particularism* leads many particularistic theories to be also *holistic*. Their qualification as *holistic* depends on the assumption that the theory's basic unit is a collectivity of humans, be it a demos, a nation, or a state, but not the individual as such. The theories that elaborate this paradigm tend toward the firm defense of the polity's interests. This is seen as an ontological datum on which any responsible understanding of international order and international law needs to be built.

Accordingly, international law is best understood as being an instrument of coexistence or perhaps of hegemonic power. As a consequence, Articles 2 para. 4 and 51 of the UNC should be interpreted in a way that accommodates the interests of those states that are capable of projecting their power globally. Any other interpretation would miss the very point of international law and would probably damage law by overstretching its normativity. This means (for example) that human rights norms should be interpreted and applied cautiously.

B. *Three Variants of the Paradigm*

The paradigm of holistic particularism has found expression in widely differing theories in the past two-and-a-half thousand years as it responded to the evolving theoretical discourse and changes in society. In particular, three variants have emerged, mostly as a reaction to deep transformations that undermined the paradigm's persuasiveness: realism, nationalism, and hegemonism.

Many of the positions that we subsume under the term *particularism* are conceived of as *realist*. This term is unfortunate. First, realism indicates two issues. One is that any scholar and any theory needs to take reality into account. This, however, is a truism, and there is no serious theory that advances what it conceives to be unrealistic positions. Therefore, this broad understanding is of no use for mapping the theoretical landscape. The second understanding of *realism* is far more narrow and only relates to a subgroup of the more broadly realist theories. Its basic tenet is that all political phenomena, within the single polities as well as between them, can be interpreted as a struggle to control the most resources. In that guise *realism* is the oldest variant of the paradigm *holistic particularism*, because its core assumptions were developed in ancient Greece. Reduced to a simple formula, the main assertion of this narrow realism is that politics is nothing but a constant struggle for power. After having been elaborated with laconic mastery by the Greek historian Thucydides (460–400 B.C.) in his report on the Peloponnesian War,[124] the "realistic" view of politics was reproposed, substantially unchanged, by Machiavelli (1469–1527) in the early modern era.[125]

However, as convincing as it may appear at first sight, a severe flaw afflicts this paradigm from the outset. Neither Thucydides and Machiavelli nor their numerous successors or epigones have been able to overcome a serious deficit of realist thought, which is its inability to explain the evident difference between internal and external politics. Whereas there is some evidence that the rule of law is not always a top priority in foreign policy, a general claim of lawlessness cannot convince if applied to the political struggle within a polity. The latter is manifestly ruled by laws that mostly succeed in establishing a certain degree of responsibility of the rulers toward their fellow members of the polity. This failure to explain in a convincing way the *whole* realm of politics as a quest for power might be one reason, why classic realism gave way, roughly half a century ago, to the so-called structural realism or neorealism of the new discipline of international relations. This limitation was necessary for "realism" to remain, at least to a certain extent, an epistemologically meaningful position.[126]

---

[124] Thucydides, *The Peloponnesian War*, trans. Thomas Hobbes, ed. David Grene (Ann Arbor: U. of Mich. P., 1959), V, 86.
[125] Niccolò Machiavelli, *Il Principe* (1513); *ibid.*, *Discorsi sopra la prima deca di Tito Livio* (1513–1519).
[126] Slaughter, *supra* note 5, at 30.

This problem becomes most evident in the writings of Hans J. Morgenthau, one of the founders of the new discipline of international relations in the United States.[127] Morgenthau maintains the pretence of explaining all politics as a struggle in defence of self-interests. However, he concedes the fundamental difference between domestic and international politics in this respect,[128] focusing his "realistic" analysis exclusively on the latter. The scholarship that grew under the umbrella of his new interpretation of realism eventually gave up the closer examination of the foundations of domestic policies. Founding the "neorealistic" approach to international relations, it came to focus exclusively on the way that states, as the sole (or at least as the main) actors on the international arena, organize their mostly hostile interactions.[129]

Trying to explain why there is rule of law in domestic politics, Morgenthau resorted to the concept of the *nation* as the consolidating factor within the polity.[130] He thereby abandoned "classic" realism in favor of the second variant of the holistic particularism, which asserts the idea of the *nation* as a *community* with its own *particular* history, *particular* destiny, *particular* culture to uphold. Nationalism as a theory asserts that the individual's belonging to a nation supports the polity's internal cohesion. This idea also justifies the quest for solidarity and inclusion inside as well as collision and exclusion outside. Although less ancient than realism, nationalism also has quite a long history, dating from the time of political Romanticism, when conservative political writers, especially in Germany, borrowed the nation-concept from the progressive lexicon of the French Revolution and adapted it to the needs of a refounded social and political conservatism.[131] Founding the cohesion of the polity on the nation in this way created a powerful new vehicle for exercising political power.

For the next century and a half, this paradigm inspired the vision of the nation and boosted the state's internal cohesion in a way that far exceeded the antiquated Aristotelian vision of the society as an enlarged family.[132] This allowed broader social classes to be involved in the polity and the political process. This development corresponded historically with and is perhaps

---

[127] Hans J. Morgenthau, *Politics among Nations. The Struggle for Power and Peace* (New York: Knopf, 1948).

[128] *Id.*, at 31, 35.

[129] Within the very voluminous literature, see, as perhaps the historically most eminent exponent, Kenneth N. Waltz, *Theory of International Politics* (New York: McGraw-Hill, 1979).

[130] Morgenthau, *supra* note 127, at 118, 244, 471.

[131] Adam H. Müller, *Die Elemente der Staatskunst* (Berlin: Haude and Spencer, 1809).

[132] Aristotle, *Politics* (Cambridge: Cambridge U. P., 1988), I, 2, 1252a *et seq.*; Jean Bodin, *Six livres de la république* (1576), I, I, 1; Robert Filmer, *Patriarcha, or the Natural Power of Kings* (1680).

connected to aggressive foreign policy, colonialism and imperialism. However, it also coincided with the creation of a body of treaties and doctrines
today often referred to as "classical international law." This body provides a
legal framework for the expansion of the nation-state, but also for peaceful
coexistence and even constructive coordination. Being constitutively *without
a spine* it worked as a "gentle civilizer of nations."[133] Also linked with these
achievements of the golden era of nation-states in establishing the fundaments
of the humanitarian international law is the essential ambivalence of *parochialism*. Indeed, the parochial understanding of human rights, stating that rights
and values need to develop a firm root in a specific culture, has always been
profoundly connected with the core tenet of holistic particularism, almost as
a kind of logical consequence of it. Nevertheless, precisely the disposition of
nation-states to recognize at least a minimal set of human rights by binding
themselves to humanitarian international law shows how parochialism can
overcome its limits. Additional evidence in the same direction can be found
in the tendency of nation-states to extend part of the rights of nationals –
namely, the rights characterizing them as humans – also to nonnationals
within the institutional range established by national constitutions. In both
cases the parochial attitude is disconnected from the basic assumption of the
particularistic paradigm, foreshadowing a possible way beyond the classical
dichotomy.

For long time, however, the overcoming of the dichotomy between particularism and universalism was hardly more than a very distant perspective: for
the time being, the most supporters of the particularistic approach to international law maintained its core dichotomous tenets, although adapting them
to the challenges of a new political situation. In fact, the national variant of
holistic particularism has had some difficulty accommodating respond to the
ongoing transition to an ever-more-closely interlinked world. An idea mainly
concentrated on the flowering and protection of a self-sufficient nation does
not provide the best conceptual precondition for developing responses to a
world in which states are ever more intertwined and ever less self-sufficient.
Because a universalistic perspective with a truly public international order is
beyond the parochial-holistic paradigm, the quest for order beyond the borders of the nation found its answer in the turn to *hegemonism* as the third
variant.

The hegemonic variant of the particularistic-holistic paradigm incorpo-
rates a global perspective without becoming cosmopolitan. An early elaboration was given by Carl Schmitt with his theory of "large-range order"

---

[133] Koskenniemi, *supra* note 15.

(*Großraumordnung*).[134] Moving from the diagnosis that the traditional concept of the European nation-state would be inadequate to cope with the new situation,[135] he proposed a *Großraumordnung* as an idea of global (yet not universal) order based on few great powers. Under this new vision, those powers would be allowed to enlarge both the range and meaning of order as well as the resources needed to achieve it.

The hegemons should guarantee the order within their respective spheres of influence, which would be in the hand of an ethnically and ideologically homogeneous group organized within a nation-state as the heart of the *Großraum*. Between the spheres of influence the principle of nonintervention should rule, and international law between these powers should maintain its "classical" form. In Schmitt's conception, the community based on pre-reflexive homogeneity assumes continental proportions because of a more comprehensive definition of the possible reasons for cohesion. Schmidt recognized no universalistic law or order as anything but a deception. For some decades Schmitt's theory of *Großraumordnung* enjoyed little interest and even less appreciation.

However, the influence of his thought remains quite strong, so that the features of his hegemonic reinterpretation of the particularistic-holistic paradigm, in general, and of its idea of international relations in particular, outlining the comprehensive definition of the political communities as the actors of international relations as well as the existentialistic dimension of conflicts, reappeared recently in Huntington's influential idea of the "clash of civilizations."[136]

C. The American Neocons

Among the variants of the particularistic-holistic paradigm, hegemonism appears to be most in tune with the challenges of globalization: it seeks to extend the reach of the polity beyond the nation for pursuing globally its interests or even values without ending in the impasse of colonialism or in a web of international governance. Recently, a new and politically powerful version of hegemonism has been developed by the neoconservative movement in the

---

[134] Carl Schmitt, *Völkerrechtliche Großraumordnung mit Interventionsverbot für raumfremde Mächte* (Berlin: Duncker and Humbolt, 1939). The concept has been later redefined, the theory being yet substantially restated, in Carl Schmitt, *Der Nomos der Erde im Völkerrecht des Jus Publicum Europeum* (Berlin: Duncker and Humbolt, 1950).

[135] Carl Schmitt, "Das Zeitalter der Neutralisierung und Entpolitisierung," in *Der Begriff des Politischen. Text von 1932 mit einem Vorwort und drei Corollarien* (Berlin: Duncker and Humbolt, 1963), at 87.

[136] Samuel P. Huntington, *The Clash of Civilizations* (New York: Simon and Schuster, 1996).

United States. Because this stream of thinking still lacks its defining work, the following discussion combines various authors to work out what can be considered the most recent gestalt of the paradigm.

Sketching tradition and innovation in a nutshell, one can state that as always under this paradigm, the assumption reigns that social, political, and juridical order based on public law can only be realized within single polities, whereas beyond them, in the realm of the relations between the polities, a truly public order is impossible. Institutions that claim to be a step toward a cosmopolitan order are to be regarded with deep suspicion. Innovation can be found in two aspects shared by most neocons. First, the *realists'* prudential restraint on using power gets lost in the neoconservative vision. Second, the democratic principle assumes a founding role within the paradigm. Democracy is used as justification for the aggressive pursuit of the national interest, intervention into nondemocratic states, and skepticism about international law.

1. The Critique of International Order through Public International Law
Skepticism about a public international order based on public international law is a widely shared attitude among the neocons. A telling example is provided by Jeremy A. Rabkin. In Rabkin's view, international law is an instrument for restraining the well-motivated and legitimate national interests of the United States, as the paladin of the free world, and of all other liberal and democratic nation-states. When it was still called "law of nations" – Rabkin argues – international law was largely about war and commerce, and therefore limited in reach and range.[137] Moreover, it was fundamentally bilateral, and preexisted international institutions. There was no room for a nebulous international community. Rabkin criticizes what he sees as international law's development into a much more ambitious and invasive enterprise, pretending to give effect to the alleged will of nothing less than humankind itself.

The consequence, according to Rabkin, has been not only a loss of efficiency but also a shift in the political meaning of international law. By building institutions, which pretend to be binding on sovereign nation-states, contemporary international law is becoming "a sheer monument to collectivist ideology."[138] That change, Rabkin claims, should pose in itself a problem for liberalism. Yet an even more serious challenge arises in a world characterized by a large

---

[137] Jeremy A. Rabkin, *Why Sovereignty Matters* (Washington, DC: American Enterprise Institute
   P., 1998), 24.
[138] *Id.*, at 95.

number of nondemocratic states, binding international institutions can represent a handicap for liberal states and for their actions taken in defense of liberty. In this light, international law often becomes an ideological weapon in support of indecent positions.

Not every thinker in this movement is totally set against international law and institutions, not least because of their possible usefulness. Robert Kagan, for example shares Rabkin's position in so far as he considers the idea of a legalization of international relations as based on "legitimacy myths."[139] The United Nations is far from being "the place where international rules and legitimacy are founded."[140] However, the United Nations and the Security Council as its main organ are useful instruments serving the interests of the nation-states. Kagan points out that this judgment holds for the foreign policy of the superpower. This is shown in cases such as the intervention in Haiti in 1994 or the Iraq bombing in 1998.[141] At the same time, international law is not able to constrain powerful states. As evidence Kagan refers to the Kosovo war in 1999, which, although waged while circumscribing or even flouting the will of the United Nations, had been considered as legitimate by France and Germany. This serves as evidence for the limits of legalization in the international order.

This skepticism is elaborated in Jack L. Goldsmith's and Eric A. Posner's book, *The Limits of International Law*. It sets out to show that international law is constitutively incapable of providing for a truly public international order.[142] Using rational choice theory, they claim to prove that international law has little normative influence on the behavior of states because states, irrespective of the law, always follow their peculiar interests, which do not include the international rule of law.

The limits of international law are not just factual, they are also normative, because of democracy. Here, they upset the Kantian theory which asserts that representative democracies are far more prone to subscribe to international law and a peaceful public international law.[143] Posner and Goldsmith claim that one of the most important reasons why democratic states do not submit themselves to international rules and international institutions involves in their specific form of domestic legitimacy – namely, the power of the people. Insofar as governments are accountable to the citizens in democracies, and the

---

[139] Robert Kagan, "America's Crisis of Legitimacy," *Foreign Affairs* 83 (2004): 65, 73.
[140] *Id.*, at 73.   [141] *Id.*, at 74.
[142] Jack L. Goldsmith and Eric A. Posner, *The Limits of International Law* (Oxford: Oxford U. P., 2005).
[143] Kant, *supra* note 105; *cf* A. Moravcsik, "Taking Preferences Seriously: A Liberal Theory of International Politics," *Intl. Org.* 51 (1997): 513–53.

citizens are not prone to prefer altruistic policies, liberal democracies would be precluded from pursuing cosmopolitan projects.[144] Moreover, international law limits the possibility of democratic self-government.

In Goldsmith and Posner's view, the more liberal and democratic the polity, the less willing it will be to submit itself to international rules not immediately supporting their interests. Yet the discrepancy between the United States and Western European states needs to be explained. Goldsmith and Posner join Kagan in ascribing this difference to the difference in power: "Powerful states do not join institutions that do not serve their interests."[145] Following the interpretation of democracy and compliance with international rules as inversely related, therefore, a democratic state will always prefer to rely on its own resources and interests, unless it is not strong enough to take full responsibility for its actions.

An extensive analysis of the epistemological deficits of Goldsmith and Posner's theory would go far beyond the purposes of the present contribution,[146] but some points need to be discussed in light of the objective of our inquiry. As a presupposition of their research, Goldsmith and Posner assume some far-reaching axioms,[147] as when they define the state as the unique significant actor in the arena of international relations, or assume a merely instrumental concept of rationality according to which the only rational behavior would consist in pursuing short-term and particular payoffs. However, these assumptions are far from self-evident. In fact, some questions arise from Goldsmith and Posner's axioms: Is it correct, first, to treat collective actors (states) in the same way as single actors (individuals)? Second, does not a purely instrumental understanding of rationality lead to an unconvincing view of human praxis? In fact, game theory was conceived to explain the actions of concrete individuals, not of complex social, political, and administrative structures, which

[144] Goldsmith and Posner, *supra* note 142, at 212.

[145] *Id.*, at 223. This is precisely one of the most important arguments articulated by Kagan in his successful book *On Paradise and Power* (New York: Knopf, 2003) to explain the differences in the foreign policy between the United States and Europe. For an analysis of content and background of Kagan's best-seller as well as for a critique of his approach, see the special issue of the *German L. J.* 4 (2003) (available at: http://www.germanlawjournal.com/index.php?pageID=2&vol=4&no=9).

[146] See, e.g., Paul Schiff Berman, "Seeing Beyond the Limits of International Law," *Tex. L. Rev.* 84 (2006): 1265; Andrew T. Guzman, "The Promise of International Law," *Va. L. Rev.* 92 (2006): 533; Oona A. Hathaway and Ariel N. Lavinbuk, "Rationalism and Revisionism in International Law," *Harv. L. Rev.* 119 (2006): 1404; Detlev F. Vagts, "International Relations Looks at Customary International Law: A Traditionalist's Defense," *Eur. J. Intl. L.* 15 (2004): 1031; Anne van Aaken, "To Do Away with International Law? Some Limits to the 'Limits of International Law'," *Eur. J. Intl L.* 17 (2006): 289.

[147] Goldsmith and Posner, *supra* note 142, at 4.

are difficult to conceptualize as single players. Goldsmith and Posner assert that their assumption is nonetheless justified by the particular shape of the international arena, where states are normally perceived as acting as a unitary whole, and because the "billiard ball" approach, considering every single state as a unity, albeit "far from perfect," is more "parsimonious,"[48] in the sense that it facilitates a useful reduction in the number and complexity of the analyzed phenomena to concentrate on the most significant among them. This argument, however, has little content in the face of one of the most relevant trends of our times: the destructuring of state unity and the progressive development of private and public networks.[49] Ignoring these new developments does not facilitate scientific analysis, but rather leads to a misunderstanding of the present reality. Either rationality should be understood in a more than purely instrumental sense[50] or, even if it is conceived as a mere instrument for the achievement of particular goals, it does not necessarily find its highest self-fulfillment in the *immediate* maximization of short-sighted payoffs. From a more far-reaching point of view, it also might be argued that the creation of norms, rules, and solid international institutions to secure their compliance would lead to a better achievement of instrumental reason insofar as it guarantees higher benefits in the long term.[51]

2. Hegemonic Order

Public order is always *particularistic* according to neoconservative thinking, and it is always *holistic*. Moreover, rights and values have in their view always a *parochial* origin. Neoconservative thought shares with all variants of the particularistic-holistic paradigm its two main characteristics: both the idea that social, political, and legal order can only be possible within a well-integrated polity and the notion that this compactness relies largely on a fact (*factum brutum*) on which to build public order. This holds true even for those who use the individualistic methodology of rational choice, such as Goldsmith

---

[48] *Id.*, at 6.

[49] Anne-Marie Slaughter, *A New World Order* (Princeton, N.J.: Princeton U. P., 2004).

[50] Jürgen Habermas, *Theorie des kommunikativen Handelns* (Berlin: Suhrkamp, 1981); Andrew Linklater, *The Transformation of Political Community* (Columbia, SC: U. of S.C. P., 1998); Thomas Risse, "'Let's Argue!': Communicative Action in World Politics," *Intl. Org.* 54 (2000): 1; Harald Müller, "Arguing, Bargaining and All That: Communicative Action, Rationalist Theory and the Logic of Appropriateness in International Relations," *Eur. J. Intl. Rel.* 10 (2004): 395.

[51] The most famous example of a non-shortsighted use of strategic rationality was delivered, at the very beginning of modern times, by Thomas Hobbes in his motivation of the transition from the state of nature to civil society. See Thomas Hobbes, *Leviathan* (1651), chapt. XIII, *et seq.* For a different – and more recent – proposal to enlarge the horizon of instrumental rationality, see Robert O. Keohane, *After Hegemony* (Princeton, NJ: Princeton U. P., 1984), 65.

and Posner, because they choose the state as their basic unit and follow a communitarian theory of democracy. To understand the state as if it were an individual is a typical feature of holistic theory.

Rejecting the idea of a public international order based on public international law, neocons will need to propose a substitute if they want to provide an answer for the challenges of the twenty-first century. At this point, two further important aspects of their conception have to be pointed out, the first locating them within the hegemonic variant of the paradigm; the second showing their extreme novelty even in comparison to the hegemonic tradition. Indeed, neocons have an outstanding characteristic in common with the postnationalistic hegemonic thought of the twentieth century, which distinguishes them from other variants of the particularistic worldview. Although realists and nationalists were thoroughly skeptical about the possibility of world order, they were generally willing to admit the necessity of a certain constraint as regards the goals pursued by the single political community in its international actions as well as in the means deployed to achieve them. On the one hand, realists such as Thucydides, Machiavelli, and, more recently, Morgenthau[152] admonish restraint in international relations, in order not to overstretch the particular community's capacities. This attitude can be traced back directly to the power-based idea of politics peculiar to the "realist" school, in which the claim for self-limitation is not a question of normative principles but only of prudential behavior grounded on a strategic understanding of practical reason. In contrast, for the exponents of hegemonism as well as for the neocons, politics is the conveyer of aspirations held by communities kept together not primarily by common interests, but rather by shared principles to mobilize all available material and spiritual resources. On the other hand, nation-states have been able, in the golden age of the *Weltanschauung* on which they were based, to develop an important body of international law. Certainly, the agreements signed in that "foundational" time did not result in enduring supranational institutions that could prevent the drive to war. They were proven impotent in the face of the aggressive tendencies deeply rooted in nationalistic thought and politics. Even so, the presence of a certain openness to international agreements testifies to how nation-states might be able, under favorable circumstances, to recognize the fundamental importance of the normative element of law, if only in a transitional way. This element is absent both in the hegemonic variant of the paradigm and in neoconservative thought. Faced with an existential fight for survival or decline, under the pressure of a worldwide battle for life or death, no normative or prudential constraint would

---

[152] Morgenthau, *supra* note 127, at 10.

apply. The community's security requires the imposition of the rules of the community on as large a scale as possible.

Although neocons share with hegemonic thought the rejection of a prudential vision of international politics aiming at the pursuit of strategic interests as well as of the normativity of international law, they go beyond the main features of the variant of the particularistic paradigm to which, at a first glance, they belong. The "classic" hegemonic approach from Schmitt to Huntington never had fully global aspirations: rather, it extended the range of the homogeneous community, aiming to create a hegemonic system in distinct spheres of influence to gather more assets for global competition. It did not aspire to impose a coherent set of values everywhere in the world. Therefore, hegemony as conceived, for example, by Carl Schmitt was limited to a large but not worldwide scale, and thus there was no global order per se, but only the competition among the enlarged hegemonic communities. Not surprisingly, we find both in Schmitt[153] and in Huntington[154] warnings against the tendency to overestimate the community's values and the ambition to impose them universally. In this perspective values are fundamental to unify the society and make it fit for competition; yet they always remain relative, and in their application not universal. To the contrary, the neoconservatives acknowledge no limitation on hegemonic expansion. The values they claim are supposed to be globally valid.

Consequently the concept of "empire," which seemed to belong to an old-fashioned political vocabulary, has reemerged in the contemporary debate. The concept is used by the critics of hegemonism to outline the features of a system that pretends to guarantee a global order, while oppressing, in reality, cultural pluralism and the just interests of the weak.[155] However, the idea of "empire" as a globalized political and legal regime is also revitalized, now with a positive connotation, by neoconservatives such as Deepak Lal. In Lal's view, empires can perform much better than nation-states in realizing the main goals of social life, including the maintenance of peace and securing prosperity.[156] Furthermore, empires can achieve these goals on a significantly larger scale. The rehabilitation of the historic function of empires is then enlarged to include the role played at the present time by the United States. Tearing the

[153] Carl Schmitt, *Positionen und Begriffe* (Berlin: Duncker and Humbolt, 1994), 151, 309.
[154] Huntington, *supra* note 136, at chapt. V, 12.
[155] Michael Hardt and Antonio Negri, *Empire* (Cambridge, MA: Harvard U. P., 2001); Detlev F. Vagts, "Hegemonic International Law," *Am. J. Intl. L.* 95 (2001): 843; Nico Krisch, *Imperial International Law* (Global Law Working Papers, No. 1, 2004).
[156] Deepak Lal, *In Defense of Empires* (Washington, D.C.: American Enterprise Institute P., 2004), 2.

"million strings" of international law that aim to tie down the superpower, casting off the Lilliputians who would hold back, the United States should accept its imperial role along with the duties arising from it. This consists, first, in securing global order, and, second, in expanding modernization. Whereas global order guarantees peace on a large scale, modernization is the condition for prosperity.[157] Extending the regime imposed by the U.S. superpower throughout the world, Lal's imperial conception globalizes hegemony in a way unknown to the tradition before the neoconservative turn.

In Lal, we find no reference to the universality of the values carried forth by the "empire." The sense of the empire's rule has to be found, Lal argues, in the security and wealth it can deliver all over the world, not in the global validity of its principles. Robert Kagan asserts, on the contrary, precisely such a global validity of Western values, as defended in particular by the United States. Herein lies the radical novelty of neoconservative thought. Far from being analogous to the despotic superpowers of the past, Kagan argues, the United States

> *is* a behemoth with a conscience. It is not Louis XIV's France or George III's England. Americans do not argue, even to themselves, that their actions may be justified by *raison d'état*. The United States is a liberal, progressive society through and through, and to the extent that Americans believe in power, they believe it must be a means of advancing the principles of a liberal civilization and a liberal world order.[158]

Liberty being a value shared, in principle, by all humans, the United States can reasonably claim to act globally. Furthermore, its intervention in the name of freedom is not a violation of the principle of equal sovereignty but a defence of a fundamental right. Kagan argues that, faced as we are with an existential threat to liberal values, it is worth thinking of a new kind of legitimacy in international relations. The protection of fundamental human rights all over the world should be recognized as superior to the principle of the equal sovereignty of states, with the consequence that actions have to be considered legitimate if they coerce dictators and autocrats to show greater respect for civil and political rights.[159] From the global validity of liberty Kagan ultimately draws the legitimacy of the worldwide American predominance:

> modern liberalism cherishes the rights and liberties of the individual and defines progress as the greater protection of these rights and liberties across

---

[157] *Id.*, at 35.
[158] Robert Kagan, "Power and Weakness," *Policy Rev.* 113 (2002): 1.
[159] *Id.*, at 78.

the globe. In the absence of a sudden democratic and liberal transformation, that goal can be achieved only by compelling tyrannical or barbarous regimes to behave more humanely, sometimes through force.[160]

Hence, as a consequence of the neoconservative turn, particularly in its more radical expression, hegemonism has reached worldwide extension and is based on the idea of imposing worldwide principles that find their truest interpretation in the hegemon's constitution. Neoconservatives seek to legitimize the global rule of the superpower and its right to intervention. They insist that "the United States can neither appear to be acting, nor in fact act, as if only its self-interest mattered."[161] In conclusion, neoconservative thought globalizes particularism without making it open for some kind of reconciliation with universalism. In the neocons understanding, the idea that every polity has a specific kind of internal order is projected beyond its limits so as to draw eventually the plan for a global order based on unilaterally specified rights and values. Universalism, understood as the inclusive order founded on the transcendental principles of the general interaction between humans and elaborated on the basis of the dialogue between cultures, still remains beyond the horizon of the neoconservative approach. Therefore, the parochialism that characterizes the neoconservative definition of rights and values keeps on being particular in the strictest sense of the word – as the sheer negation of an inclusive attitude.

IV. UNIVERSALISM: THE POSSIBILITY OF GLOBAL ORDER

The second paradigm of international law starts from the assumption that one order can in principle be extended over the entire world, to all humans and in all polities, not only in their internal relations, as accepted by supporters of the particularistic paradigm, but also in their interaction beyond the borders of each state. In this understanding, there are rights and values that are universal because they are shared by all individuals and all peoples. They are enshrined in the set of rules that build the core of international public law. Following this understanding, international law is more than a mere technique of coexistence and coordination between states.

Universalism has developed two strands: the first bases universalistic principles on metaphysical assumptions such as religious beliefs or ontological postulations about the "true" nature of human beings and their innate and

---

[160] Robert Kagan, "America's Crisis of Legitimacy," *Foreign Affairs* 83 (2004): 65, 78.
[161] *Id.*, at 85.

spontaneous sociability; the second interpreting universal order as the construct of individuals – as the original bearers of rights and values – and as the consequence of their correct use of reason. In the first case, universalism is rooted in society, although society embraces here the whole world; in the second, it is traced back to the faculties of individuals, particularly their reason.

A. *Two Strands*

1. The Metaphysical Tradition: The Legacy of Christianity and the Theory of the Natural and Universal Sociability of Humans

It took many thousand years before humans, although already living in complex societies expressing a high level of culture, could conceive of themselves as part of a common humanity. At the beginning of Western philosophical thought, in ancient Greece and Rome, the only laws thought to be universal were the laws of nature. The laws of humans – those laws, called *nomoi* in ancient Greek political philosophy, which humans give to themselves to rule their societies – were conceived to be specific for every political community. No *nomos* was assumed to be shared by all societies and all human beings.

The idea of the universal validity of a general law for all of human society appeared for the first time in the later stages of antiquity. Stoicism developed a radically new idea in Western philosophy, the concept that the whole world – physical as well as social – is ruled by only one fundamental law, the *logos*.[162] This perspective, represented a true "revolution" in the way Western thought conceived social, political, and legal order, and it had two consequences: first, the social world was now thought to be ruled by a law valid, in its essence, for all humans and applicable, even if not without cautious arrangement, in principle to all communities. This was a kind of "universal *nomos*" directly derived from the universal *logos*. Second, to be valid, the *nomoi* of the different polities had to be in accordance with the "universal *nomos*" that had been placed above them.

The Stoics had introduced a new understanding of moral and legal order. Nevertheless, their view remained largely speculative, with little impact on politics. In the best case their political philosophy could be seen as a vision of cosmopolitan fellowship within Hellenistic society or the Roman Empire. To become a paradigm of international relations and international law, universalism had to abandon this connection with the indefinitely expanding boundaries of a single political community and accept the burden of creating

---

[162] Johannes von Arnim, *Stoicorum veterum fragmenta* (Lipsiae (Leipzig): Teubneri, 1905).

universality within the complex context of political diversity. Yet this became the historical task not of Stoicism, but of Christianity.

Many elements of the Stoic philosophy became a part of Christian doctrine. Among these were the perception that there is a universal *logos* and the idea that all humans belong to a single community. However, whereas Stoicism never attained the status of an "official state philosophy," Christendom achieved in a few centuries such a prominent political position that the question how to translate the commandment of universality into a realistic political and legal program could not be passed over in silence. The Western world had become a Christian world: because the universalistic principle was now embedded in Christian doctrine, a Christian world had to develop universalistic approaches to the realms of law and politics.[163]

At first, Christian scholars tried to make this vision concrete by suggesting the idea of a universal political system. Just as the Christian Gospel was thought to be a message of love for the whole of humanity and the papacy claimed to embody the spiritual leadership of the entire world, so, too, a Christian universal monarchy had the right and the duty to rule over all peoples worldwide. Yet the principle of the "universal monarchy" was impossible to achieve, and this matter of fact became evident even before its most impressive conceptual formulation.[164] On the one hand, Christianity could never gain truly global power: even in the period of its most powerful expansion and despite the often merciless methods of its propagation, the allegedly universal message of the Gospel never reached more than a minority of humans. Furthermore, within the Christian world the growing differentiation of the territorial – and then national – states after the decline of the Holy Roman Empire undermined the very idea of unity.

The response of Christian philosophy to increasing political diversity even within the range of the Christian community was the conception of a *jus inter gentes* – that is, of an international law conceived as a set of rules governing the interactions between peoples on the basis of shared principles.[165] These principles were thought to be derived from the core commandments of

---

[163] In the early centuries of Christianity, when Christendom was yet largely distant from political power or even persecuted, this necessity to formulate a concrete political program according to Christian principles was not felt as strongly as it would be later. This is the time of the distinction between the *civitas dei* and the *civitas diaboli*, whereas the second one – the City of the Devil – corresponds to the real political situation on earth, and the first – the City of God – is projected, along with its universalistic aim, into a purely spiritual dimension. See Augustinus (413–426), *De civitate Dei*, Moretus, Antverpiae 1600.

[164] Dante Alighieri, "De Monarchia (1310–1314)," in *Opere minori*, vol. II (Torino: Utet, 1986).

[165] Francisco Suarez, "De legibus, ac Deo legislatore (1612)," in *Selections from Three Works* (Oxford: Clarendon P., 1944).

Christian religion, but the political framework, in which they had to be realized, changed significantly with the passing of the unrealistic vision of a universal monarchy. In fact, this is the moment of the foundation, in the Western world, of a modern law of nations. This development is evident in the works of Francisco Suarez, who accepted the plurality of polities, each of them governed by specific rules, but set within an all-encompassing legal framework that requires certain minimal standards of interaction. Therefore, the vision grounding the first formulations of modern Western international law can be interpreted as a kind of anticipation of a multilevel legal system, going beyond the global state as well as the interstate lawlessness of particularism. Herein lies its ongoing topicality.

Despite its significant contribution to developing the foundations of modern international law, the Christian vision of the relations between peoples was affected by a bias. In fact, although the message of love extended by Christianity claimed to address every human on earth, it has always been linked to one specific religion. Resting as it does on faith, the Christian religion could never achieve the global homogeneity or all-encompassing unity necessary to accomplish this political vision. As a consequence of its link to a peculiar religious community, the Christian law of nations became one-sided. Only Christians were allowed to be full members of the order of peace, security, and cooperation based on the commandments of divine law. Other peoples were treated as enemies or, in the best case, as marginal components of the system of international law, curtailed in their rights and dignity.[166] Even an author such as Francisco Vitoria, who was sincerely keen to overcome the most outrageous injustices that characterized the treatment of non-Christians at the dawn of the era of colonization, pleaded for a consideration of the respective claims of European and non-European peoples that, if seen from the point of view of our sensibility, reveals the signs of open discrimination.[167]

The growing ascertainment of the bias embodied from the outset in the system of Western international law led some authors to the conviction that even its core concept would be characterized by structural discrimination.[168]

---

[166] Jörg Fisch, *Die europäische Expansion und das Völkerrecht. Die Auseinandersetzungen um den Status der überseeischen Gebiete vom 15. Jahrhundert bis zur Gegenwart* (Stuttgart: Steiner, 1984).

[167] Francisco de Vitoria, "Relectio prior de Indis recenter inventis (1538–1539)," in *De Indis recenter inventis et de jure belli Hispanorum in Barbaros*, ed. Walter Schätzel (Tübingen: Mohr Siebeck, 1952).

[168] Ram Prakash Anand, *Studies in International Law and History*, (Leiden: Nijhoff, 2004); Antony Anghie, *Imperialism, Sovereignty and the Making of International Law* (Cambridge: Cambridge U. P., 2005).

Because the origins of Western international law were deeply Christian, its universalism came to seem fraudulent. Many dark episodes in Western history give this criticism a certain weight. The first step toward overcoming this innate bias embedded in Western international law would therefore be to purge it of its Christian presuppositions. Curiously, the conditions for undertaking this step were first laid down within a doctrinal dispute concerning the correct Christian interpretation of the relation between the law of humans and the law of God. In the theology of the Middle Ages and then in Catholic doctrine, the universal nature of the most general law made by humans – that is, of international law – is deduced directly from the universality of the divine law of the Christian God. However, the Reformation introduced at the very beginning of the modern era a new understanding of the relation between human and divine law that established the basic elements of a nonreligious philosophy of international law. Because the law of God, from the Protestant point of view, is inscrutable, international lawyers influenced by the theology of the Reformation had to search – if they did not want to forsake the universalistic claim of their newborn doctrinal system – for a new foundation that made no the direct reference to the Christian God. This task was accomplished by the third founder after Vitoria and Suarez of modern international law, Hugo Grotius.

The new, nonreligious foundation of the universalistic approach to international law was located by Grotius in an ontological postulate about human nature, concerning the alleged natural and universal disposition of human beings toward sociability.[169] Insofar as humans naturally tend to build societies and this tendency is not, as Aristotle thought,[170] limited to the boundaries of each people and country but can be extended globally, international law can be seen as the common law of humankind, containing the general rules defending universal sociability. This interpretation of Western cosmopolitanism makes no primary reference to the Christian God and grounds the law of nations on a view of natural reason possessed by every human being irrespective of cultural or religious background. This universal sociability is less "thick" than its counterpart within the borders of the single polities; nevertheless, it is strong enough to bear the responsibility of setting general, "thin" norms to regulate the interaction of peoples and individuals beyond the borders of their own countries.

---

[169] Hugo Grotius, De Jure Belli ac Pacis (Buffalo, NY: reprinted by William S. Hein & Co., 1995), Prolegomena, 6.
[170] Aristotle, Politics, at 2, 1252 et seq.

The idea of international law as the common law of a naturally sociable humankind has been extremely powerful in shaping its universal application. This provides the core philosophical concept supporting one of the most important theories about meaning and scope of international law, which posits an "international community." In the narrative of progress developed by the supporters of universalism the international community rests on a set of values shared by all humans. This theory views international law as protecting principles of a universal interaction based on the assumption of a naturally reasonable human sociability.

Notwithstanding its great significance, the ontological variant of the universalistic approach to international law shows at least one significant weakness. The existence of a global community including all individuals and states and sharing fundamental values seems in fact to be more a profession of faith than a proposition that can be proven or an evident axiom on which everyone must agree. To be clear about how little evidence there is to support such assumptions, imagine the case that a "realistic" critic would introduce. Historic experience suggests caution in supposing a worldwide brotherhood and sisterhood of humanity. Experience demonstrates the human capacity for social interaction, but this can lead to competition, as well as solidarity. Given the open possibilities of human interaction, the case for a worldwide community of humans turns out to be founded on a metaphysical principle derived from the old-fashioned argument about the "true" nature of humankind. However, a metaphysical assertion about the "natural" goodness of our fellow humans does not provide a very solid basis for a system of law intended to be binding on everyone, everywhere.

2. Contract Theory

This weakness at the heart of the metaphysically grounded idea of universalism lead to a second strand in this paradigm. The preconditions were created by a great "revolution" in political thinking that occurred at the beginning of Western modernity. Until that time individuals were thought of as part of the society in which they lived. The community was the totality, the "holon," superior to its members: the individuals had to serve the community, not vice versa. At the edge between the Middle Ages and modernity, these close community ties were broken. The consequence was a demand for a new philosophy of social and political life. This new vision was delivered by Thomas Hobbes, the first political philosopher who overturned the hierarchy between individual and community. Hobbes put individuals at the heart of political life: they are the bearers of the fundamental rights and the starting point of any legitimation of authority.[171] Just as Copernicus reversed the position between earth and sun, giving for the first time centrality to the latter, so Hobbes signaled a "Copernican revolution in political thought"[172] turning the order of society upside down. In Hobbes's viewed the Commonwealth is not as the highest entity in the ethical world, but rather a tool that humans create for themselves to establish a better safeguard of life, security, and property.

Following this understanding, political institutions are the product of a contract among individuals. As applied to the theory of international law, the central question is how far a society built on such institutions can reach. Must such societies be national, serving the interests only of a limited, albeit large, number of individuals? Or can we imagine that a society based on contract could expand itself to comprehend all humans? For one and a half centuries after its first formulation contract theory showed little interest in international law and, insofar as the question of international order was mentioned, the most important exponents of contractualism were rather skeptical about the possibility of guaranteeing a peaceful interaction on a global scale.[173] On the other hand, there was no conceptual reason not to apply contractualism to a system of global peace and security. If the central building block in any society is made by separate individuals and if it is assumed that all individuals are endowed with essential rights and faculties, in particular with the capacity to reason, then no insurmountable obstacle stands between our condition and the construction of a world order based on a general agreement among fellow human beings.

This consequence of contractualism, which was already implicit in the very core of its conception, was first drawn by Immanuel Kant.[174] In his political philosophy, the passage from the state of nature to the civic condition is not only, as for Hobbes, the practical output of reasoning based on expediency, but also the fulfillment of a higher moral duty. In fact, in Kant's view only the civilized human is a morally accomplished human, and, insofar as the perfect moral accomplishment can only be reached if every interaction is civilized,

[171] Thomas Hobbes, *De Cive* (London: Royston, 1651); *ibid., Leviathan, or the Matter, Form, and Power of a Commonwealth, Ecclesiastical, and Civil* (London: Crooke, 1651).
[172] Norberto Bobbio and Michelangelo Bovero, *Società e stato nella filosofia politica moderna* (Milano: Il Saggiatore, 1979).
[173] Hobbes, *Leviathan, supra* at note 171, at XXX; Baruch de Spinoza, "Tractatus politicus," in *Opera*, vol. 3 (Heidelberg: Winters 1924), III; *ibid.*, "Tractatus theologico-politicus," in *Opera*, vol. 3, XVI; John Locke, *Two Treatises of Government* (London: Awnsham-Churchill, 1698), II, 2, 12, 16.
[174] Immanuel Kant, "Zum ewigen Frieden. Ein philosophischer Entwurf," in *Werkausgabe*, vol. XI (Frankfort: Suhrkamp, 1977), 191; Kant, "Die Metaphysik der Sitten" in *Werkausgabe*, vol. VIII (Frankfort: Suhrkamp, 1977), 309.

the creation of an international order can be seen as the most difficult, but also as the noblest, duty we can pursue. As a consequence of these conceptual premises, Kant inserted in his systematics of public law, for the first time in history, a level specifically called "cosmopolitan law" (*jus cosmopoliticum*),[175] which contained not only – as it was before – the general principles of a universal *nomos*, nor simply the core elements of a natural law-based *civitas maxima*, but rather the rights that should be granted to individuals when they interact beyond state borders. In doing so, he laid down in an unprecedented way the essential tenets of what we now call *cosmopolitanism* and, therefore, also the fundaments of the *cosmopolitan view of rights and values*.

Summing up, in the contractualistic version of a cosmopolitan global order depends on the following:

• the centrality of individuals,
• some essential assumptions about the equality of humans,
• the cognizance of mutual interdependence,
• the awareness that individual long-term self-interest is in building a common society,
• the conviction that we can pursue self-fulfillment only in peace and in a global interaction based on freedom and justice,
• the principle that the definition of the rules binding all members of any society has to be based on inclusive procedures, and
• the commitment to create institutions and procedures to put the previous cognitive tenets into practice.

It was precisely on this last issue – the traditional rupture point between theory and praxis – that Immanuel Kant as the father of contractualistic universalism had to tackle the most tenacious problems, also revealing a significant uncertainty affecting his actual understanding of cosmopolitanism. We find in fact in Kant's work two solutions for the institution accomplishing world order: on the one hand the "world republic" (*Weltrepublik*) as a kind of global superstate, on the other hand the rather unpretentious idea of a "league of nations" (*Völkerbund*). Whereas the second proposal is, also in Kant's eyes, too weak to guarantee world order, the idea of a "world republic" seems too abstract and, insofar as it is conceived as a global state endowed with general authority and supreme sovereignty, also somehow dangerous for freedom. As a consequence, cosmopolitanism, as the idea that there is a set of rights and values that belong to all humans, is considered by Kant as realizable only within the framework of a "world state" – a perspective that runs against the evidence

---

[175] Kant, *Zum ewigen Frieden, supra* note 174, at 203.

that collocates the roots even of universal rights and values in the parochial terrain, as well as against the justified need for subsidiarity and respect for local specificity.

Considering the strengths and weaknesses of the philosophical approaches to universalism and cosmopolitanism, we can transitively conclude that an international law aspiring to be universalistic and cosmopolitan should resolve two problems: first, its conceptual foundation should not resort to religious or metaphysical assumptions; second, it should search for institutional solutions capable of conciliating the need for global values and rules with the respect for the equal sovereignty of peoples. The following discussion analyze some proposals for achieving this purpose.

B. Constitutionalism as the Most Visible Contemporary Offspring

Constitutionalism is the latest offspring of the universalistic-cosmopolitan scholarly tradition that strives for a global legal community that frames and directs political power in the light of common values and a common good.[176] It is often associated with international scholarship in Germany, but international constitutionalism is also taught in other countries.[177] The idea of understanding current international law as a building block of a global legal community has been a constant thread of thinking among many German international law scholars. In 1974, Hermann Mosler held the General Course at the Hague under the title "The International Society as a Legal Community."[178] Because the course was given during the Cold War, it provides a dampened version of constitutionalism. Yet it echoes the core concept of Walter Hallstein, his former superior in the nascent German Foreign Service and first

---

[176] It has deep roots in prewar projects, see Hans Kelsen, *Reine Rechtslehre* (Wein: Deuticke, 1934), 115 *et seq.*, 328; Georges Scelle, *Le Pacte des Nations et sa liaison avec Le Traite de Paix* (Paris: Sirey, 1919), 101 *et seq.*, 105 *et seq.*; *ibid., Précis de droit des gens*, vol. 1 (Paris: Sirey, 1932), 188 *et seq.*; Walther Schücking, *Die Organisation der Welt, in Festschrift für Paul Laband,* ed. Wilhelm van Calker (Tübingen: Mohr, 1908), 533; Alfred Verdross, *Die Verfassung der Völkerrechtsgemeinschaft* (Berlin: Springer, 1926).

[177] See, e.g., Pierre-Marie Dupuy, "The Constitutional Dimension of the Charter of the United Nations Revisited," *Max Planck Yearbook U.N. L.* 1 (1997): 1. In the Netherlands a chair for international constitutional law has been created at Amsterdam University in 2004, whose first and current incumbent is Erika de Wet, see Erika de Wet, the International Constitutional Order, inaugural speech 2005, on file with the author; see also *ibid.,* "The Prohibition of Torture as an International Norm of Jus Cogens and Its Implications for National and Customary Law," *Eur. J. Intl. L.* 15 (2004): 97.

[178] Hermann Mosler, "The International Society as a Legal Community," in *Recueil des cours,* vol. 140 (1974), 1; *ibid., The International Society as Legal Community* (Alphen aan den Rijn: Sijthoff/Noordhoff 1980). On this course see Robert Kolb, *Les cours généraux de droit international public de l'Académie de La Haye* (Brussels: Bruylant, 2003), 541 *et seq.*

president of the European Economic Community. Hallstein had devised the term *legal community* to conceive and direct the embryonic European integration project.[179] It succeeded in inspiring the "constitutionalisation" jurisprudence of the European Court of Justice (ECJ),[180] laying the conceptual basis for the enormous power that the Commission's Legal Service wielded for decades, as well as generally framing the political discourse.

After the fall of the Iron Curtain, Christian Tomuschat taught a much bolder course in 1999 titled: "Ensuring the Survival of Mankind on the Eve of a New Century."[181] To present the basic structure of constitutionalist thought, we focus on certain elements of his teleological reconstruction of core concepts of current international law.[182] The strengths of this approach, as well as its inherent tensions, give clear examples of the state of contemporary international constitutionalism. Tomuschat's ideas about the roles and the normativity of international law are presented first. Among the various roles of international law, of particular importance is its constitutional function of legitimating, limiting, and guiding politics. As a consequence, Tomuschat turns the dominant

[179] Walter Hallstein, *Der unvollendete Bundesstaat* (Berlin: Econ Verlag, 1969), 39, 252–255.

[180] On this, see Joseph Weiler, "The Transformation of Europe," in *The Constitution of Europe* (Cambridge: Cambridge U. P. 1999), 10.

[181] Tomuschat, *supra* note 27, at 1999. On this course Kolb, *supra* note 177, at 1057 *et seq.*

[182] There is an enormous variety of ideas, *cf.* Bruno Simma, "From Bilateralism to Community Interest in International Law," in *Recueil des cours*, vol. 250 (1994), 6, 221; Bardo Fassbender, "The U.N. Charter as a Constitution," *Columbia J. Transnational L.* 36 (1998): 574; Michael Cottier, "Die Anwendbarkeit von völkerrechtlichen Normen im innerstaatlichen Bereich als Ausprägung der Konstitutionalisierung des Völkerrechts," *Schweuzeruscgen zeitschrift für internationals und europäisches Recht* 9 (1999): 4, 403; Jochen Frowein, "Konstitutionalisierung des Völkerrechts," *Berichte der Deutschen Gesellschaft für Völkerrecht* 39 (2000): 427, 431; Giovanni Biaggini, "Die Idee der Verfassung," *Zeitschrift für Schweizerisches Rect* 119 (2000): I, 445; Jost Delbrück, "Structural Changes in the International Legal Order and Its Legal Order," *Schweuzeruscgen zeitschrift für internationals und europäisches Recht* 11 (2001): 1; Robert Uerpmann, "Internationales Verfassungsrecht," *Juristenzeitung* 56 (2001): 11, 565; Christian Walter, "Constitutionalizing (Inter)national Governance," *German Yearbook Intl. L.* 44 (2001): 170; Hauke Brunkhorst, *Solidarität: von der Bürgerfreundschaft zur Globalen Rechtsgenossenschaft* (Berlin: Suhrkamp, 2002), 20; Otfried Höffe, *Demokratie im Zeitalter der Globalisierung*, 2nd ed. (München: Beck, 2002); Brun-Otto Byrde, "Konstitutionalisierung des Völkerrechts und Internationalisierung des Verfassungsrechts," *Der Staat* 42 (2003): 1, 61; Thomas Cottier and Maya Hertig, "The Prospects of 21st Century Constitutionalism, *Max Planck Yearbook U.N. L.* 7 (2003): 261; Stefan Kadelbach, "Ethik des Völkerrechts unter Bedingungen der Globalisierung," *Harvard J. Intl. L.* 64 (2004): 1; Matthias Ruffert, *Die Globalisierung als Herausforderung an das Öffentliche Recht* (Stuttgard: Boorberg, 2004), 38. Much debated has been Ernst-Ulrich Petersmann's constitutional approach to international trade law, among his writing *cf. Constitutional functions and constitutional problems of international economic law* (Fribourg, Switzerland: University Press Fribourg 1991); *ibid.*, "The WTO Constitution and Human Rights," *3 J. Intl. Econ. L.* (2000): 19–25; *ibid.*, "Constitutional Economics, Human Rights and the Future of the WTO," *Aussenwirtschaft* 58 (2003), 49.

understanding of the relationship between international law and municipal constitutional law upside down, making the state an agent of the international community. The third step looks at the organization of the international community and discusses Tomuschat's understanding of international institutions. This raises the issue of international federalism. Yet Tomuschat does not use this term for his model. His reticence may be explained by his view that international law possesses merely derivative democratic credentials and by his uncertainty about its "social substratum" in the "international community."

1. International Law as a Common Law of Humankind

Christian Tomuschat's construct attributes new prominence to international law, which he sees as having become paramount to all other law in many respects. This importance largely results from the challenge of globalization: "[T]he concept [of globalization] captures in a nutshell the current state of increased transnationalism, which constitutes the background against which the adequacy and effectiveness of international law and its institutions must be carefully tested. It is part and parcel of the empirical context from which international law receives its major impulses. To the extent that the state forgoes or is compelled to relinquish its role as guarantor of the common interest of its citizens, common institutions should be established at regional levels or the universal level to compensate for the losses incurred."[183]

In Tomuschat's view, some rules of international law fulfill a constitutional function with respect both to the international realm *and* the municipal realm, "namely to safeguard international peace, security and justice in relations between States, and human rights as well as the rule of law domestically inside States for the benefit of human beings, who, in substance, are the ultimate addressees of international law."[184] The core principles of international law address and limit all forms of political power: this is the essence of the constitutional argument.

Thus the traditional function of international law – to regulate interstate relations – is supplemented not only with a constitutional function, but also with a further function similar to that of municipal administrative and private law: the new international law presents a "comprehensive blueprint for social life."[185] International law is seen as a multifaceted body of law that permeates all fields of life, wherever governments act to promote a public purpose; accordingly, international law now is "a common legal order for mankind as a whole."[186] The traditional understanding of international law and municipal

---

[183] Tomuschat, *supra* note 27, at 42.   [184] *Id.*, at 23.
[185] *Id.*, at 63.   [186] *Id.*, at 28, and passim.

law as dealing mostly with separate issues is replaced by one in which fundamentally the same issues are addressed and regulated. Tomuschat's vision is not one of separate spheres, but rather one of an integrated, multilayered system. His understanding of an integrated international system is not a defense of the "ancien régime" of international law with the ICJ at its pinnacle. The ICJ actually plays quite a limited role in Tomuschat's construction. Rather, the integration is provided by scholarly effort and practical reason.

Tomuschat's understanding rests on the premise that international law can direct and control social reality and (in particular) political power in the same way that municipal constitutional or administrative law do. Others would disagree. The New Haven School, for example (similar in this respect to the Critical Legal Studies movement), does not consider international law as being able to direct political behavior. From this perspective, international law is deemed to lack municipal law's determinacy and normativity (contrafacticity); rather, it is understood as usually following the practice of the most powerful states.

Tomuschat's defence of international law does not deny that its norms are often vague and contested. Nor does he ignore the permanence of state sovereignty and the lack of strong global institutions, which do not allow international law and municipal law to be regarded in fully parallel terms. Despite these limits, he advocates a "positivist" legal discourse on international law and assumes that it can operate in the same way as to municipal public law. This assumption rests above all on a moral imperative:

> [D]iscourse on issues of international law must... be couched in language that allows everyone affected by its operation to make its voice heard, fully to grasp arguments invoked by others and thus to engage in meaningful dialogue permitting to highlight on a common basis of understanding any controversial issues.... Discourse on what is right or wrong must be crystal-clear and should not fall into the hands of a few magicians who invariably are able to prove that law and justice are on their side.[187]

Tomuschat is an enlightened positivist. He knows the shortcomings of international law as an instrument of social order as well as the rational limits of established legal reasoning. Nevertheless, he sees this established form of legal reasoning as the best way available for lawyers to live up to undisputed postulates on how to carry out their profession. Moreover, social theory and political philosophy, in particular, have never been able to lead the debate on

---

[187] *Id.*

"right or wrong" better than have the established paths of legal reasoning.[188] The twentieth-century Kantian pragmatic response to relativism – the philosophy of the "als ob"[189] – can support this methodological and constructive approach, the foundation of which is an ethical premise. This explains why this position is sometimes termed as idealistic.

2. A Revolutionized Understanding of the Institutional Order

One of Tomuschat's conceptual innovations that has become part of common scholarly discourse is the qualification of such important international treaties as "völkerrechtliche Nebenverfassungen," in other words, as international law having a supplementary function for municipal constitutional law.[190] He radicalized this concept in his General Course in which the core principles of international law assume a foundational, rather than a merely supplementary, function for the state and its constitution.

In the history of international scholarship, one finds several attempts to turn the relationship between municipal and international law "upside down," reversing the correlation between the state and the international community.[191] Developments in international law after 1990, when the law formulated in 1945 appeared to have acquired substantial normativity (mainly, although by no means exclusively, through the Security Council's activities), allowed for a fresh attempt to redefine this relationship. The foundational role of international law is not conceived in formal terms as a relationship of delegated competences (Kelsen) or according to the doctrine of *dédoublement fonctionnel* (Scelle). Tomuschat's construction is based rather on substance, in particular on international human rights, a conception only possible after World War II: "The fact that the international community is progressively moving from a sovereignty-centered to a value-oriented or individual-oriented system has left deep marks on its scope and meaning."[192]

Even for Tomuschat, the state remains the most important *actor* on the international plane; this corresponds to the universalistic position of

---

[188] This is confirmed by authors who earlier on paid little importance or even criticized "legal formalism"; see Habermas, *supra* note 111, at 182, 187; Koskenniemi, *supra* note 15, at 502 *et seq.*
[189] Hans Vaihinger, *Die Philosophie des Als Ob* (Hamburg: Meiner, 1920).
[190] Christian Tomuschat, "Der Verfassungsstaat im Geflecht der internationalen Beziehungen," in *Veröffentlichungen der Vereinigung der deutschen Staatsrechtslehrer* 36 (Berlin: de Gruyter, 1978): 7, 51 *et seq.*; Robert Uerpmann-Wittzack, "The Constitutional Role of Multilateral Treaty Systems," in *Principles of European Constitutional Law*, eds. von Bogdandy and Bast (Oxford: Hart Publishing, 2006), 145.
[191] In particular, Hans Kelsen, *Reine Rechtslehre* (Wein: Deuticke, 1934), 150; Hans Kelsen, "Die Einheit von Völkerrecht und staatlichem Recht," *Harvard J. Intl. L.* 19 (1958): 234.
[192] Tomuschat, *supra* note 27, at 237.

state-centered integration.[193] However, the state assumes a *role* – and herein lies the innovation – in a broader production written and directed by the international community. "[P]rotection is afforded by the international community to certain basic values even without or against the will of individual States. All of these values are derived from the notion that States are no more than instruments whose inherent function it is to serve the interests of their citizens as legally expressed in human rights."[194] "The international community [...] views the State as a unit at the service of the human beings for whom it is responsible. Not only is it expected that no disturbances for other States should originate from the territory of the State, it is also incumbent upon every State to perform specific services for the benefit of its citizens."[195]

This understanding of statehood as an instrument through which the international community implements its core legal values does not correspond to the general understanding in legal scholarship, political science, or the media. Tomuschat himself concedes that "the transformation from international law as a State-centered system to an individual-centered system has not yet found a definitive new equilibrium."[196] It is, moreover, by no means clear which one of the two rival understandings, sovereign equality or protection of basic values by the international community, prevails in case of conflict. This "weakness" does not necessarily diminish the value and usefulness of Tomuschat's construction. Rather, it may be proof of the potential for normative legal evolution within legal texts through innovative legal scholarship – or as Hegel put it: Once the ideas have been revolutionized, reality will not resist.

According to Tomuschat, fundamental rights codified in a municipal constitution form the basis of all municipal public power, and these rights are in turn based on universal values, which are now enshrined in international human rights. Although this vision has to struggle with some of the problems of natural law thinking, it is supported by the fact that most documents (municipal as well as international) referring to fundamental rights do not "enact," but rather "recognize" such rights. This suggests that these rights, although formally elaborated and ratified by states, are considered to exist independently of the municipal legal order.[197] Accordingly, comparative constitutionalism

---

[193] See "The Universalistic-Cosmopolitan Responses: Universal Law versus State-Centered Integration," *supra* sect. II.C.1.
[194] Tomuschat, *supra* note 27, at 161 *et seq.*
[195] *Id.*, at 95.   [196] *Id.*, at 162.
[197] See, e.g., *La Déclaration des droits de l'homme et du citoyen* (adopted 1789): "l'Assemblée nationale reconnaît et déclare, en présence et sous les auspices de l'Être suprême, les droits suivants de l'homme et du citoyen"; in detail Maria Zanichelli, *Il discorso sui diritti* (Milano: CEDAM, 2004), 101 *et seq.*

acquires a substantial function for constitutional adjudication within the various municipal legal orders. As Tomuschat demonstrates throughout his course,
his construction of the state as an agent of the international community provides a coherent explicative framework for many elements of current international law as well as a helpful indication of which meaning should be attributed
to a norm in case of its legal indeterminacy.

International law, as construed in this line of thinking, supports a system of
international governance. In current discussions, the institutional features of
this system are hazy and disputed. Tomuschat enriches the pertinent debate by
linking up the notion of "international governance" with public-law thinking
on state government as developed over the past three hundred years. This
is a thoroughly legal approach: it looks (at least with one eye) to the past to
meet a new challenge, which is the analogical nature of legal thinking.[198]
His argument is based on the premise that the international community – as
with any community – needs "a sufficiently broad set of legal norms in order
to be able to deal efficiently with the many challenges arising in the course
of history":[199] *ubi societas, ibi ius.* Satisfying this need requires institutions
with the following traditional governmental functions: a "legislative function"
for enacting a "broad set of legal norms" and particularly for making basic
political decisions; an "executive function," – that is, a "machinery mandated
to translate into concrete facts the law produced"; and a function concerning
the "settlement of disputes" – that is, the "application of these rules in disputes."
Thus, at least the functions of the global institutions are fixed, something that
gives direction for interpretation, further research and political proposals.

For Tomuschat, municipal constitutional law can only inform, it cannot
determine future developments. The international system cannot adopt a
blueprint provided by comparative (municipal) constitutional law for one
specific reason: the continuing significance of state sovereignty. Although state
sovereignty undergoes a substantial transformation in Tomuschat's thinking,
he nevertheless acknowledges state sovereignty as a normative and factual
reality which for the foreseeable future will profoundly shape the international
sphere: "it may be said that the different elements of the executive function
in the international community have never been established *more geometrico*
as they would be under a national constitution, which seeks to organize the
system of governance in a transparent way, taking as its point of departure the

---

[198] Ulrich Schroth, "Hermeneutik, Norminterpretation und richterliche Normanwendung," in
Einführung in Rechtsphilosophie und Rechtstheorie der Gegenwart, eds. Arthur Kaufmann
et al., 7th ed. (Heidelberg: C. F. Müller, 2004), 270, 278.
[199] Tomuschat, *supra* note 27 at 305.

principle of the separation of powers. The international system still rests on national sovereignty."[200]

If a convincing form of global governance needs international legislative, executive, and judicial institutions, the question arises whether this governance requires the creation of a global federation. Tomuschat uses the terms *federal* and *federation* most carefully. They do not figure prominently in his text. One might assume that he has learned a lesson from the hostile reactions these terms encounter when used with respect to the European Union.

It is possible to qualify his vision as a federal one, for the basic understanding of federalism deems as "federal" any multilevel system of governance.[201] The international system as proposed by Tomuschat is such a multilevel system, in which the state "must accept to live in a symbiotic relationship with the institutions of the international community at regional and universal levels."[202] Moreover, the overall system features further integrative elements. First of all, it is the constitutional character of the international system, which is understood as enshrining and securing (although not always successfully) the fundamental legal values. The principles of Article 2 of the UNC and the core of international human rights enshrine those values "which humankind must uphold in order to be able to continue to live under peaceful conditions which permit individuals real enjoyment of human rights."[203] Hence, some international obligations are fundamental for municipal legal orders and may therefore be considered as performing a constitutional function for the entire world. Secondly, Tomuschat proposes an international political system with a considerable degree of autonomy vis-à-vis the constituent states. This is particularly true of the legislative function:

> The international system cannot rely any more solely on treaty-making, where the sovereign State holds an unrestricted power of unilateral determination. In principle, treaties are instruments of self-commitment. No State can be forced to adhere to a given conventional régime, no matter how important that régime may be with a view to furthering community interests. To the extent that in international society other values are recognized, values

---

[200] *Id.*, at 389.
[201] Mauro Cappelletti, Monica Seccombe, and Joseph Weiler, "Integration through Law: Europe and the American Federal Experience. A General Introduction, in Methods," *Tools and Institutions*, vol. 1 (Berlin: de Gruyter, 1985), 3, 7–8, 12 *et seq.*
[202] Tomuschat, *supra* note 27, at 436.
[203] *Id.*, at 85; in more detail Christian Tomuschat, Die internationale Gemeinschaft, *Archiv des Völkerechts* 33 (1995), 1, 7. C. Tomuschat, "Human rights: between idealism and realism," in *Collected courses of the Academy of European Law*, vol. 13 (Alphen aan den Rijn: Kluwer Law International, 2003).

that deserve protection irrespective of consent given by an individual State, treaties must lose their primary role as instruments for the creation of legal norms.[204]

In addition, he finds that the autonomy of the international executive branch should also be increazed: "It stands to reason that it would be much to be preferred to have a centralized agency which would itself take sanctions against a State remiss of its obligations, or which would at least co-ordinate the measures taken by individual States. Such a hierarchically organized superstructure does not yet exist, however, except in certain fields."[205]

Tomuschat's vision of international governance partially resembles the specific form of federalism realized in Germany and the European Union. In both systems, legislation that is enacted by the institutions at the higher level is executed by lower-level bodies. At the same time he holds that "it would be an erroneous assumption [. . .] that the most promising way of facing up to the challenges of the future would be to centralize ever more functions in the hands of a world bureaucracy as the nucleus of a world government. International supervision and monitoring play an essential role [. . .]. But there can be no genuinely sustainable international legal order if national systems of governance disintegrate."[206]

Tomuschat does not conceive or propose the creation of a global federal state in any traditional sense, as can be deduced from the importance he attributes to sovereign states as constituent elements of the envisaged global system. Yet as Kant[207] and the discussion on the "nature" of the European Union prove, it might be useful to refer to transnational nonstate entities as being federal.[208] Whenever an organization within a multilevel political system is vested with the competence to enact unilaterally binding decisions, the issues of legitimacy and delimitation of competences arise. These are precisely the issues that beset federal states. Thus, conceptualizing transnational entities in multilevel systems as federal entities allows reference to experiences accumulated in the municipal context.

---

[204] Tomuschat, *supra* note 27, at 306 *et seq.* This understanding is elaborated in Christian Tomuschat, "Obligations Arising for States without or against Their Will," in *Recueil des cours*, vol. 241 (Leiden: Martinus Nijhoff, 1993), 4, 199.

[205] Tomuschat, *supra* note 27, at 377.   [206] *Id.*, at 435.

[207] Kant, *supra* note 105, at 115, 133.

[208] Eric Stein, Lawyers, "Judges and the Making of a Transnational Constitution," *Am. J. Intl. L.* 75 (1981): 1; Ulrich Everling, "Zur föderalen Struktur der Europäischen Gemeinschaft," in *Festschrift für K. Doehring* (Berlin: Beck, 1989), 179; Koen Lenaerts, "Constitutionalism and the Many Faces of Federalism," *Am. J. Crim. L.* 38 (1990): 205; Kalypso Nicolaidis and Robert Howse (eds.), *The Federal Vision* (Oxford: Oxford U. P., 2002).

The importance that Tomuschat attributes to international law and the autonomy with which public functions binding on the states should be exercised at the international level conceivably qualifies his vision as "federal." Yet (again), he is reticent to use this qualification. The same is true with respect to the question whether the European Union provides an example of how to shape and develop a global system of governance. Some authors believe the EU indicates the direction the international system should take,[209] whereas Tomuschat presents European integration as exemplary for the global level far more cautiously. At the same time, nowhere does he assert that the experience of integration within the EU is limited to its specific regional setting or that such developments cannot be replicated in a broader international context.

Tomuschat's hesitance to draw parallels between his understanding and vision of international law on the one hand and the evolution of European integration on the other is also evident in his narrative on the evolution of international law. Under the heading "The Growing Complexity of the International Legal Order," he divides this evolution into the following four successive stages: (1) a law of coexistence, (2) a law of cooperation, (3) international law as a comprehensive blueprint for social life, and (4) international law of the international community.[210] The conceptualization of stages 3 and 4 are peculiar, for one would expect cooperation (second stage) to lead to integration. According to most understandings, it is precisely this feature of law – being directly important to social life (i.e., the "blueprint" in the third stage) – that should mark the law of integration and distinguish it from the law of cooperation.[211] Yet the term "integration" hardly appears in Tomuschat's text.

Accordingly, one might suspect that Tomuschat is attempting to further international federalism "by stealth." This assumption may, however, miss an important aspect of his thinking. In fact, he poses the last stage of his narrative

---

[209] For a more outspoken view, see Daniel Thürer: "From the point of view of world global order the EU seems to me to represent the most promising way of creating some structure capable of checking the abuse of economic and social power, and of directing social activities towards overriding common ends. The EU seems to be making the most successful effort so far to cope with the problematic effects of globalization and, perhaps it offers a model for new legal institutions to be created on a world-wide basis"; Daniel Thürer, "Discussion," in *Non-State Actors as New Subjects of International Law*, eds. Rainer Hofmann et al. (Berlin: Duncker & Humblot, 1999), 92; from a sociological point of view, see Klaus Friedrich Röhl, "Das Recht im Zeichen der Globalisierung der Medien," in *Globalisierung des Rechts*, ed. Rüdiger Voigt (Berlin: Nomos, 2000), 103.

[210] Tomuschat, *supra* note 27, at 56 *et seq.*

[211] Hans Peter Ipsen, *Europäisches Gemeinschaftsrecht* (Tübingen: JCB Mohr, 1972), 66 *et seq.*

(on the evolution of international law) as a question: "Is there an international community?" This question points out the major difficulty in designating the international order as federal.

3. The Substratum and Legitimacy of International Law

A "thick" federal system requires not just an overarching organization of government, but also a genuine "social substratum" – a people or citizenry that provides the organization with original (not just derived) legitimacy.[212] Municipal law rests on and refers to a people, a citizenry. Municipal public institutions (parliaments, governments, and courts) are institutions of that group; the municipal institutional actors (politicians, lobbyists, and officials) are – in one way or another – representatives of interests or values of that people. The concept *people* itself represents the focal point of reference for all political and legal processes. If international law increasingly assumes functions previously exercised by municipal law, a question arises concerning its point of reference. As long as this issue has not been settled, there is good reason to be cautious in using the term *federal*.

Under the traditional doctrine of international law, the focal point of reference is "the states." Whereas municipal law originates from the people, international law originates from the states. States are usually understood as unitary actors that animate and control the international political and legal processes. Thus, "China" presents a position in the UN Security Council; "Germany" is concerned about the human rights situation in Congo; "Thailand" ratifies an international agreement. However, in international discourse "the states" are being increasingly replaced by a new term: the international community. In a growing number of discourses, the notion of *international community* plays a role for international law and international politics similar to that played by the concept of the *people* in the municipal realm. The increasing significance of the term *international community* in discourses on international law and politics might indicate a conceptual shift that could result in the basic transformation of these disciplines. Should the view become generally accepted that international law and politics refer to a social group called the *international community*, to which all human beings belong, the realization of Tomuschat's vision and construction will be much facilitated.

The term *international community* has different functions and carries diverse meanings in Tomuschat's text. Tomuschat uses the term mostly as an underlying premise for his construction and sometimes even as a straight normative

---

[212] Stefan Oeter, *Federalism and Democracy*, in *Principles of European Constitutional Law*, eds. A. v. Bogdandy and Bast (Oxford: Hart Publishing, 2006), 53.

argument.[213] At times, he uses the term *international community* as the term *people* would be used in a municipal context – meaning a self-aware and organized group of human beings, a collective subject. This is indicated by the following passages: "As any other human community, the international community requires a sufficiently broad set of legal norms in order to be able to deal effectively with the many challenges arising in the course of history"; "the international community has realized in the last decade of the twentieth century that national efforts of combating crime must be complemented by international machinery."[214]

The international community is presented above all as a community of values, enshrined in the international obligations *erga omnes* and in *jus cogens*.[215] The role attributed by Tomuschat to states fits nicely into this understanding of the international community. States have legitimacy only to the extent that they respect and implement those fundamental obligations. The international community is even considered to have some institutions of its own. Thus, according to Tomuschat, "the Secretary-General should always promote the interest of the international community with resolute determination"; he is "an agent of the international community."[216] Even the Security Council is seen as an embryonic "community" institution.[217]

Yet he recognizes that many differences remain between the international and national communities. International community institutions are far less developed than their national counterparts. Perhaps for this reason, Tomuschat only asserts the existence of a lawmaking process *in* the international community" but not *of* the international community. The reification of the international community does not go as far as has occurred with municipal communities. Thus, Tomuschat capitalizes the word *State*, but never does so for the term *international community*.

Among the various differences between the international community and national communities, the one that appears fundamental to Tomuschat's thinking, concerns the concept of the *people*. As stated, the "people" is the fundamental point of reference in municipal law, because it is seen as the

---

[213] See, e.g., Tomuschat, *supra* note 27, at 346: the idea that "the international community has an overriding interest" is the decisive argument why a unilateral act is irrevocable.

[214] *Id.*, at 305, 431; a much more outspoken view is presented by the Russian judge Vereshchetin at the ICJ: "Mankind as a whole . . . tries to manifest itself in the international arena as an actor, as an entity"; "Discussion," in *Non-State Actors as New Subjects of International Law*, *supra* note 208, at 136.

[215] Tomuschat, *supra* note 27, at 75 *et seq.*   [216] *Id.*, at 399.

[217] *Id.*, at 89; this understanding sits uneasily with the assertion that "*International Organizations* . . . possess no social substratum of their own, but operate essentially as common agencies of their members." *Id.*, at 91.

source of democratic legitimacy, which in turn serves as the foremost source of governmental legitimacy. In other words, the concept of the people gives an ultimate point of reference to the legitimacy discussion. With respect to international law, Tomuschat sees the *international community* as providing a source of legitimacy through (common) values, but it is not a source of democratic input. He concedes that international law "as a blueprint for social life" is problematic when examined under the democratic principle because "the quantity and quality of international obligations has reached a level that in jeopardy the right of framing independently the internal constitutional order."[218] In Tomuschat's thinking, there is no substitute at the international level for the municipal source of democratic legitimacy that lies with the people.[219] Accordingly, the term *international community* does not appear in his construction as a substitute for *the people*.

Some scholars consider NGOs as the embryo of an international community that might provide democratic legitimacy to the global legal order.[220] Tomuschat rejects this approach: "Since they [i.e., the NGOs] are products of societal freedom, they lack the kind of formal legitimacy which a government emerging from free democratic elections may normally boast of. Apart from their membership, there is no one to whom they are institutionally accountable. Therefore, NGOs have never been regarded as the true voices of the peoples they are representing."[221] It is a defining feature of Tomuschat's construction that international law has no source of *democratic* legitimacy on its own: its democratic credentials rest on the democratic processes within the states, and he sees no way to overcome this dependency. Tomuschat's reticence with respect to federalism is due to an understanding that the upper level of a federal system requires its own democratic base. His skepticism in this respect distinguishes his approach from cosmopolitan federalism.[222]

In many instances, Tomuschat presents the international community as a group of human beings that serves as the "social substratum" (although not as

---

[218] *Id.* at 184.

[219] See "The Universalistic-Cosmopolitan Responses: Universal Law versus State-Centered Integration," *supra* sect. II.C.1.

[220] Daniel Thürer, "The Emergence of Non-Governmental Organizations and Transnational Enterprises," in *International Law and Changing Role of the State, in Non-State Actors as New Subjects of International Law, supra* note 208, at 37, 46.

[221] Tomuschat, *supra* note 27, at 155.

[222] For a taxonomy of the various positions, see Armin von Bogdandy, "Globalization and Europe: How to Square Democracy, Globalization, and International Law," *Eur. J. Intl. L.* 15 (2004): 885. For example, Gráinne de Burca's and Oliver Gerstenberg's contribution in this issue derives/deduces a democratic value (out) of international law from its empowerment function.

a source of democratic legitimacy) of international law and a possible point of reference similar to the "people" in the municipal context. On the other hand, sometimes his usage is far more restricted and only succinctly indicates a number of legal developments without reference outside the law. He even defines the term *international community* "as an ensemble of rules, procedures and mechanisms designed to protect collective interests of humankind, based on a perception of commonly shared values."[223] This is far less than asserting the existence of a social group that might form a reference point for international law similar to that held in municipal law by the concept of the *people*. This definitional uncertainty may be explained by the novelty of the phenomenon. A global community of values can only be asserted in a world that is fundamentally at peace with itself:

> As long as international society consisted of three different ideological blocs pursuing different and even contradictory objectives, each side could have the suspicion that general principles were the opening gate for attempts to introduce political bias into the international legal order. Controversy has not disappeared altogether from the international stage. On many issues, Western States, Russia, China and developing countries continue to hold different views, with many intermediate shades. But the sharp ideological divide has disappeared. No group of countries is opposed in principle to the recognition of human rights as an important element of the international legal order, almost no group rejects democracy as a guiding principle for the internal systems of governance of States. Given this rapprochement towards the emergence of a true international community, objections to general principles of law are progressively losing the weight which they carried 25 years ago.[224]

Tomuschat shows that current international law contains many features that allow for its evolution into a "common law of humankind" – a law through which humankind might address its pressing problems. Yet this evolution will only happen if most human beings acquire a global perception of themselves as being part of a common group. There are hints that such a shift in self-perception is under way, but the new perception has not yet established itself to the extent that it substantially informs many decisions on the international plane. However, Tomuschat's construction of international law in his General Course may well contribute to developing such a perception in future decision makers.

---

[223] Tomuschat, *supra* note 27, at 88.   [224] *Id.*, 339.

C. A More Cosmopolitan Vision of Global Order

Tomuschat's understanding of contemporary international law is surely universalistic and to some extent even cosmopolitan. Nevertheless, it denies one of the core principles of cosmopolitanism as the theory of a legal and political order for world citizens – namely, the possibility of an international democratic process; rather, he puts almost all his faith in national governments reconstructed as agents of the international community. A more cosmopolitan approach in the tradition of Immanuel Kant is presented by Jürgen Habermas. Habermas has posed the question: *Is there still a chance for the Constitutionalization of Public International Law?*[225] This question demonstrates his broad sympathy with Tomuschat's core assumption that international law plays a constitutional role in *any* exercise of public authority. Habermas considers this understanding of international law and international relations to be in competition with three other approaches: first, the traditional approach under the particularistic paradigm in its realist or national variant, that sees the plurality of diverse states as the ultimate horizon of international law; second, the approach that advocates a world order based on liberal values, but subject to American hegemony rather than international law and common international institutions – the particularistic paradigm in its hegemonic variant; third, the approach that asserts a waning of public power undermining the premises of any constitutional rule.[226] From Habermas's perspective, the cosmopolitan *telos* is conceptually and normatively most convincing.

For Habermas, practical reason mandates that the *telos* of all law be the assurance of peace and freedom under the rule of law, rather than mere security, as in a Hobbesian perspective, via brute force (or American hegemony).[227] The theoretical centerpiece of the Habermasian text consists of a reconstruction of Kant's thought meant to overcome a conceptual problem that afflicts many "Kantian" approaches. Habermas proves that Kant's fluctuating preference between *Weltrepublik* and *Völkerbund* results from an unnecessary conceptual straightjacket: the understanding of sovereignty as *indivisible*.[228] Under this understanding, developed during the French Revolution, there can be only one political center. As a consequence, global institutions would govern the world as Paris has governed France since the eighteenth century. Such a centralized political order would probably trample on the plurality of forms of life that many citizens cherish, leading to a *seelenlosen Despotism* (soulless despotism) under which freedom vanishes.[229] However, as the U.S.

[225] Habermas, *supra* note 111.
[226] See "New Approaches," *supra* sect. II.D.   [227] Habermas, *supra* note 111, at 120.
[228] Habermas, *supra* note 111, at 125 *et seq.*   [229] Kant, *supra* note 105, at 147.

Constitution has shown since 1787, sovereignty *is* indeed divisible. This allows for conceiving a federal system that consists of different layers of public authority. Thus, international federalism with operative international institutions is not conceptually inconsistent with the organization of political life in "thick" political communities, or states.

The core issue is not an either/or question, but rather how to design a multilevel system in such a way that each layer of authority exercises only those powers matching its resources of legitimacy. Like Tomuschat, Habermas is well aware of the limited resources of democratic legitimacy on which global institutions can rely; and like Tomuschat, he finds that such legitimacy is largely derived from democratic states.[230] Neither the participation of NGOs nor global parliamentarian institutions appear – at least to date – as possible sources of a legitimacy for global institutions comparable to that at the municipal level. Thus, the powers of international institutions should be confined to fields in which *democratic* legitimacy can be assumed even without having recourse to perfectly inclusive deliberative processes. According to Habermas, this is the case both for the *enforcement* of peace and for the basic requirements of human rights, but not of democratic government in the Western sense. These principles enjoy broad legitimacy already because serious infringements meet throughout the world with the same moral indignation. This community of moral indignation could be seen as an agent of Tomuschat's *international community*. As to the question of determinacy, there exists a consistent number of possible and relevant infringements that are clearly covered by these principles.

Habermas advocates two types of global regimes. One is centered in a reformed UN Security Council, which, as a supranational institution, is vested with true powers to *enforce* international peace and (the more) basic requirements of human rights. The other regime, which must deal with all legislative issues,[231] is not supranational, but rather transnational, in nature:

In the light of the Kantian idea, one can imagine a political constitution of a decentralized global society, based on currently existing structures, as a multi-level system that for good reasons lacks statal [*staatlichen*] character *in general.* Under this conception, an appropriately reformed global organization would effectively and non-selectively be able to fulfill vital, yet precisely specified, peacekeeping and human rights functions on the *supranational*

---

[230] Habermas, *supra* note 111, at 140 *et seq.*
[231] Habermas therefore also validates the contested use of the separation of powers doctrine on the international level. D. Fiedler, *Non-State Actors as New Subjects of International Law, supra* note 209, at 158–60, 173.

level without having to assume the statal form of a global republic. On a middle, *transnational level*, the large globally competent actors would deal with the difficult problems not only of coordinating, but of configurating world domestic policy, particularly problems of the global economy and of ecology, in the framework of standing conferences and negotiating systems. . . . In the various regions of the world, nation-states would have to band together as continental regimes in the form of "foreign-policy-competent" EUs. On this middle level, international relations in a modified form would continue – modified already because under an effective United Nations security system the *global players* as well as others would be barred from resorting to war as a legitimate means of conflict resolution.[232]

A constitutionalized international order is not as utopian as it might appear at first glance. Alongside numerous empirical observations, Habermas places a conceptual reminder. The international realm is not properly understood if conceived as the Hobbesian state of nature. At least some of the main actors are constitutional democracies with constitutional tenets that direct their action on the international plane.[233] Therefore, less evolutionary effort is needed to proceed from a largely horizontal international system to one with global institutions safeguarding core constitutional principles. International constitutionalism, in this sense, is simply a complement to municipal constitutionalism and a further step in a process of civilization. Thus, unlike municipal constitutionalism with its polarized extremes of the "state of nature" and "police state," international constitutionalism is not one of the alternatives in an either/or situation.

This position's understanding of the democratic legitimacy of international law can be best explained by a critique of Jed Rubenfeld.[234] Rubenfeld presents European openness to international law as reflecting a democratic deficiency, and U.S. resistance to international law is praised as living up to the democratic ideal. This is certainly in line with particularistic thinking: under this paradigm, any self-respecting polity is normatively required to minimize the influence of international law on itself. However, the issue looks totally different under the universalistic paradigm. Here, democracy is not considered primarily as the auto-determination of a macrosubject, but as a number of procedures that give a voice to those affected. From this angle, a self-respecting

---

[232] *Id.*, at 134–35; see also reform proposals for the Security Council, *id.*, at 172 *et seq.*
[233] See U.S. Supreme Court decision, *Rasul v. Bush*, 542 U.S. 466 (2004).
[234] Jed Rubenfeld, "The Two World Orders," in *European and US Constitutionalism*, ed. Nolte (Cambridge: Cambridge U. P., 2005), 280, 297; A. v. Bogdandy, "*Comment on 'The Two Orders' from Jed Rubenfeld*," in *European and US Constitutionalism*, ed. Nolte (Cambridge: Cambridge U. P., 2005), 280, 297.

democratic polity is one that attempts to provide for the necessary avenues of participation of affected individuals.

In an interdependent world, many decisions of the authorities of one polity substantially affect individuals living abroad who do not have standing in domestic procedures. This situation is one of the undemocratic features of globalization: increasingly, purely "domestic" decisions have a transnational impact with ever greater significance. There is almost no remedy in the domestic democratic process. It is the nature of the domestic political process that the interests of the polity's citizens enjoy a priority over those of foreigners. Even when the process does not aim at hurting noncitizens, domestic interests tend to be favored and foreign interests are relegated to the fringe. International law, with all its deficiencies, is thus the only instrument that provides a voice to foreign persons affected by the adoption of measures of another polity. A state open to international law is therefore not limiting its democratic life, but rather realizing a new dimension of it.

The partcularists' as well as the parochialists' argument is tainted by a further problem. Let us call it the "Carl Schmitt fallacy." Some representatives of the American intellectual establishment are late disciples of "old" Europe, in particular of Carl Schmitt as an advocate of a political order that Europe as it is today has overcome. Carl Schmitt ridiculed the Weimar Republic by comparing and delegitimizing the reality of the Weimar political process against an ideal of parliamentarianism. In a similar vein, in Rubenfeld's essay the reality of the international legal process is pitted against an idealized American democracy. This idealization is reminiscent of Carl Schmitt in another way. Schmitt's basic understanding of democracy is that of the identity of ruled and rulers, amalgamated in a homogeneous "we." "We" is a very important word in particularistic and parochialist thinking, and therefore in Rubenfeld's piece in which all internal differences have disappeared. And that "we" is forged above all – as with Schmitt – by enmity: anti-Americanism is a crucial part in Rubenfeld's argument; it is an essential argument in many theories under the parochial paradigm.

v. CONCLUSION

The paradigms of particularism and universalism help to map the theoretical landscape and to explain the premises that inform interpretations and understandings of core issues of international law.[235] Considering parochialism and

---

[235] It is important to stress that we do not argue that the paradigms or the corresponding theories determine concrete interpretations in a given case. What we do argue is that the paradigms and the theories inform the interpretation.

cosmopolitanism, we have seen how parochialism finds its origin within the conceptual framework of the particularistic paradigm. Nonetheless, parochialism, insofar as it points out the unconfutable necessity of historic roots and legal implementation of universal human rights at the level of the political and legal systems of the single polities, displays its capacity, historically as well as conceptually, to overcome its narrowness, finding a way – beyond the traditional dichotomy – for a coexistence or even a reconciliation with its theoretical opponent. On the other hand, cosmopolitanism originates from the broader background of universalism, addressing the need for a level of public law that explicitly contains the norms regulating the interactions of humans as such, regardless of their status as citizens. However, cosmopolitanism was first affected by a tendency to locate the implementation of this level in the institutions of a global state.

A review of the paradigms has shown universalism and cosmopolitanism on balance – despite the deficits that concerned them for a long part of their history – to be more useful than particularism and parochialism in understanding international law: universalistic and cosmopolitan principles seem more likely to solve global problems because they apply to all human beings.[236] The institutions of such an order would be public in nature. National governments could help to develop such an order, but would no longer be in a position individually to block the enactment or enforcement of international law. International institutions would be in turn conscious of their largely state-mediated (and thus limited) resources of democratic legitimacy and therefore respectful of the diversity of their constituent states. A democratic global federation cannot exist, but there can be a better, more peaceful, and more integrated world of closely and successfully cooperating states, supported by more efficient international institutions. It is incumbent on the profession of international legal scholarship to contribute to realizing this objective. This vision provides a conceptually coherent conception that builds on the history of American and European constitutionalism. This scholarship also has a sufficient basis in current law.

This does not mean that the universalistic paradigm as well as cosmopolitanism and the theories inspired by these approaches do not have some serious conceptual problems, affecting not only – as already mentioned – their historical formulations but also their contemporary elaborations. The terms *constitutionalism* and *constitutionalisation* (like the term federal) – which are

---

[236] For a reconstruction of the relevant philosophical thought, see Georg Cavallar, "Cosmopolis. Supranationales und kosmopolitisches Denken von Vitoria bis Smith," *Deutsche Zeitschrift für Philosophie* 53 (2005): 49–68.

part of this conceptual horizon – imply, for example, a (somewhat unrealistic) progression toward global democratic institutions, an aspiration that only a few scholars consider viable in our times. In this way, the arguments that contend against conceiving the international order as "federal" are well founded. Sometimes the term *legalization* is used,[237] but it underrates the political impact. Others address this approach as *institutionalism* or *new institutionalism*.[238] However, this approach embodies more than just the assertion that "institutions matter." Perhaps the term *supranationalism* used by Habermas captures this concept best, despite its technocratic overtones. The terminological difficulty might be indicative of the need for further elaboration and clarification.

The advocates of this approach do not deny that the current law can be read in different lights, nor that current developments on the global scale run counter to their vision, given the resistance toward a strong international public order by the governments of countries such as China, India, Russia, and the United States. At the same time, there is no reason to abandon a scientific project simply because it is politically difficult to realize. Martti Koskenniemi accuses the project of having a hegemonic nature.[239] It is, however, difficult to see how this could be so – except perhaps that by presenting itself as a meaningful construction for all concerned, cosmopolitan law asserts itself as being universally acceptable.[240] There may be more substance to the criticism that fundamental differences will remain between the normativity of public law in developed liberal states compared with that in public international law, as long as there are no strong international institutions with a strong international law ethos. As a *legal* project, international constitutionalism might lead to normative overextension.[241] Much of this may depend on the success of international

---

[237] Judith Goldstein et al., "Legalization and World Politics," *Intl. Org.* 54 (2000): 385 *et seq.*; Stefan Oeter, "Chancen und Defizite internationaler Verrechtlichung: Was das Recht jenseits des Nationalstaats leisten kann," in *Verrechtlichung – Bausteine für Global Governance?* eds. Michael Zürn and Bernhard Zangel (Berlin: Dietz-Verlag, 2004).

[238] For a detailed analysis of the various approaches, see Andreas Paulus, *Die internationale Gemeinschaft im Völkerrecht* (München: C. H. Beck Verlag, 2001), 97 *et seq.*, 188 *et seq.*

[239] See also Martti Koskenniemi, "International Law and Hegemony: A Reconfiguration," *Cambridge Rev. Intl. Affairs* 17 (2004): 2, 197.

[240] It must be conceded that the constitutionalist reconstruction needs to take into account more closely the relationship between the principles of current international law and the dramatic situation in the South. However, Koskenniemi's critique that "the global public order . . . is fully implicated in what can only be seen as a deeply unjust system of distributing material and spiritual values" also necessitates further proof. *Id.*, at § 2 of conclusion.

[241] This argument has been elaborated for international trade law; see A. v. Bogdandy, *supra* note 78, at 615 *et seq.*; Robert Howse and Kalypso Nicolaidis, "Legitimacy and Global Governance: Why Constitutionalizing the WTO Is a Step Too Far," in *The Role of the Judge in International Trade Regulation: Experience and Lessons for the WTO*, eds. T. Cottier and P. C. Mavroidis (Ann Arbor: U. of Mich. P., 2003), 307–48.

criminal law as outlined in the Rome Statute of the International Criminal Court, which may strengthen the normativity of the fundamental principles of international law. There is a risk inherent in establishing powerful (yet possibly evasive and irresponsive) international bureaucratic regimes.[242]

Despite these weaknesses, a final evaluation needs to look at the alternatives. Koskenniemi has argued for the development of international law in empowering disenfranchised groups largely outside of international institutions.[243] Objectively seen, it is difficult to understand this as the better alternative given the global challenges posed by sustainable development, poverty, climate change, and international crime. This is particularly true if one perceives legal scholarship above all as a practical science. In the current world, the practical proposals of "constitutionalist" authors appear in many instances preferable to the alternatives. Paraphrasing Kant: This vision might be vulnerable in theory, but in the current state of international relations, it provides a convincing orientation for the responsible practice of international law.

Although we endorse the historic paradigm of universalism and the necessity of a cosmopolitan level of public law, we do not deny the scientific value of scholarship under the particularistic paradigm and the parochial understanding of the origin of rights and values, nor do we hold that its claims are altogether untenable. Concerning the future of the tension between universalism and particularism, as well as between cosmopolitanism and parochialism in international law, scholars should be open to integrating the idea of a truly universalistic-cosmopolitan order with some ideas emerging from the tradition of parochialism. A renewed conception of cosmopolitanism would accept the important role played in legitimation of law by democratic participation within existing political communities, and reject any strictly vertical structure of law and political institutions. Cosmopolitanism should strive to avoid the dangers of "universal monarchy" and focus instead on defending universal rights and values belonging to all human beings.

In any event, scholars should try to find solutions for international problems that are acceptable under both paradigms. Lawyers in general and international lawyers in particular should take pride in finding (or creating) common ground between seemingly conflicting points of view. A famous example is the Antarctic Treaty.[244] Article 4 left the contrasting positions seemingly

---

[242] Joseph Weiler, "The Geology of International Law – Governance, Democracy and Legitimacy," *Harvard J. Intl. L.* 64 (2004): 547, 561–62.

[243] Martti Koskenniemi, "Global Governance and Public International Law," *Kritische Justiz* 37 (2004): 241, 253 *et seq.*

[244] Antarctic Treaty, 402 U.N.T.S. 71 (December 1, 1959).

unaffected, but this did not prevent the development of one of the most successful existing international treaty regimes. This type of approach could be applied to many forms of international conflict. For example, the principle of subsidiarity would fit well with both cosmopolitanism and parochialism.[245]

The universalistic paradigm and the cosmopolitan approach to rights and values offer the better model for a strong and justifiable international legal regime, but sensitivity to particular (i.e., parochial) concerns will make the international legal order more effective, and also more legitimate, by taking local interests more fully into account.

---

[245] In detail I. Feichtner, "Subsidiarity," in *Encyclopedia of Public International Law*, ed. Wolfrum (Oxford: Oxford U. P., 2008), 1–7.

4 Liberal Cosmopolitanism or Cosmopolitan Liberalism?

Ileana M. Porras

Since the 1990s there has been a notable surge of interest in the subject of cosmopolitanism in a variety of disciplines, from philosophy, literary theory, and cultural studies; to political theory and international relations; to most recently international law. Variously influenced by the accretion of meanings and associations, the term has acquired over the years since its coinage in fourth-century B.C.E. Greece,[1] drawing much of its inspiration from the work of Kant on cosmopolitanism[2] and informed by Rawls's thought on distributive justice,[3] the resulting literature has proved rich and diverse and curiously

---

[1] Diogenes the Cynic (d. 323 B.C.E.) is usually credited with having coined the term during the time he lived as an exile in Athens. Diogenes' claim to be a citizen of the world (*kosmopolites*) was understood to be a challenge and a critique of the traditional Greek view of the exclusive connection among rights, participation, virtue, citizenship, allegiance, and the city (*polis*). According to Martha Nussbaum, the Greek Stoics then theorized the term to explore the possibility of a moral allegiance beyond the *polis* to the community of humanity as a whole. See Martha C. Nussbaum, "Patriotism and Cosmopolitanism," in *For Love of Country: Debating the Limits of Patriotism*, ed. Joshua Cohen (1996): 1–17. Over time, the term has taken on a multiplicity of alternative meanings and associations. For instance, at various times, the term "cosmopolitanism" has been strongly associated with the project of world government. In a different register, it has come to be associated with an inclination to travel and explore the world and its cultures, and, consequently, the term is often used to denote a kind of "foreign" worldliness and sophistication that contrasts with parochialism. Nonetheless, cosmopolitanism is also critiqued as an attitude that encourages self-alienation and misanthropy. Most recently the adjective "cosmopolitan" has been used to convey the idea of multiple cultures, and, consequently, the moniker "cosmopolitan city" has been adopted to characterize large cities at ease with a high degree of multiculturalism.

[2] The three main essays in which Kant sketched out his thinking on cosmopolitan right are Immanuel Kant, "Idea for a Universal History with a Cosmopolitan Purpose" (1784), *Political Writings*, 41 (Hans Reiss ed., 2nd ed. 1991); "Perpetual Peace: A Philosophical Sketch" (1795), *ibid.* at 93; and "The Metaphysics of Morals" (1797), *ibid.* at 131.

[3] John Rawls, *A Theory of Justice* (Cambridge, MA, 1971). Rawls was no cosmopolitanist; indeed in his later work, he expressly rejected the extrapolation of his principle of distributive justice from the domestic societal sphere (bound by a social contract) to the international domain. John

contradictory. There is no single common understanding of cosmopolitanism, and consequently there is wide disagreement among the new cosmopolitanists[4] as to its specific social, political, and legal implications. The term has been used to promote a wide range of projects, from a radical form of global redistribution to alleviate poverty in the Third World[5] to military intervention in non-liberal states.[6] It has been used to account for the emergence of the so-called global civil society with its new forms of governance[7] on the one hand, and to describe the unique character of the European Union's legal and institutional structures on the other.[8] Despite this diversity and the apparent malleability of the concept, it is nonetheless possible to make some general statements about the ethics, geography, and attitude that are distinctive to cosmopolitanism and that, to one degree or another, underlie all modern cosmopolitanist projects.

Cosmopolitanism, I posit in this chapter, is first premised on a claim concerning the meaning and scope of community.

The starting point for cosmopolitanism is that all persons are born into a universal worldwide community of human beings. Because in the cosmopolitanist's view the defining characteristic or essence of the human being is sociability,[9] the claim that he or she belongs in the first place to the global community implies that each human being owes a duty of care to every other human being. A central tenet of a cosmopolitan conception of the world is that every human community smaller than the original worldwide

Rawls, "The Law of Peoples" (1999). Despite this, many of Rawls's disciples have espoused cosmopolitanism as a means of realizing Rawls in the international. See, e.g., Thomas W. Pogge, *Realizing Rawls* (Ithaca, NY, 1989).

[4] In this essay I refer to authors espousing cosmopolitan principles as "cosmopolitanists" rather than "cosmopolitans" to avoid imposing on them collectively the attributes most commonly associated with the label "cosmopolitan," viz. worldly, sophisticated, and well traveled. Although this historical derivation of the term inevitably colors any modern appropriation of "cosmopolitan," it does not adequately reflect the authors' primary objective in advocating cosmopolitanism. Nonetheless, it is interesting to note that many cosmopolitanists are, as a matter of personal history, also cosmopolitan.

[5] See, e.g., Charles R. Beitz, "Cosmopolitan Ideals and National Sentiment," *Journal of Philosophy* 80 (1983): 591–600; Thomas W. Pogge, "Cosmopolitanism and Sovereignty" in *Ethics* 103 (1992): 48–75.

[6] See, e.g., Allen Buchanan, "In the National Interest," *The Political Philosophy of Cosmopolitanism* (2005): 110–126; Fernando Teson, "The Rawlsian Theory of International Law," *Ethics and International Affairs* (1995): 79–99.

[7] See, e.g., John Kean, "Global Civil Society," *Global Civil Society 2001* (2001): 23–47.

[8] See, e.g., Pavlos Eleftheriadis, "Cosmopolitan Law," *European L. J.* 9 (2003): 241–63.

[9] Cosmopolitanists need not consider sociability the sole fundamental characteristic of human beings. Most would, instead, agree with Hobbes that self-interest is an essential driver of human choices. The difference is that cosmopolitans view sociability as being an equally strong motivator and take humans as always already existing in community.

community is in a strong sense contingent. Such contingent communities may make claims on and impose particular duties and obligations on their members, but such attachments can never completely displace or erase the primary duties and obligations that arise from each individual's belonging to the universal and global community. Cosmopolitanists can and do diverge in their attitude to existing communities such as nation-states and their particular claims on individuals, and they have quite different takes on the degree to which such communities are socially, culturally, or psychologically necessary, useful, or desirable, but all share the conviction that behind these contingent arrangements lies the inescapable fact of a preexisting global community in which each human being is, whether we are aware of it or not, already in relationship with every other human being.[10] Exactly what this implies in practical terms is, of course, open to debate and much disputed among the different strands of cosmopolitanists.

If cosmopolitanism refers to an undivided original human moral community it may also be said to describe a corresponding geography. The preferred image of cosmopolitan space is the earthly globe. Cosmopolitan space is one unmarked by political boundaries that precedes and coexists with the familiar geopolitical terrain organized around nation-states. Furthermore, because the cosmopolitanist views all human communities smaller than the one global community as equally contingent, the cosmopolitanist is able to accommodate a multiplicity of alternative claims about the geopolitical boundaries of human communities, whether these be substate or transnational. All such boundaries are merely superimpositions on the underlying unmarked cosmopolitan geography, and the cosmopolitanist can breach these by a simple act of the imagination. The cosmopolitanist pictures the individual and human communities as always potentially on the move, traversing the globe, irrespective of boundaries. Indeed, classic cosmopolitan space is not scored by the

---

[10] The modern Cosmopolitanists are, as David Hollinger has most effectively described it, all stranded somewhere on the continuum between universalism and pluralism. See David A. Hollinger, "Not Universalists, Not Pluralists: The New Cosmopolitans Find Their Own Way," *Constellations* 8:2 (2001): 236. The new trend for a hyphenated style of cosmopolitanism that Hollinger identifies (rooted, situated, national, vernacular, critical, etc.) is, it seems, an attempt to respond to one of the most traditional critiques of cosmopolitanism, one highlighted by Kant in his "Doctrine of Virtue," that to love all men (cosmopolitan love) is to love none in particular. According to Kant the right balance between local and global is achieved by the "cosmopolite" who possesses "a moral sense with dutiful global and local patriotism" and who "in fealty to his moral country must have an inclination to promote the well-being of the entire world." Quoted in Sankar Muthu, "Justice and Foreigners: Kant's Cosmopolitan Right," *Constellations* 7:1 (2000): 23.

political boundaries that separate humanity but rather is crisscrossed by the trade routes, communications networks, and other flows of people, goods and ideas that bring human beings into practical relationship.

Although it is commonly assumed that cosmopolitans are suspicious of the nation-state, drawn by means of territorial boundaries, the cosmopolitanist is not necessarily opposed to it. Indeed some modern cosmopolitanists, far from rejecting the nation-state, have concluded that political boundaries, even if contingent, are after all morally significant.[11] However, all cosmopolitanists agree that under some circumstances, political and other boundaries can and should be treated as morally irrelevant, because of the superior claims of the underlying cosmopolitan geography. At the very least, then, we can argue that a cosmopolitan approach is one that stands always ready to challenge the claims of the national and particular to be the sole legitimate source of moral obligation. Cosmopolitanism does this, moreover, not by proposing an alternative cosmopolitan politics but by providing an alternative way of understanding the meaning and value of human community above and beyond civil society (and the social contract it supposedly embodies).

In addition to referring to an ethic and describing a geography, cosmopolitanism also expresses an attitude, an approach, a sensibility, or a way of being in the world. Traditionally, a key component of cosmopolitanism, related to the assertion of a shared worldwide humanity and a shared space, was the insistence that human beings adopt an attitude of engaged curiosity and tolerance when faced with the practical reality of found cultural difference.[12] Cultural differences are for the cosmopolitan merely variations on the theme of humanity and should not be allowed to separate us further. In theory at least, the cosmopolitanist claim is that there is no one right expression of humanity, no single right culture to which all others must be reduced. Nonetheless, as many commentators have pointed out, in practice the modern cosmopolitanist engages in a process of triage and ultimately concludes that only some limited forms of cultural difference are worthy of toleration, and others are beyond

---

[11] See, e.g., Kwame Anthony Appiah, *Cosmopolitanism: Ethics in a World of Strangers* (New York, 2006); see also Jocelyne Couture and Kai Nielsen, "Cosmopolitanism and the Compatriot Priority Principle," in *The Political Philosophy of Cosmopolitanism* (Madison, WI, 2005): 180–95. In this at least the new cosmopolitanists may be said to be following in the footsteps of Kant, for Kant, far from rejecting the nation-state, saw it as one of the conditions of the tripartite justice order that would lead eventually to a perpetual peace.

[12] I use the term "engaged curiosity" to distinguish it from the more familiar form of distanced, arms-length curiosity. Engaged curiosity invokes the sense of community and relatedness that cosmopolitanism presupposes. For cosmopolitanism there is no such person as the unrelated stranger: we are all kin, albeit in some instances, distant kin.

the pale. In this respect the cosmopolitanist is almost indistinguishable from the liberal universalist who is convinced that all human beings deserve to be governed by liberal principles and institutions and that it is the duty of liberal peoples (a duty arising out of a coincidence of self-interest and love of other) to bring the rest of the world to the truth of this message.[13]

The question I seek to explore in this chapter concerns the intersection between cosmopolitanism and international law. Recent interest in the subject of cosmopolitanism across disciplines raises hope that a cosmopolitan approach could offer new insights and might help define new projects or even a new agenda for international law. At a time when international law and institutions appear weak and ineffectual and seem more than ever captive to sovereign will and raison d'état, cosmopolitanism's appealing alternative vision of a worldwide moral community inhabiting an undivided geography and its recommendation that we adopt an attitude of engaged curiosity and tolerance vis-à-vis cultural difference, appear to promise an avenue for renewal. To date few of the new cosmopolitanists have addressed the intersection between law and cosmopolitanism directly, although many of those writing from a political science or international relations perspective have touched on the subject.[14] Curiously enough, the two legal and institutional fields to which the term "cosmopolitan law" have so far been attributed have been human rights and the European Union.[15] Other legal and institutional subjects that have given rise to some cosmopolitan speculation include international trade, asylum, refugee and immigration law, international criminal law, international humanitarian law, international environmental law, and conflicts of law.[16]

In this chapter I pose the question of what the new cosmopolitanism can offer to international law. As a way to approach the question, I focus on three interconnected themes that have long been of vital interest to international law theory: first, the political theory of liberalism; second, the aspiration of international peace; and third, the role of international commerce in achieving

[13] See Maxwell Chibundu, Chapter 6 in this volume.
[14] I would include in this category David Held; see, e.g., David Held, "Principles of Cosmopolitan Order," in *The Political Philosophy of Cosmopolitanism*, eds. Gillian Brock and Harry Brighouse (2005): 10–27.
[15] See, e.g., Eleftheriadis, "Cosmopolitan Law," *supra* note 8, who considers both the human rights regime and the EU legal institutions as a species of cosmopolitan law; see also Buchanan *supra* note 6.
[16] An excellent recent review of some of the new cosmopolitanist literature from the point of view of law is Noah Feldman, "Cosmopolitan Law," *Yale L. J.* 116 (2007): 1022. See also Paul Schiff Bermann, "Conflict of Laws, Globalization, and Cosmopolitan Pluralism" *Wayne L. Rev.* 51 (2005): 1155.

that goal. Because Kant's work on cosmopolitan right has been the seminal influence on the new cosmopolitanists, I proceed to explore the particulars of cosmopolitanism through a close reading of Kant's texts on the subject. I argue that, not coincidentally, the three international law themes – liberal theory, peace, and commerce – lie at the heart of Kant's influential work on cosmopolitanism, for Kant, like many before him, was in effect engaged in that most familiar endeavor of international law theory: the search for a viable principle of constraint in the international. I conclude that the core concepts of cosmopolitanism are all familiar to the international law tradition. Cosmopolitanism, I suggest, is thus best understood as already intrinsic to international law rather than considered as a new development. For this reason, many of the projects been promoted under the guise of a new cosmopolitanism have a familiar air to them. To the extent that the new cosmopolitanists rely on a traditional Kantian conception of cosmopolitanism, it seems unlikely they can offer any truly new insights to international law.

Although the traditional concepts of cosmopolitanism are integral to international law, it could be argued that some of the new cosmopolitanists nevertheless provide a radical challenge to the status quo by importing into the international arena the distributive justice principle developed by John Rawls for the domestic sphere.[17] A similar claim may be made in favor of those who have adapted the concept of cosmopolitanism to the project of global governance by emphasizing the state-free character of the new globalized world community. To round out my analysis of the relationship between cosmopolitanism and international law, I briefly consider the question of these new cosmopolitanists. Rather than evaluate their projects on their own merits, I pose the question of where they stand in relation to Kant's cosmopolitan solution to the problem of international law. I conclude that in both cases, their novel use of the concepts of cosmopolitanism, and in particular their determination to substitute the cosmopolitan community for the civil and international communities, tend to undermine Kant's particular solution to the liberal paradox in the international arena. In other words, to the extent that their projects are still inscribed within the liberal tradition, they can no longer rely on Kant and must find an alternative theory to justify collective constraint beyond mere force.

[17] These post-Rawlsian cosmopolitanists have adopted the term "cosmopolitan justice" to describe global justice that takes global distributive justice into account. Under this view the interests of individuals are entitled to equal consideration without regard to nationality, which is treated as merely contingent. See, e.g., Beitz; Nussbaum; and Thomas W. Pogge, "Cosmopolitanism and Sovereignty," *Ethics* 103 (1992): 48–75. There is much internal disagreement among post-Rawlsians as to the practical distributional requirements of global justice.

I. LIBERAL THEORY: FROM THE NATION-STATE
TO THE INTERNATIONAL

Born of the European enlightenment, classic liberal political theory was in large measure designed to justify yet delimit the coercive capacity of the emergent nation-state. It is, in other words, first and foremost a theory about the internal domestic order. Due in large part to its adaptability over time, liberalism has proved to have impressive staying power and has become the dominant political ideology around the globe. This is so despite, or perhaps precisely because, its edifice is balanced on a core paradox or tension between the two competing poles of liberal theory: individual autonomy and collective decision making. The starting point for liberal theory is the individual abstract human being who is taken to be endowed with rationality and human dignity (liberty and equality). The defining characteristic of this human being is his or her capacity for unfettered free choice. However, given the unavoidable fact that human beings live in physical proximity to one another, that their actions have an effect beyond themselves, and that the choices of one fully free individual will often conflict with the equally free choices of another, liberal theory holds that human beings must as a matter of right reason come together into political communities (civil societies), the function of which it will then be to make collective decisions (laws) that will be binding on the members and to arbitrate between them. In this sense liberalism as a project may be said to be in search of a principle of conflict resolution beyond mere force. Briefly stated, the liberal paradox is that there is, in practice, no way to avoid the unfortunate fact that collective decision making will have some constraining effect on the free choices of some individuals, yet the classic liberal meaning of freedom is the absence of externally imposed constraints (or in Kant's more nuanced definition, freedom is the possibility of free consent).[18] The traditional liberal solution to the problem was to posit an original contract freely and rationally entered into by the individual that would bind him or her into the future and limit (or civilize) his wild freedom.[19]

---

[18] "In fact, my external and rightful *freedom* should be defined as a warrant to obey no external laws except those to which I have been able to give my own consent." Kant, "Perpetual Peace: A Philosophical Sketch," *supra* note 2 at 99.

[19] "The highest task which nature has set for mankind must therefore be that of establishing a society in which freedom under external laws would be combined to the greatest possible extent with irresistible force, in other words of establishing a perfectly just civil constitution. . . . Man, who is otherwise so enamoured with unrestrained freedom, is forced to enter this state of restriction by sheer necessity. And this is indeed the most stringent of all forms of necessity, for it is imposed by men upon themselves, in that their inclinations make it impossible for them to exist side by side for long in a state of wild freedom. But once enclosed within a precinct

Because of this, early liberals thought it necessary (or at least useful) to provide a narrative history of mankind's transition from their initial state as absolutely free individuals to their willing gathering into civil societies with their concomitant and inevitable constraints on the individual's freedom. Such narratives, whether intended as fact or legal fictions,[20] varied in tone from Hobbes's famous account of man's desperate escape from a violent state of nature to Kant's more positive version in which the need to enter into civil society arises not only from something like the at times unpleasant fact of human physical proximity and the inevitable antagonism of unfettered freedom, but also from the deep human need for recognition from one's fellows.[21] In any case, the existence of civil societies (ultimately in the form of nation-states) is treated by classical liberals as a natural, inevitable, and desirable outcome for rational human beings.[22] The consequent constraints on freedom are considered a valid trade-off because the individual gains the advantages of security and predictability from the order imposed by civil society. Where liberal accounts have differed over time is the degree of constraint that is deemed acceptable and the conditions under which domestic governance institutions will be deemed legitimate. Although modern liberals no longer (at least overtly) rely on the traditional historical narratives, they nonetheless seem caught in the narrative

like that of civil union, the same inclinations have the most beneficial effect." Kant, "Idea for a Universal History with a Cosmopolitan Purpose," *supra* note 2 at 45–46.

[20] Kant makes it clear that the original social contract that creates the civil union is both necessary and a fiction, or in his terminology, "an *idea* of reason." Kant, "On the Common Saying: *This May Be True in Theory, but Does Not Apply in Practice*," in Kant, *Political Writings* 79 (Hans Reiss ed., 2nd ed. 1991).

[21] Although on occasion, Kant's view of human beings' original depravity is reminiscent of Hobbes's equally negative view of human nature. See Kant, "Perpetual Peace: A Philosophical Sketch," *supra* note 2 at 103.

[22] In an argument situated somewhere between Adam Smith's "invisible hand" and St. Augustine's "felix culpa," Kant claimed that civil society and the greatest achievements of civilization were the direct and indirect result of man's natural antagonism and "unsocial sociability": "*The means which nature employs to bring about the development of innate capacities is that of antagonism within society, in so far as this antagonism becomes in the long run the cause of law-governed social order.* By antagonism, I mean in this context the *unsocial sociability* of men, that is, their tendency to come together in society, coupled, however, with a continual resistance which constantly threatens to break this society up." Kant, "Idea for a Universal History with a Cosmopolitan Purpose," *supra* note 2 at 44. "All the culture and art which adorn mankind and the finest social order man creates are fruits of his unsociability." *Ibid.* at 46. A few years later in his essay "Perpetual Peace," Kant added that even if "people were not compelled by internal dissent to submit to the coercion of public laws, war would produce the same effect from the outside. For [given the spherically bounded character of the earth] each people would find itself confronted by another neighboring people pressing in upon it, thus forcing it to form itself internally into a *state* to encounter the other as an armed *power*." Kant, "Perpetual Peace: A Philosophical Sketch," *supra* note 2 at 112.

structure of the absolutely free and autonomous individual who somehow precedes civil society and whose voluntary submission to the constraints of collective decision making must always be both explained and demonstrated.[23] The result is that liberal theory seems in the end always to be concerned with the problem of justifying (and delimiting) legitimate constraint by the state, while the originally free autonomous individual is taken uncontroversially as a simple given.

Although liberal theory's primary purpose was to justify and delimit the coercive power of the nation-state over the otherwise free, equal, and autonomous individuals over whom the state ruled, it was evident that it could not ignore the calamity of violence or war outside the nation state. All the more so, as Rousseau saw quite clearly, because international violence was exacerbated by the division of mankind into political communities of interest, the very mechanism that was designed to reduce the original violence.[24]

The transposition of liberal theory to the international arena, however, has always posed a particularly tricky challenge. Here the classical liberal move has been to substitute the nation-state as the moral agent. The absolutely free and autonomous individual that anchors liberal theory in the municipal sphere is thus in the international arena replaced by the absolutely free and autonomous or "sovereign" nation-state. Pushing the liberal analogy further, these autonomous sovereigns are said to coexist in the sovereign equivalent of a state of nature, which according to authors as diverse as Grotius,

---

[23] Recognizing the obvious limits of the historical contractarian myth, much liberal political theory has been concerned with explaining that a "rational" individual would, of necessity because he is rational, enter into such an agreement. At the point when free choice is reduced to a matter of abstract rationality, the question of the "content" or "nature" of the contract becomes more pressing. A rational human being ought to choose to enter into a just or legitimate compact and will therefore be held to have done so. The characteristics that are considered to be required for the compact to be just and legitimate have varied over time, but today consist of some mix of liberal principles such as republican and democratic government and a commitment to respect for individual human rights.

[24] As Jean-Jacques Rousseau so powerfully framed it in a tract that influenced Kant's ideas on cosmopolitanism:

> If the social order were really, as it pretended, the work not of passion but of reason, should we have been so slow to see that, in the shaping of it, either too much, or too little, has been done for our happiness? that each one of us, being in the civil state as regards our fellow citizens, but in the state of nature as regards the rest of the world, we have taken all kinds of precautions against private wars only to kindle national wars a thousand times more terrible? and that, in joining a particular group of men, we have really declared ourselves the enemies of the whole race?
>
> (Jean Jacques Rousseau, "A Lasting Peace" [1756], 38)

Hobbes, and Kant is the same as saying in a state of constant war (actual or potential).[25]

However tricky the transposition of liberal theory from the domestic order to the international domain, it is important to note that many of the early political theorists whose ideas influenced liberal theory developed their views about the relationship between individuals and collectivities by engaging in what we might describe as a backward analogy from sovereigns (or states) to individuals. Grotius, for instance, and Hobbes and Kant after him, used the still-ungoverned state of nature inhabited by sovereigns to illustrate the now-abandoned precivil society "state of nature" inhabited by individuals.[26] Indeed, one could argue that the ungoverned and violent intersovereign state of nature was used as a foil to prove the advantages of an ordered and well-governed civil society. For Kant, for instance, the violent state of international relations, unconstrained by law, serve to exemplify the original depravity of man: "Although it is largely concealed by governmental constraints in law-governed civil society, the depravity of human nature is displayed without disguise in the unrestricted relations which obtain between the various nations."[27] It is, of course, well known that the birth of liberalism coincided with and contributed to the development of the sovereign nation-state. It is perhaps less apparent that there is a kind of inevitable intimacy between the project of producing a theory of the internal domestic order that constructs the sovereign state and the need to theorize an external international order that gives the sovereign its coherence. The sovereign state makes sense only in the company of other sovereign states, with whom it can relate in peace or war, in the same way that the concept of the individual requires the presence of other individuals. Thus we could argue that even though liberal political theory was developed primarily to justify and delimit the collective constraint of the nation-state, it had to do so within the context of an original international disorder that it then also sought to tame.

Nonetheless, the structure of liberal theory was designed in such a way as to virtually preclude the possibility of resolving the liberal paradox within the international. Within the liberal framework, the sole legitimate source of legal obligation, as opposed to moral obligation, was the command of the sovereign. That legitimate authority arose not from a relationship of force but from the reciprocal and mutually advantageous liberal compact entered

---

[25] "[O]ne state, as a moral person, is considered as existing in a state of nature in relationship to another state, hence in a condition of constant war." Kant, "The Metaphysics of Morals," *supra* note 2 at 165 (citing Grotius and Hobbes).

[26] Grotius, *de Iure Praedae*; Hobbes, *Leviathan*.

[27] Kant, "Perpetual Peace: A Philosophical Sketch," *supra* note 2 at 103.

into by the members of a particular civil society – an authority then backed up by force.[28] As Hobbes's *Leviathan* describes it so well, in entering into a compact, individuals created something greater than themselves, which then took on a life of its own. Individuals, it seems, could do this without compromising their essential character and dignity as human beings. On the contrary, a civil society based on liberal principles came to be seen as the precondition for human flourishing. At first glance it would seem that the analogous solution is available to sovereign states. Why not, after all, imagine the states entering into a mutually reciprocal compact that would create a higher-level authority empowered to make legally binding decisions on the sovereigns? The essential difficulty is that we lack the concept for an entity of an essentially higher order than a sovereign; neither an empire nor a political federation will do. An empire is no more than an extension of a single sovereign will over others, and a voluntary federation is either too weak, not capable of making binding law and enforcing it, or too strong such that it would compromise the essential character and dignity of the sovereign and eventually supersede it.[29] Seemingly, the only viable alternative is the possibility of sovereigns making voluntary commitments to bind themselves to law, through a kind of international agreement or contract, but under the terms of liberal theory, this solution makes for an exceedingly precarious international order. In terms of the liberal tension, the balance is weighted too heavily on the side of autonomy and insufficiently counterbalanced by collective constraint. Given that the absence of legitimate collective constraint is a recipe for disorder – a descent into the world of violence and politics, the very place from which liberal international law seeks to escape – the difficulty for the international liberal lies in locating a valid alternative principle of constraint on nation states.

---

[28] At the domestic or state level, modern Rawlsian liberalism added a distributive justice dimension to the mix of what it takes for a civil society to be legitimate. It is to address this concern that Rawls introduced his now famous idea that the rules a well-governed liberal society should choose should reflect those any rational person would choose under the veil-of-ignorance condition. See Rawls, *A Theory of Justice, supra* note 3.

[29] Kant was obviously sensitive to this dilemma, and although he ultimately proposes a political arrangement he terms a (con)federation, he is careful to distinguish it from the kind of federation that amounts to a unified state. "But a federation of this sort would not be an international state. For the idea of an international state is contradictory since every state involves a relationship between a superior (the legislator) and an inferior (the people obeying the laws), whereas a number of nations forming one state would constitute a single nation. And this contradicts our initial assumption, as we are here considering the rights of nations in relation to one another in so far as they are a group of separate states which are not to be welded together as a unit." Kant, "Perpetual Peace: A Philosophical Sketch," *supra* note 2 at 102. See also *ibid.* at 113.

International law theorists have sought to bridge the divide in a variety of ways. In every era of international law some source of law or other valid principle of constraint outside of sovereign consent has been posited to free states collectively from the chaotic and war-prone state of nature in which they must otherwise reside. In the still-religious world of Vitoria and Grotius, natural law principles derived from a combination of divine law and human reason were thought sufficient to ground international law in something beyond sovereign will.[30] Conceptually, this might have been satisfying, but in practice, state practice continued to be guided by self-will. In any case, in the postsecular age of Wolff and Vattel, divine backing for natural law could no longer be taken for granted, and so the place of natural rights was taken by what Vattel termed "necessary law,"[31] whereas in the positivist age that followed the balance was held by customary law and the almost iconic category of *jus cogens*, until finally, as David Kennedy and Martti Koskenniemi have so thoroughly demonstrated, the deep ground of international law came to reside in the elliptical argumentative structure of international law itself.[32] Regardless, at every stage of this history, Kant's remonstration against the "sorry comforters" of international law would have been equally apt.[33] What these tactics had in common, however, was that each was an attempt to counterbalance the predominance of sovereign will by gesturing to some universal and unchanging principle that could be anchored in the intrinsic character of the human being. What was being sought was an ordering principle that could serve to justify collective constraint in the international beyond mere force.

II. COSMOPOLITAN PEACE: REPUBLICAN STATES, (CON)FEDERATION, AND COSMOPOLITAN RIGHT

Within this tradition, in the late eighteenth century, Kant's proposed solution to the liberal dilemma in the international domain depended on the voluntary

---

[30] The most influential recent exploration of natural rights from political theory is Richard Tuck, "Natural Rights Theories: Their Origin and Development" (1979). For a more limited discussion of Grotius's explicit reliance in his early work on natural rights derived from a mix of divine law and reason, see Ileana M. Porras, "Constructing International Law in the East Indian Seas: Property, Sovereignty, Commerce and War in Hugo Grotius' *De Iure Praedae* – The Law of Prize and Booty," or "On How to Distinguish Merchants from Pirates," *Brooklyn J. Int'l L.* 31 (2006): 741, 756.

[31] For a careful analysis of Vattel's construction of "necessary law," see Emmannuelle Jouannet, "Emer de Vattel et l'émergence doctrinale du droit international classique" (1998).

[32] David Kennedy, "International Legal Structures" (1987); Martti Koskenniemi, "From Apology to Utopia: The Structure of International Legal Argument" (1989).

[33] Kant, Perpetual Peace: "A Philosophical Sketch," *supra* note 2 at 103.

creation of a (con)federation ("free federation") of republican nation-states that would serve as a substitute for the union of civil society.[34] As Kant understood it, war (actual and potential) was the natural condition of the international society of nations-states.[35] Sovereigns, existing in a "state of nature" were in a state of permanent natural enmity with all other sovereigns. The particular or immediate cause of any given war might be the undisciplined greed for riches, property, and power of uncontrolled sovereigns, but absent an ordering principle that could triumph over the underlying state of nature; such wars were inevitable, although their frequency might be reduced by a generalized adoption of republican forms of government. Kant believed that in states where the executive was constitutionally separate from the legislature and there was some significant degree of representation, the people, who would suffer the deprivations, pains and loss of war, were not likely to authorize their sovereign to take them to war lightly.[36]

For Kant, the ultimate goal of the international system was the achievement of true or perpetual peace, for war was not only destructive in its active phase, but also the incessant preparation for war, whether aggressive or defensive, needlessly consumed vast resources. These wasted resources, the disruption of the economy occasioned by war, and the crippling debt burden that modern war implied, diverted the states' resources from its proper purpose, that of education, culture, and the promotion of the arts of civilization. The consequence was a slow down of human progress or, in Kant's terms, an impediment to the development of human capacities. Kant, however, did not despair, for

[34] Kant, "Perpetual Peace: A Philisophical Sketch, *supra* note 2 at 104. Since Kant's day various international institutions have been touted or promoted as the functional equivalent of Kant's "free federation," including the League of Nations, the UN, and most recently the EU, which to many observers seems to echo a number of the themes highlighted by Kant; a union of nations that is not a unitary state, a community of democratic, republican states that happen also to be neighbors, an ideology of peace, and a central preoccupation with international trade.

[35] "A state of peace among men living together is not the same as the state of nature, which is rather a state of war. For even if it does not involve active hostilities, it involves a constant threat of their breaking out." *Ibid.* at 98. In a footnote Kant adds the comment that in the state of nature the "other" injures me by virtue of the very state in which he coexists with me, without need to determine active injury. He injures me, says Kant, by the very "lawlessness of his state (*statu iniustu*), for he is a permanent threat to me, and I can require him either to enter into a common lawful state with me or to move away from my vicinity." *Ibid.* Here Kant seems to go further than Grotius or Vattel who did require some cognizable positive injury beyond mere coexistence in a state of nature. The idea of a natural enmity is applied to peoples and nations: "Peoples who have grouped themselves into nation states may be judged in the same way as individual men living in a state of nature, independent of external laws; for they are a standing offence to one another by the very fact that they are neighbors." *Ibid.* at 102.

[36] *Ibid.* at 100.

in his view, man's reason was naturally oriented toward the achievement of justice. Furthermore, according to Kant, the design of nature, which in his view took advantage even of man's negative impulses, would both lead inexorably to the same end: perpetual peace and a universal cosmopolitan existence.

> The history of the human race as a whole can be regarded as the realiza-
> tion of a hidden plan of nature to bring about an internally – and for this
> purpose also externally – perfect political constitution as the only politi-
> cal state within which all natural capacities of mankind can be developed
> completely.... [T]he highest purpose of nature, a universal cosmopolitan
> existence, will at last be realized as the matrix within which all the original
> capacities of the human race may develop.[37]

Kant recognized that the ideal means to achieve this end was "a universal *union of states* (analogous to the union through which a nation becomes a state)."[38] What Kant had in mind here was a political entity distinguishable from an Empire, for Kant was at heart an anti-imperialist. Indeed he went as far as to argue that although the international state of nature is essentially a state of war, it was still preferable to the "false" peace imposed by an empire, for such an empire was merely a powerful state seeking to impose its will on other states.[39] Furthermore, in Kant's view, the peace imposed by such an empire was, in any case, bound to fail because nature willed it otherwise: using linguistic and religious differences to separate peoples.[40] Although Kant's ideal universal union of states was to be something other than an empire, it was, as Kant foresaw, subject to similar limitations. For in Kant's words:

> If an international state of this kind extends over too wide an area of land, it
> will eventually become impossible to govern it and thence to protect each
> of its members, and the multitude of corporations this would require must
> again lead to a state of war.[41]

---

[37] Kant, "Idea for a Universal History with a Cosmopolitan Purpose," *supra* note 2 at 50–51 [Eighth proposition]

[38] Kant, "The Metaphysics of Morals," *supra* note 2 at 171.

[39] "The idea of right presupposes the separate existence of many independent states. And such a state of affairs is essentially a state of war, unless there is a federal union to prevent hostilities breaking out. But in the light of reason, this state is still to be preferred to an amalgamation of the separate nations under a single power which has overruled the rest and created a universal monarchy. For the laws progressively lose their impact as the government increases its range, and a soulless despotism, after crushing the germs of goodness, will finally lapse into anarchy." Kant, "Perpetual Peace: A Philosophical Sketch," *supra* note 2 at 113.

[40] *Ibid.*

[41] Kant, "The Metaphysics of Morals," *supra* note 2 at 171.

Accordingly, a permanent universal union of states, the precondition for a true perpetual peace, must remain an unrealized ideal that must nevertheless be pursued.

> It naturally follows that *perpetual peace*, the ultimate end of all international right, is an idea incapable of realization. But the political principles which have this aim, i.e. those principles which encourage the formation of international alliances designed to *approach* the idea itself by a continual process, are not impracticable.[42]

Kant's alternative, and in his view practicable, proposal was the formation of a community of autonomous sovereign states that would voluntarily enter into a common regime of mutual and reciprocal obligations with the purpose of pursuing the ultimate goal of perpetual peace. In place of the ideal universal international state, Kant thus proposed a loose (con)federal system that would not infringe on state sovereignty. Instead, Kant's (con)federation relied on state sovereignty: on the power of sovereignty to enter into binding treaties and on the rational determination of sovereign states to abide by their agreements. Kant's project for a (con)federation relied on the strength of liberal republicanism in the domestic sphere of a number of states for its realization. Guided by the same principles, and sharing broadly similar values and the ultimate goal of peace, these liberal states would be willing and able to enter into reciprocal agreements to for go the option of war (self-help) to resolve their disputes among themselves. Kant's imagined (con)federation would be limited to those states sharing the same republican liberal principles and values. It was, however, universal in potential, for Kant was convinced that republican liberalism was the only domestic political theory congruent with right reason and therefore with justice. All sovereign states, he believed, would eventually come to understand this from the inside and could in any case be expected to evolve in that direction. In the end, world peace would be achieved through a republican liberal world order entered into voluntarily that would progressively approximate the ideal universal international state.[43] As Kant well understood, however, even his more modest initial project still needed to be grounded in something beyond civil law and sovereign will. Indeed, Kant had little faith in the capacity of international law alone to achieve perpetual peace. For, as his famous reference to Grotius, Puffendorf, and Vattel as "sorry comforters," still dutifully quoted in justification of military aggression, demonstrates, he was acutely aware of the malleability of international law in the hands of

---

[42] *Ibid.*
[43] On Kant and republican liberalism, see M.N.S. Sellers, "Republican Legal Theory" (2003), chapter 15.

opportunistic sovereigns, even those purportedly guided by liberal republican principles in the domestic sphere. In his words:

> For Hugo Grotius, Puffendorf, Vattel and the rest (sorry comforters as they are) are still dutifully quoted in *justification* of military aggression, although their philosophically or diplomatically formulated codes do not and cannot have the slightest *legal* force, since states as such are not subject to a common external constraint.[44]

Kant had, in other words, come squarely up against the international face of the liberal paradox. It was in this context that Kant recast and theorized the ancient concept of cosmopolitanism, and it was Kant's version of the concept that came to dominate all subsequent reflection on the subject. Kant's turn to cosmopolitanism, must then be understood as part of the ongoing history of international law's attempt to resolve the liberal paradox. Kant's interest in the term had little to do with its ancient association with statelessness, worldliness, or world travel, although he was, as was common for a cultured man of his generation, a fascinated armchair traveler. He was an avid reader of travel literature and scientific accounts and taught and promoted the study of geography and anthropology before these were recognized university disciplines.[45] Kant used the term instead to refer to a preexisting, permanent and irreplaceable global community, not unlike the *civitas maxima* depicted by Christian Wolff that later served as the backdrop for Vattel's "necessary law."[46] Interestingly, however, Kant's "original" global community is defined in spatial and relational terms:

> Thus all nations are *originally* members of a community of the land. But this is not a *legal* community of possession (*communio*) and utilization of the land, nor a community of ownership. It is a community of reciprocal action (*commercium*), which is physically possible, and each member of it accordingly has constant relations with all the others. Each may offer to have commerce with all the rest, and they all have a right to make such overtures without being treated by foreigners as enemies. This right in so far as it affords the prospect that all nations may unite for the purpose of creating certain universal laws to regulate the intercourse they may have with one another, may be termed *cosmopolitan (ius cosmopoliticum)*.[47]

---

[44] See Kant, "Perpetual Peace: A Philisophical Sketch," *supra* note 2 at 103.
[45] Cosgrove; David Harvey, "Cosmopolitanism and the Banality of Geographical Evils," *Public Culture* 12:2 (2000): 529–64.
[46] There has been much debate as to whether Vattel's influential interpretation of Wolff was consistent with or a departure from Wolff. On this topic, see Jouannet, Vattel 216 et seq.
[47] Kant, "Idea for a Universal History with a Cosmopolitan Purpose," *supra* note 2 at 172.

Kant's vision of the global or cosmopolitan community was based on an image of humankind inhabiting a physical globe, the bounded earth. It was a community based neither on shared possession nor on shared ownership of the earth. Instead, it was a community based on coexistence itself. In Kant's view, man's nature was inherently sociable in orientation. Coexistence for human beings thus implied the necessity of safeguarding the possibility of nonhostile human encounter between strangers. In consequence, the global community imagined by Kant was a moral community that gave rise to an actual, albeit minimal, common and universal reciprocal obligation of each human being to the other – a duty that Kant termed "cosmopolitan right." As Kant presented it, the term cosmopolitan right did not simply describe an ethical proposition, it was a right that always produced legal obligation. Yet although cosmopolitan right was a fact, it was also, like justice, a necessary aspiration of the human race. Indeed, according to Kant, cosmopolitan right was the inevitable end point toward which universal history must tend, for only through the realization of cosmopolitan right could mankind hope to create the required conditions for human flourishing.[48] In Kant's analysis, cosmopolitan right still needed to be realized and operationalized through the establishment of a (con)federation that brought together liberal republican states. Within such a (con)federation the states would be able to enter into truly binding international agreements among themselves, and perpetual peace would come into reach.

In Kant's scheme, the success of the (con)federal system depended on the recognition and the interplay between the three legal political orders and their associated rights: civil society, international law, and in a significant innovation, what he termed "cosmopolitan law" (or right). Cosmopolitan law was not presented as a substitute for civil or international law, but as a supplement. Civil law was designed to govern the relationship between citizens within a polity and could impose its regulations on foreigners (noncitizens) who chose to dwell among them. International law, on the other hand, regulated the conduct between sovereign states and was concerned with "the relationship between individual persons in one state and individuals in the other or between such individuals and the other state as a whole."[49] The fundamental function of cosmopolitan law, however, was to give content to and govern a crucial relationship that was not properly served by either of the other two justice regimes – the relationship between a sovereign state and a foreigner who reached its shores without evil intent, as well as, concomitantly, the relationship between local inhabitants and the arriving foreigner. Such a foreigner was

---

[48] Ibid. at 50–51.
[49] Kant, "The Metaphysics of Morals," supra note 2 at 165.

the moral equivalent of an uninvited visitor. Elsewhere Kant is careful to distinguish between an (uninvited) visitor and a "guest" – who has a right to be entertained.[50] Yet although the stranger arriving on foreign shores was no guest and was not entitled to "entertainment," a visitor, according to Kant, should be accorded a minimum degree of hospitality.

> [H]ospitality means the right of a stranger not to be treated with hostility when he arrives on someone else's territory. He can indeed be turned away, if this can be done without causing his death, but he must not be treated with hostility, so long as he behaves in a peaceable manner in the place he happens to be in.[51]

In practice, the right of hospitality, invoked by Kant, created only the simple obligation that a visitor not be treated automatically as an enemy and met with hostility absent some kind of provocation. It did not imply that such a visitor should be welcomed, it imposed no duty that the stranger be received with kindness, it did not even rule out the possibility that the stranger might be turned away without a hearing (so long as it could be done without endangering his life).

Minimalist as it was, Kant's cosmopolitan right of hospitality, stood in sharp contrast and served as a necessary corrective to the implications that could be derived from the tradition expounded by Kant, that in the state of nature the other injures me by virtue of the "very lawlessness of his state (*statu iniustu*), for he is a permanent threat to me." Following this logic, absent something like the cosmopolitan right of hospitality, the stranger arriving on foreign shores stood to be treated as an enemy. Indeed, we could argue that treating the uninvited visitor preemptively as an enemy was the rational thing to do. Under such conditions, the prospect of peace was slight. The cosmopolitan right of hospitality, by contrast, reversed the assumption, by providing that the uninvited stranger should not be treated as an enemy unless he had acted as one. The duty to hold off treating the stranger as an enemy opened up the possibility of communication and amity. It should be stressed that in Kant's view, the right of hospitality had a reciprocal character for the rules of hospitality bound both visitor and host, in a manner reminiscent of the rules of etiquette. If the host performed his duty to the visitor, the latter in turn was obliged to behave as a nonhostile guest. Consequently, there were two ways to violate the duty of hospitality, as a host and as a guest – both in such a situation could be said to act inhospitably.

---

[50] In Perpetual Peace. Kant, "Perpetual Peace: A Philosophical Sketch," *supra* note 2 at 107.
[51] *Ibid.* at 105.

Kant's theory of international relations has understandably been labeled cosmopolitan. His world, however, was organized around the role of nation-states. In a sense, then, Kant's was a thin cosmopolitanism. To the extent that he considered there to be a morally relevant global human community[52] outside or before the state, this community imposed few claims or constraints on either states or individuals. Thin it might be, Kant's cosmopolitan right was a necessary matter of justice. The duty of hospitality was presented not as a matter of cultural choice but as a matter of right. Perpetual peace could only be attained when justice could be achieved at each of the three interrelated levels of human community (domestic, international, and cosmopolitan). Absent any one of these, the whole system would collapse, and war and violence would once again become endemic.[53]

III. COSMOPOLITAN PEACE: COSMOPOLITAN RIGHT
AND THE WAY OF COMMERCE

The nexus between cosmopolitanism and peace initially drawn by Kant has indelibly colored the modern understanding of the "purpose" of cosmopolitanism. So too, I would argue, has the association that Kant envisioned between cosmopolitan peace and international commerce. As we have already seen, Kant's cosmopolitan right, in substantive terms, was composed of the limited right not to be treated with hostility on arrival to foreign shores. It is tempting, of course, to conceive of Kant's right to hospitality as a kind of precursor to our modern conception of human rights. A proper understanding of the meaning and function of this right, however, requires us to reconsider it from within its historical context. From this perspective it becomes evident that Kant's cosmopolitan right – the right to hospitality – was concerned with the objective of facilitating international commerce. That it was so should come as no surprise, for in adopting a right to hospitality Kant signaled his embrace of a long-standing tradition, mediated by Vitoria and Grotius,[54] which

[52] Kant in fact says little about the way in which the original global cosmopolitan community can be said to have a practical existence or how such a community would intersect with contingent local communities. At one point, however, he intriguingly seems to suggest that the global cosmopolitan community has become manifest: "The peoples of the earth have thus entered in varying degrees into a universal community, and it has developed to the point where a violation of rights in *one* part of the world is felt *everywhere*." *Ibid.* at 107–8. This statement of course can be read as a precursor to our more modern claims about globalization.

[53] Kant, "The Metaphysics of Morals," *supra* note 2 at 174. ("It can indeed be said that this task of establishing a universal and lasting peace is not just a part of the theory of right within the limits of pure reason, but its *entire ultimate purpose*"; emphasis added).

[54] For a discussion of the role of commerce and the discovery of a right to engage in commerce in Grotius's and Vitoria's early work, see Ileana M. Porras, "Constructing International Law in

professed that international commerce was a form of interstate relations that brought humanity back together in mutual interest and thereby led them to peace. For this reason, Kant envisioned that one of the central functions of the (con)federation would be to encourage and facilitate international commerce, for through international trade the international community would come to approximate the cosmopolitan community.

Beginning with Vitoria in *De Indis*, the natural law tradition had theorized a right to hospitality. Vitoria's and Grotius's accounts of a natural right to hospitality differed in some significant respects, yet both men had based their claims for this right on what has been termed "the doctrine of the design of divine providence in favor of commerce."[55] Simply stated, according to this doctrine, international commerce was desired by God as a means of bringing separated humanity back into friendship. The classic elements attributed to God's design included the provision of different resources across the nations, so that the peoples would need each other and duly go in search of one another to exchange goods. Under this view the oceans, which seemed to separate the nations, were reimagined as highways that would bring the peoples together in the reciprocal benefaction of exchange. Kant, a child of the Enlightenment, was unconvinced that "natural law" could be considered a form of law rather than a code of ethics. For this reason, for the most part, Kant eschewed the terminology of natural rights. Indeed, as we have already seen, Kant's great innovation was to posit a third order of right: cosmopolitan right, which coexisted with the two familiar orders of right, civil and international. Perpetual peace could be achieved only when these three orders of justice were pursued simultaneously and brought into collaboration. In this scheme, the importance of the right of hospitality could not be overestimated, for it was the keystone of cosmopolitan right.

Although Kant sought to recast the right of hospitality in this radical manner, his source for the origin of a right of hospitality bears an unmistakable family affinity to Vitoria's and Grotius's earlier discovery of a natural right to hospitality in God's evident interest in promoting commerce. Kant's allusions to the elements of the doctrine of the design of divine providence in favor of commerce are muted yet recognizable in his discussions of cosmopolitan right and the right to hospitality.[56] In place of God's design or providence,

---

the East Indian Seas: Property, Sovereignty, Commerce and War in Hugo Grotius's *De Iure Praedae* – The Law of Prize and Booty," or "On How to Distinguish Merchants from Pirates," *Brooklyn J. Int'l L.* 31 (2006): 741, 756.

[55] *See* Jacob Viner, "The Role of Divine Providence in the Social Order: An Essay in Intellectual History" (1972) 32 et seq.

[56] *See ibid.*

Kant substitutes the design of nature: "The mechanical process of nature visibly exhibits the purposive plan of producing concord among men, even against their will and indeed by means of their very discord."[57] In this same passage, Kant makes it clear that he is not discounting the religious (Christian) claim of divine providence. Rather, he argues, that it is more in keeping in a work of theory to speak of nature and not of providence, for, he adds: "[m]odesty forbids us to speak of providence as something we can recognize."[58] Whether it is best understood as the design of inscrutable providence or that of a more modestly observable nature, the design retains a similar structure (dispersal/abundance-need/trade) and the same objective: peace. In Kant's version, nature by means of war has "despotically" driven human beings to inhabit even the most inhospitable regions of the earth. Necessity, lack of resources, and the hard struggle for survival that ensued had forced men to settle down and establish civil society (law). The final step was the discovery of trade: "Salt and iron were next discovered, and were perhaps the first articles of trade between nations to be in demand everywhere. In this way, nations first entered into *peaceful* relations with one another, and thus achieved mutual understanding, community of interest and peaceful relations, even with their most distant fellows."[59]

Other elements of the doctrine of God's providential interest in commerce can be found throughout Kant's texts in passages where they are linked explicitly to the right to hospitality. Kant, for instance, repeatedly emphasizes the closed spherical character of the planet. In "Perpetual Peace," he emphasizes that the earth is a bounded sphere (the spatial basis of cosmopolitan geography), necessarily shared by all human beings.[60] The "right of resort" – the right to present yourself in the society of others – one aspect of the right to hospitality, is premised on mankind's communal habitation of the earth's surface and the impossibility of getting away from one another:

> Since the earth is a globe, [human beings] cannot disperse over an infinite area, but must necessarily tolerate one another's company.... The community of man is divided by uninhabitable parts of the earth's surface such as oceans and deserts, but even then, the ship or the camel (the ship of the

---

[57] Kant, "Perpetual Peace: A Philosophical Sketch," *supra* note 2 at 108.
[58] *Ibid.* at 109.   [59] *Ibid.* at 111.
[60] The image of the bounded globe is a common representation of cosmopolitan space and is used to evoke the inescapable relational nature of the cosmopolitan community. Yet, as Denis Cosgrove points out, the image of the globe has also long been a constant of the imperial imagination. The image of the globe was amenable to the universalizing gaze as well as to the appropriating gaze, for one could look down on the whole world from one's own perspective. Denis Cosgrove, "Globalism and Tolerance in Early Modern Geography," *Annals of the Association of American Geographers* 934 (2003): 852–870.

desert) make it possible for them to approach their fellows over these owner-less tracts, and to use as a means of social intercourse that *right to the earth's surface* which the human race shares in common. . . . But this natural right of hospitality, i.e. the right of strangers, does not extend beyond those conditions which make it possible for them to *attempt* to enter into relations with the native inhabitants. In this way, *continents distant from each other can enter into peaceful mutual relations* which may eventually be regulated by public laws, thus bringing the human race nearer and nearer to a cosmopolitan constitution.[61]

Man's ability to disperse and separate is thwarted by the closed character of the globe, and he must make the best of it. In a classical reversal, the geographic features that seemed at first designed to separate mankind can now be see as part of the plan to bring nations together, for they can be traversed in the pursuit of trade: "The ocean may appear to cut nations off from the community of their fellows. But with the art of navigation, they constitute the greatest natural incentive to international commerce, and the greater the number of neighboring coastlines there are (as in the Mediterranean), the livelier this commerce will be."[62] So long as the most minimal right to hospitality was recognized, the encounters between peoples would bring prosperity and peace – bringing to fruition nature's design.

From this reading it is apparent that Kant subscribed to a modified version of the doctrine of the design of divine providence in favor of commerce. If international commerce was part of nature's plan to bring mankind to peaceful coexistence, then commerce must be enabled. It was evident, however, that international commerce would be rendered almost impossible, at least with those not already formally one's friends, if those undertaking the initial contact were most likely to be met by preemptive violence on arrival in foreign shores. As Kant saw, for international trade to be possible, the rules governing the relationship between a foreign visitor and the sovereign or local inhabitants had to be fundamentally reordered. The nonhostile reception of a foreigner arriving in native shores was the precondition for the possibility of commerce. In Kant's hands, this moment of contact between strangers became almost sacred, for in it lay the seed of peaceful international communication and exchange. The new cosmopolitan right of hospitality was designed to safeguard the possibility of encounter, an encounter that was for Kant the most evocative manifestation of the global or cosmopolitan community of interest, giving man the opportunity to express his natural sociability while furthering the obvious

---

[61] Kant, "Perpetual Peace: A Philosophical Sketch," *supra* note 2 at 106 (emphasis added).
[62] Kant, "Idea for a Universal History with a Cosmopolitan Purpose," *supra* note 2 at 172.

and desirable economic advantages of trade. The right of hospitality was at the service of commerce, yet in Kant's view nature fortunately did not rely solely on the realization of this cosmopolitan right to achieve her aims, but could depend equally on that most powerful driver of human action – self-interest: "[N]ature also unites nations which the concept of cosmopolitan right would not have protected from violence and war, and does so by means of their mutual self-interest. For the *spirit of commerce* sooner or later takes hold of every people, and it cannot exist side by side with war."[63]

Interestingly, the images of international travel and foreign commerce that Kant deployed in his work on cosmopolitanism were almost exclusively those associated with sea voyages.[64] When he describes the geographic features that separate the nations or bring them together, he mentions oceans and coastlines (rather than, for instance, mountains or rivers). The desert itself becomes an ocean, traversed by means of the camel – the ship of the desert. Indeed, when he posits a cosmopolitan right of hospitality, Kant appears to have the particular conditions of the long-distance seaborne trade in mind, as had Vitoria and Grotius. Furthermore, in line with Vitoria and Grotius before him, the "stranger" he pictures, who is to be protected by the right of hospitality (and commerce) is quite clearly the European trader engaged in "visiting" the distant shores of foreign lands in pursuit of trading opportunities. Thus, for instance, despite the wealth of possible examples of "inhospitable" behavior closer to home, Kant's illustrations draw on the behavior of distant foreigners – the inhabitants of the Barbary coast and the Bedouins, and in an interesting twist that reminds us that Kant's right of hospitality also imposes a duty on the stranger who is received without hostility, on the acts of "civilized states" vis-à-vis distant foreigners – for Kant criticizes as inhospitable the behavior of the seaborne commercial states who have turned visiting into conquering.[65]

[63] Kant, "Perpetual Peace: A Philosophical Sketch," *supra* note 2 at 114.

[64] Perhaps this was due, at least in part, to the fact that Kant was born and spent his entire life in the city of Königsberg, East Prussia (now Kaliningrad, Russia), a major Baltic seaport.

[65] See *ibid.* at 106. Although Kant was by no means free of the Eurocentrism and cultural racism of his age, he was also aware of and outraged by the excesses of the European commercial empires in Asia and the Americas. In the late eighteenth century, as he wrote on the subject of cosmopolitan right and the crucial role of international commerce in the pursuit of perpetual peace, Kant could not ignore that the Honourable British East India Company had fought a seven-year war against the French army in India to consolidate its influence and virtual trading monopoly; that it had become the military ruler of a large swathe of the subcontinent; and that during the governorship of Warren Hastings, a Company employee, Bengal had suffered a famine that left a third of its population dead while the Company nonetheless sought to extract its profit. Furthermore, by the end of the eighteenth century, the scandal of the African slave trade and of the exploitation of slaves for the Caribbean sugar trade could no longer be ignored by Enlightenment thinkers.

International "commerce," of course, was not in Kant's time exclusively, nor even predominantly, ocean based. Kant's focus may be read as attesting to the fact that in the late eighteenth century, it was still the long-distance seaborne trade that filled the imagination. Equally, however, it serves as a reminder of the continuity between the work of Vitoria, Grotius, and Kant, for the context in which the earlier authors discovered the right of hospitality was that of the long-distance seaborne trade.

There is one significant way, however, in which Kant may be said to have broken with the tradition. Vitoria writing in the context of the Spanish conquest of the New World, and Grotius writing in the context of the incipient Dutch challenge to Iberian control over the trade routes to the East Indies, both positioned the right of hospitality within a just war equation. Simply put, both men, in slightly different ways, discovered a right, the inevitable violation of which provided a cause for just war. Thus, although the right of hospitality was ostensibly intended to facilitate trade – in pursuit of God's providential design to bring men to peace – in practice, it served to justify war. Kant was also concerned with the questions of war and peace, and the role of law in achieving and securing peace, but he was not much interested, at least in his writings on cosmopolitanism, in the doctrines of just war. Thus, Kant's right of hospitality does not function as a justification for war in a complex algorithm of just war. On the contrary, Kant seems aware of the fact that the right of hospitality had been much abused by European traders voyaging to distance lands:

> Yet these visits to foreign shores, and even more so, attempts to settle on them with a view to linking them to the mother land, can also occasion evil and violence in one part of the globe with ensuing repercussions which are felt everywhere else. But although such abuses are possible, they do not deprive the world's citizens of the right to *attempt* to enter into a community with everyone else and to *visit* all regions of the earth with this intention.[66]

Curiously, however, although Kant was aware of the violence, exploitation, and conquest that accompanied much of the European long-distance seaborne trade to the Americas, Africa, and Asia,[67] he nonetheless continued to be optimistic about the peace-generating potential of international commerce. The constant warfare that was of concern to Kant was the endemic intra-European warfare of the period. That the European powers fought each other over the control of colonial resources (including access to land and labor) did not seem to overly disturb Kant in his conviction that international commerce

---

[66] Kant, "Idea for a Universal History with a Cosmopolitan Purpose," *supra* note 2 at 172.
[67] See Kant, "Perpetual Peace: A Philosophical Sketch," *supra* note 2 at 106–7.

might put an end to war. It was as though Kant held in his mind a notion of pure commerce, which could remain undisturbed despite the many distortions undergone by the practice of international commerce. "Commerce" was simply the term ascribed by Kant to the positive form of international relations, whereas war was its negative counterpart. Although he understood that commerce (like war) was driven by self-interest, he considered the self-interest that led to commerce as constructive – for commerce, at least in its ideal form, was based on reciprocity and voluntary exchange. In this view, the self-interest of one party to a transaction was mirrored in that of the other party, and after the exchange, both would be better off. Both would profit. It was precisely this prospect of rendering each other a reciprocal benefit that would lead to amity between peoples and an end to war. This innocent image of international commerce could only be upheld if one ignored the reality of the coercion inherent in most forms of international exchange, and the uncomfortable fact that the most profitable exchange was usually one in which one party controlled the terms of the exchange. It could only persist if one disregarded the equally complicating factor of competition in commerce, and the problem that one trader's profits was another's lost opportunity. There were, in other words, never really only two parties interested in an act of exchange. As soon as a third party entered the game, the potential for conflict increased. Competition for the trading opportunities of the East and West Indies and Africa had exacerbated intra-European conflicts from the moment the long-distance seaborne trade had become technically practicable. That Kant could nonetheless continue to promote international commerce as a means to international peace speaks to the imaginative power of the doctrine of the design of divine providence in favor of commerce. For it is clear that the form of commerce that providence or nature had planned for mankind was that of the ideal exchange.

IV. THE NEW COSMOPOLITANISTS AND THEIR PROJECTS

Through a close reading of Kant's work on cosmopolitanism, I have sought to demonstrate that his cosmopolitanism can be understood as already inscribed within the international law tradition: he was trying to solve the liberal paradox at the international level, through a project that aimed to substitute peace for war, and the primary means proposed was more commerce. To the extent that the new cosmopolitanists rely on Kant, I would argue, it is unlikely that they can deliver on the promise of renewal that some in the world of international law had hoped for. Perhaps for this reason, many of the projects that have been promoted under the guise of a new cosmopolitanism feel very familiar.

Yet although the traditional concepts of cosmopolitanism can be shown to be integral to international law, it could be argued that some of the new cosmopolitanists nevertheless provide a radical challenge to the status quo. The two strongest candidates are cosmopolitanists who have imported Rawls's distributive justice principle into the international arena and those who apply the rhetoric of cosmopolitanism to the project of global governance.

A. *Distributive Justice and the Cosmopolitan Project*

Many modern cosmopolitans have been heavily influenced by the twentieth-century political philosopher John Rawls, whose groundbreaking work, *A Theory of Justice*, sought to introduce a principle of distributive justice to the Kantian theory of justice. Rawls, however, was concerned with the meaning of justice within a single polity. His famous conceit – the requirement that our policy choices be made as though from behind a veil of ignorance about our given or eventual identity and social, cultural, or economic position – did not contemplate citizenship as one of the variables about which we would be ignorant. Rawlsian liberals, working on issues of international justice, however, rapidly extended Rawls's theory into the domain of the global. Toward the end of his life, Rawls sought to distance himself from this application of his work, and in his book *The Law of Peoples*, he expressly denied that a distributive justice principle was required for justice at the international level. Rawls thus left an uncomfortable legacy for his internationalist followers. Simply stated, according to Rawls, the principle of distributive justice he had earlier elaborated could only make sense within a bounded associational community, and, in his view, no such community could be identified in the international context.

Rawlsian internationalists were thus forced to go in search of a theory of international community that might serve to compensate for this apparent deficiency that the master had identified at the international level. Conveniently enough, given that Rawls identified as a Kantian, they found an answer in Kant's work on cosmopolitanism and particularly in his identification of "cosmopolitan right." Recalling the existence of a global community that precedes and is not replaced by the bounded nation-state or any alternative constructed community – a global community that Kant contended imposed reciprocal obligations on human beings in the form of cosmopolitan right – the new cosmopolitanists (contra Rawls) concluded that distributive justice was a necessary tenet of international justice. Combining the idea of a morally precedent cosmopolitan community and the principle of distributive justice, these new cosmopolitanists proceeded to derive something like a global obligation of solidarity, which gave rise in turn to an individual duty of care (of different weights and degrees).

Paradoxically, of course, the result is that the new cosmopolitanists have stretched Kant's limited cosmopolitan right to breaking point while leaving it unsupported by the tripartite justice structure that Kant envisaged. They have done so in two ways: first, by populating cosmopolitan right with substantive principles that reflect a modern sensibility of individual human rights or capacities (as explained by Martin Nussbaum);[68] second, by inferring a degree of reciprocal cosmopolitan duty in every individual, the mere fact of a worldwide cosmopolitan community and an originally shared globe can hardly support, especially in the face of the closed sociopolitical entities that are nation-states. The projects of global redistribution that these cosmopolitanists propose may seem attractive in theory, but in practice they suffer from the limitation that they can be quite easily dismissed as ethical proposals without legal obligation. Kant was very clear that the cosmopolitan right to hospitality he elaborated was to be conceived as a legal right rather than simply a moral right. He was equally clear, however, that it could only function as a legal right if it was guaranteed within a carefully balanced tripartite system of justice built on the nation-state. This tripartite system, as we have already seen, depended on the strength of republican liberalism in the domestic order (civil law) in the form of liberal nation-states and on the strength of the international order created by liberal nation states (international law) in the form of a (con)federation. In this structure cosmopolitan right was best seen as the glue that held the other two orders together. The new cosmopolitanists, on the other hand, seek to expand the scope of cosmopolitan right while reducing the relevance of the nation-state.

B. Global Governance and the Cosmopolitan Project

Another tendency among the new cosmopolitanists that seems to promise to challenge the status quo of international law is that which employs the vocabulary of cosmopolitanism to elaborate global governance projects in the face of the new phenomenon of globalization. Global governance cosmopolitanists use "cosmopolitanism" to convey their understanding of globalization – the ever-increasing interdependence and de-territorialization of the means of production, finance, services, and communication – as relating to or presaging

---

[68] For a nuanced account of Nussbaum's critique of Rawls and her attempt at getting beyond the social contract idea that has dominated political theory since Hobbes, see Feldman, "Cosmopolitan Law," *supra* note 16.

the advent of a new form of global community outside the nation-state. Essentially, their idea is that the processes of globalization have made state territorial
boundaries irrelevant and thus given birth to a new global community and that
this community is the cosmopolitan community made manifest. From their
point of view, the nation-state has lost its purchase and is no longer the most
significant source of law. The new global community inhabits cosmopolitan
space, which they imagine as a postnational regulatory space. Those who
inhabit this space and participate in the production of norms include transnational corporations, multilateral organizations, and international civil society
(rather than the familiar individuals and states). In a sense, these cosmopolitanists are the least influenced by Kant's particular vision of a state-based
cosmopolitanism. Instead, global governance proponents are attracted to cosmopolitan theory only to the extent that it allows them to put the state in
its place. Global governance proponents substitute a non-state-based global
civil society for the traditional domestic civil society as the locus of politics.
They assume that the emergence of this new transnational civil society is good
and should be encouraged. The emerging transnational civil society is said to
prefigure a new form of international democracy in a generous and tolerant
cosmopolitan social-cultural space – after the demise of the nation-state. This
is not the place to undertake a critique of the assumptions underlying the
global governance projects of this strand of the new cosmopolitanists. However, at first glance it would appear that their cosmopolitanism bears little
resemblance to that of Kant.

Be that as it may, it is perhaps worth remembering that Kant's version of
cosmopolitanism was elaborated in the context of an earlier wave of globalization. The "new" commercial, labor, financial, religious, ideological and
military movements, and "linkages" that seemed to characterize Kant's world
made it possible for him to claim that what happened in any part of the world
had an impact everywhere else.[69] In a sense there is, after all, a connection
between Kant and the globalization cosmopolitanists. Kant's cosmopolitan
right of hospitality, was, as we have seen, a right designed to uphold the possibility of international commerce, for Kant saw in commerce the positive face
of international relations that could be set up in opposition to war. Cosmopolitanists may not take such a rosy view of international commerce, yet they accept
the proposition that globalization is driven by economics. Their cosmopolitan
space is first of all a global marketplace inhabited by economic actors, including corporations and consumers. Kant believed that international exchange
based on reciprocal benefit would ultimately lead to the recognition of mutual

[69] Kant, "Idea for a Universal History with a Cosmopolitan Purpose" *supra* note 2.

interest among the nations of the world and therefore to peace. Likewise, globalization cosmopolitanists appear convinced that the global marketplace will produce a global community of interest. Freed from the demands (and the distortions) of the nation-state, they seem to say, human beings will be better able to regulate their affairs. The assumption is that this will lead to greater harmony and less conflict.

As with the cosmopolitan distributivists discussed earlier, from an international law perspective, the main flaw in the position of the globalization cosmopolitanists is that they seek to mount a cosmopolitan peace without the benefit of a cosmopolitan architecture. The problem is that although they reject the nation-state and, with it, a traditional state-based international law, these cosmopolitanists still subscribe to the basic assumptions of liberal political theory, including in particular the view of the human being as inherently autonomous, rational, and fully free. Thus the problem of justifying collective constraint remains. In the absence of the guarantees of the republican liberal state, the problems of accountability, legitimacy, and enforcement grow more, rather than less, pressing. In practice, of course, proponents of global governance have not yet done away with the state. Rather, they emphasize the multiplicity of sites of overlapping governance (regulatory management structures that may well include some formal legal regime) that already exist in our globalized world. To some extent, they seem to rely on the diffuseness and multiplicity of disciplinary sites to guard against the production of empire. Empire is not the only danger, however. As commentators have pointed out, global governance tends to become managerial and expert-driven and not sufficiently accountable or open to political contestation.

v. CONCLUSION

The subject of cosmopolitanism has given rise to a vibrant new literature across many disciplines in the past twenty years. Most recently, international law theorists have also begun to explore the possibilities inherent in the terminology of cosmopolitanism at a time, when yet again, it seems that international law is in need of shoring up. This chapter has raised the question of what, if anything, the new cosmopolitanism can offer to international law. Because Kant's work on cosmopolitanism has been foundational, an answer to this question requires a close exploration of the relationship between Kant's work and the tradition of international law. The starting point is a focus on three themes that have been central in this tradition. One is of liberalism, and the paradox on which it is constructed: the tension between the free choice of the autonomous individual and the need for collective constraint. As is well known, in the domestic sphere liberal theory resolves the paradox by positing some version of the social contract, which provides the justification for collective constraint. According to liberal theory, the purpose of the legitimate collective constraint imposed by the state on its citizens is to put an end to the unfettered violence that would otherwise erupt in the unregulated state of nature. The problem of unfettered violence is equally a concern on the international plane, and not surprisingly those concerned with international relations have turned to liberal theory. I argue that in this transposition from the domestic to the international sphere, in which nation-states take the place of individuals, liberal theory has come up against the familiar liberal paradox, yet the old solution is not available. International law's history can be read as a search for an ordering principle that would substitute for the social contract and the state in the domestic realm and provide a justification for collective constraint in the pursuit of peace. Kant's turn to cosmopolitanism in the eighteenth century should be understood, then, as one attempt to devise an ordering principle that would bring the world to peace. Kant's innovation was to posit the existence of a third order of justice – cosmopolitan right – that was to stand alongside the civil order and the international order. Kant's substantive cosmopolitan right, the right to hospitality, was derived not from the consent of states but from the reality of a preexisting worldwide moral community, yet it was to be put into effect through the cooperation of an international community of republican liberal states. Further, Kant's limited right of hospitality should not be read as a precursor "human right," but understood in connection to the promotion of international commerce. In this Kant joined the ranks of early international law theorists, such as Vitoria and Grotius, who discovered a right to hospitality or commerce, but grounded it in natural law. Moreover, Kant's emphasis on the positive role of international trade in the achievement of cosmopolitan peace stands in a long tradition within international law, which has viewed international commerce as the obverse of war. Exploration of the three themes of liberal theory, peace, and commerce leads to the conclusion that cosmopolitanism has been at work in international law since its inception, for cosmopolitanism, in Kant's version at least, is merely an interesting repackaging of some of the central themes of international law.

Most of the new cosmopolitanists trace their ideas back to Kant. Some, such as the group concerned with distributive justice and those involved in promoting global governance in the face of globalization, have attempted to go beyond Kant. However laudable the goals of some of the new cosmopolitanists, to the extent that they continue to subscribe to liberal theory, they cannot avoid the liberal paradox with which Kant grappled; a liberal paradox that has both a domestic and an international expression. For Kant cosmopolitan right is the glue that holds the other two justice orders (civil and international) together. The glue is essential, of course, but Kant is clear that the attainment of perpetual peace will be impossible without first constructing a just republican liberal order within nation states and the voluntary cooperation of these nation-states within the framework of positive international law. The new cosmopolitanists, on the other hand, seem intent both on reducing the hold of the domestic order on the increasingly autonomous individual, who is to be recognized as having substantive and far-reaching (cosmopolitan) rights and obligations outside of the ambit of the nation-state, and on retracting the province of international law because of its excessive dependence on sovereign will.[70] For these cosmopolitanists, the glue has become the whole.

---

[70] For a strong critique of the new cosmopolitanists on the grounds that they are undermining the present flawed yet effective system of state-based rights, international law, and democratic accountability and substituting for it abstract normative claims of cosmopolitanism without any evident gains, see David Chandler, "New Rights for Old? Cosmopolitan Citizenship and the Critique of State Sovereignty," *Political Studies* 51 (2003): 332–349.

5 Are Human Rights Parochial?

James Griffin

1. A QUICK SKETCH OF THE PERSONHOOD ACCOUNT OF HUMAN RIGHTS

We agree that human rights are rights that we have simply by virtue of being human. That does not get us far, however, because we lack agreement on the relevant sense of "human." Thus, our notion of a "human right" suffers from no small indeterminateness of sense. During the seventeenth and eighteenth centuries, when thinkers increasingly accepted that human rights were available to reason alone apart from belief in God, the theological content of the notion was gradually abandoned, and nothing was put in its place. The term was left with so few criteria for determining when it is used correctly and when incorrectly that today we often have only a tenuous, and sometimes a plainly inadequate, grasp on what is at issue. One of our pressing jobs now is to remedy the indeterminateness.

A term with our modern sense of "a right" emerged in the late Middle Ages, probably first in Bologna, in the work of the canonists, who glossed, commented on, and to some extent brought system to the many, not always consistent, norms of canon and Roman Law.[1] In the course of the twelfth and thirteenth centuries the use of the Latin word *ius* expanded from meaning a law stating what is fair to include also our modern sense of "a right": that is, an entitlement that a person possesses to control or claim something. For instance, in this period one finds the transition from the assertion that it is a natural law (*ius*) that all things are held in common and thus a person in mortal need who takes from a person in surplus does not steal, to the new form of expression, that a person in need has a right (*ius*) to take from a person in

---

[1] I present here what I take to be the present state of scholarship: see James Brundage, *Medieval Canon Law* (London: Longman, 1995); Brian Tierney, *The Idea of Natural Rights* (Atlanta: Scholars Press, 1997).

surplus and so does not steal.[2] The prevailing view of the canonists was that this new sort of *ius*, a right that an individual has, derives from the natural law that all human beings are, in a very particular sense, equal: namely, that we are all made in God's image, that we are free to act for reasons, especially for reasons of good and evil. We are rational agents; we are, more particularly, normative agents.

This link between freedom and dignity became a central theme in the political thought of all subsequent centuries. Pico della Mirandola, an early Renaissance philosopher who studied canon law in Bologna in 1477, gave an influential account of the link. God fixed the nature of all other things, he said, but left man alone to determine his own nature. It is given to man "to have that which he chooses and be that which he wills."[3] This freedom constitutes, as it is called in the title of Pico's book, "the dignity of man."

This same link between freedom and dignity was at the center of the early-sixteenth-century debates about the Spanish colonization of Latin America. Many canonists argued emphatically that the American natives were undeniably agents and, therefore, should not be deprived of their autonomy and liberty, which the Spanish army was everywhere doing. The same notion of dignity was also central to political thought in the seventeenth and eighteenth centuries, when it received its most powerful philosophical development at the hands of Rousseau and Kant. This notion of dignity, or at any rate the word "dignity," appears in the most authoritative claims to human rights in the twentieth century. The United Nations says little in its declarations, covenants, conventions, and protocols about the grounds of human rights; it says simply that human rights derive from "the inherent dignity of the human person,"[4] but the most plausible interpretation of their use of "dignity" is that it is the use of the philosophers of the Enlightenment.

Now, the human rights tradition, which I have condensed into very few words, does not lead inescapably to a particular substantive account of human rights. There can be reasons to take a tradition in a new direction or to break with it altogether. Nonetheless, the best substantive account of the existence conditions for human rights is, I should say, very much in the spirit of the tradition and goes like this.

Human life is different from the life of other animals. We human beings reflect; we form pictures of what a good life would be and try to realize these

---

[2] See Tierney, *Idea of Natural Rights*, 261–62.

[3] Giovanni Pico della Mirandola, *On the Dignity of Man*, trans. Charles Glenn Wallis (Indianapolis: Hackett Publishing, 1998).

[4] See Preamble to the International Covenant on Economic, Social, and Cultural Rights, 993 U.N.T.S. 3, (1966); preamble to the International Covenant on Civil and Political Rights, 999 U.N.T.S. 171 (1966).

pictures. That is what we mean by a characteristically *human* existence. It does not matter if some animals have more of our nature than we used to think, nor that there might be intelligent creatures elsewhere in the universe also capable of deliberation and action. So long as we do not ignore these possibilities, there is no harm in continuing to speak of a characteristically human existence. We value our status as human beings especially highly, often more highly even than our happiness. Human rights can then be seen as protections of our normative agency – what I shall call our "personhood."

But personhood cannot be the only ground for human rights. It leaves many rights too indeterminate. For example, we have a right to security of person, but what does that exclude? Would it exclude forcefully taking a few drops of blood from my finger to save the lives of many others? Perhaps not. To up the stakes, would it also not exclude forcefully taking one of my kidneys? After all, the two weeks it would take me to recover from a kidney extraction would not deprive me of my personhood. Where is the line to be drawn? The personhood consideration on its own will not make the line determinate enough for practice. Further, if a proposed right cannot become a practicable claim that one person can make upon another, then it will not be a right. That degree of determinateness is one of the existence conditions for rights. To fix a sufficiently determinate line, we should have to introduce considerations such as these: given human nature, have we left a big enough safety margin? Is the right too complicated to do the job we want it to? Is the right too demanding? And so on. We must consider how human beings and societies actually work. Thus, to make the right to security of person determinate enough we need another ground, call it practicalities. I propose, therefore, two grounds for human rights: personhood and practicalities. The existence conditions for a human right would, then, be these. One establishes the existence of such a right by showing, first, that it protects an essential feature of personhood, and, second, that its determinate content results from the sorts of practical considerations that I have roughly sketched.

My statement here of the personhood account is too abbreviated to persuade doubters, but I have discussed it more fully elsewhere.[5]

II. A QUICK SKETCH OF THE EPISTEMOLOGY OF HUMAN RIGHTS

There is a "taste model" of value judgment, given its classic statement by Hume and still highly influential in philosophy and the social sciences. According to it, value judgments are a matter of taste or attitude. Our attitudes can be

[5] Griffin, *On Human Rights* (Oxford: Oxford University Press, 2008), chap. 2.

corrected for factual or logical error, but once that is done, there is no further ground for regarding one value judgment as better than another. Factual judgments can be true or false; value judgments are neither. Factual judgments are objective; value judgments are subjective.

The taste model seems to me to collapse from its own explanatory inadequacy. According to the taste model, our preference fixes on an object, which thereby becomes valuable. However, value cannot be explained so simply. There is no reliable correlation between our *actual* preferences and what is *valuable* to us.

So we might, as many philosophers and social scientists do, drop *actual* preferences in favor of *rational* preferences. We must understand more fully or more accurately what the natural world is like, and only then, in this enhanced state of knowledge, might our reactions of desire be directed at what can count as a value. This "rational preference account" is much the more plausible, and among philosophers now the more common, form of the taste model. Yet what standard does "rational" represent? We might say, as Richard Brandt proposes, that a desire is rational if it persists when I have become aware of all the relevant natural facts and when I have purged my thought of logical error.[6] Nonetheless, is this enough? Take an instructive example that we owe to John Rawls.[7] A man has a particularly crazy aim in life – say, counting the blades of grass in various lawns. He knows that no one is interested in the results, that the information is of no use, and so on; he commits no logical error. Nonetheless, we should be hard put to it to see the fulfillment of this obsessive desire as enhancing his life – apart, that is, from preventing anxieties and tensions that might be set up by frustrating his desire, but that is to introduce other values. What we should be hard put to see is the fulfillment of his desire as, in itself, improving the quality of his life.

What this example suggests is that our standard for "rational" has not yet become strong enough. The way to make it stronger, however, is to make desires "rational" in some such sense as "formed in appropriate appreciation of the nature of their object." Yet although this seems to handle the counterexamples, it seems also to undermine the preference account of value. It stresses an *appropriate* reaction of desire, and so suggests that there is an element here of getting things right. Once the idea of the "appropriateness" of a response enters, standards of correctness and incorrectness also enter.

So I believe that judgments about human interests can be correct or incorrect. They report deliverances of a recognition of certain things going on in

[6] Richard Brandt, *A Theory of the Good and the Right* (Oxford: Clarendon Press, 1979), 10.
[7] John Rawls, *A Theory of Justice* (Oxford: Clarendon Press, 1972), 432–33.

the world – namely, interests being met or not met. These interests are part of human nature, and not just human nature as seen by a particular person or society. These judgments seem to be true or false in the way that statements of natural fact can be.

But these are judgments about human interests – that is, prudential values. Can judgments about how people ought to behave – that is, moral norms – also be correct or incorrect, true or false?

Let me take two examples. "That's painful" is paradigmatically a judgment about a human interest. "That's cruel," however, goes beyond human interests; it encapsulates a moral norm. A person who acts cruelly intends to make another suffer without compensating good; that intention is both necessary and sufficient. The obviousness of the judgment "That's cruel" comes from its generally being made within certain motivational limits: it is well within the capacities of the human will not to be cruel. So the condemnation built into the word "cruel" is apt. Its obviousness also comes from its not going much beyond claims about pain and intentions. The property "cruel," being a combination of pain, cause, and intentions, has whatever epistemological standing they have – standing as natural facts, I should say.

Now turn to a second kind of example – one that may involve considerable change in epistemic standing. Human life is of especially high value. From that we derive an especially strict norm, "Don't deliberately kill the innocent." Part of the content of the right to life – indeed in the seventeenth century much of it – is not killing another person without due process, although as far back as Locke (indeed, much earlier) philosophers were including certain further protections – for example, aiding the desperately needy. However, when we make the move from human interests to moral norms, certain limitations of human agents enter the picture, especially limitations in will and understanding. There are limits to what may be demanded by human agents, and those limits help to shape the content of the human right to life – for example, the matter of how much aid for the needy may be demanded of one. Further, the limits of understanding limit what is available to us to decide the content of human rights. Sometimes we can calculate reliably enough – that is, to a degree of probability on which we should be prepared to act – the consequences of large-scale, long-term social arrangements. We can, if the changes in question are extreme enough. In less extreme cases, however, often in just the cases we regard as live options, we cannot – cases such as deliberately killing noncombatants in war, using terrorism as a political instrument, killing one patient to save five others, and so on. Here too we often cannot do the calculation of consequences to a reliable degree of probability. There is no obvious remedy for this failure. In the absence of a remedy, we find some other way to conduct our moral life. Or rather, in many cases a sufficiently reliable, all-encompassing calculation of consequences has never been available to us, so we have simply carried on with our moral life pretty much in the piecemeal, not fully systematic way that mankind has always done. We have at times raised our standards and broadened the considerations that concern us, but we have not convincingly risen to an overarching system. Instead, we long ago developed a different approach to ethical decision making. The very great value of human life has led to our having very great respect for it; we allow that there can be exceptions to the norm "Don't deliberately kill the innocent," but out of our great respect for human life we demand that the case for any exception be especially convincing. That is, we respect life: we do not try to promote it, for example, by maximizing it. There is an element of policy in this approach, and we can see that another society might adopt a somewhat different policy. Because this norm constitutes a large part of the content of the human right to life, there is therefore an element of policy in the human right as well.

If this element of policy is a necessary determinant of the content of many human rights, as I think, what does this mean for their epistemic standing? The norm "Don't deliberately kill the innocent" expresses a policy. An expression of a policy is not true or false in the way that a statement that a human interest is or is not met is; it is not a matter of natural fact. We shall have to consider what opening this element of policy may provide to relativity or ethnocentricity or some other parochial condition.

III. ETHICAL RELATIVITY

Ethical relativism, as I understand it, makes two claims: first, that ethical judgments are made within a framework of basic evaluations, which may take the form of beliefs, preferences, sentiments, and so on; and, second, that there are divergent frameworks for judgments on the same matter, no one framework being most authoritative.[8] We can then specify the framework further case by case – the basic evaluations of individual persons, of social classes, of cultures, and so on.

Ethical relativism, as most commonly expressed, is universal: *all* ethical judgments are relative to a framework. Its contradictory is therefore particularly negative: some are not. I argued in the last section that some ethical judgments – namely, judgments about basic human interests – are objective, where "objective" means dependent not on a person's subjective states but on

[8] For fuller discussion of ethical relativity see Griffin, *On Human Rights*, ch. 7.

considerations that would lead all successfully rational persons to the same conclusion. So universal ethical relativism is, I conclude, false. However, philosophers tend to treat values as if they were uniform: all are objective, or none is; all are a matter of knowledge, or none is; all are relative to a framework, or none is. But in the last section I also questioned this assumption of uniformity. Some complex moral norms, such as "Don't deliberately kill the innocent," have an element of policy to them, and so lack empirical truth-value, whereas the judgments that a particular human interest is or is not met have one.

Relativism need not take a universal form. Consider relativity to the evaluative framework of individuals, based on their different desires and sentiments. Value beliefs can be subjected to criticism by facts[9] and by logic.[10] Many ethical beliefs are shaped by a person's understanding, often misunderstanding, of the empirical world: of the consequences of our acts, of what the objects of our desires are really like, and so on. Once one's desires and attitudes have been corrected, one may come to change them; over time they may increasingly converge with the desires and attitudes of others. What a relativist must maintain, however, is that some divergent beliefs will remain, and remain for the reasons relativists give. In any case, our interest here is human rights. Are *they* relative to a framework?

How can one make a case for ethical relativism? The commonest way is to cite, with little in the way of argument, certain examples of particularly stubborn ethical disagreement, which are meant to leave one thinking that the best explanation of the disagreement is the relativist's. This is, of course, an extremely weak form of argument. Establishing the best explanation of stubborn ethical disagreements requires understanding all the possible origins of these conflicting beliefs and all the possible resources that might resolve the conflict – no quick or easy job. That the job is so difficult leaves many relativists, despite its inadequacy, doing no more than citing examples. Let me give a brief sampler of the examples that they have offered.

Some societies regard theft as a serious crime; others do not even have the concept of private property, on which the idea of "theft" depends.[11] It is hardly obvious that relativism provides the best explanation of this difference. If one lives where food is plentiful without cultivation, there may be no pressure to develop an institution of private property. However, if one's survival depends on

---

[9] See David Hume, "Of the Standard of Taste," in various collections of his essays.
[10] See Richard Brandt, *A Theory of the Good and the Right*, 10.
[11] This is one of Gilbert Harman's examples of relativity to an ethical framework; see Gilbert Harman and Judith Jarvis Thomson, "Moral Relativism," in *Moral Relativism and Moral Objectivity* (Oxford: Blackwell, 1996), 9.

clearing land and shouldering the burdens of growing one's own food, some
form of control over the land and the crop is highly likely to emerge. The
best explanation may be difference not in ethical framework but in material
conditions.

Some societies have tolerated infanticide; others condemn it.[12] Consider,
however, the extreme case of life-threatening poverty. Tolerance of infanticide
is an adaptation that most of us would make if forced to it by the direst
poverty: say, if one were faced with the awful choice between the survival
of one's newborn baby or one's young child. A plausible explanation of the
disagreement over infanticide between a society of such abject poverty and
one better off may not be a difference in evaluative frameworks but, again, a
difference in material conditions.

Many people are committed to preserving the environment; others see no
objection to exploiting it.[13] This is a conflict that does indeed look irresolvable.
To my mind, we can coherently talk about the value of the environment not
just when changes in the environment affect human beings – say, our health or
enjoyment – but also apart from any effect on sentient life. The environment
has a value in itself. The idea of the environment's being intrinsically valuable
rests, I believe, on an idea of appropriateness of attitude. The only appropriate
response to, say, the enormous age, biological complexity, and beauty of the
Great Barrier Reef is wonder and awe. And wonder and awe prompt respect.
There is something lacking in a person who does not have some such response.
The wanton destruction of the Great Barrier Reef would be a monstrous act.
Ethics, I should say, is broad enough to encompass standards not just of *right*
and *wrong* but also of *appropriate* and *inappropriate*. Now, if the natives on
an island in the Great Barrier Reef decide to improve their quality of life by
mining, and thereby destroying, the reef, the apparent rational resolution of
the conflict between the preservationists and the exploiters would be to weigh
the costs and benefits to sentient creatures against the intrinsic value of the'
reef. That, I suspect, is a piece of weighing we cannot do. We must remember
that some values may be incommensurable, in this sense of the term: two
values are incommensurable if and only if they cannot be ranked against one
another as "greater than," "less than," "equal to," or "roughly equal to."[14] For

[12] *Ibid.*, 8–9.
[13] For the citation of incommensurable values as an example of moral relativity, see Maria
Baghramian, *Relativism* (London: Routledge, 2004), chap. 9
[14] For fuller treatment, see James Griffin, "Mixing Values," in *The Aristotelian Society, Supplementary Volume LXV* (1991); *idem.*, "Incommensurability: What's the Problem?" in Ruth
Chang (ed.), *Incommensurability, Incomparability, and Practical Reason* (Cambridge, MA:
Harvard University Press, 1997).

a pair of values to be commensurable in this sense, there must be a bridging notion in terms of which the comparison between them can be made. For example, most, perhaps all, human interests, I should say, lend themselves to comparison. They do not because there is a substantive supervalue behind them, but because there is a formal value notion in terms of which we can, and regularly do, compare them: for example, "prudential value," "quality of life," or "human interest" itself. We thus have the conceptual materials to judge that "this would enhance the quality of my life more than that," "this is a more major human interest than that," and so on. Yet sometimes – not often, I believe – two competing values are so different in nature from one another that there is no bridging notion available. In this conflict over the environment, for example, there is no bridging notion; comparison breaks down. This is indeed an intractable difference, but it does not derive from difference in ethical framework but from incommensurably different values. There is even a possible resolution of this disagreement: bringing both parties to see that the values they purport to commensurate are incommensurable.

A last example. Many of us think that abortion is prohibited; many others think that it is permitted.[15] Most often a person who holds that abortion is forbidden also holds background religious beliefs. Then is this, after all, an example of ethical relativity? Virtually all of us would accept that abortion is prohibited if we believed that an all-good, all-wise God had told us so, but with such a background, this intractable disagreement seems to have arisen not from different ethical frameworks but from different metaphysical beliefs. Perhaps, however, this just means that we should reconsider our definition of ethical relativism as relativity to a framework of basic *evaluations*. Evaluations cannot be sharply divided from empirical and metaphysical beliefs; our basic evaluations are what they are in part because of nonethical beliefs. Yet if this truth is to support the relativity of a belief about the morality of abortion, it must be because of the further relativity of facts or of metaphysical conceptual schemes. Ethical relativity would then not stand alone. Although these further relativities seem much shakier than ethical relativity, perhaps that impression is mistaken.

Still, not all ethical disagreements about abortion arise from differences over religion. When they do not, what best explains the stubbornness of the divergence? No doubt, many different things, but one explanation that is hard to make plausible is that there are two different frameworks of fairly

---

[15] David B. Wong offers this as an example of what he would regard as ethical relativism; see David B. Wong, *Moral Relativity* (Berkeley: University of California Press, 1984), chap. 12 sect. 5.

well-articulated and well-defined ethical beliefs producing this disagreement. That would make thought at this level far clearer and more inferential than it is. What might these ethical beliefs be? Nor is it plausible that these divergent beliefs about abortion are themselves basic ethical beliefs. They do not have quite that depth; they need justification themselves. What is more plausible, I should say, is that the framework for each of these conflicting views is a complex mixture of ethical beliefs, factual beliefs, and sentiments. They might be beliefs such as, "A fetus is already a fully biologically formed potential person, as much so as a newborn baby" or "An early fetus is too biologically primitive to be a person." Or they might be sentiments such as revulsion at the very thought of killing a fetus or, on the contrary, equanimity in the face of it. These beliefs are vague, however, and their implications for action are by no means clear. We should have to decide what weight to attach to these sentiments of revulsion or equanimity. What authority do they have?

My discussion of each of the four examples I have given is, I admit, inconclusive – neither decisively for nor against their relativity. That is my point. One would have to dig much deeper before one could reach a satisfactory conclusion. Merely citing an example is no case at all. Let me now try to dig somewhat deeper in the example that primarily concerns us: human rights.

IV. THE RELATIVITY OF HUMAN RIGHTS

Human rights are suspected – by Westerners as much as by Easterners – of being relative to Western culture. Human rights are undoubtedly a Western product: introduced by Christians in the late Middle Ages and further developed there in the early modern period and in the seventeenth and eighteenth centuries.[16] They were part of the growth in individualism in that particular time and place; they were part of a new sense in Europe and the Americas of "the dignity of man" and the great value of human autonomy and liberty.

Yet why think that human rights are, as well as a product of the West, also relative to the values of the West? One argument might be that the values from which human rights are derived – most prominently autonomy and liberty – are themselves peculiarly Western values. Some societies, it is true, value autonomy highly, seeing in it the peculiar dignity of the human person, whereas other societies value autonomy much less, seeing in it the threat of social atomism and the loss of solidarity and fraternity and of the harmony that comes from our all serving the same values. Yet anyone who thinks seriously about the value of our status as normative agents and the benefits of living in

---

[16] See Griffin, *On Human Rights*, sects. 1.1, 2.2.

a cohesive fraternal community will recognize that both are highly important. They will also recognize the same about both others' having to respect our individuality and our having duties of concern and care for others. It may be that realizing certain of the values of individualism is incompatible with realizing certain of the values of community, but incompatibility of values is not their relativity. Besides, the frequency of the incompatibility is exaggerated. Not all forms of autonomy are the autonomy to which we attach great value.[17] I would display more autonomy, in one correct use of the word, if I calculated my own income tax each year and decided for myself the plausibility of the Big Bang, instead of relying on the expertise of others. Neither of those is the autonomy to which we attach great value, however. What we attach great value to is the autonomy that is a constituent of normative agency, and relying on a tax accountant or an astrophysicist does not derogate in the least from one's normative agency. The form of solidarity to which we attach such great value does not require surrendering our normative agency, although it may require greater trust in one another and greater convergence in public standards. The form of solidarity that is of great value is a joint commitment to the members of one's community and to the community's successful working. The plausible explanation of the fact that different societies rank autonomy and solidarity differently is not that they are rankings of the relativist sort. Everyone, on pain of mistake, has to admit that autonomy and solidarity are both highly valuable. No one would maintain that any loss in autonomy is worse than any loss in solidarity, or vice versa. The more specific a choice between the two becomes – a certain loss of autonomy, say, to achieve a certain gain in solidarity – the more convergence in choice one will expect there to be. We do seem able, if only roughly, to compare these competing values.

A second argument for the relativity of human rights – indeed, an argument arising from my own personhood account – is this. We just saw how certain moral judgments – for example, "That's cruel" – could be derived from judgments about human interests – for example, "That's painful."[18] The judgment "That's cruel," goes so little beyond claims about pain, cause, and intention that it inherits the epistemic standing they have – standing as natural facts, I proposed. This suggests – merely suggests – that a human right (a moral standard) might similarly be derived from a certain human interest (a prudential value), again inheriting from it a sort of objectivity that would defeat the claim of relativity. Take the derivation of autonomy (the human right) from autonomy (the prudential value). I also admitted, however, that the

[17] See Griffin, *On Human Rights*, sects. 8.2, 8.3.
[18] See Griffin, *On Human Rights*, sect. 6.4.

derivation of still other human rights from human interests was less simple – for example, the right to life, which has an element of policy to it. The norm "Don't deliberately kill the innocent," which is one of the correlative duties of the right to life, in part expresses a policy, and different societies might adopt different policies. Some human rights thus have a clear conventional element. Do they thereby have an element of relativity?

Take the right to autonomy. Once one recognizes the value of autonomy, one recognizes also a reason to be autonomous oneself and a reason not to deny other people their autonomy. Human rights are protections of one's personhood, and so protections of, among other things, one's capacity for and exercise of autonomy. Is the objective epistemic status of the judgment that autonomy is prudentially valuable transferred to the judgment that autonomy is a human right? We should ask: What more comes into the second judgment than is already present in the first? The obvious answer is: the first is a prudential judgment, the second a moral judgment. I find it very hard to understand the nature of the transition from prudence to morality, but, despite my uncertainty, I think that at least there is a kind of rationality to it. It is reasonable to treat the reason-generating consideration that moves me when my autonomy is at stake as different from the one that moves me when yours is at stake. The obvious difference between these two cases is that in the one it is *my* autonomy, and in the other it is *yours*. However, the most plausible understanding of the engine of these two judgments is *autonomy: because a person's quality of life is importantly at stake*. The *my* and *your* are not part of the reason-generating consideration. The clause *because a person's quality of life is importantly at stake* lacks reference to me or to you, but it lacks nothing of what we understand the reason to be. To try to deny "autonomy" its status as a reason for action unless it is attached to "my" would mean giving up our grasp on how "autonomy" works as a reason for action.

Return now to my question: What more is present in the second judgment than is already contained in the first? There is, of course, whatever is added by calling autonomy a "human right." Many philosophers say that the judgment that something is a human right carries with it a claim that it has a particular moral importance: for example, it has the status of a "trump" or a "side constraint." However, human rights are neither trumps nor side constraints – a large claim but one that I have tried to justify elsewhere.[19] Autonomy – or, more generally, personhood – is not necessarily the most important human interest. Human rights make only an overrideable claim that a person's autonomy be given due respect – that is, the respect due to the sort of autonomy at

---

[19] See Griffin, *On Human Rights*, sect. 1.4.

stake in any particular case. That much follows simply from autonomy's being a prudential value. It is true that to know that autonomy is a prudential value is also to know how valuable it is: that it is generally highly valuable to us, valuable enough to attract, as it has, special protection, but of varying value from case to case, and overrideable by other important values.

When I speak here of the "derivation" of the human right to autonomy, I do not mean an entailment. I mean only that a reasonable person who recognizes the prudential value of autonomy will also recognize the respect that it is due. The reasonableness of that transition is enough to deny a relativist a foothold here.

Another important qualification. The transition from prudence to morality is, of course, too complicated a matter to be dealt with as briskly as I have just done – so complicated that there is no point in my embarking on a few more brisk comments. I have discussed the subject more fully elsewhere and will again fall back on that.[20] So let me leave my brief sketch of the kind of rationality involved in the transition from prudence to morality as a kind of marker: I need a fuller argument at this point, but so too would a relativist who wants to resist the objective tendency of my line of thought.

Let me turn to the second example I mentioned: the human right to life. Does a relativist find a foothold at least here? There is, I said, an element of policy in this right. Such policies are, it is true, social artifacts. All that we can say, however, is that a different society might choose a *somewhat* different policy. There are strong constraints on the policies that can be chosen. The nonarbitrary determinants of the content of the policy are the prudential value of human life, facts about human nature, and facts about how societies work. The great value of life would lead nearly all societies to adopt severe restrictions on deliberately taking an innocent person's life, the severity manifesting itself in reluctance to recognize many exceptions, especially, given what people are like, exceptions that cannot themselves be clearly enough limited or that have to rely on agents' being capable of highly subtle distinctions. Some societies may, even so, turn out to be relatively liberal about the restrictions, whereas others are relatively conservative, but that fact offers no appreciable support for relativity. If the convention adopted by one society could be seen to be working rather better than the convention of another, then there is strong rational ground for the second to adopt the convention of the first. If, as is common, we cannot tell whether any one convention is working better than the others, then no society would have good reason to resist an obvious solution

[20] James Griffin, *Value Judgement: Improving Our Ethical Beliefs* (Oxford: Clarendon Press, 1996), chap. V.

to the divergence: agreement on a common convention. This sort of difference between societies represents not a different framework of basic evaluations but merely a highly constrained difference in a rational opting.

What may we conclude? I have carried my discussion both of the epistemology of human rights and of their relativity only so far. I did not argue earlier for the reality of prudential values, but only for their factuality: judgments about human interests, I concluded, can be true or false in the way that judgments about natural facts – say, about an ointment's being soothing – can be. I want to conclude at this point that judgments about human interests and about human rights do not offer appreciably more scope for relativism than do judgments about natural facts. I must acknowledge, however, that one can be a relativist about natural facts – for example, the sort of comprehensive relativism that Wittgenstein is sometimes thought to hold: relativity to a form of life. The assessment of this radical form of relativism I leave to others.[21]

v. WHAT IS THE PROBLEM OF ETHNOCENTRICITY?

There are those who maintain that, even if ethical relativism were false, the problem of ethnocentricity would remain.[22]

What exactly *is* the problem of ethnocentricity? Perhaps this.[23] Human rights are, or are widely held to be, universally applicable. Yet if the only available justification for them is in Western terms, then they are not universally authoritative. If this were the problem, it would be overcome by establishing an objective justification of human rights authoritative for all rational beings. An objective justification of this sort would be sufficient, but perhaps not necessary. Certain forms of intersubjective justification might also do.

Still, if such an objective or intersubjective justification were forthcoming, a problem of ethnocentricity might even then remain. Such justification may be a long way off, or may take some societies a long time to come around to, and the language of human rights is something that we use now and have reason to go on wanting to use now. Perhaps we need a case for human rights, or even a variety of cases, not made in what for many are alien Western terms. Perhaps we must still aim to avoid ethnocentricity.

---

[21] For a good recent assessment, see Paul Boghossian, *Fear of Knowledge: Against Relativism and Constructivism* (New York: Oxford University Press, 2006).

[22] See, e.g., John Rawls, *The Law of Peoples* (Cambridge, MA: Harvard University Press, 1999), sect. 17.1.

[23] John Tasioulas adopts this interpretation in his "International Law and the Limits of Fairness," *European Journal of International Law* 13 (2002): 993–1023, sect. 2.

This does not follow. Hundreds of thousands of Westerners have adopted Asian religions, and not because they have managed to find Western metaphysical and ethical counterparts for these often culturally remote Asian beliefs, but, on the contrary, because they have looked into these religions on their own terms and been attracted by what they found. No one regards their Eastern origins as, in itself, an unscaleable barrier. The alien can be baffling, but if this problem can be overcome by Westerners in the case of Eastern religions, why not Easterners in the case of the much more accessible Western human rights?

Full, definitive rational justification aside, there seem to me to be two ways to bring about unforced agreement on human rights. One would be to put the case for human rights as best we can construct it from resources of the Western tradition and hope that non-Westerners will look into the case and be attracted by what they find. The other would be to search the ethical beliefs of various non-Western societies for indigenous ideas that might provide a local case for human rights, or for something not unlike them. This search is a valuable component of the current debate about Asian values, and many writers have helpfully explored the conceptual resources of Islam, Buddhism, Confucianism, and so on to that end. At first glance it will seem that this second approach (let me call it the less ethnocentric approach) is clearly the better one simply because less ethnocentric. However, on a longer look, the first approach (let me call it the more ethnocentric approach) is, I want to propose, on balance, preferable.

We now, in these cosmopolitan times, tend to exaggerate the differences between societies; societies change faster than foreigners' pictures of them.[24] It is true that different parts of the world have sometimes had radically different histories, which still exert an influence on their vocabularies, their ways of thinking, their religions, their values. However, the influences on the members of virtually all societies are now much more a mix of local and global than they were even a hundred years ago. Since then there has been a massive increase in global communication, convergence on economic structures, homogenization of ways of life due to growing prosperity, and widespread travel and study abroad precisely by the persons most likely to be influential in their society. We today face considerable problems about individuating cultures. It is by no means clear even that each of us is a member of *a* culture, let alone which culture it is. A culture is, roughly, a linguistic group with its own art, literature, customs, and moral attitudes, transmitted from generation to generation. I do not doubt that we can individuate *some* cultures. The clearest conditions for

---

[24] See Griffin, *On Human Rights*, sects. 1.5, 13.4.

the use of the term are when groups develop largely independently of one another. One could apply the term to an isolated Indian tribe just discovered in the depths of the Amazon. However, it became increasingly difficult to speak in those terms in modern conditions. Let me take a concrete (egocentric) example. To what culture do I belong? To the United States, where I was born and raised? Or should I say New England? Or do I belong to the culture of Britain, where I have spent my entire adult life? Or should I say, England, to exclude Scotland and Wales? Or is there now only an omnibus "Western" culture?

Too many contemporary writers merely echo Rawls's belief that a pervasive and ineradicable feature of international life is a radical intersociety pluralism of conceptions of justice and the good. Rawls's reasons for regarding these differences as ineradicable are difficult to find, however. We exaggerate, in particular, the disagreement between societies over human rights. Several Asian governments emphatically affirmed human rights in the Bangkok Declaration of 1993, however, it is true, also insisting that "while human rights are universal in nature, they must be considered in the context of a dynamic and evolving process of international norm-setting, bearing in mind the significance of national and regional particularities and various historic, cultural and religious backgrounds."[25] To declare that human rights are "universal" but qualified by "particularities" makes one alarmed about what that qualification will be used to justify. Still, there are loopholes in human rights themselves; no human right is absolute. Westerners themselves often contribute to the exaggeration of differences between East and West by exaggerating the strictness of the Western conception of human rights. Much of the flexibility and qualification in the Eastern conception is there, too, in the Western conception, on an accurate account of it. There is a wide variety of conditions that outweigh or qualify human rights: for example, if the very survival of a good government is at stake, or if a large number of lives can be saved from terrorist attack.[26] There is also a great difference between possessing a freedom and its possession being of value. This raises the question, also prompted by the Bangkok Declaration, of whether social and economic rights have priority over civil and political rights. I think that the arguments go heavily against such a priority,[27] but these are all legitimate questions, as the United Nations Universal

---

[25] Bangkok Declaration (1993), preamble and Articles 1, 8.
[26] See Griffin, *On Human Rights*, sect. 3.2.
[27] For reasons given by, e.g., Partha Dasgupta, *An Enquiry into Well-Being and Destitution* (Oxford: Clarendon Press, 1993), chap. 5.

Declaration (1948) perhaps too amply acknowledged,[28] and they deserve serious answers. Still, these legitimate questions are raised by the "particularities" not of Asian societies but of any society in certain circumstances of emergency, or at certain stages of development, or in facing certain ethical choices that we all face (e.g., between the values of individualism and the values of community).

How might the less ethnocentric approach go today? An obvious move would be for members of each society to look for their own local understanding of what, according to the United Nations, is the ground of human rights – "the dignity of the human person." One's local explanation of that idea need not repeat my explanation: namely, autonomy, liberty, and minimum provision. It might also include, for example, forms of justice and fairness and well-being that my account does not.[29] There is a problem for this whole strategy for reducing ethnocentricity, however. The less ethnocentric approach, on the present interpretation, would come down to finding local values similar to the Enlightenment values of autonomy, liberty, justice, fairness, and so on. It would look for local counterparts of whatever Western values back human rights. It would then have to rely on the indigenous population's seeing how valuable these values or close counterparts of them are, and how they can serve as the ground of human rights. This is virtually what the more ethnocentric approach does.

The less ethnocentric approach might, of course, aim for greater independence of the Western approach to human rights. It might look not for local counterparts of Enlightenment values, but for possibly nonequivalent indigenous values that can serve as that society's own peculiar ground for human rights. The Western ground and various non-Western grounds might turn out to support pretty much the same list of human rights. The advantage, it might be thought, in indigenous societies' aiming for independence of Western ideas, would be that they would then accept human rights discourse more readily. Global conversation in terms of human rights could start straightaway. The drawback, however, is that the conversation would be likely to break down early. A useful human rights discourse is not made possible just by agreeing on the *names* of the various rights, which is all that agreement on the list secures. We need also to be able to determine a fair amount of their content to know how to settle some of the conflicts between them. Think of how the

---

[28] Universal Declaration of Human Rights, G.A. res. 217A (III), U.N. Doc A/810 (1948), Article 29.2.
[29] See Griffin, *On Human Rights*, sect. 2.9.

international law of human rights would be constrained if it knew only their names. To know their content and ways to resolve their conflicts requires knowing what the values are that ground human rights and to reach some measure of agreement on them. That is, international law requires such knowledge if, as I believe, international law aspires, and should aspire, to incorporate basic human rights with ethical weight. It is hard to tell how well the international community could scrape along agreeing only on the names of human rights; perhaps we are not far from that position now, and the discourse of human rights has, nonetheless, had some undeniably good results. Yet we should be much better off if we could agree on the contents of human rights and how to resolve their conflicts. This constitutes a strong case for favoring the more ethnocentric approach, if it were found feasible.

It is feasible. The deepest cultural divide in history is not between the West and China (e.g., Confucianism, leaving Buddhism aside as an Indian import), and certainly not the West and Islam (Islam is an Abrahamic religion), but the West and India (Hinduism and Buddhism). The West aims at progress, at the growing achievement of the goods of human life; Hinduism at timeless, changeless being. Westerners see understanding as largely analytic – breaking things down into parts and discovering their interaction; for Hindu metaphysicians knowledge is an intuition of an indivisible whole, and differences between things are illusory. Westerners regard knowledge, in large part, as knowledge of the behavior of external objects, as in paradigmatically that largely Western achievement, the natural sciences; in contrast, Hindus regard reality as a distinctionless, entirely static nirvana. And so on.[30]

This deep cultural difference is not, however, evidence of a serious current "problem of ethnocentricity." It is perfectly proper to use the word "culture" in this context. The differences between the West and India go far back: the European idea of human rights goes back to the late Middle Ages, and the idea that human beings are made in God's image goes back to Genesis 1.27. The Buddha was born about 563 BCE; Hinduism emerged centuries before that. Each of these religions developed at a time when Europe and India were sufficiently isolated for there to be criteria of identity for their "cultures." That was millennia ago, however. To address *our* problem of ethnocentricity, we must take account of where each of us is *now*.

Also, the ultimate religious ideals are usually considerably different from, and far less influential in ordinary life than, the rules for everyday conduct that

---

[30] These contrasts are more fully drawn out by Archie J. Bahm, *Comparative Philosophy: Western, Indian and Chinese Philosophies Compared*, rev. ed. (Albuquerque, NM: World Books, 1995), chap. III.

they also teach. Buddhism tells us to extinguish the self, but it also has rules for the whole pack of squabbling, thieving, lying ordinary people. Buddhism has its Five Precepts: do not kill, do not steal, do not lie, do not be unchaste, do not drink intoxicants. Jesus set unattainable standards: be ye therefore perfect; love thy neighbor as thyself. Christianity never abandoned the down-to-earth Jewish Ten Commandments, however: thou shalt not steal, nor commit adultery, and so on. Thus, although Indians may have heard occasionally about ultimate goals and ultimate reality, most of them, like most of the rest of humanity, lived their lives well this side of the "ultimate."

The picture of India as spiritual, mystical, antirational, in sharp contrast to a West of science, rationality, and progress, is a gross oversimplification. It became, nonetheless, the dominant European picture of India, not least because it was a self-serving picture for European colonists in need of a justification for their presumptuous civilizing mission. As Amartya Sen and others have shown, however, India has a long tradition of secular rationality, scientific investigation, and freedom of thought. It goes back at least to Ashoka, Buddhist emperor of India in the third century BCE, and to the late medieval and early modern period – a striking example given by Sen is the liberal thought of Akbar, the late-sixteenth-century Mughal emperor of India.[31] And these rational, liberal ideas spread widely among a middle-class elite during the nineteenth and twentieth centuries.

When Indians came in contact with the development of the natural sciences of the West, they had no trouble whatsoever, despite reality's being unchanging, understanding and contributing to the laws of its change. Similarly, when Indians campaigned for their independence from Britain, they had no trouble at all, despite autonomy's and liberty's being illusions, articulating what their aims were. When they were told by the British that they were not yet ready for self-government, that they would make mistakes, Gandhi replied: "Freedom is not worth having if it does not connote the freedom to err and even to sin."[32] It may well be the case that the Hindu tradition, with its caste structure as the source of rights and privileges, contains no concept of the rights one has simply in virtue of being human.[33] It may also be the case that the Buddhist tradition, with its focus on perfecting the individual through meditation and insight rather than on improving society, also lacks the

---

[31] Amartya Sen, *The Argumentative Indian: Writings on Indian History, Culture, and Identity* (Harmondsworth, England: Allen Lane, Penguin Press, 2005), chaps. 1, 4, 13.

[32] Mahandas Gandi, *The Collected Works* (Delhi, 1984), 253.

[33] Jack Donnelly thinks so; see Jack Donnelly "Traditional Values and Universal Human Rights: Caste in India," in *Asian Perspective on Human Rights*, eds. Claude E. Welch Jr. and Virginia A. Leary (Boulder, CO: Westview Press, 1990).

concept.[34] This does not matter. The Hindus (and Muslims) who made up India at Independence seem to have had no trouble grasping the values of liberty and autonomy, and their constitution (1950) puts beyond doubt that they had no trouble handling the language of human rights.[35]

The case of India and the West reveals no serious, present-day divergence in understanding what human rights are and why they are important.

vi. TOLERANCE

There may be "decent" peoples, as Rawls calls them,[36] who reject some of the items on the Enlightenment list of human rights. Some rights may be contrary to deep, sincerely held commitments of theirs – religious beliefs, say, about the role of women. So long as a people count as "decent," however, it deserves our tolerance. "To tolerate," Rawls says, "means not only to refrain from exercising political sanctions . . . to make a people change its ways," but also "to recognise these nonliberal societies as equal participating members in good standing of the Society of Peoples."[37] Granting decent, nonliberal peoples this form of respect may encourage them to reform themselves, or at least not discourage reform, while denying them respect might well do so.[38] There is also a noninstrumental reason to grant them respect: it is their due.

Rawls takes as his example of a decent, nonliberal people an imaginary hierarchical Islamic society, Kazanistan.[39] He attributes the difference in political structure between Kazanistan and a Western liberal country largely to their cultural, particularly religious, differences. For the reasons just given, this seems to me highly doubtful. Rawls's question about tolerance, however, need not

---

[34] Robert E. Florida thinks so; see Robert E. Florida, *The Buddhist Tradition*, vol. 5 of *Human Rights and the World's Major Religions*, series ed. William H. Brackney, (Westport, CT: Praeger, 2005).

[35] Part III of the Constitution is devoted to "fundamental rights," which include guarantees of equality before the law (Art. 14); no discrimination on grounds of religion, race, caste, sex, or place or birth (Art. 15); freedom of speech and expression, assembly, association, movement, and residence (Art. 19); freedom of religion (Arts. 25–28); and rights to life, personal liberty (Art. 21), and due process (Art. 22). What is more, the Indian drafters took Western constitutional practice as a model. See Pratap Kumar Ghosh, *The Constitution of India: How It Has Been Framed* (Calcutta: World Press, 1966), 70: "The framers of our [Indian] Constitution shared the American view [viz. Jefferson's view that a democratic constitution should include a bill of rights] and, therefore, incorporated in our Constitution a list of fundamental rights." See also M. V. Pylee, *India's Constitution* (Bombay: Asia Publishing House, 1962), 3: "The makers of the Indian Constitution draw much from the American Constitution though not its brevity. . . . Thus the Constitution of India is the result of considerable imitation and adaptation."

[36] Rawls, *The Law of Peoples*, 61–67.   [37] *Ibid.*, 59.
[38] *Ibid.*, 62.   [39] *Ibid.*, 5, 75–8.

be motivated by cultural differences. A decent hierarchical people, according to Rawls, has two defining properties. One is that such a people does not have aggressive aims. The other is that its system of law secures human rights for all, imposes genuine moral obligations on its members, and its legal officials sincerely and not unreasonably believe that the law is guided by a common good conception of justice.[40] Recall, however, that Rawls substantially shortens the list of human rights and reduces their function. His list omits such typical human rights as freedom of expression, freedom of association (except for the limited form needed for freedom of conscience and religious observance), the right to democratic political participation, and any economic rights that go beyond mere subsistence. He also reduces human rights to two functions: fixing both the rules of war and the grounds for international intervention.

A great obstacle to our accepting Rawls's shortened list of human rights – especially if, like Rawls, we want a list with a realistic chance of being adopted – is that it would never be accepted by the international community. The United Nations' list of human rights is too deeply entrenched for it to be changed quite so greatly. It could no doubt be amended here and there, but not subjected to Rawls's radical surgery at its very heart. The international community would firmly resist the reduction of the discourse of human rights to Rawls's two functions only; it would carry on using human rights to assess the behavior of a single nation and institutions within a nation; and many of us, I believe, would go on using them to assess even the conduct of individual persons. Rawls, it is true, does not deny that the rights he drops from the list could appear among a people's "fundamental" or "international" rights. They are not, however, human rights proper, he says; they are merely "liberal aspirations." This is a radical demotion in their status, and it is this demotion that would be resisted. That raises a question about a strong, unexamined assumption of Rawls. "I leave aside," he says, "the many difficulties of interpreting . . . rights and limits, and take their general meaning and tendency as clear enough."[41] There is, of course, some clarity to them; they are not nonsense. Nonetheless, I would argue (and have elsewhere) that there is an intolerable degree of indeterminacy of sense in what a human right is – an indeterminacy that leaves unclear the criteria both for what should be on the list of human rights and, even more worryingly, what the contents of the individual rights are. This applies also to all the rights on Rawls's own shortened list: for example, the rights to life, liberty, health, and welfare. We can make our understanding of these rights adequate for our own thought only with the addition of some further substantive value. It need not be my addition, only *some* addition. Once the value is added,

[40] *Ibid.*, 64–67.					[41] *Ibid.*, 27.

however, it will determine which human rights there are, and they cannot then be restricted in the arbitrary way that Rawls chooses to do.

There is another worry. There are grounds for intervention that are not violations of human rights. I have argued elsewhere that the domains of human rights and of justice overlap, but are not congruent.[42] Some matters of justice – for example, certain forms of retributive and distributive justice – are not matters of human rights. Imagine, for instance, a country structured socially so that nearly all of its great prosperity goes to a small white colonial elite, leaving the mass of the black native population just at subsistence level. If this gross injustice were also likely to persist for some time, diplomatic or economic sanctions might well be justified. Think of a country somewhat like South Africa under apartheid, but with a decent consultation hierarchy that works well enough to raise the poor to subsistence level but not higher. So far as his theory goes, Rawls is free to amend it to say that serious violation of human rights is sufficient, but not necessary, to justify intervention, and that certain violations of justice (and perhaps yet more) are also sufficient. Actually, Rawls treats observance of human rights as definitive of a decent hierarchical society, without mention of retributive or distributive justice.[43] Admittedly, he does mention as also definitive the possession of "a common good conception of justice,"[44] but it is doubtful that that requires acceptance of a principle for distribution of welfare at fairly high levels.[45] Rawls cannot believe that a common good conception requires a society to raise its members above subsistence level, because a decent hierarchical society need not do more than that. My example of the South Africa–like country raises doubts that subsistence level is high enough. A satisfactory case that the level must be higher than subsistence is likely to make appeal to something especially valuable about human status that will not be protected by mere subsistence, and once that special value starts generating rights, no arbitrary stopping points are allowable.

The serious weakness in Rawls's functional explanation of human rights is that it leaves the content of his shortened list – the content both of the list itself and of each individual right – unworkably obscure. How do we determine, for example, the minimum of welfare required by human rights? If one has a further substantive value to appeal to – say, the value attaching to normative agency – then the minimum would be the somewhat more generous provision of what is necessary to function effectively as a normative agent. It looks as if Rawls could, if he wanted, avail himself of an altogether

---

[42] Griffin, *On Human Rights*, sect. 2.6.   [43] Rawls, *The Law of Peoples*, 65–67.
[44] *Ibid.*, 65.   [45] *Ibid.*, 88.

different approach to fix the minimum. He could ask: At what level of welfare would its neglect start to provide prima facie justification for intervention by other peoples? Confronted with that question, we would not know how to answer. We should need help from some further substantive ethical thought. We might, for instance, appeal to the idea of "the dignity of the human person," but that suffers badly from vagueness. We should lose the dignity of our normative agency, for instance, before we sank as low as mere subsistence. Subsistence that forced us to labor all our waking hours just to scratch out an existence from the earth, without leisure, reflection, or hope, brutalized by our conditions, would lack the dignity of normative agency. So, if this were our line of thought, we should still need to determine what sort of "dignity" is at work in human rights. In any case, Rawls does not seem to avail himself of this approach. Instead, as we have just seen, he assumes that "the general meaning and tendency" of human rights are already "clear enough." But, as I have argued, they are not.

I am not trying here to make a contribution of my own to the understanding of tolerance, important though that matter is. My interest now is human rights, and my conclusion negative. We should not follow Rawls's lead in commandeering the language of human rights to explain intervention. The language that he can provide is too indeterminate in sense to do so, and, once its sense is made more satisfactorily determinate, it will contain what is needed to justify the ampler list of human rights that, for so long, the tradition has championed.

6 The Parochial Foundations of Cosmopolitan Rights

Maxwell O. Chibundu

[I]nternational human rights are not the work of philosophers, but of politicians and citizens.[1]

I. INTRODUCTION

Louis Henkin titled a collection of his essays published in 1990 *The Age of
Rights*.[2] Although it turned out to be a prescient description of what international law was to become in the next decade and a half, it was hardly
an accurate description of the international order into which the book was
launched. The previous year had witnessed the fall of the Berlin wall, but its
ramifications for human rights were, in 1990, uncertain. In contrast, there was
no denying the completeness of the destruction of "rights" that had occurred
in Tiananmen Square. *The Age of Rights* had not been written with either of
these two events in mind, however, nor was it necessarily crafted to explore
the emerging policies of glasnost in the Soviet Union. In some ways, the title
seemed misplaced against the backdrop of the privations of famine, hunger,
ill health, imprisonment, and outright death flowing from responses to World
Bank– and International Monetary Fund–imposed "structural adjustment programs" in Africa and Latin America; the large-scale deprivations of life (and
other atrocities) in Lebanon, the Palestinian camps, and the wars of Central
America, all of which featured prominently in the news stories of the 1980s.
Rather, most of the essays in the collection had been written primarily against
the backdrop of an emerging trend in the United States to treat "international
human rights" less as a moral engagement, and more as a legal and political
tool. The successful inclusion in the Helsinki Declaration of the recognition

[1] Louis Henkin, *The Age of Rights* (New York: Columbia University Press, 1990), p. 6.
[2] *Ibid.*

172

by states that the claims of their citizens to more or less free movement was a matter of international concern, and the enshrining of this philosophy in United States trade policies had given "rights" a new salience in international diplomacy.[3]

Illustrative of this emerging philosophy of rights is a signal essay in the collection: "Rights: American and Human." Initially published in a law journal in 1979,[4] Henkin devoted as much time in this essay explicating the concept of "rights" enshrined in the American Declaration of Independence and the American Constitutional order as he did elaborating on claims about the nature and sources of international human rights. The purpose was to identify and associate American parochial conceptions of Constitutional rights with the international rights embodied in the Universal Declaration of Human Rights (UDHR).

The timing of the essay could not have been more exquisite. Barely a year later, the Second Circuit of the United States Courts of Appeals rendered what is unquestionably a seminal judicial decision on international human rights: *Filartiga v. Pena-Irala*.[5] That decision, relying on a hitherto obscure United States domestic statute, ruled that alleged torture by a Paraguayan official of a Paraguayan citizen in Paraguay could be adjudicated in and remedied by a U.S. Court. The Court of Appeals justified its ruling on the ground that torture violated international human rights laws, and that the torturer, "like the pirate and slave trader before him," could be made to account in any court regardless of the place of the act or the nationality of the torturer.[6] It is not an exaggeration to assert that this decision virtually single-handedly launched the coercive era of human rights adjudication and enforcement. Coercive adjudication in support of international human rights thereafter flourished not only in the United States, but also through much of Europe, as national courts asserted their "right" under the doctrine of "universal jurisdiction" to make Third World dictators account for wrongs allegedly perpetrated in their own countries.[7] In time, the rank of wrongdoers

---

[3] Final Act of the Conference on Security and Co-operation in Europe, Helsinki, August 1, 1975, (1975) 14 ILM 1292 (Helsinki Declaration); Trade Act of 1974, Pub. L. No. 93–618, title IV, § 402, 88 Stat. 1978, 2056 (1975), codified at 19 USC § 2432 (2006) (Jackson-Vanik Amendment).
[4] Louis Henkin, "Rights: American and Human" (1979) 79 *Columbia Law Review* 405–25, in Henkin, *Age of Rights*, pp. 143–56.
[5] 630 F 2d 876 (2nd Cir. 1980).   [6] *Filartiga*, 630 F 2d at 890.
[7] E.g., Heraldo Muñoz, *The Dictator's Shadow: Life under Augusto Pinochet* (New York: Basic Books, 2008); Richard Alan White, *Breaking Silence: The Case That Changed the Face of Human Rights* (Washington, DC: Georgetown University Press, 2004); William J. Aceves, "Liberalism and International Legal Scholarship: The Pinochet Case and the Move Towards a Universal System of Transnational Law Litigation" (2000) 41 *Harvard International Law*

and victimizers expanded to include multinational companies engaged in resource extractions in the "Third World." These corporations were seen as conspiring in (or at least facilitating) violations of rights by the governments and officials of those countries.[8]

Despite being grounded primarily on conceptions of human rights dominant within the United States legal order, Henkin's essays presciently provided a memorable tag that gave voice to a significant movement in international law during the next decade. The collapse of communism as a viable competing political movement to liberal democracy and removal of the Soviet Union as a check on the exercise of power by the United States and its West European and NATO allies, coupled with vicious ethnic and religious-based conflicts in the Balkans and sub-Saharan Africa, provided a milieu in which actions by the United Nations Security Council effectively reinforced the use of judicial tribunals to enforce "rights" asserted as being universal.[9] The adoption of the Rome Treaty of the International Criminal Court and the consequent creation of a permanent judicial tribunal charged with individualized enforcement of "international humanitarian law" added to the strengthening substantiation of the "age of rights."

Beyond litigators, moral and political philosophers began to speak in glowing terms about rights that transcend philosophical abstractions into the realm of concrete legal realities.[10] Rights were "cosmopolitan," it was said, and inhered

---

Journal 129–84; Wolfgang Kaleck, "From Pinochet to Rumsfeld: Universal Jurisdiction in Europe 1998–2008" (2009) 30 *Michigan Journal of International Law* 927–80; Beth Stephens, "Translating *Filártiga*: A Comparative and International Law Analysis of Domestic Remedies for International Human Rights Violations" (2002) 27 *Yale Journal of International Law* 1–57.

[8] E.g., *Sinaltrainal v. Coca-Cola Co.*, 578 F 3d 1252 (11th Cir. 2009); *Wiwa v. Royal Dutch Petroleum Co.*, 226 F 3d 88 (2nd Cir. 2000); *Bowoto v. Chevron Texaco Corp.*, 312 F Supp 2d 1229 (N.D. Cal. 2004); *Doe v. Unocal Corp.*, 110 F Supp 2d 1294 (C.D. Cal. 2000), vacated, 403 F 3d 708 (9th Cir. 2005). Sarah H. Cleveland, "The Alien Tort Statute, Civil Society, and Corporate Responsibility" (2004) 56 *Rutgers Law Review* 971–88; Richard L. Herz, "The Liberalizing Effects of Tort: How Corporate Complicity Liability Under the Alien Tort Statute Advances Constructive Engagement" (2008) 21 *Harvard Human Rights Journal* 207–39.

[9] As will become evident, a core contention of this chapter is that there is no such thing as "universal human rights." This should not be confused with a claim that there are no "universals." Some ideas and concepts may in fact have legitimate claims to being "universal" – that is, that they exist in some readily articulated form across most, if not all cultures, and that they have done so across both space and time. Ideas of "the good," or "happiness," of "justice" and of "fairness," and even possibly of "dignity," "liberty," or "equality" may all be "universals" in this sense, but they are not, most certainly, "rights" – at least in the legal sphere. As concepts, these values, to be made usable as legal rights, must undergo highly particularistic transformations that both depend on and embody very specific parochial interests, circumstances, and mind-sets.

[10] E.g., Seyla Benhabib, *Another Cosmopolitanism*, Robert Post (ed.), (New York: Oxford University Press, 2006); K. Anthony Appiah, "Grounding Human Rights," in Amy Gutmann

in the person not by virtue of membership in a particular political community, but simply by virtue of being a person, or a member of the community that is human. The possession of rights that were universal reconciled the "liberal's" professed acceptance of the validity of "multicultural difference" with the claim of "cosmopolitan pluralism." "Relativism," a concept that had been invoked in the past by liberals to undercut the hubris of a dichotomized world of "the civilized West" and the "primitive" rest, became a term of unqualified opprobrium. Rights were and could only be one thing: "universal."

But facts, however malleable, are indeed stubborn, and the most persistently stubborn reality of international law has been the organization of international society into more or less self-regulating political entities at the apex of which stands the "nation-state." That fact could be disregarded in the name of a universalized conception of human rights when the malefactors were the potentates of peripheral member states of the system; but when the virility of its dominant member was challenged by a terrorist attack on its soil, the meaning and reach of even the most central of those hitherto universal claims were suddenly up for grabs. What, if any, human rights claims were involved when a person suspected of terrorism is targeted for summary execution without the benefit of a trial? Was it consistent with human rights norms for such persons to be picked up in complete secrecy, indefinitely detained with no notice to anyone, subjected to "harsh" interrogation methods, and tried, if at all, by special tribunals with special rules of evidence? How much "collateral damage" would be deemed acceptable in the targeting of those deemed responsible for terrorism? The disclosure of activities that, if engaged in by minor states, would have been condemned as unquestionably illegal, became no more than occasions for debating their scope and legality, with "legitimate" arguments being offered on "both sides."

Guided by the central theme of this volume, in this chapter I reflect on the dichotomy between the purported universality of three related and sometimes intertwined concepts – liberalism, human rights, and the state – and the particularisms entailed in the various conceptions or formulations of these concepts.[11] Much of the contemporary confusion extant in the discourses on these three topics may be explained by the conflation of the treatment of these ideas. A concept requires that the speaker take a stance outside of the normative

(ed.), *Human Rights as Politics and Idolatry* (Princeton, NJ: Princeton University Press, 2001), pp. 101–16; Martha C. Nussbaum, "Capabilities and Human Rights" (1997) 66 *Fordham Law Review* 273–300.

[11] For an illustration of the distinction between an idea (e.g., law) as a concept and conceptions of the idea, see H. L. A. Hart, "Postscript," in Joseph Raz and Penelope Bullock (eds.), *The Concept of Law*, 2nd ed. (New York: Oxford University Press, 1994), p. 238.

validity or otherwise of the idea; a position that appears especially difficult for contemporary "liberal" philosophers and their legal acolytes. This is especially true with regard to human rights, but it infects the ideas of liberalism and of the state as well. My proposition, simply summarized, is that liberalism, as a cosmopolitan idea, has begotten two concepts that, in the 1990s, were at war with each other: "international human rights" and "the state." Lawyers in the victorious West, certain as to where justice lay, employed their advocacy skills to delegitimize the state, and in the process, they thought, to enhance international human rights. However, the policies of many Western states – policies for which both legal and moral justifications were not hard to come by – suggested the very qualified nature of that success. In the aftermath of the attacks on the World Trade Center and the Pentagon (and no less important, of the failed attempt on either the White House or the Congress), the state has reemerged as the dominant institution of international society, with the claims of international human rights being made subservient to the imperatives of its security. In what follows, I seek to explain this dynamic by illuminating the intellectual forces that invariably try to situate concepts – here, those of the state, international human rights, and cosmopolitan liberalism – on a universalizing pedestal but leave their particularistic conceptions within the framework of parochial differentiation.

I begin by dissecting the ambiguities in the concept of human rights. Then I consider ambiguities inherent in the idea of the state. Finally, I explain how those ambiguities were played out in the post–Cold War world order of the 1990s and early twenty-first century. I conclude by drawing out the lessons these ambiguities hold for the future direction of the discourses of international human rights and of the state in the current (post–Iraq War, post–financial crisis) world order.

II. AMBIGUITIES IN THE CONCEPT OF RIGHTS

The contributions in this volume make explicit two very distinct ways of think-ing about "rights" generally, and "international human rights" in particular. For ease of presentation, they can be referred to as the "philosophical" and the "legal." The philosophical examines the idea of rights primarily by inquiring into their nature and attributes and what makes them human. It takes as a given their existence, and it is less interested in their ontological sources. It is of course the latter with which the legal is primarily concerned. The philoso-pher, as an epistemological matter, wants to know the extent to which rights can be said to inhere in the person, or the extent to which they are artifacts of social organizations and political communities. The mode of the discourse is to provide justifications for these competing visions of the idea of rights by appealing to certain deontological values. These values, of which three are especially noteworthy – "liberty," "equality," and "dignity" – are taken as foundational elements of a liberal society. Moral and contemporary political philosophers, therefore, do not quibble over whether "human rights" – international or otherwise – are framed by a particular sociopolitical ethos – say, that of "liberalism," "Confucianism," "capitalism," or "Marxist socialism." Nor do these philosophers dispute that liberal institutions furnish superior (if not exclusive) normative grounding for the realization of human rights.[12] Issues of relativism and of particularism are therefore of secondary importance in the discourse of rights. Philosophical inquiry does not so much concern the particularism or universality of rights as how best to establish their content and how to relate them to the core liberal values of liberty, equality, and dignity.[13]

The discourse of law (and even more so, its practice) is primarily functional rather than deontological. To be sure, legal discourse overlaps with that of the moral philosopher inasmuch as both worry about the content of rights, but because of the differences in the purposes for which the discourses are undertaken, the conceptions of and approaches to rights among lawyers differ (or, perhaps more accurately, should differ) from those of moral and political philosophers. For lawyers, rights are about the validity of claims that can be asserted against and that are redressable through governmental power. The existence of the state and the use and abuse of governmental power are real, not abstractions that are fashioned and circumscribed by discursive needs. The lawyer may believe that that rights-based claims flow from or are enhanced by the values of liberty, equality, and dignity, but such an argument is at least one step removed from the practical needs of the rights claimant for immediate relief from a particularized harm or threat of such harm. It is true that academic lawyers do not (and preferably should not) function as advocates for particular individuals, groups or causes, yet their discourse and modeling must, as an ontological matter, take account of the institutional framework within which claims of rights function – that is, not as an abstraction of political jostling within a normatively constructed just liberal political order (cosmopolitan or otherwise), but in a world of diffused social systems with myriad political arrangements with varied degrees of acceptance, effectiveness, and legitimacy. Legal discourse is thus less a statement of normativity than it is a presentation of description and prescription, with the validity of the latter in no small

---

[12] Compare John Rawls, *The Law of Peoples* (Cambridge, MA: Harvard University Press, 1999).
[13] For further elaboration on this discourse, see Part IV.

measure a product of the accuracy with which the former has been rendered.[14] Unhappily, much of the discourse on human rights in both disciplines fails to distinguish among or pay particular attention to these differences. Each pretends that the idea of human rights is uniformly interdisciplinary.

The looseness of the intellectual articulation of the concept of rights is illustrated by divergences in the sourcing of its pedigree. In his contribution in this volume, James Griffin, a philosopher, dates its conceptualization to the canonists of Bologna in the late European Middle Ages.[15] Others find its foundational articulation in the thoughts of the European Enlightenment, and especially in the revolutionary movements of France and the United States in the late eighteenth century.[16] Some scholars have gone much further back and situated the idea in the Roman Empire,[17] the Greek City States,[18] and even the Persian Empire.[19] For most international lawyers, however, the idea of human rights is either "timeless," existing as an "inherent" attribute of "personhood," or it is the product of the UDHR, and the post–World War Covenants and treaties that seek to implement the provisions of the declaration.[20]

Can all these positions be correct? The answer depends on whether we are talking about the concept of human rights (of which international human rights would be but one iteration) or conceptions of human rights, including various conceptions of international human rights. Philosophy and jurisprudence as intellectual discourses do worry about concepts as constructs because in them lie the essences of the idea.[21] For a lawyer – even an academic

[14] As I explain in Part IV, this is not an argument against normativity in legal discourse on rights, but it is a claim about the nature of that normativity, and why it is different from that in which moral and political philosophers are engaged.

[15] Chapter 5 in this volume. *See also* James Griffin, *On Human Rights* (New York: Oxford University Press, 2008), p. 30.

[16] E.g., Stephen P. Marks, "From the 'Single Confused Page' to the 'Decalogue for Six Billion Persons': The Roots of the Universal Declaration of Human Rights in the French Revolution" (1998) 20 *Human Rights Quarterly* 459–514; Michael J. Perry, *The Idea of Human Rights: Four Inquiries* (New York: Oxford University Press, 1998), p. 5 (rooting human rights in Christian principles and stating that "there is . . . no intelligible . . . secular version of the conviction that every human being is sacred; the only intelligible versions are religious").

[17] Orlando Patterson, *Freedom in the Making of Western Culture* (New York: Basic Books, 1991).

[18] E.g., Maurice Cranston, "Are There Any Human Rights?" (Fall 1983) *Daedalus*, 1, 3 ("But we must go back even farther in time to trace the origin of the idea of human rights. Citizens of certain Greek city-states enjoyed such rights as . . . freedom of speech . . . or equality before the law.").

[19] E.g., Pierre Briant, *From Cyrus to Alexander: A History of the Persian Empire*, Peter T. Daniels (trans.) (Winona Lake, IN: Eisenbrauns, 2002), p. 47 ("Even today, Cyrus is presented by his modern acolytes as the inventor of 'human rights.'").

[20] Professor Henkin's discussion of rights in his *Age of Rights* illustrates this standard legal conception of human rights. Henkin, *Age of Rights*.

[21] It is not fashionable in modern discourse to speak of the essence of an idea, but it is surely the case that any idea possesses some core that unites its various articulations, even if it is sometimes

one – a concept in and of itself has little practical purchase. A concept is essentially descriptive. It attempts to state what is. Lawyers prefer to work with ideas that are formulated in prescriptive normative terms, and it is "conceptions" that satisfy this pragmatic billing. Conceptions cannot be "universal," however, which is precisely the practical legitimating purpose for which the international human rights pedigree often is invoked. There is nothing timeless about a concept, anymore than there is about conceptions. Indeed, because a concept is constructed by seeking to model and make sense of the multiple ways in which an idea is interpreted by those engaged in its practice, the statement of a concept may well change if there is a radical transformation in the extant conceptions of the essential attributes of the idea. What can be categorically said, however, is that a concept aims toward a universal formulation of the core elements of an idea, while fully recognizing the existence of multiple variations in the conceptions of the idea. Conceptions, on the other hand, present particularized and sometimes atavistic views of the concept. Given a human propensity for megalomania, it is hardly surprising that conceptions not infrequently are advanced as concepts.

Whatever view one takes of the concept of human rights (i.e., about its nature and scope), there seems little doubt that for most contemporary international lawyers, the UDHR least controversially articulates its current incarnation or conception. That conception is worth spelling out in some detail because, as I show in Part IV, it differs in some crucial ways from the portrayal of international human rights that gained ascendancy in the 1990s.

First, the obvious may be worth restating. The UDHR was a direct product of two human catastrophes of the 1930s and 1940s: the global economic depression and the even more brutal worldwide killing field that was World War II. Against this backdrop, the UDHR draws important distinctions between intermediate and ultimate objectives (which I here call "values") and the means for the realization of those values – namely, "rights." Importantly, the UDHR does not see human rights as ends in and of themselves. Rather, they are means – important, to be sure – through which states must strive to achieve core objectives. The structure of the UDHR importantly conveys the conception that its framers had of the relationship of community values, the relationships

difficult to frame with precision what that core might be. Thus we can speak of a chair or a cat and meaningfully convey an idea that differentiates the two, even though both have four legs. Or, for that matter, we can speak of a chair and a table and still convey meaningful distinctions among the two even though each comes in quite a variety of forms and both share quite a good deal of similarities. We likewise differentiate between a cat and a dog. The idea of the essence of the thing was a central concept in earlier Western philosophical discourses, notably those of classical Greece and of Thomas Aquinas.

among those values, the intersection of rights and values, and the function of the state in furthering both values and rights. Let us unpack these claims by taking a closer look at the structure and text of the UDHR.

The core values of the UDHR are stated in the Preamble. They are presented in the form of intermediate and of ultimate objectives. Thus, the first preamble asserts as a value the "recognition of the inherent dignity and of the equal and inalienable rights of all members of the human family"; but such *recognition* is called for not because of its intrinsic worth but because it is the "foundation of freedom, justice and peace in the world."[22] As jarring as it may appear to current advocates of human rights, neither dignity nor the equality of rights are "rights"; they are values to be striven for, and then only in the context of other core values – namely, those of "freedom," "justice," and "peace." Similar explanations can be offered with regard to "[the protection of] human rights [under] the rule of law,"[23] "the promotion of universal respect for and observance of human rights and fundamental freedoms,"[24] and indeed, the entire project of specifying the content of human rights. As one of the preambles straightforwardly explains, "faith in fundamental human rights, in the dignity and worth of the human person and in the equal rights of men and women," is to be prized as long as it promotes social progress and better standards of life.[25] Putting aside the obligation of the state to ensure security to all through the maintenance of peace and friendly relations among states – an obligation extensively covered under the Charter of the United Nations – the promotion of social progress, better standards of life, and freedom were the end objectives claimed by the framers of the Universal Declaration. The promotion of human rights was a tool in the service of these objectives.

Rather than being "promulgated" as legal rules, the declaration is *proclaimed* as "a common standard of *achievement for all peoples and all nations.*" Its provisions are directed to "every individual and every organ of society with the exhortation that keeping the declaration in mind, they "shall strive by teaching and education to promote respect for these rights and freedoms and by progressive measures, national and international, to secure their universal and effective recognition and observance." The declaration thus put forward a set of precepts that were deemed to be of universal acceptance. It went beyond that, however. It also elaborated, consistent with these general statements, some quite specific doctrines. These varied in their specificity. The

---

[22] Universal Declaration of Human Rights, Preamble, first paragraph, 10 December 1948, GA Res. 217A(III), UN Doc. A/810, at 71.
[23] Preamble, third paragraph of the Universal Declaration.
[24] Preamble, sixth paragraph of the Universal Declaration.
[25] Preamble, fifth paragraph of the Universal Declaration.

first article, for example, contains the very broad declaratory and indisputably hortatory statements that "[a]ll human beings are born free and equal in dignity and rights. They are endowed with reason and conscience and should act towards one another in a spirit of brotherhood." In contrast, Article 4 is a model of succinctness and, on the face of it, would seem to present a categorical prohibition against slavery and the slave trade, whereas Article 23 asserts the existence of an affirmative "right to work." However, none of these provisions, on their own terms, impose legally enforceable duties on nor create remediable rights for particular persons. Indeed, the phrasings of the declaration in fact leave unclear whom the specific subjects of the declaration might be: each individual natural person, any and all legal persons (natural and corporate), the state, subunits of the state, all of humanity, or all of the above and others?

In a real sense, the answer matters little, for the lack of precision as to the subjects of the declaration was not accidental. The document was intended as a political statement of the philosophical underpinnings of international human rights, not a legal promulgation of those rights. The legal work was to be done through other instruments that were substantially more specific in the mandates that they issued and the corrective action to be taken for failure to comply with those mandates. Thus, the International Covenant on Civil and Political Rights, like the Covenant on Economic, Social and Cultural Rights, makes plain that the obligations spelled out in their provisions are undertaken by the state, that the beneficiaries are persons within the jurisdiction of the state, and that the state must periodically submit compliance reports to an impartial body. In certain instances, other signatories may file complaints of noncompliance against a state that is in violation of its duties, and in some instances, notably the Convention against Torture, a state is explicitly required to provide judicial or administrative means through which individuals alleging violation of specified legal rights can seek vindication and remedy for those violations.

Framing the declaration as a set of precepts rather than rules did not of course mean that its proponents were opposed to or thought little of the use of enforceable legal rules in the international human rights arena – on the contrary. Contemporaneous with the proclamation of the declaration, the United Nations system engaged in a significant amount of related international lawmaking. There were, for example, the adoption of the four Geneva Conventions that were intended to formally humanize the conduct of warfare, the outlawing of genocide, and the regulation of the obligation of states in the grant of asylum to refugees. As with the declaration, World War II provided the catalyst for these actions. Unlike the declaration, these became formal rules rather than mere assertions of principles. These different choices were not inadvertent nor uninformed. The framers of the declaration were interested in the legal formulation and implementation of the principles embodied in the declaration, but they also recognized that the legal regulation of the diverse principles articulated in the declaration required extended discussion, negotiation, trade-offs, compromises, and textual specificity. These proponents accepted a basic reality of lawmaking: that legal rules necessarily are formulated against a backdrop of doctrines that are anything but categorical or "universal." Indeed, it took almost two decades for the first of the legal formulations to be agreed to, and the process remains incomplete. The International Covenant on Civil and Political Rights; the Covenant on Economic, Cultural and Social Rights; and the conventions against torture, on the elimination of all forms of racial discrimination, of discrimination against women and "persons with disability," and on the "rights of the child," unlike the UDHR, indisputably are legal statements of rights and obligations. The texts of the rules provide reasonably specific notice about the identity of their subjects and objects, the scope of the announced rights and duties, grounds for exceptions from the rule, compliance and enforcement mechanisms, remedies for violations of the rule, and centrally, the means through which one becomes subject to the rules.

All of these facts are well known. Why are they worth rehearsing? Primarily because in the wake of the *Filartiga* decision, the dominant narrative about the declaration in particular, and international human rights, generally, took on a revisionist cast that presented human rights as a set of categorical universalist rules that were to be enforced through coercive measures. However, because this recasting violated the original understandings, it has had significant consequences both for the idea and reality of international legal ordering, and particularly for those members of the system who operate at or close to its margins. Before exploring the nature and costs of those consequences in Part IV, I want to take up, however briefly, an exploration of the idea of the modern state and its place in the formulation and development of international human rights concepts.

III. LIBERALISM, HUMAN RIGHTS, AND THE STATE

If the UDHR was unfocused as to the identity of the recipients of its mandates, the covenants and conventions adopted pursuant to its visions made clear that the state (including persons acting for it) is the primary – if not exclusive – legal obligor. Yet one of the paradoxes of our cosmopolitan "age of rights" has been to undermine the legitimacy of the state as the source of rights.[26] This paradox may be unavoidable in an environment characterized by misconceptions of the ideas of rights and of the state, but when properly understood, the two concepts can and should form a harmonious whole in delivering that most basic of human needs: the security of the person in collaborative association with others. Grasping the idea of the state is thus helpful both to explain where contemporary cosmopolitan notions of human rights have gone off the rail and to provide justification for a vision of an associational relationship among persons that is not antagonistic to the mediating function of the state.

Preliminarily, it should be acknowledged that the hostility of international human rights scholars in the 1990s, although in rhetoric directed generally at the state (and more particularly its core attribute of "sovereignty"), was in reality an attack on a particular group of states: the non-Western, nonliberal, nondemocratic (i.e., the so-called illiberal or rogue) states. However, because the rhetoric drove the discourse while the reality constrained the prescriptive choices that were advanced, human rights proponents were faced with either having to accept a misdiagnosis of the problem or with having to provide inconsistent rationales for reconciling the diagnosis with their prescribed cures. The alternative, forthrightly acknowledging the "problem of the state," was in fact the problem of the "illiberal" (read as "Third World") state flouted yet another norm of the human rights movement – namely, that of "equality."[27] Cosmopolitanism offered the easy (if unsatisfactory) way out.[28] However, because the state qua state has been portrayed as the problem, it is first worth investigating in its generality as a philosophical, legal, and practical proposition.

The ubiquity of the modern state is indisputable. Its presence in the life of the person can be expressed along three dimensions: as the definer and regulator of persons and interactions within its sphere of competence or jurisdiction; as the provider of benefits to such persons; and as an anchor for emotional or quasi-spiritual attachments. Although it may share each of these attributes with at least one other contemporary social, cultural, or economic institution (such as the family, religion, the corporation, and a host of civic-minded benevolent associations), it is unique in the comprehensiveness, effectiveness, and the finality with which it claims and exercises prima facie authority over all three, and it does so through politics, or, more accurately, the regulation

---

[26] For a critical evaluation of this paradox, see Louis Henkin, "That 'S' Word: Sovereignty, and Globalization, and Human Rights, Et Cetera" (1999) 68 *Fordham Law Review* 1–14.

[27] Some commentators, recognizing the difficulty, either chose to laugh it off by invoking the familiar cliché that "hypocrisy is the homage that vice pays to virtue" or by asserting that equality, no less than dignity, is the right of the individual, not that of the state.

[28] I develop and support this claim in Part IV.

of communal life through coercion – explicit or internalized. The individual more or less takes the legitimacy of that regulation as a given, quibbling only as to its scope in particular cases. In exchange for that unquestioning loyalty, the state claims to confer a wide range of benefits, ranging from the provision of protection of "property rights" to the safeguarding of personal and national security to its citizens, and the conferring of discrete benefits under the programs of the "welfare state." The existence of political communities serving many of the functions of the state have of course been around for millennia, dating at least as far back in recorded history to the Sumerian civilization of Babylonia. What makes the modern state distinctive is that it was the product of a quite conscious rejection and explicit attempts at rebalancing of the three features of the regulation of political association just outlined.

By the beginning of the seventeenth century, influential European thinkers no longer found sustainable the fiction that the authority of the ruler flowed from his divine relationship with an omniscient and ever-living deity. These thinkers tried articulating alternative grounds of legitimacy of persons to the state and for regulating the conduct of persons within the state. In the process, they created alternative models or fictions, in which concepts of "natural rights" and of "legal positivism" came to be dominant.[29] By the end of the eighteenth century, views were beginning to coalesce around what we now call "liberalism." The core of the thought was and remains that the legitimacy of the relationship of persons to the state and toward each other is grounded in the existence of reciprocal or contractual arrangements between the conferring of benefits and the surrendering of rights. Although thinkers differed significantly about the source of the rights to be surrendered or the scope of the benefits to be conferred, the idea that the individual had a say in which or how many rights to give up, and which benefits were to be purchased with those rights was indisputably a revolutionary concept.

What is noteworthy for our purposes here is that ideas natural rights and of positivism, the state and law, and liberalism (that is, the philosophical underpinnings and justifications of the modern state) were direct products of the European experience.[30] Yet they were not and could not be confined to

---

[29] The most eloquent statement of the relationship between natural rights and positivism is Thomas Hobbes's *Leviathan*. Thomas Hobbes, *Leviathan* (London: Guernsey Press Co., 1987) (1651). See in particular Chapter 14, in which he explains how the sovereign authority of the state inexorably flows from the interplay of the human faculty for reason, the desire for peace, and the innate or natural right of the person to engage in the defense of the self.

[30] Hobbes's work again is illustrative. His writings, as Quentin Skinner has amply demonstrated, had their roots in the experiences of the English Civil War. Quentin Skinner, *Reason and Rhetoric in the Philosophy of Hobbes* (Cambridge: Cambridge University Press, 1996). However, this parochial underpinning of cosmopolitan thought is also found in the writings of well-known

Europe. For as Europe became the dominant actor on the world stage in the nineteenth and twentieth centuries, it carried and exported these ideas in its commercial, military, and political dealings with other societies. The spread of these products of the "European Enlightenment" took varied forms – some of it peaceful, much of it extremely coercive. Whether through commerce or colonialism, religious proselytization, or benevolent educational or science missions, Europe both persuaded and coerced other societies into sharing its particularistic view of the relationship of the person to the state that grew out of and was molded by the European experience. The modern international system, clearly the offspring of liberalism and of European power, thus absorbed a particular logic of legitimacy that however universal it might now seem to be, grew out of a particular set of experiences. That was the logic proclaimed and endorsed in the UDHR and which has informed the covenants, conventions, and treaties that have been adopted in its wake. But these arrangements are themselves part of the broader scheme for international order.

Although liberalism spoke to relationships within the state, the international legal order initially overlooked that this was a quite different setting from relations among – rather than within – societies. Until the 1990s, the general view was that the international system, like the individual, more or less took the legitimacy of the state as it found it. The doctrine, which was (and arguably remains) a mainstay of the United Nations Charter, long preceded the twentieth century. In effect, the stricture against the international system or its individual members "interfering" in the political independence of any other member of the system gave effect to the doctrine of sovereignty that had been developed by European societies as a means of constraining the religious wars that had bedeviled the continent for centuries. This idea of "sovereignty" sought to foster "peaceful coexistence" through a principle of "mutual independence."

Despite much discussion in international law as to the constitution of a state (i.e., what makes a state a state), the standards for the acceptance of the existence of a state were always quantitatively derived, thereby endowing the concept with an aura of objectivity. This was so even with regard to the most subjective of the standards identified in the Montevideo Convention on the Rights and Duties of States – namely, those of "effective" control over a population and the "capacity" to engage effectively in relations with other

---

international lawyers such as Hugo Grotius and Samuel von Pufendorf. This recognition, however, does not necessarily undercut the profundity or generality of their thoughts, but it does argue against the implicit claim in the idea of their universality – that is, as being somehow divinely ordained or immutable.

states.[31] One might have supposed that in view of the ethnonationalist ground-ings of both the Great Depression and World War II, the post–World War II international arrangements would have sought to standardize and interna-tionalize the criteria for state formation and recognition. Far from such an approach, the United Nations Charter unequivocally confirmed and indeed reinforced the particularistic conception of the principle of "self-determination" by which a population or people got to determine for them-selves free from outside influences whether to create a state, and if so the nature, institutions, and identity of the state. Furthermore, members of the United Nations – and indeed the United Nations itself – were prohibited, with one exception, from interfering in the internal affairs of member states.[32] When one remembers that in 1945 the subjugation of peoples of non-European ancestry to colonial domination was the rule rather than exception, and that over the next thirty years, the principle of self-determination and the prohibi-tions against intervention in the internal affairs of a state formed the backbone of the decolonization process, the radical importance of the principle and the prohibition become manifest.

The history of international law in the thirty years following the UDHR was that of the assertion of state sovereignty over all else.[33] Buttressed by prin-ciples of self-determination and territorial inviolability, the shield of political independence became a sword by which nation-states, especially the emerg-ing decolonized states of Africa and Asia, sought not only to gain their places within the international order but to bludgeon that order into according them respect, deserved or otherwise. A generation after San Francisco, however, and for a variety of reasons, the West European and North American states began to rebel against the extant order, and claims of human rights provided one anchor for that rebellion.

---

[31] Montevideo Convention on the Rights and Duties of States, Montevideo, December 26, 1933, (1936) 49 Stat 3097. E.g., R. R. Baxter, "Multilateral Treaties as Evidence of Customary International Law" (1968) 41 *British Yearbook of International Law* 275–300 at 300 ("[T]he four elements of statehood listed in the Montevideo Convention on the Rights and Duties of States have become a standard expression of the definition of a State." [footnote omitted]); Thomas D. Grant, "Defining Statehood: The Montevideo Convention and Its Discontents" (1999) 37 *Columbia Journal of Transnational Law* 403–57.

[32] That one exception was when the Security Council determined that such action was necessary to maintain "international peace and security" or to remove a threat to the maintenance of such security. UN Charter Articles 2(7), 39–51.

[33] For an unusually thorough and thoughtful probing of the conscientiousness with which non-Western actors on the international scene wrestled and sought to reconcile the conflicting demands of national independence and international human rights, see Roland Burke, *Decol-onization and the Evolution of International Human Rights* (Philadelphia: University of Penn-sylvania Press, 2010).

The post–San Francisco international order was characterized by two phenomena, neither of which had been fully anticipated, let alone planned for under the United Nations Charter, and both challenged the "universality" of the aspirations articulated in the UDHR. First, at the core of the charter was the idea of "collective security." This was not a new concept, but was in fact carried over from the charter's predecessor, the Covenant of the League of Nations. The charter's innovation was to give teeth to the enforcement of the concept by creating the Security Council, the decisions of which, once it had determined that there had occurred a breach of collective security (or the threat of such a breach), became binding on all members of the system.[34] This reinforced regime of collective security was, however, premised on continuing cooperation among the major powers that had triumphed in World War II. These "permanent members" of the Security Council each had the power by use of a "veto" to prevent action by the council, even if every other state believed such action to be necessary.[35] Within four years of the adoption of the charter, however, the international system had effectively been reconstituted by the creation of two permanent blocs of states that invariably pitted the preferences of permanent members – typically the United States and the Soviet Union – against each other. The idea of "collective security" enforced through the cooperation of the permanent members of the Security Council was thus effectively neutered.

The second unanticipated post-charter event that effectively reconstituted the international order was the rapidity and breadth of the decolonization process. The charter, borrowing from the League of Nations, recognized and indeed privileged the principle of self-determination. At its creation, however, no one anticipated the rapidity of the decolonization process that was to sweep through the non-European world. The charter's endorsement of high-minded paternalism in the form of provisions on international "trusteeships" and the specific creation of an international Trusteeship Council, alongside its silence on the merits of colonial governance, were affirmations of the expected deliberateness with which subjugated Asian and African societies were to be weaned from colonial tutelage.[36] However, the subjugated peoples proved to be otherwise disposed. Beginning with the independence of Indonesia from the Netherlands, Asian and African societies took matters into their own hands and obtained political independence in remarkably quick succession. Events

---

[34] Articles 25 and 39 of the UN Charter. Furthermore, in pursuance of such Collective Security, the charter carved out the one exception to the prohibition against interference in the domestic affairs of member states. Article 2(7) of the UN Charter.
[35] Article 26 of the UN Charter.   [36] Articles 75–91 of the UN Charter.

that had been anticipated to occur over many generations were more or less concluded within a decade.

The decolonization process – and more particularly, the speed with which it occurred – had profound consequences for the international order and for the legal framework of international human rights. Notably, the international system that had become accustomed to functioning as a "gentleman's club" of "statesmen," "diplomats," and "plenipotentiaries" under European cultural conventions became subjected to the brash rhetoric of politicians reared in and answerable to persons of a different sociocultural milieu. These politicians of the "Third World," rather than quietly going along with the vision of the international system as an evenhanded umpire that, subject to the claims of "collective security" shielded "domestic policy" from international scrutiny, argued for the recognition of distinctions among such policies. For these politicians, a clear hierarchy of views existed in international law that the system could not disregard in the name of the evenhanded application of established doctrine, whatever its pedigree.

At the apex of the international legal order envisioned by these newcomers was the principle of the self-determination of peoples – a collective human right – that could not be subordinated to any other right or group of rights. It was this principle that grounded and legitimized their participation in international politics, and it was this principle of equal recognition and participation that the ancient doctrine of sovereignty was supposed to guarantee.[37]

Next, and in a related vein, the collective human rights of peoples rendered illegal those practices such as racial discrimination and apartheid that denied equal treatment to whole population groups because of their assigned status in society. Here, the doctrine of sovereignty could no more function as a shield than it could within the sphere of the international recognition of

---

[37] To the extent that human rights is about dignity (see *supra* note 22), it is not uncommon for its proponents to denigrate the notion that state sovereignty can be defended in terms of dignity. The argument seems to be that the attribute of dignity can be possessed only by human beings (or at least sentient beings), and not by corporate entities or conceptual abstractions. I have yet to find any satisfactory explanation of why the idea of dignity has to be so limited. As a social construct, it is unclear why its creators cannot bestow it as readily on inanimate conceptions as on biological organisms. In any event, history is replete with instances in which human beings have given up their lives in defense of the abstraction that is the state, and there are enough instances in which they have endowed the state with such similar attributes as honor, pride, and even courage, that the burden surely ought to be on those who claim that states cannot possess dignity. Compare *Alden v. Maine*, 527 US 706 (1999) (Kennedy, J.) ("[States] are not relegated to the role of mere provinces or political corporations, but retain the dignity, though not the full authority, of sovereignty.").

self-determination. Rather, the concept of collective human rights operated as a sword with which international society could compel equal justice for the downtrodden in colonial and apartheid societies.

A similar orientation to rights as expressive of the collective claims and interests of a subordinated group explains the third stance of the Third World during the heady era of decolonization. Their politicians, diplomats, and international lawyers contended that integral to the idea of statehood was the exercise of "permanent sovereignty" over the natural resources of the society. This meant that governments – certainly colonial and precolonial adminis- trators – lacked the authority permanently to alienate, through concessions, contracts, and the like, the "national patrimony" of the state. Nor could con- tractual provisions that purported to grant special rights to foreign investors in the natural resources of a society bind a people and their rulers; for the rights of the people when exercising sovereignty over their natural resources (through their leaders, of course) trumped any contractual or property claim by those investors in the purportedly transferred communal interests. A cen- tral debate within this conception of rights thus focused on the identity of the creator and distributor of the rights in question: the domestic law of the host state, the law (if any) stipulated in the concession or contract, or "international law." That Third World international lawyers insisted that natural resource investment agreements be subject to the domestic law of the host country was not simply a matter of power politics, but a reflection of a significant jurispru- dential concept – namely, that rights are creatures of the social institutions against whom they are asserted, a principle that is often overlooked in the current cosmopolitan debate about the universality of rights.

For the new statesmen (and, occasionally, stateswomen) of the nascent "Third World," then, human rights was as much (perhaps even more so) about the dignity of the political community as it was about the treatment of the individual. In their conceptions of international human rights, they were aided and abetted by the division within the international system. It is here that the unanticipated rapidity with which decolonization occurred becomes decisive in shaping international law's conception and validation of international human rights. Members of the socialist camp who subscribed to an ethic that privileged collective over individual interests naturally enough agreed with the collectivized interpretation of human rights. The elite and politicians of the so-called First, capitalist, or industrialized World were simply caught unawares. This was a consequence of several factors. In the first place, like any schoolmaster, the West did not expect that its Third World pupils would so readily abandon the teachings that had been drummed into them for at least two generations.[38] Furthermore, because many of the students continued to mouth the platitudes, the West was even slower in accepting the reality that practices were in fact different. Thus, the human rights and humanitarian disasters of the "partition" of India and those of the "crisis" in the Congo went essentially unacknowledged within the international system. It took the Indonesian conflict of 1965–1966 and the Nigerian–Biafran civil war of 1967–1970 to make unavoidably clear that the student after all may have a quite different set of values and considerations than did the schoolmaster.

Second, the West's slowness in accepting (if not recognizing) the deviations of their former students was in no small part a reflection of the fact that this teacher did not often practice what it preached. In its suppression of colonial dissidents, whether in Malaya, Kenya, or Algeria (to give the most notorious and well-documented examples), the West's policy makers and practitioners either actively employed or countenanced means that flouted the letter and spirit of the UDHR and its related covenants. Nor was the United States an exception. Internally, widespread policies of racial segregation and, externally, the means sometimes resorted to in the waging of the wars in Southeast Asia were condemnable under the UDHR. Although fear of being called to the carpet for hypocrisy or double standard rarely has functioned as an effective deterrent, it can sometimes blind one to the recognition of a reality, or at least its articulation. It was not until the major powers of the West had unequivocally extricated themselves from the last of these colonial wars – Vietnam in 1974[39] – that Western scholars could unequivocally promote their particularized vision of human rights, as claims of individuals against their own governments.

iv. NEOLIBERALISM, HUMAN RIGHTS, AND THE PROBLEM OF THE "PARIAH STATE"

Notwithstanding the UDHR and the several covenants and treaties drafted under its inspiration and influence, international human rights were at best a secondary concern for international society in the thirty years preceding the publication of Professor Henkin's essay on the intersections of American

---

[38] The reasons for the Third World's departure from these teachings are beyond the scope of this chapter, although many are hinted at in the text that follows. For those interested in my own take on some of those reasons (at least in the African context), see Maxwell O. Chibundu, "Law in Development: On Tapping, Gourding and Serving Palm-Wine" (1997) 29 *Case Western Reserve Journal of International Law* 167–261.

[39] That Americans may prefer to see the Vietnam War in benevolent terms as an anti-Communist crusade, and that, not infrequently, decolonization was followed by internecine conflict among the decolonized, do not detract from the validity of the claims advanced in the text.

Constitutional and international human rights laws.[40] Nonetheless, intimations of change were already present. In 1975, the two dominant post–World War II military alliances – the North Atlantic Treaty Organization (NATO) and the Warsaw Pact – although acting outside of the specific framework of the United Nations but under what fairly can be characterized as a "collective security" arrangement within the framework of the Organization for Security and Cooperation in Europe (OSCE), adopted provisions that recognized as a valid concern of signatories the regulation by a signatory of the ability of that signatory's citizens to depart voluntarily from the territory of the signatory.[41] The obvious purpose was to clarify (if not to create) an international legal basis for the expressions of concern by NATO members regarding the Jewish emigration policies of the USSR. That the USSR accepted international oversight of the freedom of travel by its citizens undermined the previously widespread view that how governments disposed of the claim of their citizens for free movement in and out of the country were solely matters of domestic law. The OSCE agreement gave added weight and legitimacy to domestic constituencies within the United States that argued that the Soviet Union's treatment of its Jewish citizens was both a violation of international human rights law, and a matter of international, not merely domestic concern.

In the ensuing incorporation in U.S. trade law of the "Jackson-Vanik" Amendment, which sought to punish countries deemed by the United States to be in violation of their international law obligations by denying them access to the U.S. market,[42] we encounter a legislative precursor to an attitude and approach that was to characterize the human rights movement in the 1980s and 1990s. Domestic interest groups, using their access to the institutions of domestic power, portrayed and converted their concerns into those of international society at large and employed domestic coercive forces and measures to fill in the notorious lacuna of enforcement in international law. The attitude first required the identification of a pariah enemy whose conduct clearly fell well outside of the boundaries of civilized humanity. The alleged wrong was thus framed not as an accidental departure from the norm, but as a systematic dehumanization of the victim that called for the assertion of "universal

---

[40] See Part I, p. 1.
[41] Final Act of the Conference on Security and Co-operation in Europe, Helsinki, 1 August 1975, (1975) 14 ILM 1292.
[42] Trade Act of 1974, Pub. L. No. 93–618, title IV, § 402, 88 Stat. 1978, 2056 (1975), codified at 19 USC § 2432 (2006); Robert H. Brumley, "Jackson-Vanik: Hard Facts, Bad Law?" (1990) 8 *Boston University International Law Journal* 363–71; Robert M. Dow, "Linking Trade Policy to Free Emigration: The Jackson-Vanik Amendment" (1991) 4 *Harvard Human Rights Journal* 128–38.

jurisdiction" over the wrongdoer. Domestic tribunals and institutions thus validated their capacity to take coercive measures in the name of international law by pointing to the shared interest of humanity in calling a pariah to account. As the *Filartiga* court so memorably framed the interaction of parochial rules and cosmopolitan visions: "[o]ur holding today, giving effect to a jurisdictional provision enacted by our First Congress, is a small but important step in the fulfillment of the ageless dream to free all people from brutal violence."[43]

Where the U.S. Congress, courts, and academics blazed the path, others eagerly followed. The decision of a Spanish magistrate to request that the United Kingdom extradite the former Chilean president, Augusto Pinochet, for his alleged responsibility in the death of Spaniards during his reign of terror in Chile precipitated a series of decisions in the English courts that effectively mainstreamed and popularized the vision of the promotion of international human rights as essentially one of coercive judicial intervention. Western judicial tribunals (fortified by the efforts of nongovernmental organizations, lawyers, journalists, and human rights activists) took on the mantle of global knights in shining armor ready, able, and willing to slay the dragons of Third World dictatorships who violate the human rights of their citizens and foreign sojourners. These judges and magistrates thus provided for international human rights law the missing ingredient of general public international law: an authoritative interpretive body that could enforce its decisions through established coercive channels.

The horrors of the atrocities of the conflicts in the Balkans and Rwanda, the seeming clarity with which the pariahs of these conflicts could be identified, the claimed moral imperative of powerful Western governments appearing to be "doing something," the need for that "something" to be retributive to address the problem of "impunity," and the ever-present reminder that past horrors occurred because good persons stood silently by all conjoined to facilitate the transformation of parochial interest-driven conceptions of human rights into seemingly unassailable altruistic universal undertakings. The ease of these transformations in substantial part has been aided and shaped by the widespread practice of rape in these conflicts. Whatever may have been the practice in the past, the coming of age of women's rights movements in the post-1960s era – and more particularly, the role that women now play in framing and shaping international legal and political discourse – has been decisively instrumental in defining the contours of the discourse – and more particularly in transforming it from an obviously parochial

43 *Filartiga*, 630 F 2d at 890.

interest-group-driven conversation into one of ostensibly cosmopolitan concern.[44]

Power – specifically, who possesses it – has not surprisingly been instrumental in the construction of the new order. The explicit discussion of power features little if any in human rights discourse. Among moral philosophers this omission is perhaps understandable. The discipline, after all, rests on abstractions. Considering the role played by power poses a significant hurdle for the philosophical project, and hence it is often preferable to elide the issue. Lawyers – even academic ones with a jurisprudential bent – have no similar justification. This is especially true of international lawyers, because power is at the heart of international affairs. To be sure, at the margins, there may be some occasional difficulty in identifying what constitutes "power," especially of the so-called soft variety. Some may dispute whether mass media distribution networks that engage in cultural propaganda possess and use power. In the human rights arena, however, the use of power has gone well beyond such "soft" sources. Coercive judicial decisions, economic sanctions, and even military force are now routinely applied as elements of the human rights agenda, and surely no one can seriously dispute that these are core elements of power. Understanding such resort to power in the advocacy of human rights is crucial both to explain the turn it took during the neoliberal "age of rights" and to help explain its likely turn in the decade and more ahead.

The most obvious demonstration of the reorientation of the distribution of power within the international order and the uses to which it would be put in the 1990s was the collapse of the Soviet Union. That collapse was seen as unequivocally proving the superiority of Western institutions and beliefs. "Democracy," "the market," "the rule of law," and of course "human rights" were presented as what made the West different and successful, where the Communists and their Third World acolytes had failed. Although the value of the first two seemed self-evident (as judged by the readiness with which they were embraced in rhetoric if not actual practice), acceptance of the last two demanded more of a political push from their intellectual backers. This may have been due in part to the obvious immediate material returns acceptance of the first two entailed, as contrasted with the abstractions, complex, and farther

---

[44] Compare *Kadic v. Karadžić*, 70 F 3d 232 at 236 (2nd Cir. 1995) (holding that the Bosnian leader "may be found liable for genocide, war crimes, and crimes against humanity," including rape and forced prostitution, in a United States federal court). Claims of rape as a weapon of war and of the use of child soldiers now constitute the stereotypical grounds for invoking international human rights as former (and, increasingly, reigning) Third World dictators or rulers are made to account for human rights violations in such fora as the International Criminal Court and so-called mixed tribunals (such as those for Sierra Leone, Cambodia, and Lebanon) that are funded, administered, and, in significant part, staffed by international personnel.

off returns promised by the institutionalization of the latter two concepts. Or it may be that the gains from the rule of law and human rights could be realized only at the expense of those already in power, or the demotion if not outright overthrow of much that had become culturally accepted within the "emerging" or "transitional" societies, the political power structures of which were put into play. In any event, proponents of universal human rights saw the use of raw power as a helpful tool in propagating their conceptions more broadly.

With the removal of the threat of a Soviet veto, the Security Council proved a good deal more willing to legitimate the use of coercive power by international society in the enforcement of human rights. The Security Council either created outright or lent its support to the creation of international tribunals that were charged with sitting in judgment over alleged human rights violators. It employed its Chapter VII powers in attempts to coerce compliance with measures deemed to be helpful in limiting potential violations. The council worked in tandem with interest groups predominantly in the West to identify and mark the violators as pariahs and to determine, calibrate, and apply the requisite economic sanctions or political or military force that would coerce obedience from pariah states and their rulers.

Acting more and more as an administrative and/or adjudicatory body (rather than a legislative or executive organ of the United Nations), the Security Council focused not simply on reining in wrongdoing by states, but on punishing individuals. For perhaps the first time in the administration of international society, a system of "justice" was created that was driven explicitly to provide an unmediated place for private interest groups within the corridors of political power in the international system. These groups were astute in the robust use of an increasingly internationalized and instantaneous media both in the communication of their preferences (which, however particularistic, were invariably presented in universalist language) and in pressuring politicians into action. However, this vision of a unified system of justice and the seemingly global coalition that underpinned it are now fraying. To understand the reasons for the brevity of the epoch is to appreciate the promise and perils of neoliberal cosmopolitanism. I explore those perils and promises in the next section, but before doing so, it is helpful to reflect on an alternative path that was readily available to the wielders of international power but only marginally explored.

International human rights scholarship may be divided between those who see the various "rights" enumerated in the UDHR as existing on a single plane (the "Flat Rights" School) and those who contend that some rights are more equal than others (the "Hierarchical Rights" School). For the latter group, the "civil" and "political" rights found in the International Covenant on Civil and Political rights are deemed fundamental and are expressive of the core of human rights, whereas those contained in the International Covenant on Economic, Social and Cultural Rights constitute second order or "second generation" rights. Although these latter rights should be respected, the Hierarchical Rights School sees them as being less consequential in the constitution of a liberal society. Civil and political rights are said to be fundamental because they privilege the rights of the individual as a citizen and person against government. Governmental power is thereby checked and made answerable to control by the political community. This is of course a restatement of the contractarian view of European Enlightenment liberalism. In contrast, the "second-generation" rights, by generally imposing affirmative welfare obligations on the state, potentially empower the government by permitting it to engage in the social redistribution of collective goods. The injurious consequences of such redistribution are best illustrated by the difficulties of judicially enforcing these second-generation rights. Ascertaining the appropriate level of redistribution would result in the devolving of political decisions to the judicial branch of government, a grant of power to an unaccountable institution that perversely weakens its legitimacy and ultimately its authority to effectively enforce those civil and political rights that properly fall within its preferred province. To the Flat Rights School's argument that the effective exercise of civil and political rights may require that the beneficiaries be properly fed, clothed, and sheltered (a claim derisively referred to as "the full-belly thesis"), Hierarchical Rights proponents respond that the argument lacks empirical or historical support.[45]

Flat Rights proponents seemed to have gained a measure of legitimation when, in one of the seminal events of the 1990s, postapartheid South Africa appeared to treat "economic and social rights" as being on the same plain with "civil and political rights." Yet even the most sympathetic observers of the South African Constitutional Court's attempts to flesh out and give effect to the contents of the so-called economic rights – notably health, housing, work, and social security – will accept that its efforts have been substantially less satisfying than had been hoped for and certainly trail those in other areas such as religious and associational rights.[46] One can of course attempt to explain these

---

[45] Compare Jeanne M. Woods, "Justiciable Social Rights as a Critique of the Liberal Paradigm" (2003) 38 *Texas International Law Journal* 763–93 (criticizing the Hierarchical Rights School while defending what I have termed the "Flat Rights" School approach).

[46] E.g., Alfred Cockrell, "Rainbow Jurisprudence" (1996) 12 *South African Journal on Human Rights* 1–38; Mark S. Kende, "The Fifth Anniversary of the South-African Constitutional Court: In Defense of Judicial Pragmatism" (2002) 26 *Vermont Law Review* 753–67.

shortcomings by pointing to the particulars of South African society, but such explanations will no more likely be conclusive than those that are grounded in the nature of the judicial process. It may be that those who gathered in Paris to frame the UDHR, and their successors who sought to provide legal texts for those rights, understood quite well the complexities and limitations of the process when they opted to leave the assurance of compliance and of enforcement to national means, self-reporting, and peer review. In deploying coercive power in the 1990s to subvert that regime, proponents of international human rights may have shown the poverty of their understanding of the nature of human rights.

v. THE AGE OF RIGHTS IN THE AGE OF TERROR

In 1998, plenipotentiaries of member states of the United Nations Organization meeting in Rome formalized a compact that created an International Criminal Court (ICC). For the first time, the international system established a permanent tribunal for the prosecution, trial, and punishment of individuals accused of engaging in systematic violations of human rights and humanitarian laws. Alongside the creation of ad hoc criminal tribunals for the former Yugoslavia and for Rwanda, and of so-called hybrid tribunals for other trouble spots (notably Sierra Leone and Cambodia), the ICC potentially promised the actualization of the fervently sought goal of international human right activists: there should be no "impunity" for violations of human rights.

We have now lived through two decades of the coercive enforcement of international human rights. We need therefore no longer predominantly dwell on the theoretical virtues of its academic and philosophical production, but must consider the practical and distributive consequences of the enforcement processes as well. This examination is particularly apt because claims of international human rights violations, however much they may have been centered in the so-called Third World during the last quarter of the twentieth century, is scarcely now their exclusive preserve.

When in 1999, members of NATO waged an air campaign against Serbia (ostensibly to prevent a repeat in Kosovo of "ethnic cleansing" that Serbs are said to have undertaken previously in Bosnia-Herzegovina), we arrive at the full flowering of the coercively interventionist mode of cosmopolitan human rights. A so-called right to protect gained widespread support, subsequently enshrined as international policy by member states of the United Nations.[47]

---

[47] United Nations Millennium Declaration, September 8, 2000, GA Res. 55/2, UN Doc. A/RES/55/2. Spencer Zifcak, *United Nations Reform: Heading North or South?* (New York: Routledge, 2009), pp. 105–27.

That policy could be invoked to legitimize "humanitarian interventions" (Articles 2(4) and 2(7) of the United Nations charter notwithstanding) in such fratricidal conflicts as those of the Democratic Republic of the Congo, Liberia, Sierra Leone, Northern Uganda, and Darfur, Sudan. In applying this policy to safeguard primarily the rights of Muslims and of Black Africans, a liberal international system dominated by Christian Europe and America demonstrated the high-mindedness, selfless altruism, and cosmopolitanism of the international human rights order. That most of the victims being protected were helpless women and children strengthened the argument. There simply was no basis for equating such systematic brutalities with the past genteel debates over cultural or moral relativism. The modern human rights violator, like the slave trade of old, was, in the memorable phrase of the Second Circuit, "*hostis humani generis,* an enemy of all mankind."[48]

Yet how selflessly "cosmopolitan" are these arguments? Have we finally arrived at the "age of [international human] rights?" Two contemporary examples of the intersection of cosmopolitan human rights and the particularities of the propagating and receiving societies suggest countervailing realities and point to the costs and consequences for human rights of the power play that has driven the human rights agenda in recent years. Before looking at them, a noteworthy but frequently overlooked paradox deserves explicit unveiling.

Within international human rights circles a good deal of genuine (if ultimately confused) disagreement centers on a purported distinction between rights as exclusively the claim of the individual and some rights as the prerogative of groups.[49] Within the first group, there are those who argue for a hierarchical ordering of rights: "first-" and "second-" generation rights. In this framework, the distinction between rights that inhere in the "individual" qua individual, and those that belong to the person because of his or her group classification or "identity" clinches the argument for privileging "political" over "social" and "economic" rights.[50] Political rights are said to inhere in the individual and are thus adjudicatorily enforceable. Economic rights, on

---

[48] *Filartiga,* 630 F 2d at 890.
[49] Professor Henkin, for example, bluntly asserts that "[h]uman rights are rights of individuals in society." Henkin, *Age of Rights,* p. 2. On the other hand, proponents of "rights of indigenous peoples," or of "right to development," posit such rights as those of a group rather than of individuals. Yet it is difficult to see how, as a concrete matter, any right – even those that supposedly belong to groups – can be experienced other than through individuals, or how individual rights can exist in the abstract other than as claims that exist by virtue of the individual's membership within a particular community or polity.
[50] There is a sense in which this distinction is utterly nonsensical, even for proponents of the hierarchy of rights. Most if not all political rights, such as those relating to freedoms of association, expression, and religious worship, derive their value for the individual precisely in her or his distinctive classification as a member of a national polity or of a religious sect.

the other hand, inherently are distributive in character and often are determined by reference to group alignments, which make them, as a minimum, extremely controversial to enforce. In either case, the focus of the argument is on the claimant or beneficiary of the right.

In looking to the ICC and the Security Council to enforce international human rights and international humanitarian laws, this comfortable dichotomy breaks down. In these proceedings, there is in fact a substantial (if unacknowledged) shift of attention from the individualized focus on the assertion of rights toward a group orientation on the definition and enforcement of those rights. Although the rights in play ostensibly remain those of the individual, it is in fact the individual violator rather than the individual beneficiary of rights that attracts attention. Because the justification for international intervention is invariably framed in terms of the systematic and massive character of the violations and consequent injuries to the victims, the focus in fact becomes on remedying alleged violations of group rights. Here, it is the institutional actors – the despotic violator and the international enforcer that command attention. The victim and the society in which he or she is victimized become pawns in the power play. Can such a shift of focus in the supposed equalizing role of human rights laws be explained in anything but political terms? As anything but a continuation of the political power game? Surely, as an often-repeated African proverb says, in this conflict among elephants, it is the grass that suffers. Yet the long-term consequences of the shift have barely registered in the discourse. Let us see what they might be by contrasting the place of human rights norms in the discussion and evaluation of two contemporary conflicts that indisputably implicate systemic issues of international human rights violations and enforcement.

As the first decade of the twenty-first century drew to its close, two examples of the construction of international human rights claims provided vivid demonstrations of the continuing interplays between parochial interests in and interpretations of those rights on the one hand, and their asserted cosmopolitan reach and relevance on the other. Those examples are to be found in the debates over the claimed "genocide" in the Darfur region of western sudan and the consistency with international human rights law of the means employed by the United States and other "democracies" in the waging of the "war" against terrorism. It is in the legal treatment of these issues, rather than in their moral acceptability, or otherwise, that I want to focus on. More particularly, the issue that is presented in both situations is the extent to which the legal language of international human rights is in fact sufficiently dispassionate so that it fairly can be said to transcend the parochial-cosmopolitan divide.

In an unfortunately all-too-frequent occurrence in postcolonial Africa, the Darfur region of Sudan has been, since 2002, the site of a civil war. The war has resulted in mass slaughters, massive population displacements, and a good deal of generalized and perhaps targeted atrocities and sufferings. For the Sudanese (and indeed other Africans who have experienced so many civil wars as part of the process of coming to grips with the consequences of the colonial construction of nation-states on the continent), a civil war fronts questions about national identity, the validity and uses of sociocultural cleavages, the fairness of the distribution of economic resources, and the possibilities (or otherwise) of political accommodations. The killings and sufferings precipitated and fostered by these wars are of course regrettable and are best done without, but they are also indisputably (and perhaps unavoidably) consequences of the process by which hitherto inorganic or artificially created states mature into organic modern political communities or states. This is a process that is not unknown to Europe nor to North America. That was the history of the former before 1945, and the truism that "civil wars are the bloodiest of wars" received its deepest confirmation in the American Civil War of 1861–1865.

For Europeans, and especially for American politicians and academics, Darfur has not been about a civil war, but rather about whether the central government in Khartoum has been engaged in "genocide," the ultimate international human rights violation. The agreed-on legal definition of genocide is that it criminalizes participation in specified acts when "committed with intent to destroy, in whole or in part, a national, ethnical, racial or religious group, as such."[51] If based solely on quantitative measures, all civil wars (at least those sufficiently bloody to be noteworthy) invariably would constitute "genocide." These wars, by definition, involve the targeting of a specific population group for a quite specific political purpose. It is precisely the existence of a politically or socially constructed cleavage between two divergent population groups that generates and fuels any civil war. What distinguishes "genocide" then from a run-of-the-mill civil war is not the nature and scope of the killings, but the purpose for which the killings are undertaken. Succinctly put, are the killings directed at the population group for an accepted or legitimate political purpose (such as the realization of self-determination or to avoid the disintegration of the state), or for an illegitimate purpose, such as the elimination of a group *"as such"*? This is of course a subjective distinction, one that relies on the ascertainable intention of the parties that engaged in the conflict.

---

[51] Convention on the Prevention and Punishment of the Crime of Genocide, Article 2, Paris, December 9, 1948, in force January 12, 1951, 78 UNTS 277; (1988) 102 Stat. 3045.

That the Sudanese central government and the various population groups in Darfur view the answer to this question through the prisms of their history and particularized experiences is entirely understandable. The propriety of viewing and presenting a war as "civil" or "genocidal" in such situations necessarily reflect not simply the objective conditions on the ground, but also on the necessity of refuting or the desirability of superimposing on the opponent a malevolent intent. In short, among the combatants, the classification of the war is as much political propaganda as it is an attempt to describe the reality on the ground. Surely, a different standard of analytical propriety is expected from witnesses of the war from without. One might think that for these outside observers, a more objective evaluation of the legal issues raised by the conflict is warranted. It's surely counterproductive for the cosmopolitanism of international human rights if the protections ostensibly afforded by such legal documents as the Genocide Convention are framed purely by the expediencies of politics and political power. Yet that is precisely the import of the debate over whether the waging of the war in Darfur constitutes "genocide."

Whether Darfur is "a genocide" has become a political litmus test. As such, the particularities and facts of the conflict have become irrelevant to the profession of the creed. What is demanded and received from politicians – irrespective of party – is a simple declaration that "what is going on in Darfur is a "genocide." All have complied. Simultaneously, however, all have declined to expend any meaningful resources to bring a halt to the asserted "genocide," and they have refused to do so despite ringing denunciations and outcries. To placate public opinions by appearing to be "doing something," politicians have uniformly resorted to a now standard playbook: shout louder about the alleged genocide, get the Security Council to pass a Chapter VII Resolution that imposes sanctions on Sudan's leadership, and refer the matter to the prosecutor of the International Criminal Court. What explains the broad and uniform denunciation of events in Darfur as a "genocide" and the unwillingness of politicians and policy makers to employ material resources to tackle the problem, while hypocritically employing the institutions of the United Nations to give a veneer of active resistance to the genocide? Does this reflect a commitment to cosmopolitanism and multilateralism in tackling the problem? Parochial interests and forces more aptly explain Western attitudes and policies toward the Darfur conflict.

To avoid a misconstruction of the arguments that follow, it should be pointed out that the issue addressed here is not the existence or genuineness of the commitment of U.S. citizens or others to human rights, but rather why the insistence that Darfur constitutes a "genocide" has become a dominant expression of that commitment. To be sure, it might be that the violations of rights by the Sudanese government is distinctively egregious, but in a world and at a time that has witnessed hundreds of thousands killed and millions displaced in such other theaters of sectarian or religious conflicts as Iraq and the Democratic Republic of the Congo, this is a claim that would not withstand serious scrutiny. The reality of Darfur is that the conflict provided one of those relatively rare opportunities in which otherwise divergent domestic interests could converge over a "cause."

Perhaps the most vociferous proponents of viewing Darfur as a genocide and demanding that something be done about it is the African American citizenry of the United States. The group's interest is perfectly understandable. The Darfur conflict has been portrayed as a conflict between an Arab-dominated radicalized Muslim central government in Khartoum that is backed by local Arab malefactors (the "Janjaweed") on the one hand, and black African Darfurians on the other. Given the history of that central government in the suppression of the Black African population of southern Sudan, that African Americans distrust the motivations of the government, even when it is purportedly waging a civil war, is entirely understandable. Yet that distrust does not explain the vigor of the pressure that African Americans have brought to bear on the U.S. government in dealing with the Darfur conflict. That explanation lies in the desired assertiveness of African Americans in the shaping of U.S. foreign policy. Having successfully pressured the U.S. federal government into according them the equal rights of citizenship in the 1960s, African Americans, by the 1980s, were seeking to demonstrate their full membership in the polity by engaging in that most quintessentially American political practice: lobbying by the African "diaspora" of the mighty American government to undertake or promote policies that favor the kinsfolk in the homeland.[52] In getting the U.S. Congress to impose "comprehensive" antiapartheid sanctions on South Africa in 1986 over the objections of the president of the United States, African Americans demonstrated that the community's power had come of age and had to be reckoned with. The release of Nelson Mandela four years later and the peaceful termination of the invidious apartheid system in 1994 seemingly demonstrated not only the effectiveness but also the wisdom of this diaspora politics. To some extent, however, the triumph over South Africa was mitigated by subsequent forays into Africa. Although African American diaspora politics was again central in getting the United States to fly the flag of the United

---

[52] Groups that have successfully practiced these politics include Greek Americans, Irish Americans, Armenian Americans, and Jewish Americans. Indeed, much of U.S. foreign policy, at least outside of Latin America (and to some extent Western Europe and East Asia) is intelligible only by taking into account the role of national, racial or religious ethnic pressure groups in the formulation of those policies.

Nations in the 1992 (ostensibly humanitarian) intervention in the Somali civil war, the hasty withdrawal of those troops the next year was a debacle that sidelined the pressure group during debates over possible intervention in Rwanda in 1994. But the widespread acceptance in the United States that the country should have done more in Rwanda, an acceptance in part generated by the supposed successful interventions in Bosnia and Kosovo gave African Americans a renewed sense of the possibilities of using U.S. power for what they considered to be good causes in Africa. Darfur presented precisely such an opportunity, one that in shaping the issue as a clash between a dominant Arab government and oppressed Black Darfurians recalled moral clarity and successful use of power to overthrow South Africa's apartheid government.

American exceptionalists also embraced intervention in Darfur. "Exceptionalist" theory arises from the view that the United States is no ordinary country, but rather a "beacon" or a "city on a hill" charged with illuminating the path for others.[53] In this order, where the United States has stood as the "sole superpower," that belief has taken on two strains that do not always coexist easily with each other. There are the so-called moralists – primarily neoconservatives – who interpret American exceptionalism as requiring that the United States employ its unparalleled power to spread certain classical liberal ideals, notably "democracy," "the rule of law," and "the free market." The promotion of human rights may be a part of the package, but only so long as its promotion reinforces the other three ideals. The United States certainly may deprive others of human rights in pursuance of those three objectives, and any criticism of that conduct is condemned as "moral equivalence." A somewhat different strain of American exceptionalism focuses on national realism in the conduct of foreign affairs. The United States is different not because of any special moral character that it has, but because of the uniqueness of its interests and institutions. Its interests are unique because no other country possesses the global reach of the United States, or has undertaken – at least since World War II – to protect and defend liberal values and institutions. American institutions are viewed as being distinctive because having been forged in the cauldron of the Enlightenment, they have continued to retain the civic ethos of that era: liberal, democratic, and republican. Both of these "moral" and

---

[53] On American exceptionalism, see, e.g., Seymour Martin Lipset, *American Exceptionalism: A Double-Edged Sword* (New York: W. W. Norton & Co., 1996). On its continuing explanatory value for current U.S. foreign policies, see, e.g., Godfrey Hodgson, *The Myth of American Exceptionalism* (Ann Arbor, MI: Sheridan Books, 2009) and Andrew J. Bacevich, *The Limits of Power: The End of American Exceptionalism* (New York: Henry Holt and Company, 2008). See also the exchange among David Rieff, George Packer, Ronald Steel, and Robert Kagan in "An Exchange: Neocon Nation?" (Summer 2008) 171 *World Affairs* 12–25.

"national" wings of American exceptionalism frame international politics as a game of self-interest in which the United States should not be judged by the same standards as other countries because its vision of national interest is less parochial than those of other societies.[54]

But do intentions matter? If, as no one doubts, there have been mass killings and sufferings in Darfur, it surely makes little difference what motivates actors within the United States (and by extension international society) to declare those to constitute genocide. Or does it? I shall take up this question in the final section of this chapter. Before doing so, I want to contrast the blunt acclamation of Darfur as a *genocide* with the much more nuanced (one might say highly evasive) discussions of the extent to which in waging its several wars on terrorism, the United States (and indeed many other Western societies) has complied with or been respectful of international human rights rules and norms.

No principled evaluation of contemporary international human rights discourse can help but be struck by the differential attitudes among academics and politicians alike in the certitude of the declaration of genocide in Darfur and the stretched contextualization and particularization of claims of human rights violations in the waging of the war on terrorism.[55] That the United States has employed morally deplorable means surely is not open to argument; that many of these means are in fact outright illegal cannot seriously be contested. The genuine debates revolve around the extent to which such illegalities can be excused, a debate that is in part facilitated (indeed necessitated) by the absence in international law of any practical coercive means for ensuring compliance with the rules by the big (and indeed, medium-sized)

---

[54] Rieff, Packer, Steel, and Kagan, "Neocon Nation."

[55] Nor is this bifurcated response limited to academic scholars and politicians. It is all too evident in the differential approach taken by the ICC chief prosecutor, Luis Moreno-Ocampo, in his investigation of whether to lodge claims of international criminal law violations with regard to the prosecution of the Iraq War on the one hand, and the Darfur civil war on the other. Compare Luis Moreno-Ocampo, "Letter to The Hague," February 9, 2006, pp. 1, 9, http://www.iccnow.org/documents/OTP_letter_to_senders_re_Iraq_9_February_2006.pdf ("The Office of the Prosecutor has received over 240 communications concerning the situation in Iraq.... While sharing regret over the loss of life caused by the war and its aftermath.... at this stage, the Statute requirements to seek authorization to initiate an investigation in the situation in Iraq have not been satisfied."), with Luis Moreno-Ocampo, "Statement to the United Nations Security Council Pursuant to UNSCR 1593 (2005)," December 4, 2009, p. 1, http://www.coalitionfortheicc.org/documents/1401_001.pdf ("[T]here have been positive developments. First, judicial proceedings in relation to the Darfur situation are progressing; second, cooperation with the African Union, the Arab League and other international bodies have been fruitful; and third, States and international organizations have maintained consistent support for the execution of the Court's arrests warrants.").

powers. Thus arguments in justification of practices that a decade and a half ago were deemed categorical violations of nonderrogatable human rights rules are now forcefully presented, respectfully listened to, dispassionately dissected and evaluated in terms of their "reasonableness," "proportionality," and/or "necessity" for ensuring national security. Legislators and commentators that in other settings routinely denounced the treatment by non-Western states of "their citizens" now have little difficulty finding or arguing for the justification, excuse, or immunization of their nationals, governments, and policy makers against liability for torturing and killing the non-Westerners. The basic claim appears to be that extraordinary measures can be justified in wars of "national security" and that the fight against "terrorism" is of such paramount importance that it must be allowed to operate outside of classical interpretations of international human rights laws.[56] Strikingly, the justifications that have been advanced in support of these violations might almost make one believe that international human rights laws, rather than forbidding discrimination on account of nationality, not only tolerates but affirmatively supports such a distinction. To be sure the question of "torture" (what it is, what justifies resort to it, and above all, on whom it may be practiced) has dominated much of the discourse, but in many ways it represents the least consequential of the differentially grounded departures *from hitherto sacrosanct human rights norms*. The use of extrajudicial killings through so-called targeted assassinations has become so normal that its legal validity is rarely commented on. Rather, the focus has been on its utility, and how much "collateral" damage (i.e., the killing or maiming of bystanders) is acceptable. Similarly, the presumption of guilt on the basis of one's association with those suspected of wrongdoing is now hardly considered to be morally objectionable, let alone legally unacceptable. The secret seizure of persons and their indefinite incarceration outside of formal legal processes are routinely defended as measures permitted in times of "war."[57] In such analysis, human rights claims are not articulated as categorical trumps of the individual, but as one of the mélange of claims that societies wrestle with and seek to accommodate through reasoned trade-offs and compromises. The balance struck in any given instance may be incorrect, but the striking of such balances are not automatically assumed to constitute nefarious behavior.

---

[56] E.g., Military Commissions Act of 2006, Pub. L. No. 109-366, 120 Stat. 2600 (2006) (expressly providing post hoc immunity for U.S. intelligence officers who may have violated U.S. law that criminalized torture).

[57] International Covenant on Civil and Political Rights, Article 20, New York, December 19, 1966, in force March 23, 1976, 999 UNTS 171.

vi. HUMAN RIGHTS, DEMOCRACY, AND THE RULE OF LAW

This chapter has sought to demonstrate that the highly moralistic and universalist tone of the claims that are asserted in contemporary human rights discourses mask the differential understandings and applications of the concept across time and space. The argument is not that the concept and its implementing doctrines necessarily are subject to cynical manipulation (although some of that certainly occurs) but that human rights are products of the particularized histories and experiences of living societies. The puzzle of contemporary human rights discourse is how and why such a rudimentary fact has been so systematically overlooked in the aftermath of the triumph of Western liberalism in the post–Cold War world. The answer lies in the spectacularly triumphalist approach that Western academics, politicians, and pundits took in relating their understandable desire to reshape the emerging new order into the likeness of the West. For these commentators, it has not been sufficient to point to the relative merits of Western ideas and institutions, but those ideas and institutions had to be presented as fully formed, complete, unchanging, unexceptionable, and, above all else, universal. Deviation from such certitude is portrayed as moral blindness or worse. The fiction has thus been created and propagated that in contemporary Western liberal institutions (not the least of which is human rights), humankind has finally reached perfection. We are living, as a popular book title put it, at "the end of history," with human rights, democracy, the rule of law, and capitalism (or "the free market") representing the ultimate culmination of the human quest for the perfect peaceful and just society.[58] A lot of the shine has gone out of that triumphalism, even among its most admiring adherents.[59] NATO, the West's military alliance, which did not lose a single soldier to enemy fire in the forty years of its existence during the Cold War, has now lost hundreds of combatants in wars outside the theater of its original jurisdiction. The United States, its principal sponsor, has lost thousands, and in the process has demolished one of the cardinal beliefs of the post–Cold War liberal triumphalists – that "democracies" are inherently pacific. As demonstrated in Part IV, in waging these wars, liberal democracies have in fact employed means that clearly violate their own cherished human rights and rule of law norms. Finally, the global financial crises; the highly interventionist fiscal, monetary, and regulatory measures that are being employed to contain and reverse the effects of the crises; and the increased

---

[58] Francis Fukuyama, *The End of History and the Last Man* (New York: Free Press, 1992).
[59] Francis Fukuyama, *America at the Crossroads: Democracy, Power and the Neoconservative Legacy* (New Haven, CT: Yale University Press, 2006); Robert Kagan, *The Return of History and the End of Dreams* (New York: Random House, 2008).

advocacy even among the strongest proponents of neoliberalism of heightened national and international regulation of the market have undermined the unalloyed enthusiasm for capitalism as a mainstay of the new global order. Nor is it inconsequential that many of the societies that have best ridden out these economic crises – Brazil and China, in particular – but do not feature prominently in that informal list of non-Western societies that human rights advocates like to point to as examples of the virtues of the universal human rights.

The triumphalist phase of neoliberalism is now over, and as a consequence many excesses of that era (including those relating to international human rights) will and ought to be jettisoned, but it would be equally destructive to be indiscriminate in rejecting its mistakes. Liberalism would not have become the dominant international ideology that it is if it did not possess some virtues that are of universal appeal. However, it is no less the case that much of that appeal flows from the material power that the West has exercised over the rest of the world during the last three and a half centuries. That the West has asserted parochial interests as universal norms is understandable; that Western academics may believe that their parochial interests constitute universal norms is less comprehensible, and certainly less acceptable. In any event, given modern technologies, non-Westerners are less likely to be easily misled. If then we are to seek the framework for an international order in which international human rights is accorded a proper place, a few basic principles merit reiteration.

First, the idea of human rights must be seen to be amorphous and understood as inherently ambiguous. Its contents and elements cannot be defined other than against the backdrop of the histories and experiences of particular societies. This is equally true of international human rights and international society. Concepts of international human rights clearly embody norms or values of "dignity," "liberty," and "equality," but the substantive content of these terms are as varied as the composition of international society, and in fact also will vary with time and experience. It is one thing for Louis Henkin to seek to elaborate for Americans an emerging era of international law by analogy to American constitutional history but quite another for Western human rights academics to infer that international human rights law is and must be based on American constitutional history or processes.

Second, to contend that a term is amorphous or ambiguous is not to assert that it lacks meaning or shape. The concept of international human rights is elastic, but it is not infinitely so. Ascertaining and delimiting boundaries is indeed a universal undertaking, but it is one that relies on the accepted tools of collaboration within the international system: cooperation rather than coercion; intellectual persuasion (through diplomacy, for example) in preference to the raw use of power. Law is a tool within the international order, and elements of international human rights norms have become legalized through treaties or the processes of customary international law formation. It is no less true, however, that the international legal order is far from being hierarchical and that many of the norms of international human rights remain aspirational. In either event, both the legal and the aspirational are susceptible to interpretation, and the concept of universality, if it has any meaning, entails a fair opportunity for as many constituent participants in the international system as is possible to participate in the interpretive process. This is especially important given the premises discussed in the previous paragraph.

Third, as much as one might crave uniformity in law, it is not an essential attribute of the international legal order. Indeed, there are good reasons to subscribe to diversity over uniformity in the creation, interpretation, and application of international rules. To be sure, the powerful will always have the desire – and perhaps the capacity – to hammer their preferences into binding rules, but any lasting and legitimate legal order demands that rules be just; that is, giving to each her or his desert. (What constitutes one's desert, of course, will always be up for grabs, and cannot be enshrined in any static a priori distribution or "rights" or benefits.) Rules may entail principles of general application, but they must also be contextualized to take account of the particular needs and circumstances of each group to whom they will be applied. The lazy desire categorical rules, especially if those purported rules conform to their cultural preferences and unexamined intuitions; but international law cannot be a party to such provincialism.

Earlier in this argument, I had left open the issue of whether, even if we all agreed on the desired outcome of a particular human rights situation – bringing an end to the killings, rapes, and mutilations in Darfur, for example – our motivations for seeking agreement matter, independently of the rationales that we offer for the agreement. The previous three paragraphs supply an answer. Our statement of human rights rules and norms are important not only because of the ends they are intended to achieve, but because the statements themselves are part of the process of being human and of creating a community of human beings. Even if a society can be given an array of fully formed rules and somehow be engineered unquestioningly to follow those rules, such a society would not be worth living in. For the maturation of a society, discovering, creating, interpreting, and applying rules are just as important as the actual content of the rules they create. This is unfortunately a lesson that many human rights advocates in the West overlook in their zeal to civilize the non-Western world, and to punish foreign autocrats for their misbehavior. Western academics, courts, and politicians cannot (and should not) substitute their preferences and interpretations of human rights norms and rules for those that will prevail in non-Western societies. This remains true even if the West furnishes all the funds and technical expertise that would be required by non-Western societies in adhering to those Western interpretations and preferences.

There are victims of human rights violations in both the Third World and the West. The pain and sufferings inflicted on these persons cannot be condoned, nor should they be tolerated. Nonetheless, genuine disagreements arise around the means for promoting these valid objectives. I have argued here against the currently dominant ethos that encourages the West to exercise its coercive power in lieu of persuasion. A criminal law culture in which outsiders sit not only as advocates or even judges, but as executioners is fatally flawed. This is so because political and cultural outsiders will never be able to impose supposedly universal norms as dispassionate arbiters but inevitably will act on the basis of their own parochial interests. Moreover, given the West's more substantial resources, its use of coercive means to enforce its parochial understandings of international human rights fundamentally distorts the concept for participants outside the West. Above all, non-Western participants are deprived of the lessons and values that would be gained from direct experience in creating, interacting with, and thereby feeling ownership for their own particularized conceptions of human rights. Everyone, including the West in the longer run, is impoverished in the process.

vii. CONCLUSION

Although I have argued that the realities of societal or national power go a long way toward explaining the tenor of the contemporary discourse of international human rights, it would be wrong to pretend that power has provided the exclusive influence on that discourse. The reality is that in a way that would have been alien to the Enlightenment liberals of the eighteenth century, non-Westerners have become participants in the shaping of current Western liberal discourse. The flow of information is no longer based on nor transmitted exclusively through the experiences of Westerners but also reflects the privileged access by some non-Westerners to the Western marketplace of ideas. Access may be provided by technologies of information and of travel, or indeed through the increased flow of immigration. In either event, the discourse of human rights in the West increasingly includes the voices of non-Westerners, the so-called cosmopolitans. Many members of the "cosmopolitan community" have argued with a good deal of vigor for a "Third World approach" to "international law." Their basic claim is that international law – including international human rights law – as currently constituted is suffused with the patterns of power relationships that were created to enable and to legitimize the colonization and domination of non-Western peoples.[60] One corrective, might be the identification and removal of those patterns, and their replacement by doctrines that in their content are more favorable to the substantive interests of the formerly colonized.[61] Current Western scholars of course are not indifferent to these claims. Indeed, many Western scholars have been pioneers of a more inclusive canon of international law.[62] Might not the views of these cosmopolitans substitute for the additional diverse voices that this chapter has contended to be essential to the discourse of human rights? I would suggest a different understanding of what it means to make international human rights law. Simply put, my argument is not for a singular international human rights law, regardless of how many voices it takes to create such law, but for the recognition that there are and will always exist a multiplicity of international human rights laws even with regard to a single topic, such as torture. I am less interested in the content or substance of the law than I am in according full recognition and acceptance to an existing reality, which is that international law is being made as much by non-Westerners employing their own processes as by Western scholars and courts. There is no singular international law, but a multiplicity of international laws.

An analogy to the difference between the conventional notion of "cosmopolitanism" as embedded in the movement for "Third World approaches to international law" (TWAIL) and the arguments advanced here may be illuminated by contrasting two ideas of cosmopolitanism reflected in the writings of two well-known "cosmopolitan" scholars.

Costas Douzinas, a Greek by birth who teaches at a British university, speaking of the "schizophrenic" and "disorientating" experience of having a "dual identity" writes: "I realised that, in matters of politics, I would remain

[60] E.g., Ien Ang, "Desperately Guarding Borders: Media Globalization, 'Cultural Imperialism.' and the Rise of 'Asia,'" in Yao Souchou (ed.), *House of Glass: Culture, Modernity, and the State in Southeast Asia* (Singapore: Seng Lee Press, 2001), p. 27.

[61] For a succinct discussion of the movement, see Jayan Nayar, "Orders of Inhumanity" (1999) 9 *Transnational Law and Contemporary Problems* 599–631. See also David P. Fidler, "The Return of the Standard of Civilization" (2001) 2 *Chicago Journal of International Law* 137–57; David P. Fidler, "Revolt against or from within the West? TWAIL, the Developing World, and the Future Direction of International Law" (2003) 2 *Chinese Journal of International Law* 29–76. On a Third World approach to International Human Rights discourse, see Makau Mutua, *Human Rights: A Political and Cultural Critique* (Philadelphia: University of Pennsylvania Press, 2002).

[62] E.g., Thomas M. Franck, "The Emerging Right to Democratic Governance" (1992) 86 *American Journal of International Law* 46–91; Henry J. Steiner, "Ideals and Counter-Ideals in the Struggle over Autonomy Regimes for Minorities" (1991) 66 *Notre Dame Law Review* 1539–60.

forever a Briton in Athens and a Greek in London. This is a condition I cannot rationally define but which has dominated my emotional experience and the discussion of politics (something that happens all the time in Athens and more rarely in London)."[63] He goes on to define cosmopolitans as positioning themselves "as enemies of patriotism and nationalism, as promoters of global social processes, institutions and world citizenship and as critics of hegemonic and imperial designs."[64]

Anthony Appiah, the son of a Ghanaian father and an English mother, educated primarily in England, and with tenure and appointments to the philosophy and African American studies departments of two of the most preeminent universities in the United States, has drawn attention to the difference between "culture" and "identity." He contrasts, for example, the claimed "diversity" of the United States with the diversity present in Ghana, terming the former as a claim to the diversity of "identities," and the latter that of "cultures."

> Language is only one of many things most Americans share. This is also, for example, a country where almost every citizen knows something about baseball and basketball. And Americans share a familiarity with our consumer culture. They shop American style and know a good deal about the same consumer goods: Coca-Cola, Nike, Levi-Strauss, Ford, Nissan, GE. They have mostly seen Hollywood movies and know the names of some stars; and even the few who watch little or no television can probably tell you the names of some of its "personalities." . . .

> Coming, as I do, from Ghana, I find the contrast with a nation of a more substantial diversity of folkways to be striking. Take language. When I was a child, we lived in a household where you could hear at least three mother tongues spoken every day. Ghana, with a population close to that of New York State, has several dozen languages in active use and no one language that is spoken at home – or even fluently understood – by a majority of the population.[65]

In framing the debates over "pluralism" and "multiculturalism," it is the asserted "pluralism" of the United States, not that of Ghanaian (or, for that matter African) diverseness, that has been taken as the norm to be striven for. It is to the "cultural toleration" of the United States, not the practicing coexistence and cohabitation of Africans that is looked to for a model. Indeed,

---

[63] Costas Douzinas, *Human Rights and Empire: The Political Philosophy of Cosmopolitanism* (New York: Routledge-Cavendish, 2007), p. 133.
[64] *Ibid.*, p. 134.
[65] Kwame Anthony Appiah, *The Ethics of Identity* (Princeton, NJ: Princeton University Press, 2005), pp. 116–17.

to the extent that anyone attempts to focus on diversity within Africa, it is the occasional "tribal" or "ethnoreligious" conflict that is asserted as the norm for that continent. The argument made here has been an appeal for greater attention to the parochialism of supposedly universal values, and greater respect for the parochial values of less powerful nations, through which they express their own understanding of universal human needs.

7   Rights in Reverse

International Human Rights as Obligations

Chios Carmody

I. INTRODUCTION

The issue addressed in this volume is whether international law, and in my case human rights law, is "parochial," a term I take to mean "restricted to a small area; narrow; limited; provincial."[1] What I want to do in this chapter is address the topic from a reverse perspective by examining what is often left out of everyday discourse about international human rights: the idea of international human obligations. In doing so, I hope to offer some observations about the contextual nature of human rights and their potential for universalization.

Obligations are not a popular topic in debate about international human rights for the simple reason that most discussions of human rights necessarily address the question of vindicating *rights*. In this, it is easier to see those rights as relatively absolute, at least in an initial phase, than it is to try to understand them conditionally as part of broader legal culture. Much of the debate about international human rights today proceeds on the assumption that the rights involved are "inherent," "inalienable," and so forth and that therefore to infer they have other things that come with them, such as obligations, is to question this orthodoxy, which naturally raises suspicion.[2]

---

[1] *Webster's New Word Dictionary*, 3rd ed., s.v. "parochial."

[2] The strong focus on rights in international human rights law also has some curious consequences. One of these is what I term "deresponsibilization," by which I mean the tendency of "rights-talk" to eclipse almost all other considerations, a tendency aided by the fact that the primary holder of corresponding obligations is the impersonal state. See Kirsten Hastrup, "Accommodating Diversity in a Global Culture of Rights," in *Legal Cultures and Human Rights: The Challenge of Diversity*, ed. Kirsten Hastrup (New York: Springer, 2001), 11; Andrew Clapham, The Human Rights Obligations of Non-State Actors (Oxford: Oxford University Press, 2005), 7.

It need not however, particularly at a time when a majority of the world can be said to be formally committed to the idea of basic human rights and when other issues, and therefore other "rights," are increasingly coming to the fore. Questions involving the environment and intergenerational equity are only two of these, but there are others. I do not propose to address those other rights here because my aim in this chapter is much more basic: I want to continue to focus on the way in which international human rights are "parochial" and to do so by emphasizing the jurisprudential arrangement of the law.

I suggest that international human rights and obligations are not the whole story when it comes to the particularity and universality of human rights, that community and legal tradition are important, and that understanding the law as part of a greater social process can help to define how far human rights can be realized. What *is* universal about rights is the set of rules that should govern this process. However, the actual product of rights discourse will vary from place to place and time to time. The central problem is to identify the boundaries of communities within which rights discourse should take place. I do not provide answers to the question of identification, but I suggest that the identification takes place, at least in part, because of the broader sense of social obligation. When actors believe themselves to be obliged, they are less likely to regard their acts as claims independent of the existing social fabric. Instead, they weigh their rights against the knowledge of what already exists, including the obligations that they are reciprocally owed. The language of international human rights is provocative in the sense that it potentially upsets this balancing.

This chapter is divided into five parts. Following this introduction, Part II deals with the nature of rights in law generally and examines how they are qualified. All rights are said to be limited, but how this qualification is manifested by the shape of obligations and other legal elements is not often considered. Part III goes on to review what other features of a legal system function to limit the assertion of rights. These include the particular orientation of the legal system, its "weave" of rights and obligations, and the need in asserting rights to develop meaningful alternatives for legal and social arrangements. Drawing on this analysis, Part IV explores the notion of community and how it is that communities constantly define and refine the legal relations that are the basis of their social arrangement. To do so, it briefly examines the case of modern-day slavery in West Africa. Part V sums up the findings in the chapter and suggests that there will continue to be parochialism as communities struggle to define the extent of rights and obligations within the greater universalism of human rights.

II. THE NATURE OF RIGHTS AND OBLIGATIONS

As mentioned in the introduction, we often refer to international human rights without context, by which I mean that we often omit a vital part of the legal matrix to which these rights belong. Here I point to the universal truth that rights are matched by corresponding obligations, whether individual or collective, private or public, and that to conceive of international human rights purely in terms of rights alone is to ignore a great deal of the legal environment in which they must be realized.

Early modern publicists of public international law like Samuel von Pufendorf were among the first to appreciate an important aspect of rights: *the correlativity of rights and obligations*. Thus, it is said that "[n]o right can be attributed to one person without at the same time attributing certain correlative duties of non-interference to others."[3]

However, whom these "others" are is open to question. Traditionally governments were considered to be the primary holders of the obligations that arise from international human rights, but recently a number of commentators have pointed out that most human rights "are not defined with regard to a specific duty-holder."[4] Instead, "[t]he focus is on inherent possession of the right[s], and references to duties can be found to society, the state, groups and individuals."[5]

Uncertainty in the locus of responsibility is being used today to go beyond the narrow, state-centered approach to human rights law and argue that at least *some* obligations found in international law, such as those involving the prohibition on genocide, war crimes, and crimes against humanity, also apply to nonstate actors. These are now said to include corporations, mercenaries, international and nongovernmental organizations, international criminals, and terrorists.

---

[3] William A. Edmundson, *An Introduction to Rights* (Cambridge: Cambridge University Press, 2004), 25.

[4] See Clapham, *Obligations of Non-State Actors*, 34; see also Theo Van Boven, "A Universal Declaration of Human Responsibilities?" in *Reflections on the Universal Declaration of Human Rights: A Fiftieth Anniversary Edition Anthology*, eds. Barend Van Der Heijden and Bahia Tahzib-Lie (New York: Springer, 1998), 73.

[5] Clapham, *Obligations of Non-State Actors*, 40. This is also true of the law of state responsibility, which does not define exactly to *whom* state responsibility is owed. Article 33(1) of the International Law Commission's Articles on State Responsibility provides that "obligations of the responsible State [for cessation and reparation] may be owed to another State, to several States, or to the international community as a whole, depending in particular on the character and content of the international obligation and on the circumstances of the breach." This is followed by Art. 33(2), which provides that state responsibility under Art. 33(1) is "without prejudice to any right, arising from the international responsibility of a State, which may accrue directly to *any person or entity other than a State*" (emphasis added).

The reasoning behind this extension is several-fold. It includes textualism, the universality of *jus cogens* norms, the intensification of globalization, the growth of private economic power, as well as the perception that, as Andrew Clapham observes, "due to the growing importance and pressures of global forces outside the state's control . . . social justice is seen as increasingly threatened."[6]

At the same time, opposition to the expansion of rights and to rights-focused discourse is located in several ideas. Human rights treaties are signed by states, are guaranteed by laws, and are protected by processes that are fundamentally *public*. There is, moreover, no clear definition of the "social justice" that, *in extremis*, is given as the underlying rationale for greater private responsibility. To project such obligations onto nonstate actors is also fundamentally unfair because it gives little consideration to their capacity to bear them and raises complex questions of derivative responsibility.[7]

Whatever conclusion may be reached about the ultimate question of who bears the burden of international obligations, the first point must be that if we seek to define what the content of those rights are, we must be clear about the extent of their corresponding obligations. Many legal systems require this kind of consideration implicitly, and some even do so explicitly. For example, Articles 6 and 7 of the Civil Code of Québec state:

6. Every person is bound to exercise his civil *rights* in good faith.

7. No *right* may be exercised with the intent of injuring another or in an excessive and unreasonable manner which is contrary to the requirements of good faith.

Similarly, Article 5 of the International Covenant on Civil and Political Rights[8] provides:

> Nothing in the present Covenant may be interpreted as implying for any State, group or person any right to engage in any activity or perform any act aimed at the destruction of any of the rights or freedoms recognized herein or at their limitation to a greater extent than is provided for in the present Covenant.

---

[6] See Clapham, *Obligations of Non-State Actors*, 5.

[7] Jan Klabbers discusses this issue in the case of international organizations in *An Introduction to International Institutional* (Cambridge: Cambridge University Press, 2003), 300–16. For debate over the ascription of responsibility to international organizations, see International Law Commission, *Draft Articles on the Responsibility of International Organizations*, A/CN.4/L.687 (July 19, 2006); *ibid.*, A/CN.4/L.720 (July 25, 2007), Arts. 28–29. For commentary see José Alvarez, International Organizations: Accountability or Responsibility? Luncheon Address to the Canadian Council of International Law (October 27, 2006) (on file with author).

[8] 999 U.N.T.S. 171 (1966).

What these statements infer is an underlying relationship between two jural elements. Rights cannot be meaningfully asserted without an appreciation of the consequences that their assertion imposes. This observation is often made in relation to economic, social, and cultural rights where the immediate lack of resources guarantees only their progressive realization.[9]

An associated feature that serves to limit rights is awareness of their *mutuality*. Human rights cannot be exercised in such a way so as to eviscerate the rights of others, a doctrine formally know as "abuse of rights" (*abus de droit*). Ian Brownlie points out that the doctrine is the alter ego of two related, but distinct, principles: the first being nondiscrimination, the second the presumption of responsibility in case of injury caused.[10]

Nor are rights and obligations the *only* jural correlatives. There are others. Wesley Newcomb Hohfeld identified privileges and the absence of right ("no rights"), powers and liabilities, and immunity and disability, as additional dyads that must be considered in any legal system to determine the content of justice.[11] These too play a role in arranging the legal matrix.

III. RIGHTS AND OBLIGATIONS IN LEGAL CULTURE

The law of international human rights therefore involves deciding what action is appropriate in a crowded legal landscape, one often referred to as a "balance." How this balance is struck, however, is a function of many culturally and contextually defined variables.[12]

---

[9] Matthew Craven, *The International Covenant on Economic, Social and Cultural Rights: A Perspective on Its Development* (Oxford: Oxford University Press, 1995), 26. Unlike the International Covenant on Civil and Political Rights, which requires states to "respect and ensure" the rights recognized, Art. 2(1) of the ICESCR merely obliges states "to take steps . . . with a view to *achieving progressively* the full realization of the rights" (emphasis added). Craven explains that this formulation reflects "the belief held during the drafting of the [ICESCR] that the implementation of economic, social, and cultural rights could only be undertaken progressively, as full and immediate realization of all the rights was beyond the resources of many [s]tates."

[10] Ian Brownlie, *System of the Law of Nations: State Responsibility, Part I* (Oxford: Oxford University Press, 1983), 70.

[11] Wesley Newcomb Hohfeld, *Fundamental Legal Conceptions: As Applied in Judicial Reasoning* (New Haven, CT: Yale University Press, 1919), 64. Hohfeld wrote that by reducing legal relations to these "lowest common denominators of the law . . . it becomes possible not only to discover essential similarities and illuminating analogies in the midst of what appears to be infinite and hopeless variety, but also to discern common principles of justice and policy underlying the various jural problems involved."

[12] For example, one Chinese commentator Liu Hainan has observed:

The idea of regarding morality as important to law, the collective as superior to the individual and justice as vital to profits advocated by Confucianism, the influence of

The "balance" I have just referred to will be struck differently from community to community and will be influenced by *preexisting ideas of what law is designed to do*. Patrick Glenn, for instance, has written about the way in which the traditional *jus* of Roman law was regarded as "a bilateral statement of legal relation" until, under the influence of corruption and change, it was reformulated as "an earthly sanction to ensure such entitlements are respected." In the process law became subjective, and in becoming subjective, it generated rights.[13]

It is also possible to acknowledge in this transition other conceptions of rights. In Islamic tradition, for instance, the notion of the law as subjective is more limited. "The purely subjective is prescribed; law does not contemplate an individual *potestas*; in the legal language there is no word corresponding to that of 'right' in the subjective sense." The same can be said for Judaism: "[t]here is no language of rights in the Talmud, no single word which conveys the same bundle of prerogatives as does the word 'right' and its equivalences in Western languages. The word which dominates is rather *mitzvah* [commandment]."[14] The English common law too was traditionally resistant to the idea of rights, at least in its more individualist and robust forms. As Glenn describes it, the English common law is "[a] law of relations, of mutual obligation, is not a law which concentrates its attention on the legal powers or interests of the individual. It is not a law of rights, and the notion of the subjective right . . . played little or no role in the history of the common law in England. The existence of rights in English law has been denied well into the twentieth century."[15]

The point of this comparative overview is, of course, that each of these views contains within it a very different notion of obligation, and consequently of right. In some traditions of law, the law is intensely relational and therefore obligation-laden; in others it is less so. As a result, there is great difficulty in conceiving of what "rights" as independent legal elements might be; the law is principally about obligation. To speak of rights – in the abstract, at any rate – is absurd.

modern Western culture and the wound inflicted upon the Chinese people by imperialist aggression; and the strong demands of independence and subsistence and the principle of building socialism with Chinese characteristics based on the practical situation have formed the basic factors that affect Chinese human rights ideas.

Peter R. Baehr et al., eds., *Human Rights: Chinese and Dutch Perspectives* (The Hague: Kluwer Law International, 1996), 23.

[13] H. Patrick Glenn, *Legal Traditions of the World* (Oxford: Oxford University Press, 2000) 130–31.

[14] *Ibid.*, 101–2.   [15] *Ibid.*, 219–20.

Then too there are, more subtly, patterns of thought that serve to mediate the idea of rights still further. In Western culture the concept of "rule of law" is used as shorthand for the notion that a well-organized society must be based on the law. Accordingly, if a dispute arises, the normal way to settle it is to have recourse to the courts.

However, a second tradition found elsewhere views recourse to formal law as incomplete and potentially offensive. A trial can do only limited good. In all circumstances, as René David points out, "the essential is to restore harmony, for harmony . . . is something which must be ensured if it is desired that the world live in peace according to the natural order."[16] This perspective regards the role of law very differently. Formal law – and the rights it vindicates – are looked on with suspicion and are used only "for external display."[17]

This prospect of absurdity, or at least a sense of the socially inappropriate, is what has motivated a number of commentators to speak of the need to think broadly about rights. Doing so provides a more accurate picture of existing legal conditions. Leon Trakman and Sean Gatien explain:

> Liberal rights that fail to encompass important interests. . . . promote only the liberty of some people, denying liberty to others. This denial of liberty is accentuated when interests that are protected as rights are not subject to responsibilities owed to those who are harmed by their exercise. The result of not subjecting rights to responsibilities . . . is the erosion of the social ties upon which our communities depend.[18]

The reality of community therefore requires consideration of rights *and* obligations *together*. Doing so provides a more accurate picture of existing conditions:

---

[16] See René David, *The Different Conceptions of the Law*, vol. II of *International Encyclopaedia of Comparative Law* (New York: Springer, 1992), 1–8.

[17] See Glenn, *Legal Traditions of the World*, 66. René David speaks of the situation in Japan where in formal court action there is the acute sense that the plaintiff has already irretrievably lost something. "The winner is no better off than the loser; by resorting to the courts, the plaintiff has alienated public opinion; by requiring execution of the decision given, he is acting as a bad citizen." *Ibid.*, 1–9. One aboriginal judge in Canada describes the strong clash between the European and aboriginal views of justice as follows:

> The Canadian justice system, like other systems in the European tradition, is based on the concepts of adversarialism, accusation, confrontation, guilt, argument, criticism and retribution. These concepts, however, are not in keeping with Aboriginal value systems. Indeed, they are antagonistic to the high value that Aboriginal traditions place on harmony and peaceful coexistence among all living beings.

Murray Sinclair, "Aboriginal Peoples and Euro-Canadians: Two World Views," in *Aboriginal Self-Government in Canada*, ed. John Hylton (Saskatoon: Purich Publishing, 1994), 32.

[18] Leon Trakman and Sean Gatien, *Rights and Responsibilities* (Toronto: University of Toronto Press, 1999), 61.

Rights with responsibilities protect the positive liberty by which both individuals and communities coexist and act in solidarity with each other. It subjects their identities and lives to human cooperation and association. It affirms, rather than denies, their autonomy as individuals.[19]

This combination requires a focus on and consideration of obligations. Understanding their role is vital to a fuller appreciation of rights:

> responsibilities safeguard both the constitutive commitments that give rise to individual choices and the impact of those commitments upon others. They do so by explicitly injecting teleological considerations into the mechanics of rights. Responsibilities thereby relate the right to the good, unity to plurality, individual and community, without supporting one to the other *a priori*. They establish a balance between the individual's right to choose and his responsibility towards others who are detrimentally affected by that choice.[20]

At the same time, the problem with an integrated perspective on rights and obligations is that it can serve as a justification of the status quo. Both Trakman and Gatien, as well as others, recognize that the particular balance struck between rights and obligations in any society is not necessarily final, that it is constantly evolving, and that the championing of rights, at least in the first instance, has frequently been the key to that evolution. Again they observe:

> How the tension between rights and responsibilities is struck is the art of life, politics, and law. What is important is that the structure of rights not preclude or distort that art. If the tension slackens to rights without responsibilities, important social interests will remain unprotected. If the tension is so taught that weight is given to responsibilities but not rights, individuality and freedom if choice will be suppressed.[21]

What their observations infer is that in the process of social evolution certain interests will *inevitably* be devalued, reclassified, even harmed. That is a foreseeable consequence of social change. What needs to happen, therefore, is not some measurement of *all* rights against their effects before the rights are recognized, as Trakman and Gatien appear to suggest, but instead, some process through which society can identify newly asserted rights and devise ways to deal with their assertion equitably. In other words, awareness of a balance between rights and obligations must be matched by awareness of the need for a balance between social stability and change.

---

[19] *Ibid.*, 74.   [20] *Ibid.*, 49.
[21] *Ibid.*, 50.

IV. RIGHTS AND OBLIGATIONS IN OPERATION: MODERN SLAVERY IN WEST AFRICA

I have referred in several places to the idea of a legal balance and to the associated idea that this balance is often fluid and contestable on many points. A given legal system will strike the balance differently at different times and on different subjects. One of the factors affecting that balance, however, is the example of balance struck in other legal systems. Today the realization of human rights in so many systems means that human rights cannot be ignored. As Kirsten Hastrup asserts, "[t]hey have taken root in the collective imagination of the natural order."[22] As such, they are a constant challenge to what already exists.

Why? Because "rights-talk" can serve to overcome the overbearing weight of obligation. We have already examined how the law in many instances is obligation-laden. To displace this weighting, which is often culturally reinforced, there is a need for action in the form of a new legal "accent." That accent can be expressed in the vernacular of rights. Legal thought and language *reflect* social realities but can also *construct* them.[23]

The example of modern slavery in West Africa is illuminating. At one time slavery – the ultimate form of human obligation – was practiced throughout the region and in the late twentieth century was still very much alive in Mauritania and Niger. In mid-2007 slavery was criminalized in Mauritania, but recent reports indicate that little has actually changed. A similar situation prevails in Niger.[24]

Thomas Kelley has done an insightful job of detailing how slavery continues to exist in practice in Niger despite successive attempts at de jure emancipation. Kelley points out that "the dichotomy between slave and non-slave remains a fundamental, defining aspect of contemporary Nigerien social order, but that extant slavery in Niger is different than Western slavery. None of the rules regarding Nigerien slavery are written, and none are intentionally supported by formal state law, yet they are adhered to strictly by most Nigeriens."[25]

The reason for continuing adherence to slavery lies in its cultural construction and communitarian ethos. Kelley refers to the fact that "[b]efore the

[22] Hastrup, "Accommodating Diversity," 9.
[23] Clifford Geertz, *Local Knowledge* (New York: Basic Books, 1983), 232.
[24] For updates from an advocacy website with information on slavery in Mauritania and Niger, see "Le Site de S.O.S. ESCLAVES MAURITANIE," S.O.S. Esclaves Mauritanie, www.sosesclaves.org/pagecentrale.htm (March 2, 2010).
[25] Thomas Kelley, "Unintended Consequences of Legal Westernization in Niger: Harming Contemporary Slaves by Reconceptualising Property," 56 *American Journal of Comparative Law* (2008): 999.

institution of Western law, a person's access to land depended on a complex web of social relations. So long as he fulfilled his obligations to his lineage and his community, he could expect reasonably secure and durable access to land."[26]

Recent emphasis on Western-style legalization, made in an attempt to spur privatization and develop the Nigerien economy, is having the perverse effect of *denying* slaves land because, according to local tradition and custom, slaves have only usufructory rights, not fee simple. Thus:

> Under the new land tenure rules, the person's obligations to the social group fade in importance as his access to land comes to depend solely on obtaining a piece of paper designating his ownership. Once he has this paper, he can, if he wishes, ignore his cultural obligations to his community, including his obligations to his *horso* [slaves].[27]

In Mauritania, slavery also remains a real phenomenon. It has repeatedly been "abolished" by successive administrations but continues to exist for many of the same reasons that it exists in Niger. One NGO has stated:

> most people held in servitude will not overcome the internalised set of values which makes people of slave descent believe that they should remain living with, and working for, the families which enslaved their parents or ancestors. Others submit to their current exploitation because they see no alternative options in terms of where they would live or work. In these circumstances physical coercion is rarely needed to prevent people from leaving.[28]

Without doubt, what is continuing to happen in Mauritania and Niger is profoundly offensive to international human rights. Slavery and servitude are expressly prohibited in every international human rights instrument that deals with the subject and, more broadly, with basic civil and political rights. The

---

[26] *Ibid.*, 1022.   [27] *Ibid.*

[28] "Forced Labour in Mauritania," presented to the 27th Session of the Working Group on Contemporary Forms of Slavery, UN Commission on Human Rights (2002), Anti-Slavery International, www.antislavery.org/archive/submission/submission2002-mauritania.htm. The Office of the UN High Commissioner for Human Rights states that "Even when abolished, slavery leaves traces. It can persist as a state of mind – among its victims and their descendants and among the inheritors of those who practised it – long after it has formally disappeared." See Office of the High Commissioner of Human Rights, "Fact Sheet No. 14 – Contemporary Forms of Slavery," United Nations, http://www.ohchr.org/Documents/Publications/FactSheet14en.pdf (accessed March 4, 2010). In October 2008 the Community Court of Justice of the Economic Community of West African States found the government of Niger liable in restitution to a young Nigerian woman, Hadjiatou Mani, who was owned as a slave for 10 years. The court ordered the government to pay Mani CFA 10 million ($19,750). See "West African Court Convicts Niger in Slavery Case," *The Independent*, October 27, 2008.

International Covenant on Civil and Political Rights states that "[n]o one shall be held in servitude."[29]

Although it is possible to sympathize with the slaves' emancipation under domestic law, the reality remains that they are part of a web of social relations that relegates them to a secondary and dependent status and that needs to be modified before their legal rights as equals in society can be fully realized. Something more than legal emancipation is necessary for them to be truly free. Disregard for this greater context is the reason Kelley concludes somewhat counterintuitively that

> what many [slaves] in Niger want is not freedom in the sense of being rid of all property claims upon them and restraints on their will, but connectedness; specifically the ability to access resources – land in particular through connection to the corporate body with which they are associated.[30]

Kelley's conclusions reveal the slaves' acute awareness of the *social* – as opposed to the purely legal – construction of their status. Their situation is akin to that prevailing in the postbellum South of the United States where slaves were freed, only to encounter political and economic obstacles that gave rise to renewed forms of legalized discrimination.[31]

Given the example of modern-day slavery in Mauritania and Niger, it is possible to despair that things will ever change. As one BBC correspondent observed in a vignette:

> When Assibit first ran away from her owners she was asked what it was like to be free, but she did not understand the question. She did not understand the concept of freedom, or even the word.

> When I arrived in Niger, I could barely believe that slavery exists in this century on such a scale, but when I left I could not see how it could end in our generation. Ending slavery in Niger would require a social revolution.[32]

---

[29] International Covenant on Civil and Political Rights, 999 U.N.T.S. 171 (1966), art. 8. Note that Niger has ratified the ICCPR but Mauritania has not. Efforts to end slavery in Mauritania therefore rely on the ILO Forced Labour Convention (C29) and the Abolition of Forced Labour Convention (C105), both of which Mauritania has ratified.

[30] Kelley, "Unintended Consequences of Legal Westernization in Niger," 1025.

[31] See generally Eric Foner, *Reconstruction: America's Unfinished Revolution* (New York: Harper & Row, 1988), 1863–77; Leon Litwack, *Been in the Storm So Long: The Aftermath of Slavery* (New York: Alfred A. Knopf, 1979).

[32] Hilary Anderson, *Born to Be a Slave in Niger*, BBC News, February 11, 2005, news .bbc.co.uk/1/hi/programmes/from_our_own_correspondent/4250709.stm (accessed March 3, 2008).

These examples reveal the need for deep-seated social change that must accompany the emergence of robust, Western-style rights. The change will not come about until the community, which Thomas Franck defines as "an ongoing, structured relationship,"[33] is reconfigured to recognize those rights. Recognition will undoubtedly modify the nature of the relationship among actors that are part of that community. There will have to be give and take in the process of reconstituting the community along different, more inclusive lines.

A point to be drawn from the situation in West Africa is that continuing indifference to slave rights runs the risk of creating social instability as ideas of equality gradually permeate Nigerien society. At the same time, the need to reconcile competing claims is something that happens in *every* community, albeit on a less socially explosive scale, from day to day. The ability to do so a measure of a particular community's resilience.

V. CONCLUSION

The example of modern slavery in West Africa is a deeply troubling one, yet the tenacity with which the institution has survived is a testament to the way in which it is woven into the social fabric. Slavery as an economic institution is an example of how long-standing social practices premised on dependency cannot be uprooted overnight.

At the same time, there are reasons to welcome a general awareness of legal rights. To some degree, speaking about human rights is, as Frantz Fanon observed, "to assume a culture, to support the weight of a civilization."[34] In human rights discourse that "civilization" is primarily Western and individualistic, yet it is also one with other resonances and expressions elsewhere, in other traditions.

This, then, is the way in which human rights are parochial: they are "restricted to a small area; narrow; limited; provincial" because *each* community has its own conception of what those rights are and how they are to be interpreted in the context of broader legal culture.

Furthermore, divergence from abstract international norms is to be expected if we are to take seriously the claim that people everywhere are rational and deserve a substantial measure of respect for the human rights they choose. To deny them this opportunity is to privilege certain conceptions of human

---

33 Thomas Franck, *Fairness in International Law and International Institutions* (Oxford: Oxford University Press, 1998), 10.
34 Frantz Fanon, *Black Skin, White Masks*, trans. Charles Lam Markmann (New York: Grove Press, 1967), 17–18.

rights and devalue others, thereby implicitly *denying* the universality of human rights.[35] Patrick Glenn has written:

> The results of [human] rights doctrines can be held up as examples; if other doctrines fall short of them they will be challenged, even internally. Insisting on the necessarily universal character of rights, however, is seen and will continue to be seen as a modern form of imperialism, using the same old private means. Universal rights are simply another form of universalizing the truths of a particular tradition. It is being illiberal about being liberal, forcing people to be free. Yet if all people are of equal potential, if all exercise human rationality . . . and if all, as human beings, are entitled to choose how they will live their lives, their choice must count. So rights doctrines eventually end up, as they should, being evaluated against other doctrines, in particular circumstances by particular people.[36]

What all of this means is that international human rights *are* necessarily parochial, although not in the way that might have been contemplated when the term was first encountered at the outset of this chapter.

The basic reason for this distinctiveness arises from the fact that these rights – including human rights – are not asserted historically or in a vacuum. Instead, they are identified and realized *within* preexisting communities that place different emphasis on the associated idea of obligation, and indeed much else. The relevant factors change over time, but human rights cannot be thought about in the abstract beyond the communities in which they exist.

---

[35] A curious tension arises in asserting the universality of human rights and neglecting their particularity. Liu Hainian observes, "[s]uch a practice not only negates the particularity of human rights, but also denies the universality of human rights." See Baehr, *Chinese and Dutch Perspectives*, 18.

[36] Glenn, *Legal Traditions*, 245.

8 Parochial Restraints on Religious Liberty

Brian D. Lepard

I. INTRODUCTION

Every day millions of human beings are deprived of the right to practice their religion or belief freely; indeed, many are tortured or killed simply for adhering to unpopular religions. These threats to religious freedom seem to be growing, despite the adoption of many laws, both national and international, purporting to safeguard this essential liberty.

The freedom to change one's religion or belief, which is guaranteed by international human rights law, is under special threat. Today, many governments, particularly but not exclusively those influenced by Islamic doctrines, are denying that such a right exists. They have challenged the principle of universalism underlying international norms of religious liberty, instead advocating a kind of "religious parochialism" according to which different states, and different religious communities, should be entitled to regulate the religious choices of their citizens and members.

I suggest that this particular challenge of reconciling universal freedom of religion or belief, including a right to change one's religion or belief, with respect for religious and cultural differences is one of the most acute in our age. This is especially so after the events of September 11 and the "war against terror" have brought into bold relief the issue of how the secular West, and the international law that it helped create, can be reconciled with religious, and especially Islamic, law.

I seek to investigate this contemporary challenge as a case study of the larger theoretical issue of cosmopolitanism and parochialism in international law that is the focus of this book. I propose that although this is a severe challenge today, it can be overcome, in particular through adoption of a concept of "unity in diversity" in international law. This concept is not only already imminent in evolving norms of international human rights law but is consistent with much religious law, including Islamic law. It thus has tremendous potential to bridge the existing divide.

II. UNIVERSALISM AND RELIGIOUS PAROCHIALISM IN THE EVOLUTION OF INTERNATIONAL HUMAN RIGHTS LAW GENERALLY

The inclusion of the concept of universal human rights, first in the UN Charter in 1945 and then in the Universal Declaration of Human Rights (Universal Declaration) in 1948, was a major breakthrough in recognition of the ideal of the universality of human rights. The UN Charter asserts that one of its primary purposes is to "reaffirm faith in fundamental human rights, in the dignity and worth of the human person, [and] in the equal rights of men and women."[1] The Universal Declaration declares in Article 1 that "all human beings are born free and equal in dignity and rights. They are endowed with reason and conscience and should act towards one another in a spirit of brotherhood."[2] It then announces many specific human rights.

The Universal Declaration and the network of treaties, declarations, and supervisory organs that it has spawned represent an effort to recognize that human rights are *universal*, and do not depend on one's culture or religion – hence the title, "Universal" Declaration. Yet from the beginning, efforts to achieve universality encountered demands for recognition of difference. Within the Universal Declaration itself there are a number of references to "communities" and individual obligations to them. For example, Article 27 affirms that "everyone has the right freely to participate in the cultural life of the community."[3] Article 29 provides that "everyone has duties to the community in which alone the free and full development of his personality is possible."[4]

Although the United States and its allies dominated the UN's initial membership that crafted the Universal Declaration, diverse government voices were heard in the process – including representatives of Muslim states such as Saudi Arabia and countries with a Confucian or Buddhist tradition like China and Japan. These states often argued for recognition of rights that were important in their cultures, including economic, social, and cultural rights, such as the right to adequate food, clothing, and shelter, and the right to work.[5]

---

[1] U.N. Charter, Preamble.
[2] Universal Declaration of Human Rights ("Universal Declaration"), Art. 1.
[3] *Ibid.*, Art. 27, para. 1.   [4] *Ibid.*, Art. 29, para. 1.
[5] For a defence of the universal character of the rights proclaimed in the Universal Declaration based in part on the inclusion of representatives of diverse cultures and religions in its drafting,

Early on in the elaboration of the Universal Declaration, the decision was made by the principal drafters to exclude any reference to the divine or to a religious basis for the rights it proclaimed. Their commendable purpose was to ensure that the declaration could be acceptable to states of varying political systems and ideologies, including those based on atheism or secularism. Nevertheless, the omission of any recognition of a divine origin for human rights helped create a sense of alienation among many believers, who came to see the Universal Declaration as a symbol of a "Western" culture that was irreconcilable with religion. For similar, but different, reasons, many members of indigenous populations viewed the declaration as a Western European cultural document that was inconsistent with their own belief systems.[6]

As James Griffin points out in his contribution to this volume, "human rights are suspected – by Westerners as much as by Easterners – of being relative to Western culture."[7] Indeed, today, despite the premise of the global human rights system that human rights are universal, many critics, including governments, are asserting that human rights are and should be relative to culture, including one's religious culture.

III. UNIVERSALISM AND RELIGIOUS PAROCHIALISM IN THE EVOLUTION OF INTERNATIONAL LEGAL STANDARDS ON RELIGIOUS LIBERTY AND THE FREEDOM TO CHANGE ONE'S RELIGION OR BELIEF

Let me turn now to a review of the respective roles of universalism and religious parochialism in the evolution of international legal standards on religious liberty in general, and freedom to change one's religion or belief in particular.

The past sixty years have witnessed a gradual recognition in international law of the ideal of freedom of religion as a facet of individual freedom generally – a recognition that naturally assumes the universality of this right as well as the right to freedom from any discrimination on religious grounds. Thus, the Universal Declaration asserts in Article 18 that "everyone has the right to freedom of thought, conscience and religion; this right includes freedom

and its incorporation of communitarian as well as liberal values, see Mary Ann Glendon, *A World Made New: Eleanor Roosevelt and the Universal Declaration of Human Rights* (New York: Random House, 2001), 221–33.

[6] See, e.g., Makau Mutua, "The Complexity of Universalism in Human Rights," in András Sajó, ed., *Human Rights with Modesty: The Problem of Universalism* (Leiden/Boston: Martinus Nijhoff, 2004), 51, 54 (arguing that "the purportedly universal" character of the global human rights movement "is at its core and in many of its details, liberal and European").

[7] James Griffin, "Are Human Rights Parochial?" Chapter 5, this volume, 158.

to change his religion or belief, and freedom, either alone or in community with others and in public or private, to manifest his religion or belief in teaching, practice, worship and observance."[8]

The 1966 International Covenant on Civil and Political Rights (ICCPR) provides, in its own Article 18, that "everyone shall have the right to freedom of thought, conscience and religion. This right shall include freedom *to have or to adopt* a religion or belief of his choice, and freedom, either individually or in community with others and in public or private, to manifest his religion or belief in worship, observance, practice and teaching."[9] The same article affirms that "no one shall be subject to coercion which would impair his freedom to have or to adopt a religion or belief of his choice."[10]

Significantly, the explicit recognition of a right "to change" one's religion was omitted in the ICCPR because of the view of some Islamic states that once one is a Muslim, he has no right to convert to another religion, which would constitute apostasy. These states also expressed concern about proselytism. The Saudi Arabian representative declared that "if the individual was to enjoy true religious freedom, he had to be protected against pressure, proselytism and also against errors and heresies."[11] To satisfy these concerns of Saudi Arabia and other Muslim countries, the drafters settled on the compromise language "to have or to adopt a religion or belief of [one's] choice."[12] So immediately the universality of a right to change one's religion came under challenge.[13]

Moreover, the ICCPR goes on in Article 18(3) to permit certain limitations on freedom to *manifest* one's religion or belief (but not freedom "to have or to adopt" a religion or belief of one's choice). These limitations are only those "prescribed by law and . . . necessary to protect public safety, order, health, or morals or the *fundamental* rights and freedoms of others."[14] It is clear that these limitations are relatively strict; for example, only the "fundamental" rights and freedoms of others, not *any* rights or freedoms, can be grounds for

[8] Universal Declaration, Art. 18 (emphasis added).
[9] ICCPR, Art. 18, para. 1 (emphasis added).
[10] *Ibid.*, para. 2.   [11] U.N. Doc. A/C.3/SR.1022 (1960), para. 27.
[12] See Mashood A. Baderin, *International Human Rights and Islamic Law* (Oxford: Oxford University Press, 2003), 118–19.
[13] On the right to change one's religion or belief as guaranteed by the Universal Declaration, see, e.g., Nazila Ghanea, *Human Rights, the UN and the Bahá'ís in Iran* (Oxford: George Ronald; The Hague: Kluwer Law International, 2002), 94.
[14] ICCPR, Art. 18, para. 3 (emphasis added). On these restrictions, see generally Manfred Nowak, *U.N. Covenant on Civil and Political Rights: CCPR Commentary*, 2nd rev. ed. (Kehl: N. P. Engel, 2005), 425–31.

limiting the right to manifest religion or belief.[15] Nevertheless, governments routinely invoke this "clawback" clause to justify restrictions on both religious conversions and manifestations of religious belief.

In 1981, the UN adopted its first and only declaration devoted to religious liberty, the Declaration on the Elimination of All Forms of Intolerance and of Discrimination Based on Religion or Belief (1981 Declaration).[16] The 1981 Declaration goes further than either the Universal Declaration or the ICCPR in specifying a number of religion-oriented rights, some of them collective as well as individual. Despite the hopes of many supporters of religious freedom that the 1981 Declaration would soon be followed by the drafting and adoption of a binding treaty on religious freedom, no such efforts have come to fruition. Thus, no new treaty norms have emerged in the past quarter century.

However, some observers contend that many of the norms enshrined in Article 18 of the Universal Declaration, Article 18 of the ICCPR, and the 1981 Declaration now have crystallized into norms of customary international law. Indeed, some scholars and international bodies such as the Human Rights Committee established under the ICCPR have opined that a general norm of religious liberty and freedom of conscience has evolved into a *jus cogens* norm – a norm from which no derogation is permitted by states on any ground.[17] Nevertheless, the status of freedom of religion or belief under customary law is murky.

A number of theoretical justifications have been offered for these contemporary international expressions of a norm of religious liberty. Each of these justifications has particular implications for the debate on universality versus religious parochialism.

First, some supporters of a universal norm of freedom of religion in international law have argued that it is necessary to prevent war and social conflict

[15] On this point, see "Report of the Special Rapporteur of the Commission on Human Rights on Freedom of Religion or Belief, Asma Jahangir," in *Elimination of All Forms of Religious Intolerance: Note by the Secretary-General*, U.N. Doc. A/60/399 (2005), para. 62.

[16] G.A. Res. 36/55 (1981).

[17] For the views of the Human Rights Committee, see Human Rights Committee, General Comment No. 24, U.N. Doc. CCPR/C/21/Rev.1/Add.6 (1994), para. 8. Legal scholar Francisco Forrest Martin, among others, has argued that "freedom of conscience" is a *jus cogens* norm. See Francisco Forrest Martin, "Delineating a Hierarchical Outline of International Law Sources and Norms," *Saskatchewan Law Review* 65 (2002), 333, 347, 347 n. 73. For a definition of *jus cogens*, or peremptory, norms, see Vienna Convention on the Law of Treaties (1969), Art. 53 ("a peremptory norm of general international law is a norm accepted and recognized by the international community of States as a whole as a norm from which no derogation is permitted and which can be modified only by a subsequent norm of general international law having the same character").

grounded in religion. Dismayed and disillusioned by the ferocity of wars waged under the banner of asserting the supremacy of this or that religion, they have pleaded for religious tolerance as a means of ensuring peace. Second, other supporters of modern-day universal norms of religious liberty have maintained that religious freedom should be protected to safeguard the religion, ethnicity, or culture of a particular group.

Finally, a third perspective on the justification for a universal norm of religious freedom is that freedom of religion must be protected by law because it is a natural outgrowth of the liberty that every individual enjoys, simply by virtue of being a human being, to make his or her own choices. This was the point of view propounded by the thinkers of the Enlightenment, and it was reflected in such documents as the U.S. Declaration of Independence, the U.S. Constitution, and the French Declaration of the Rights of Man and of the Citizen. Moreover, this perspective apparently animated many of the drafters of the Universal Declaration of Human Rights.

IV. CONTEMPORARY CHALLENGES TO FREEDOM TO CHANGE ONE'S RELIGION OR BELIEF

I now examine various contemporary challenges to the universality of the norm of freedom to change one's religion or belief. Some of these challenges are bold and forthright. Others, however, are more subtle, and in fact have been lodged under the banner of one or more of the theories I have just outlined that typically support the universality of religious liberty.

A. Challenges from Advocates of Religious Preferences

First, a number of religious leaders, and governments, have asserted the right to prevent individuals from changing their religion from a favored one on the grounds that that favored religion is the "true" religion and that no one accordingly has the right to abandon it. Religion-inspired discrimination, with accompanying limitations on freedom to change one's belief, appears to be on the upsurge.

Many countries with an Islamic background have openly discriminated against non-Muslims. For example, the Government of Iran has persecuted the Bahá'í religious community solely on grounds of religion or belief. Iranian Bahá'ís have been arbitrarily arrested, dismissed from their jobs, tracked through a systematic national campaign of espionage by government officials, and denied fundamental human rights. Iranian Bahá'í youth have been forbidden to pursue higher education. Bahá'ís are widely regarded as "apostates" of Islam who have abandoned the true religion and thus have forfeited all rights.[18]

More generally, the Organization of the Islamic Conference (OIC) has in recent years launched a campaign against so-called defamation of religion. UN human rights bodies and the General Assembly have responded by adopting a series of resolutions under this rubric. Although these resolutions criticize defamation of any religion, they focus in particular on alleged defamation of Islam.[19] In March 2008, the Human Rights Council, which succeeded the Commission on Human Rights, observed with concern "the increasing trend in recent years of statements attacking religions, including Islam and Muslims, in human rights forums." It acknowledged freedom of expression, but went on to emphasize that "the exercise of this right carries with it special duties and responsibilities, and may therefore be subject to certain restrictions, but only those provided by law and necessary for the respect of the rights or reputations of others, or for the protection of national security or of public order, or of public health or morals."[20]

These resolutions should be of great concern, for a number of reasons. They imply that Islamic governments should be shielded from criticism of human rights violations. Indeed, the UN's former Special Rapporteur on Freedom of Religion or Belief, Mrs. Asma Jahangir, has expressed these kinds of fears. She has emphasized that the right to freedom of religion or belief, "as enshrined in relevant international legal standards, does not include the right to have a religion or belief that is free from criticism or ridicule."[21] The Special Rapporteur highlighted the importance of freedom of expression. She said in this regard that "criminalizing defamation of religion can be counterproductive. . . . There are numerous examples of persecution of religious minorities as a result of excessive legislation on religious offences or overzealous application of laws that are fairly neutral. As a limit to freedom of expression and information, it can also limit scholarship on religious issues and may asphyxiate honest

[18] See generally www.bahai.org/dir/worldwide/persecution.
[19] See, e.g., Commission on Human Rights Res. 1999/82 (1999), paras. 2,3; G.A. Res. 61/164 (2006), paras. 4, 6, 8. On the defamation of religion resolutions in the Human Rights Council, see generally "Religion and Human Rights: The Limits of Freedom and Faith," *The Economist*, April 3, 2010, 62–63.
[20] Human Rights Council Res. 7/19 (2008), Preamble, para. 12. The Human Rights Council also adopted resolutions on defamation of religion in 2009 and 2010, with slightly different language. See Human Rights Council Res. 10/22 (2009); Human Rights Council Res. 13/16 (2010). In a welcome development, in March 2011 the Council abandoned the "defamation of religion" concept and adopted a resolution entitled "Freedom of religion or belief" that focused on this vital right while emphasizing that "no religion should be equated with terrorism." See Human Rights Council Res. 16/13 (2011), esp. para. 7.
[21] U.N. Doc. A/HRC/2/3 (2006), para. 36.

debate or research. . . . Criminalizing speech that defames religions, whilst not amounting to forms of expression prohibited by international law, can limit discussion of practices within religions that may impinge upon other human rights."[22]

Of course, many Islamic governments impose punishments for "apostasy" – leaving the "true faith" of Islam – under some interpretations of *shari'a* law. Mrs. Jahangir has noted that in a variety of countries the "punishment for conversion can consist of arrest and trial for 'apostasy,' imprisonment, and sometimes the death penalty."[23] She says further that in "some countries, legislation prohibits conversion without prior notification of the authorities or defines 'forcible' conversion in broad terms."[24] Indeed, blatant infringements of religious freedom, and the right to change one's religion, are not limited to the Islamic world. For example, a number of states in India have passed "anti-conversion" laws aimed at "protecting" the Hindu majority from efforts by members of other faiths to teach their religion. These worrisome laws impose criminal sanctions.[25]

B. Challenges from Advocates of Interreligious Peace

A second challenge to religious freedom, and in particular, the right to change one's religion, comes from a friendlier source – advocates of interreligious harmony. Legitimate concerns about religious divisions in the world today, including between the Christian and Islamic worlds, have spawned a new language of "tolerance," one that seems to see respect for freedom of religion primarily as a way of assuaging tensions between religious communities.[26] One implication of this view, however, is to open the door to limitations on individual freedom to share one's belief with others on the ground that unqualified freedom to teach religion could inflame animosities between religious groups.

---

[22] *Ibid.*, paras. 42–43.   [23] U.N. Doc. A/60/399, para. 43.
[24] *Ibid.*, para. 45.
[25] See, e.g., Arpita Anant, "Anti-Conversion Laws," *The Hindu*, December 17, 2002, available at http://www.hindu.com/thehindu/op/2002/12/17/stories/2002121700110200.htm; "Gujarat to Ban Faith Conversions," *BBC News*, February 25, 2003, available at http://news.bbc.co.uk/2/hi/south_asia/2798771.stm.
[26] This perspective is implied in the "Dialogue among Civilizations" initiative launched by the UN General Assembly in 2001. See G.A. Res. 56/6 (2001), Preamble (recalling the UN Millennium Declaration of September 8, 2000, "which considers, inter alia, that *tolerance* is one of the fundamental values essential to international relations in the twenty-first century and should include the active promotion of a *culture of peace and dialogue* among civilizations, with human beings respecting one another, *in all their diversity of belief*, culture and language, neither fearing nor repressing differences within and between societies but cherishing them as a precious asset of humanity") (emphasis added). .

Moreover, anticonversion laws have been defended as necessary to prevent interreligious conflict.

C. *Challenges from Advocates of the Rights of Religious Communities*

A third challenge to freedom to change one's religion or belief emanates from a desire to respect the rights of religious communities. Advocates of religious community rights have tended to view religion as merely another facet of culture or ethnicity and the protection of religious communities as part of a larger effort to safeguard minority cultures and communities and allow them not only a measure of self-determination, but also the right to maintain their unique identity vis-à-vis the majority population.[27]

However, one feature of this approach is that it tends to discourage the mixing of members of different religions and to justify restrictions on the right to teach one's religion to others, an individual right that could be viewed as infringing on a collective right of an existing community to "keep" its current religion, free of external interference. This perspective, even when adopted by "liberal" thinkers, may have some sympathy for the types of anticonversion laws described earlier.

D. *Challenges from Advocates of a Liberal or "Social Contract" Theory*

Finally, and perhaps most ironically, the traditional "liberal" or "social contract" view of human rights that underpins the UN human rights system, and that generally advocates religious liberty, nevertheless can aid and abet those who seek to place restrictions on this freedom, and in particular, restrictions on freedom to change religion or belief. The problem is that the liberal view begins with the proposition that human beings should be free to do whatever they please, subject only to those limitations that are reasonably necessary to protect the rights and freedoms of others. It thus emphasizes "freedom from" unwarranted governmental regulation rather than "freedom to" pursue particular actions.

Accordingly, one regrettable tendency of this liberal view is to diminish the unique importance of religious liberty. Many liberal theorists appear to give short shrift to freedom of thought, conscience, and religion. This is certainly true in the case of those liberal theorists who advocate a version of "communitarianism." We can see this tendency in John Rawls's influential book,

---

[27] This view might draw some support from Article 27 of the ICCPR, which affirms that "in those States in which ethnic, religious or linguistic minorities exist, persons belonging to such minorities shall not be denied the right, in community with the other members of their group, to enjoy their own culture, to profess and practise their own religion, or to use their own language." ICCPR, Art. 27.

The Law of Peoples.[28] Rawls suggests that in a "second" original position entered into by diverse "decent" but not necessarily "liberal" "peoples," they would fail to agree on full rights to "equal liberty" of conscience, among many other rights. He proposes accordingly that these rights should not form part of a list of philosophically defensible "universal" rights, which should be limited to "urgent rights."[29]

Moreover, beyond the domain of theory, there are a number of recent decisions of the European Court of Human Rights – a court generally known for its advocacy of a high standard of human rights protections – that have upheld the right of states to impose significant restrictions on freedom of religion. In these decisions the court has validated governmental restrictions on the freedom to teach one's religion to others and the freedom of Muslim girls or women to wear a head covering.

Article 9 of the European Convention on Human Rights proclaims that "everyone has the right to freedom of thought, conscience and religion; this right includes freedom to change his religion or belief and freedom, either alone or in community with others and in public or private, to manifest his religion or belief, in worship, teaching, practice and observance."[30] Similarly to Article 18(3) of the ICCPR, it affirms that the liberty to manifest one's religion or belief can be subject "only to such limitations as are prescribed by law and are necessary in a democratic society in the interests of public safety, for the protection of public order, health or morals, or for the protection of the rights and freedoms of others."[31]

The European Court of Human Rights has decided a number of cases involving criminal charges of proselytizing and whether proselytizing activities are protected by Article 9. In general, it has affirmed that freedom of religion includes the freedom to teach one's religion to others. Thus, in the 1993 case of *Kokkinakis v. Greece*, it stated:

> While religious freedom is primarily a matter of individual conscience, it also implies, inter alia, freedom to "manifest [one's] religion." Bearing witness in words and deeds is bound up with the existence of religious convictions.
>
> According to Article 9 (art. 9), freedom to manifest one's religion is not only exercisable in community with others, "in public" and within the circle of those whose faith one shares, but can also be asserted "alone" and "in

---

[28] John Rawls, *The Law of Peoples with "The Idea of Public Reason Revisited"* (Cambridge, MA: Harvard University Press, 1999).
[29] See *ibid.*, 32–34, 62–63, 65, 74–75, 78–79.
[30] Convention for the Protection of Human Rights and Fundamental Freedoms (1950), ("European Convention on Human Rights"), Art. 9, para. 1.
[31] *Ibid.*, Art. 9, para. 2.

private"; furthermore, it includes in principle the right to try to convince one's neighbour, for example through "teaching," failing which, moreover, "freedom to change [one's] religion or belief," enshrined in Article 9 (art. 9), would be likely to remain a dead letter.[32]

Despite this strong language, the European Court of Human Rights, in that case and others, has held that states may impose reasonable limitations on the right to teach one's religion – in particular, for the purpose of restricting "improper proselytism, such as the offering of material or social advantage or the application of improper pressure with a view to gaining new members for a Church."[33] It has, of course, indicated that these types of measures must be "justified in principle and proportionate."[34] In *Kokkinakis* and *Larissis and Others v. Greece*, a case decided in 1998, it found that criminal prosecutions of individuals for certain acts of proselytism of civilians did not satisfy this standard.[35] However, in *Larissis and Others*, the court also decided that proselytizing activities could be prosecuted as a crime when they were conducted by military superiors with respect to their subordinates. The court was concerned with the potential for these activities to constitute harassment or an abuse of power.[36] This recognition of the legitimacy of *criminal* prosecutions for religious teaching activities is disturbing.

The European Court of Human Rights has also upheld governmental prohibitions of the wearing of an Islamic headscarf by a primary schoolteacher in Switzerland (in *Dahlab v. Switzerland*)[37] and by an adult student in classes at a state university in Turkey (*Sahin v. Turkey*).[38] In December 2008 it likewise ruled that there was no violation of Article 9 of the Convention when Muslim schoolgirls in France were expelled for their refusal to remove their Islamic headscarves during physical education classes.[39] It has emphasized in these cases that states have a wide "margin of appreciation," in other words, discretion, to implement the policies they view as best to protect the rights and freedoms of others, and ensure public safety and public order, so long as these are necessary in a democratic society. Moreover, the court has again expressed concern in these cases about religious "proselytizing."[40]

---

[32] *Kokkinakis v. Greece* (1993), para. 31.
[33] *Larissis and Others v. Greece* (1998), para. 45. See also *Kokkinakis v. Greece* (1993), para. 48.
[34] See *Kokkinakis v. Greece* (1993), para. 47; *Larissis and Others v. Greece* (1998), para. 46.
[35] See generally *Kokkinakis v. Greece* (1993); *Larissis and Others v. Greece* (1998), paras. 56–61.
[36] See *Larissis and Others v. Greece* (1998), para. 51.
[37] *Dahlab v. Switzerland* (2001).   [38] See *Sahin v. Turkey* (2005).
[39] See *Dogru v. France* (2008); *Affaire Kervanci c. France* (2008).
[40] But see *Affaire Ahmet Arslan et Autres c. Turquie* (2010) (court held that there was a violation of Article 9 where the government prosecuted individuals belonging to a particular Muslim

Many defenders of religious liberty have viewed these decisions with concern because of the wide latitude they give to states to regulate religious conduct.[41] It is particularly problematic that the court has consistently been willing to bless states' regulation of a relatively innocuous manifestation of religion, the wearing of a headscarf, on the ground that doing so helps protect public order, public safety, and the rights and freedoms of others.[42]

These weaknesses in explicit protections of religious liberty in international documents and in judicial decisions by the European Court of Human Rights have in turn contributed to the uncertain status of religious freedom under customary international law. The International Court of Justice has already recognized many human rights norms, such as those prohibiting genocide and racial discrimination, as norms of customary international law.[43] Moreover, it has classified some of them as *jus cogens* norms. As noted earlier, however, the status of the norm protecting religious freedom is much more ambiguous.

v. TOWARD "UNITY IN DIVERSITY" IN INTERNATIONAL HUMAN RIGHTS LAW ON RELIGIOUS FREEDOM

How should the international law community respond to the challenges I have just outlined? How can we cultivate a theory of religious freedom, including a right to change one's religion or belief, that can adequately answer these challenges? In the balance of this chapter, I sketch the skeleton of such a theory.

I suggest, in particular, that these challenges can be answered on the basis of ethical principles that (1) are found, explicitly or implicitly, in contemporary international human rights law and (2) are logically related to a preeminent principle of "unity in diversity." Let me explore each of these criteria in turn.

First, it would be entirely possible to articulate a theory of religious freedom that is completely independent of contemporary legal norms. In fact, most philosophical theories of human rights are built on a freestanding philosophical foundation. Assuming that one accepts their fundamental philosophical premises, they can provide a means to assess the morality of norms and behavior and to critique the morality of contemporary international legal

---

denomination for wearing religious apparel in the public streets as opposed to public institutions such as schools and where there was no evidence they were engaged in proselytizing).

[41] See, e.g., Peter G. Danchin, "Suspect Symbols: Value Pluralism as a Theory of Religious Freedom in International Law," *Yale Journal of International Law* 33 (2008), 1, 7–8.

[42] Peter Danchin appears to adopt a similar view. See *ibid.*

[43] See Brian D. Lepard, *Customary International Law: A New Theory with Practical Applications* (Cambridge: Cambridge University Press, 2010), 3.

norms from the "outside." However, these theories suffer from an inherent weakness. In particular, their divorce from the international legal system often renders them of little utility either to international lawyers generally or to officials of governments that recognize international human rights standards and in principle have committed themselves to complying with these standards.

One example of this potential weakness is John Rawls's book, *The Law of Peoples.* Rawls, starting from a framework totally independent of contemporary international human rights law, has constructed a theory of human rights that is minimalist in comparison to the long and comparatively robust list of rights already recognized by governments in international law.[44] In fact, many scholars have appropriately criticized this philosophical framework for neglecting important ethical principles recognized in contemporary international law. For example, James Griffin argues that "a great obstacle to our accepting Rawls's shortened list of human rights – especially if, like Rawls, we want a list with a realistic chance of being adopted – is that it would never be accepted by the international community."[45]

Second, and on the other hand, one could attempt to erect a theory of religious freedom grounded solely in contemporary legal norms. That is, one would look at the text of relevant documents, such as the Universal Declaration, and infer from them answers to the various challenges I have outlined. Yet this approach, too, has some inherent flaws. Most important, it is ethically emasculated. Lacking any clear philosophical foundation of its own, and wedded to the text of international legal documents, which itself is often "watered down" as a result of long and excruciating diplomatic negotiations, the approach can fail to solve some of the most difficult issues presented by attacks on religious freedom.

For example, Article 18 of the Universal Declaration affirms a right to religious freedom, including a right to "change" one's religion and a right to "teach" it. However, Article 29 also authorizes limitations on rights, as I have noted. Likewise, Article 18 of the ICCPR, after similarly affirming a right to religious liberty, explicitly permits limitations on manifestations of religious belief for various social purposes. Where do we draw the line, then, between permissible expressions of religious belief and permissible governmental limitations on these expressions? The international documents are silent on this

---

[44] For a similar critique, see Griffin, "Are Human Rights Parochial?" Chapter 5, this volume, 168–70.
[45] *Ibid.*, 169.

question. Only a philosophical theory can help us work through these tough cases.

The approach suggested here integrates both agreed norms of international human rights law and a more rigorous philosophical analysis and is based on ethical principles that satisfy both of the earlier-mentioned criteria. This integrated approach can help solve some of the difficult questions I have raised, but in a way that comports with contemporary international human rights law.

A. "Unity in Diversity," Freedom of Moral Choice, and Open-Minded Consultation as Fundamental Ethical Principles in International Law

I begin with the assertion of a preeminent ethical principle: that of "unity in diversity." According to this principle, all human beings are first and foremost members of a single human family and should act toward one another as family members. However, diversity of nationality, race, ethnic origin, language, sex, thought, opinion, and religion is to be cherished as enriching this one human family. Individuals have a right to associate with, and take pride in, this array of lesser communities, and these communities have certain rights to self-governance, but all within the framework of participation in a global community of humankind. This is why the principle is referred to as one of "unity in diversity."

There are many provisions of contemporary international law, including the UN Charter and the Universal Declaration, that support a principle of unity in diversity. For example, the Universal Declaration calls for recognition "of the inherent dignity and of the equal and inalienable rights of *all members of the human family*" and asserts, as we have seen, that all human beings "should act towards one another *in a spirit of brotherhood*."[46] The Declaration simultaneously values respect for diversity by calling for education that "shall promote understanding, tolerance and friendship among all nations, racial or religious groups."[47] Likewise, Article 27 of the ICCPR provides that "in those States in which ethnic, religious or linguistic minorities exist, persons belonging to such minorities shall not be denied the right, in community with the other members of their group, to enjoy their own culture, to profess and practice their own religion, or to use their own language."[48]

Although I cannot here mount a robust philosophical defense of this principle as a foundational principle for an ethical system, I will note that many of the great Western philosophers have endorsed its underlying theme of the unity of the human family. For example, in his essay, "Perpetual Peace," Immanuel

---

[46] Universal Declaration, Preamble, Art. 1 (emphasis added).
[47] *Ibid.*, Art. 26, para. 2.   [48] ICCPR, Art. 27.

Kant declared that the "peoples of the earth have . . . entered in varying degrees into a universal community, and it has developed to the point where a violation of rights in *one* part of the world is felt *everywhere*."[49] John Stuart Mill, in his essay, "Utilitarianism," supported an impartial concern for the happiness of all mankind that could be nurtured based on "the social feelings of mankind; the desire to be in unity with our fellow-creatures."[50] Furthermore, many contemporary philosophers have advocated a similar principle. Thus, Peter Singer has made the case for a "principle of equal consideration of interests" that implicitly acknowledges the unity of the human family by forbidding racial or national preferences.[51]

These and other theorists have simultaneously emphasized the value of diversity and dialogue. In fact, a number of the contributors to this book have done so. For example, John Tasioulas has stated that public international law "will be impaired in its legitimacy to the extent that it is not appropriately responsive" to diversity in ways of specifying the content of human rights, and trading them off "against countervailing considerations in cases of conflict."[52]

The principle of unity in diversity logically leads to recognition of many other associated ethical principles that also reflect the requirement I have established of being recognized in contemporary international law. I refer to these particular principles as "fundamental ethical principles" and provide a much more complete list of them in my book, *Rethinking Humanitarian Intervention*.[53]

One such related and important fundamental ethical principle, of direct relevance to the problem I am considering here, is that of freedom of thought, conscience, religion, opinion, and expression – or what might be termed more broadly "freedom of moral choice."[54] We have already seen that this freedom is generally endorsed in contemporary global texts, such as the Universal

---

[49] Immanuel Kant, "Perpetual Peace: A Philosophical Sketch," in *Kant: Political Writings*, ed. Hans Reiss and trans. H. B. Nisbet, 2nd ed. (Cambridge: Cambridge University Press, 1991), 93, 107–8 (emphasis in original).

[50] John Stuart Mill, "Utilitarianism," in John Stuart Mill, *Utilitarianism, On Liberty, Essay on Bentham, Together with Selected Writings of Jeremy Bentham and John Austin*, ed. Mary Warnock (New York: New American Library, 1974), 251, 284. See also *ibid.*, 268.

[51] See Peter Singer, *Practical Ethics*, 2nd ed. (Cambridge: Cambridge University Press, 1993), 16–26, esp. 21; 232–34. See also Peter Singer, *One World: The Ethics of Globalization* (New Haven, CT: Yale University Press, 2002).

[52] John Tasioulas, "Parochialism and the Legitimacy of International Law," Chapter 2, this volume, 37.

[53] See generally Brian D. Lepard, *Rethinking Humanitarian Intervention: A Fresh Legal Approach Based on Fundamental Ethical Principles in International Law and World Religions* (University Park: Pennsylvania State University Press, 2002), 39–98.

[54] I note that John Tasioulas seems to have a similar freedom in mind when he defines "freedom" as "both autonomy (having and exercising the capacity to choose from a range of options) and liberty (having and exercising the capacity to pursue, without interference, the option one has

Declaration of Human Rights, which declares that everyone has the right to "freedom of thought, conscience and religion" and to "freedom of opinion and expression."[55]

Importantly, however, freedom of moral choice is also a direct corollary of the principle of unity in diversity. When applied to individuals as well as communities, it becomes clear that this principle holds that diversity of opinion is a good *and* a right. All people must have a fundamental right to formulate their own thoughts and opinions. This is especially true for matters involving ethics, morality, and religion, which give people a higher meaning in their lives. In the apt words of Peter Danchin: "Religious traditions . . . provide their adherents with a comprehensive understanding of the world and identify the place and role of human beings and other sentient beings within that world."[56]

Freedom of moral choice is not only a fundamental right; it is what I call an "essential" human right. This means that it is so closely connected with the principle of unity in diversity that it deserves the highest weight morally and should normally preempt any potential reasons for not respecting it. Indeed, without this freedom, individuals lack the capacity to choose to recognize fundamental ethical principles and attempt to implement these principles in their lives.[57] This capacity is recognized in the first article of the Universal Declaration, we have seen, which affirms that all human beings "are endowed with reason and conscience and should act towards one another in a spirit of brotherhood."[58] This language implies the imperative of protecting the exercise of reason and conscience in the interest of promoting the realization of ethical values, like human brotherhood (and sisterhood).

Of course, freedom of moral choice is not free of all restrictions. In particular, the external behavior of individuals in acting on this freedom (as opposed to their internal thoughts or convictions) must comport with appropriately defined social duties. However, the freedom is vital and cannot lightly be restricted.

Another critical ethical principle related to that of unity in diversity, and recognized today in international law, is a principle of open-minded consultation. Open-minded consultation is a means of solving difficult ethical dilemmas. It requires us to consult with others about how to solve these dilemmas, actively seek out their views, be detached from and willing to revise our own

chosen)." Tasioulas, "The Legitimacy of International Law," 17 (manuscript on file with the author).
[55] Universal Declaration, Arts. 18, 19.
[56] Danchin, "Suspect Symbols," 46.
[57] On this point, see Lepard, *Customary International Law*, 359–60.
[58] Universal Declaration, Art. 1.

opinions, and be motivated primarily by a desire to seek truth and attempt to find the most ethically defensible course of action in collaboration with others rather than by our own self-interest.[59]

Again, this principle follows logically from those of unity in diversity and freedom of moral choice. These principles together imply the importance of encouraging an honest exchange of viewpoints, involving the participation of as many affected actors as possible. However, the ideal of unity likewise indicates that this exchange must occur in an atmosphere of humility and mutual learning. Importantly, the principle of open-minded consultation is distinct from negotiation or bargaining, both of which seek a compromise of competing self-interests, rather than a transcending of those self-interests. As in the case of unity and diversity and freedom of moral choice, many foundational texts of international law make direct or indirect reference to this ideal. For example, the UN Charter affirms that the organization's purposes encompass the cultivation of "friendly relations among nations" and the achievement of "international co-operation in solving international problems" and in "promoting and encouraging respect for human rights."[60]

The principle of open-minded consultation has direct implications for freedom of religion or belief. Because religion or belief is intimately linked with each person's identity as a moral agent, it must be freely chosen and accepted, according to each individual's conscience and personal search for spiritual truth. It cannot be compelled. Every individual must be free to search out religious truth for himself or herself, to change his or her belief, and to share his or her conscience, beliefs, and religion with others in a mutual exploration of truth. Indeed, it is morally imperative that individuals representing diverse religious and belief systems engage in this kind of mutual open-minded dialogue.

I note that a number of the other contributors to this volume endorse a similar perspective in their thoughtful contributions. Likewise, Peter Danchin calls for "value pluralism." He says that "this approach opens up new pathways and dynamic possibilities for rights discourse between diverse points of view – a process which, rather than imposing one, totalizing outlook, is capable of transforming each of them."[61] John Tasioulas seems to advocate an approach to international law that pairs a claim of ethical objectivity "advocacy of intercultural dialogue, conducted in an inclusive and fallibilist spirit, as a vital

[59] See generally Lepard, *Customary International Law*, 90–91; Lepard, *Rethinking Humanitarian Intervention*, 68–71.
[60] See UN Charter, Art. 1, paras. 2, 3.
[61] Danchin, "Suspect Symbols," 46.

epistemic conduit to the truth."[62] Both these scholars thus endorse a form of open-minded consultation.

I suggest that any interpretive problems relating to legal texts like the UN Charter, the Universal Declaration, or the ICCPR relating to religious freedom ought to be resolved by reference to the ordinary meaning of their terms and their legislative history, if possible, but also in light of fundamental ethical principles, including the three fundamental principles I have just identified: unity in diversity, freedom of moral choice, and open-minded consultation. These fundamental ethical principles, in other words, should serve as a "background value system" in applying more traditional legal interpretive methodologies.

B. *"Unity in Diversity" and Other Fundamental Ethical Principles in Religious Law*

The fundamental ethical principles I have just reviewed relating to freedom of conscience and religion have a strong claim to guide decision making about the application of contemporary international legal norms based on their recognition in these norms and their relationship to the principle of unity in diversity. However, it is important to emphasize, also, that these principles find echoes in the world's great religious traditions – and certainly in the revered moral texts of these religions. These moral texts proclaim the highest-order ethical norms within each tradition and hold a place within each system comparable to that of a national constitution in domestic legal systems. I explore common principles in these texts in more detail in my book *Hope for a Global Ethic: Shared Principles in Religious Scriptures.*[63] This congruence with the world's revered moral texts lends additional credibility to these principles as a "global ethic" that can serve as a background value system in the interpretation and application of international law and helps to refute claims that they are culturally relative.[64]

In my books *Rethinking Humanitarian Intervention* and *Hope for a Global Ethic*, I explore passages from revered texts of seven religions demonstrating a belief not only in the moral ideal of human unity, but also in the value of

---

[62] Tasioulas, "Parochialism and the Legitimacy of International Law," Chapter 2, this volume, 31.

[63] Brian D. Lepard, *Hope for a Global Ethic: Shared Principles in Religious Scriptures* (Wilmette, IL.: Baháʾí Publishing, 2005). On the possibility of a global ethic based in part on shared religious principles, see also, e.g., Singer, *One World*, 141–44.

[64] James Griffin mentions a similar approach that searches "the ethical beliefs of various non-Western societies for indigenous ideas that might provide a local case for human rights, or for something not unlike them," but finds that a "more ethnocentric approach" constructed "from resources of the Western tradition" is, "on balance, preferable." See Griffin, "Are Human Rights Parochial?" Chapter 5, this volume, 163.

human diversity and in encouraging the formation and expression of diverse viewpoints. I will give just a few examples here.

The Hebrew Scriptures proclaim that we should love our neighbors as ourselves (Leviticus 19.18) and declare, "Have we not all one Father? Did not one God create us?" (Malachi 2.10).[65] In the New Testament, Jesus confirmed the Torah's commandment to love our neighbors as ourselves. In the story of the Good Samaritan, he eloquently explained – to a skeptical lawyer no less – that everyone in need is our "neighbor" for purposes of applying this commandment. (See Luke 10.25–37.) However, the New Testament also endorses loyalty to government and respect for members of one's own family (see, e.g., Romans 13.1–7 and 1 Timothy 5.8).

The holy book of Islam, the Qur'ān, which Muslims revere as the Word of God, proclaims that all human beings were the creation of one God and by virtue of their common origins, they are endowed with an inviolable dignity and common bond: "Mankind, fear your Lord, who created you of a single soul" (4.1).[66] A revered *hadīth*, or tradition concerning the conduct of the Prophet Muhammad, affirms that the "whole universe is the family of Allah," and another *hadith* asserts that people are as "alike as the teeth of a comb."[67] At the same time, the Qur'ān affirms that all nations and peoples have been created with diverse characteristics for the divine purpose of being united: "O mankind, We have created you male and female, and appointed you races and tribes, that you may know one another. Surely the noblest among you in the sight of God is the most godfearing of you" (49.13).

Finally, the sacred scriptures of the Bahá'í Faith announce that "all peoples and nations are of one family, the children of one Father, and should be to one another as brothers and sisters!"[68] At the same time, they value diversity and refute any attempt to impose uniformity of thought. Bahá'í texts clarify that the purpose of this principle of human unity taught by the Prophet of the Bahá'í Faith, Bahá'u'lláh, "is neither to stifle the flame of a sane and intelligent patriotism in men's hearts, nor to abolish the system of national autonomy so essential if the evils of excessive centralization are to be avoided. It does not ignore, nor does it attempt to suppress, the diversity of ethnical

[65] From *Tanakh: A New Translation of the Holy Scriptures According to the Traditional Hebrew Text* (Philadelphia: The Jewish Publication Society, 1985).

[66] All quotations from the Qur'ān are from the translation by A. J. Arberry. See *The Koran Interpreted*, 2 vols., trans. A. J. Arberry (New York: Simon and Schuster, 1955).

[67] Quoted in C. G. Weeramantry, *Islamic Jurisprudence: An International Perspective* (New York: St. Martin's Press, 1988), 133.

[68] 'Abdu'l-Bahá, *Paris Talks: Addresses Given by 'Abdu'l-Bahá in 1911* (Wilmette, IL: Bahá'í Publishing, 2006), 177.

origins, of climate, of history, of language and tradition, of thought and habit, that differentiate the peoples and nations of the world."[69]

I now focus on the most revered texts of Islam to demonstrate that claims by some Islamic governments that the earlier-mentioned principles are "Western" in origin and un-Islamic in fact have no foundation. The Qur'ān, like other sacred scriptures – and contrary to the horrific violations of religious freedom committed in their name throughout human history – unequivocally affirms liberty of thought, conscience, and religion, as pointed out by many modern-day Muslim scholars.[70] An oft-cited Qur'ānic verse proclaims: "No compulsion is there in religion" (2.257). Another verse also clearly endorses religious diversity and freedom of religion: "To you your religion, and to me my religion!" (109.5). The Qur'ān forbids contention with nonbelievers and instead requires Muslims to collaborate with them to bring about a more just and moral society: "Help one another to piety and godfearing; do not help each other to sin and enmity" (5.3).

Furthermore, at the societal level, the Qur'ān, while recognizing the right of Muslims to associate in a community, or *umma* (see, e.g., 3.100), simultaneously recognizes a similar right on the part of Jews, Christians, and other "People of the Book." Indeed, it teaches that all of these religions were revealed by one and the same God and that Muslims must in fact accept the teachings of Moses and Christ. Thus, the Qur'ān states: "Say: 'We believe in God, and that which has been sent down on us, and sent down on Abraham and Ishmael, Isaac and Jacob, and the Tribes, and in that which was given to Moses and Jesus, and the Prophets, of their Lord; we make no division between any of them, and to Him we surrender'" (3.78). The Qur'ān also affirms that Christians have the right to govern themselves according to the laws of the New Testament, not Islamic law: "So let the People of the Gospel judge according to what God has sent down therein" (5.51).

VI. TOWARD A NEW SYNTHESIS RELATING TO FREEDOM
TO CHANGE ONE'S RELIGION OR BELIEF

What implications do these principles have for interpreting relevant provisions of international law relating to freedom of religion or belief, and freedom to

---

[69] Shoghi Effendi, *The World Order of Bahá'u'lláh: Selected Letters by Shoghi Effendi*, 2nd rev. ed. (Wilmette, IL: Bahá'í Publishing Trust, 1974), 41.

[70] See, e.g., Abdulaziz A. Sachedina, "Freedom of Conscience and Religion in the Qur'an," in David Little, John Kelsay, and Abdulaziz A. Sachedina, *Human Rights and the Conflict of Cultures: Western and Islamic Perspectives on Religious Liberty* (Columbia: University of South Carolina Press, 1988), 53, 76.

change one's religion or belief and teach it to others? What response do they offer to the various challenges to these freedoms I have earlier outlined?

First, freedom of thought and conscience, and freedom to choose or change one's religion or belief, must be seen as absolute freedoms. There are no grounds whatsoever for restricting them. Indeed, a careful reading of Article 18(1) of the ICCPR confirms this view, as asserted by the Human Rights Committee as well as the UN's former Special Rapporteur on Freedom of Religion or Belief, Mrs. Asma Jahangir.

For example, in General Comment No. 22, the Human Rights Committee affirmed that "Article 18 distinguishes the freedom of thought, conscience, religion or belief from the freedom to manifest religion or belief. It does not permit any limitations whatsoever on the freedom of thought and conscience or on the freedom to have or adopt a religion or belief of one's choice. These freedoms are protected unconditionally, as is the right of everyone to hold opinions without interference in article 19.1."[71] The committee also declared that freedom of religion or belief includes the right "to replace one's current religion or belief with another or to adopt atheistic views, as well as the right to retain one's religion or belief."[72] To the extent the text of Article 18 of the ICCPR or other relevant provisions of international law, such as Article 18 of the Universal Declaration, is open to different interpretations, fundamental ethical principles confirm this point of view.

Second, freedom to *manifest* one's religion or belief in external action is also a vital freedom. Of course, external actions have the potential to impinge on the rights and freedoms of others. Thus, it may be necessary for states to subject these actions to some limitations, as acknowledged in Article 18(3) of the ICCPR. However, these limitations must be interpreted and applied in the strictest way possible.[73]

Turning to the various challenges to freedom to change one's religion or belief, first, religious or secular extremism must be forthrightly rejected. There are simply no ethical grounds, based on fundamental ethical principles, for accepting a form of religious or secular parochialism that denies to adherents of disfavored beliefs, whether religious or nonreligious, the right to accept and act on those beliefs. This is particularly true where this denial is

---

[71] Human Rights Committee, General Comment No. 22, U.N. Doc. CCPR/C/21/Rev.1/Add.4 (1993), para. 3. See also U.N. Doc. A/60/399, para. 46 (former UN Special Rapporteur Asma Jahangir affirms that the rights to adopt, change, or maintain a religion "have an absolute character and are not subject to any limitation whatsoever").

[72] Human Rights Committee, General Comment No. 22, para. 5.

[73] See *ibid.*, para. 8 ("The Committee observes that paragraph 3 of article 18 is to be strictly interpreted.").

justified by the asserted need to "protect" one or more favored religions, or to prevent "defamation" of them. The free choice of individuals to leave a particular religion, express criticism of it, or join another cannot legitimately be restricted.

Freedom of moral choice, as an essential human right, can be subject to no significant restrictions. Individuals must always be free to choose their own beliefs and, within reasonable bounds, to pilot a course of ethical action that comports with those beliefs, regardless of which religion or belief system currently enjoys the privileges of state power. Moreover, in light of the fundamental ethical principle of open-minded consultation, individuals should also be free to have access to new ideas and to share their own ideas and religious perspectives with others. There must be an ongoing discussion and debate among people of different religious and nonreligious beliefs that should not be chilled by overzealous concern with protecting religious or governmental sensibilities.

Second, according to a perspective anchored in unity in diversity, freedom of religion or belief can indeed reduce conflict and lead to reconciliation between nations and religious groups, which is a desirable goal. In fact, the ideal of unity means not only that the absence of conflict between religious groups is laudable, but also that members of all belief systems should strive toward greater positive understanding and mutual cooperation. They should, ideally, work to recognize ethical principles shared by all the great religions.

Nevertheless, as I have earlier pointed out, an immoderate concern for averting religion-based conflict can lead to accommodations of claims to suppress freedom to change religion or belief in the interest of preventing interreligious strains and strife. The essential ethical principle of freedom of moral choice insists that no such accommodations are permissible. Any individual should always have the right to change his or her belief system, regardless of the impact on the sensibilities of others. Open-minded consultation is required, not forcible suppression of individual conscience. It is only such open-minded consultation, not mere appeals for mutual restraint and "tolerance," that can lead to the deeper interreligious understanding that is a prerequisite for eliminating religion-inspired conflict.

Third, the principle of unity in diversity points to the importance of respecting not just individual liberties, but also the rights of various communities and religious groups. Freedom of religion *is* a right that must be enjoyed by communities as well as individuals.[74] Nevertheless, group rights must be

---

[74] Thus, Peter Danchin rightly says that "some forms of group difference require certain 'group-specific' rights." Danchin, "Suspect Symbols," 37.

exercised within the boundaries of the essential ethical principle of individual freedom of moral choice, and also with regard for the moral ideal of the unity of the entire human family. In short, some rights of religious groups should be regarded as legitimate, but others as illegitimate.

What are legitimate rights of religious communities? In keeping with respect for individual religious liberty, it should be permissible for individuals freely to agree to abide by particular moral rules in their chosen religion, as well as certain governance structures. Indeed, there may well be a place for secular (or religious) governments to confer on religious authorities limited lawmaking and judicial functions with respect to members of their religious communities, particularly in relation to personal status. Some states today give such a role to religious authorities. Furthermore, we have seen that the Qur'ān itself endorses just such a delegation, while simultaneously affirming the impermissibility of any coercion in matters of religion. So long as this delegation does not infringe on the rights of members to choose to exercise their fundamental human rights or not, there is room within international human rights standards for such diversity.

This last caveat is critical. Anyone governed by religious law should freely choose to be so governed and should be free at any time to leave the religious community with which he or she is currently affiliated. Under no circumstances can religious law that enjoys the sanction of state authorities contravene international human rights standards unless adult individuals have consciously and voluntarily consented to accept the authority of that religious law. Individuals are at liberty not to exercise their internationally recognized rights, but this must always be a full and conscious choice that should be freely revocable at all times.

This perspective has obvious implications for "anticonversion" laws aimed allegedly at "protecting" particular communities from outside religious influences, including proselytizing. Although it may be legitimate to restrict proselytizing activities that amount to coercion, in keeping with the overarching principle of freedom of moral choice, restrictions that target teaching activities beyond this narrow category should be regarded as illegitimate. The state has no business making judgments for individuals about the appropriateness of their changing religious beliefs. In fact, to the extent that religious coercion can properly be restricted, only the individual engaging in the coercion, and not the alleged "victim," should be subject to restrictions.

Given the moral importance of freedom of conscience, it would seem that unless the coercive means used are criminal, considered without regard to their connection with proselytizing, it is wrong for governments to penalize this type of conduct using the criminal law. Former UN Special Rapporteur

Mrs. Asma Jahangir has expressed similar doubts about the legality of anticonversion laws under international law. She has affirmed that "conversion is an
essential part of the right to freedom of religion" and that "freedom of conscience is absolute and cannot suffer any limitation."[75] And she has declared
that a "law prohibiting conversion would constitute a State policy aiming at
influencing [an] individual's desire to have or adopt a religion or belief and is
therefore not acceptable under human rights law."[76]

Mrs. Jahangir has furthermore defended the right of missionaries to propa-
gate their religion as a freedom guaranteed under Article 18(1) of the ICCPR.
She affirms that "missionary activity cannot be considered a violation of the
freedom of religion and belief of others if all involved parties are adults able
to reason on their own and if there is no relation of dependency or hierarchy
between the missionaries and the objects of the missionary activities."[77]

Finally, a perspective grounded in unity in diversity has obvious affinities
with certain long-standing liberal theories of rights, but it also differs from them
in a number of respects. We have already seen that it endorses the legitimacy
of recognition of religious communities and thus has a "communitarian"
dimension. At the same time, it emphasizes the ideal of the unity of the whole
human race, not merely mutual tolerance among individuals or disparate
societies.

Perhaps most important, this perspective does not view freedom of religion
or belief as merely one freedom among others. In fact, given the ethical
primacy of the free exercise of individual conscience, this perspective sees
freedom of thought, conscience, and religion as a, if not the, *paramount*
freedom. Because individuals are moral agents with the capacity to recognize
fundamental ethical principles and help humanity to become more united
in its diversity, freedom to change one's religion or belief must be given the
strongest protection by international law. One must have the freedom *to* form
and act on one's conscience and religious beliefs, in addition to, as provided
by the traditional liberal doctrine, freedom *from* governmental interference
with private thought and action.

Accordingly, religious freedom in general, and the freedom to change one's
religion or belief in particular, must be given appropriately firm safeguards in
international law. This means, for example, that any doubts about the character
of a norm protecting religious freedom and freedom to change one's religion
as a norm of customary international law should be resolved in favor of such

[75] *Report of the Special Rapporteur on Freedom of Religion or Belief*, in *Elimination of All Forms
of Religious Intolerance: Note by the Secretary-General*, U.N. Doc. A/61/340 (2006), paras. 55,
59.
[76] U.N. Doc. A/60/399, para. 52.   [77] *Ibid.*, para. 67.

a status. For similar reasons, the norm should be recognized as a *jus cogens* norm, although I cannot fully defend this conclusion in the space available here.[78]

Moreover, it is imperative to strengthen international legal protections for religious freedom, including ideally through the adoption of a treaty that spells out clearly and unequivocally the broad range of specific rights that must be part and parcel of this preeminent right, such as an absolute right to change one's religion or belief and a right to teach one's religion or belief to others. These specific rights must be enjoyed by both individuals and religious communities. As noted earlier, any limitations on them must be narrowly circumscribed. Individuals who believe their religious freedom has been violated should have appropriate avenues of legal recourse. Indeed, it is important to develop international judicial remedies for victims of religious human rights violations, so that no human being is bereft of a remedy for violations of this essential right. Most important, these endeavors should be motivated by a growing recognition among the leaders of the world that freedom of religion or belief, including the liberty to change one's religion or belief, is a prerequisite for the building of a more peaceful and unified world.

---

[78] For a more detailed analysis of the status of freedom to change religion or belief as a norm of customary international law and a *jus cogens* norm, see Lepard, *Customary International Law*, 346–67.

9   Parochialism, Cosmopolitanism, and Justice

Mortimer Sellers

Any careful consideration of the international legal order will reach the same conclusion as every author in this volume, which is that parochialism and cosmopolitanism stand together at the center of the theoretical and historical foundations of international law. The first problem in global justice is where to draw the boundary between the two. The modern law of nations as developed by Grotius, Vattel, and Wheaton began with "those rules of conduct which reason deduces, as consonant to justice and common good, from the nature of the society existing among independent nations."[1] This doctrine assumes both a cosmopolitan standard ("reason") and parochial communities ("nations"). The difficulty lies in distinguishing the proper borders between the jurisdiction of international law, national law, individual autonomy, and other parochial communities of specialized legal order. Justice and the common good determine what is cosmopolitan, what should be parochial, and where to draw the legal boundaries of blood, soil, power, and authority.

Hugo Grotius stated the problem very well when he refuted Carneades' primitive realism at the beginning of his discussion of the laws of war and peace.[2] Law arises from the desire to maintain social harmony,[3] and each person and every social group has its own role to play in doing so.[4] We owe a duty of care and obedience to our fellow citizens, but also to our fellow human beings.[5] The trick is to avoid confusing the law of nations with what is the law

---

[1] See Henry Wheaton, *Elements of International Law*, 8th ed. R. H. Dana (Boston, 1866), chap. I §14 (p. 20), quoting James Madison, *An Examination of the British Doctrine which subjects to capture a Neutral Trade not open in a Time of Peace* (London, 1806), p. 41. For the history and significance of this doctrine, see M. N. S. Sellers, *Republican Principles in International Law* (Basingstoke, 2006).

[2] Hugo Grotius, *De Iure Belli ac Pacis libri tres, In quibus jus Naturae et Gentium, item juris publici praecipua explicantur* (revised ed., Amsterdam, 1646) prolegomena §5.

[3] *Ibid.*, §8.   [4] *Ibid.*, §10.

[5] *Ibid.*, §18; §§22–23.

only of certain peoples and vice versa.[6] Grotius understood that international law governs matters of international concern.[7] Other questions belong to states, or to the people themselves.[8] Tradition excluded rules governing (for example) the acquisition of property from international law,[9] or the seizure of goods for debt,[10] or the decision of nations whether to trade (or not) with others.[11]

Emer de Vattel made a similar distinction. States have their own affairs and interests, about which they deliberate and decide themselves, which makes them moral persons, with rights and obligations of their own.[12] States, like real persons, should therefore remain free and independent, constrained by the rules that are necessary for their common society, but otherwise autonomous.[13] So the laws of international society (as of any society) are legitimate only to the extent that they advance the real interests and happiness of their subjects, both collected in states and separately, as real persons.[14] Vattel recognized that the particular needs and therefore the specific laws of different states will vary vastly from nation to nation.[15] Regulations or practices that make one nation more just may be harmful in another set of circumstances.[16] This means that certain matters of purely national concern should be beyond the interference of any foreign power. Vattel calls these matters the "domestic affairs" of states.[17] For example, every nation has the right to enter into commerce (or not), according to its own judgment.[18] Vattel identified questions of religion[19] and property as being primarily parochial concerns.[20]

Henry Wheaton also distinguished the proper provinces of international and domestic law.[21] Because there is no legislative or judicial authority recognized by all nations (he observed), international law must therefore rest more directly on universal principles of justice than is true in most other jurisdictions,[22] and specifically those rules of international conduct "which . . . best promote the general happiness of mankind."[23] This means that legal requirements may vary, according to the exigencies of different times and circumstances.[24] As independent moral beings, states have zones of "sovereignty" in which others

[6] *Ibid.*, §53.

[7] *Ibid.*, II.7 §1.1. at 170.

[8] *Ibid.*, I.1 §14.1 at 7.

[9] *Ibid.*, II.7 §1.1 at 196.

[10] *Ibid.*, III.2.7. 1 at 447.

[11] *Ibid.*, II.2.13.5 at 118.

[12] Emer de Vattel, *Le Droit des Gens ou principes de la loi naturelle appliqués à la conduite et aux affaires des Nations et des Souverains* (London, 1758), préliminaires §§1–2. at 1.

[13] *Ibid.*, §23.

[14] *Ibid.*, chap. II, §15 at 23–24.

[15] *Ibid.*, §25 at 30.

[16] *Ibid.*, §25 at 30.

[17] *Ibid.*, book I, chap. III, §37 at 38.

[18] *Ibid.*, I. VIII §§90–92 at 84–86.

[19] *Ibid.*, chap. XII.

[20] *Ibid.*, chap. XX.

[21] Henry Wheaton, *Elements of International Law*, 8th ed. R. H. Dana (Boston, 1866).

[22] *Ibid.*, part I, chap. I §1 at 3.

[23] *Ibid.*, I.I.§5 at 6.

[24] Quoting Leibniz, *ibid.*, §11 at 16.

may not interfere.[25] Wheaton viewed some such rights as "absolute" and others as "conditional," according to time and place.[26] Among the "absolute" rights of states are their choices of government[27] and how to regulate property.[28] Within those areas properly subject to the jurisdiction of international law, however, Wheaton repeated August Heffter's observation that all men and all states should be able to claim this global law's protection – and remain subject to its rules.[29]

The necessary balance between cosmopolitan justice and parochial interests, as described by the great publicists of the seventeenth, eighteenth, and nineteenth centuries, reappeared in the twentieth in the carefully worded provisions of the United Nations Charter, which speaks not only of "the equal rights of men and women" but also the rights "of nations large and small."[30] On the one hand, the Security Council may "take such action by air, sea, or land forces as may be necessary to maintain or restore international peace and security,"[31] on the other, "nothing contained in the present Charter shall authorize the United Nations to intervene in matters which are essentially within the domestic jurisdiction of any state."[32] How then to distinguish "domestic" from international concerns? The United Nations Charter speaks of "peace and security,"[33] the "equal rights" of peoples,[34] economic and social development,[35] "human rights" and "fundamental freedoms,"[36] as all being appropriate subjects of international concern[37] – and all members of the organization pledge to take joint and separate action to achieve these purposes.[38]

What is it about commerce, property, and religion (subject to parochial control, according to traditional conceptions of international law) that separates them from peace, security, and rights (more cosmopolitan concerns)? The simplest answer may be that commerce, property, and religion *can* be justly regulated locally, whereas peace, security, and individual human rights *cannot*. Peace between nations *requires* transnational cooperation. The security of nations *requires* transnational enforcement. The rights of individuals against the state *require* some outside authority to make them real. In contrast, local regulation of commerce, property, and religion can continue without harming

---

[25] *Ibid.*, II.1 §60 at 75.
[26] *Ibid.*
[27] *Ibid.*, II. 1 §72 at 100.
[28] *Ibid.*, II.2 §78 at 111.
[29] *Ibid.*, I.I §10 at 14.
[30] Charter of the United Nations (1945), Preamble.
[31] *Ibid.*, Article 42.
[32] *Ibid.*, Article 2 §7.
[33] *Ibid.*, Article 1 §1.
[34] *Ibid.*, Article 1 §2.
[35] *Ibid.*, Article I §3.
[36] *Ibid.*
[37] *Ibid.*, Article 1.
[38] *Ibid.*, Article 56. *Cf.* Article 55.

international relations or violating individual rights too much. International law has a presumption in favor of localism and national (and personal) independence. International standards apply only when justice and the common good require their enforcement. The Charter of the United Nations identifies a fundamental human need when it speaks of developing "friendly relations among nations based on respect for equal rights and self-determination of peoples"[39] and "fundamental freedoms for all."[40] Both people and peoples want and should have as much independence as possible, consistent with justice and the common good.

1. PAROCHIALISM

The justified parochialism protected by international law reflects the same simple truth that animated the movement for decolonization, the great revolutions of the eighteenth century, and human resistance everywhere against tyranny and oppression: that liberty consists in the freedom to do everything that injures no one else,[41] and that law may legitimately constrain us *only* to serve the common good of society as a whole and for no other purpose.[42] Otherwise the law should leave us free to govern our own lives – individually and collectively – as we see fit.[43] International law has recognized these parochial benefits of liberty and independence from the beginning and has applied them to states as well as to individual human beings.[44] The Universal Declaration of Human Rights reaffirmed the same values as a General Assembly Resolution,[45] and the International Covenant on Civil and Political Rights[46] and the International Covenant on Economic, Social and Cultural

---

[39] *Ibid.*, Article 1 §2. [40] *Ibid.*, 1 §3.
[41] Déclaration des droits de l'homme et du citoyen (1789), Article IV.
[42] *Ibid.*, Article V.
[43] See Mortimer Sellers "An Introduction to the Value of Autonomy in Law," in M. N. S. Sellers (ed.), *Autonomy in the Law* (Dordrecht, 2008), 1 ff.
[44] See, e.g., Emer de Vattel, *Le Droit des Gens ou principes de la loi naturelle appliqués à la conduite et aux affaires des Nations et des Souverains* (London, 1758), préliminaires §4 at 2: "Les Nations étant composées d'hommes naturellement libres et indépendans et qui avant l'établissement des Sociétés Civiles, vivoient ensemble dans l'état de nature; les Nations, ou les Etats souverains, doivent etre considérés come autant de personnes libres... [et] le Corps de la Nation, l'Etat, demeure absolument libre et indépandant, à l'égard de tous les autres hommes." *Cf.* Emmanuelle Jouannet, *Emer de Vattel et l'émergence doctrinale du droit international classique* (Paris, 1998).
[45] Universal Declaration of Human Rights (December 10, 1948), General Assembly Resolution 217 A (III).
[46] International Covenant on Civil and Political Rights, adopted for signature 16 December, 1966, entered into force 23 March, 1976.

Rights[47] comprehensively restated them in the form of treaties. Both covenants begin by recognizing that "the inherent dignity" and "equal and inalienable rights of all members of the human family" are "the foundation of freedom, justice and peace in the world"[48] and that "all peoples have the right of self-determination" and therefore to "freely determine their political status and freely pursue their economic, social and cultural development."[49]

The commitment to the self-determination of persons and of peoples that is at the heart of modern international law regards states or nations as rightfully free and independent because the real individual persons that compose them are rightfully free and independent.[50] This essentially parochial commitment to freedom and independence is also cosmopolitan, because it rests on universal recognition of "the equal rights of men and women and of nations large and small."[51] Because law exists to vindicate these individual and collective rights, coercion and the use of "armed force" may be justified only to promote the "common interest,"[52] sometimes equated with the "purposes of the United Nations."[53] Thus the "self-determination" or parochial jurisdiction of states arises by analogy and direct delegation from the self-determination and rightful autonomy of real human beings, who associate in states to promote their collective welfare. The direct dependence of international (and justified domestic) law on the common good of the people reconciles the universal standard of reason with the parochial circumstances of particular states.[54]

The international human rights covenants identify the political status of peoples, their economic affairs, and their social and cultural development as being the primary focus of their "self-determination" and therefore of the parochial jurisdiction of states.[55] "Self-determination" in this sense, as elaborated in the International Covenant on Civil and Political Rights, takes place through "genuine periodic elections which shall be by universal and equal suffrage" and "held by secret ballot, guaranteeing the free expression of the will

---

[47] International Covenant on Economic, Social and Cultural Rights, adopted for signature 16 December, 1966, and entered into force 3 January, 1976.

[48] This phrase begins the preamble in both covenants and is taken from the Preamble to the Universal Declaration of Human Rights (1948).

[49] Both covenants contain these phrases in Article 1, Section 1.

[50] Vattel, *Le Droit des Gens*, at préliminaires §4 at 2.

[51] United Nations Charter (1945), Preamble.

[52] *Ibid.*   [53] *Ibid.*, Article 2, Section 4.

[54] See M. N. S. Sellers, "The Republican Foundations of International Law," in Samantha Bessen and José Luis Martí (eds.), *Legal Republicanism* (Oxford, 2009), pp. 187–204.

[55] See the shared article 1 §1 of the International Covenants on Civil and Political and Economic, Social and Cultural Rights.

of the electors."[56] Each people's collective right separately to pursue its own economic, social, and cultural development in this way nevertheless remains subject to the economic, social, and cultural rights of individual persons, and also to their civil and political rights, which constrain the scope of the self-determination of the community as a whole.[57] Every state party to the international human rights covenants undertakes "to respect and ensure to all individuals subject to its jurisdiction" their civil and political rights[58] and "to achiev[e] progressively" their subjects' individual economic, social and cultural rights.[59]

States exercising their parochial jurisdiction over economic, social, and cultural questions must therefore use "all appropriate means" including "particularly" the adoption of legislative measures to achieve the "full realization" of their subjects' economic, social, and cultural rights.[60] This leaves them some latitude in practice but also considerably constrains the nature of "domestic" laws concerning the right to work (as described in Article 6 of the International Covenant on Economic Social and Cultural Rights), the right to fair wages (Article 7), to trade unions (Article 8), to social security (Article 9), to marriage (Article 10), to an adequate standard of living (Article 11), to health (Article 12), to education (Article 13), and so forth.[61] This detailed list, as elaborated in the International Covenant on Economic, Social and Cultural Rights, gives a more nuanced sense of the class of economic, social, and cultural interests that are subject (broadly speaking) to the self-determination of peoples, as expressed through parochial legal institutions.

The common thread in these economic, social, and cultural questions, which differentiates them from the more universal or cosmopolitan standards of civil and political justice, is their susceptibility to local conditions. The availability of work, the nature of fair wages, what constitutes social security, or would count as an adequate standard of living are all highly variable, depending on local circumstances. The state's capacity to offer health care or the nature of a suitable education will also vary, depending on a state's history and stage of development. In contrast, the individual right to life (as expressed

---

[56] International Covenant on Civil and Political Rights (1966), Article 25 (b).
[57] See the shared preamble of the International Covenant on Civil and Political Rights and of the International Covenant on Economic Social and Cultural Rights, which seek to create conditions "whereby everyone may enjoy" fully both their civil and political and their economic, social and cultural rights.
[58] International Covenant on Civil and Political Rights (1966), Article 2.1.
[59] International Covenant on Economic, Social, and Cultural Rights (1966), Article 2.1.
[60] *Ibid.*
[61] For a unified list of universal human rights, including economic, social, and cultural rights, see the Universal Declaration of Human Rights (1948).

in Article 6 of the International Covenant on Civil and Political Rights), the right not to be tortured (Article 7), not to be held in slavery (Article 8), or imprisoned for debt (Article 11) are all standards that can be met instantly and with ease in almost all circumstances (except perhaps in cases of extreme public emergency, which threaten the very life of the nation).[62] These are also the areas in which governments or national majorities, expressing their will directly or through freely chosen representatives, can do the most harm to disfavored minorities, in violation of universal standards.

The underlying parochialism of international law arises because the liberty of peoples, like the liberty of individual persons, can tolerate subjection *only* to laws made for the common good and *never* to laws made to serve private purposes or interests. International law therefore properly extends *only* to those subjects for which the common interests of all peoples (and persons) clearly benefit from transnational jurisdiction. Traditional international law, as expressed by the most influential early publicists and perpetuated in the United Nations Charter, has recognized questions of international peace and security, the independence and liberty of peoples, and human rights and fundamental freedoms as being essentially cosmopolitan concerns, whereas economic, social, and cultural questions deserve more parochial consideration. Throughout most of human history, the basic structures of the economy, society, and culture have been primarily local in their development and properly so. Economic, social, and cultural institutions arise in particular times and places, to serve the needs of particular peoples and nations. Most of what is sweetest in life is built in parochial circumstances, among our families, neighbors, and friends.

II. COSMOPOLITANISM

International law arises as different societies come into contact with one another and seek to live together in peace. This leads them to respect certain obvious practices necessary for human cooperation, such as the sanctity of legates, the binding nature of treaties, the duty of good faith, and certain basic limitations on warfare, protecting noncombatants.[63] Each society or state appeals to its own traditions and divinities to justify these standards, but their

---

[62] International Covenant on Civil and Political Rights (1966), Article 4 §1. Cf. The Universal Declaration of Human Rights (1948), Articles 3 to 21 for a similar list of universal civil and political rights.

[63] On very early international law, see David J. Bederman, *International Law in Antiquity* (Oxford, 2001).

central content is obvious, once one accepts the value of occasional cooperation between even generally hostile populations.[64] The Treaty of Kadesh,
for example, concluded between the Hittites and Egyptians, in the thirteenth
century before the Christian era, records its text in both languages and appeals
to the gods of both peoples as guarantors of their agreement.[65] As commerce
and prosperity advance under these primitive standards of diplomacy, communication with others encourages deeper reflection about human cooperation,
as in Rome, where Marcus Tullius Cicero viewed the world as "a single society of all the peoples and the gods together,"[66] required by justice and the
law of nations, as well as by their separate national laws, not to harm one
another.[67]

A cosmopolitan in the strictest sense might see this world community as
the only one that matters. Diogenes of Sinope, generally credited with having
coined the term "cosmopolitan" to describe his own views, disdained local
attachments in favor of a broader human society.[68] One need not go so far as
he did to embrace cosmopolitan justice as the basis of international law. Hugo
Grotius inaugurated the modern era in the law of nations when he said that
basic doctrines of international law and justice would remain true even if one
were to concede (*etiamsi daremus*) that there is no God.[69] Bypassing divinity
in this way makes cosmopolitan standards possible, separating international
law from local authority or religious affiliation. Once reason and society (not
a particular God or temporal authority) became the shared foundation of
international law,[70] then lawyers could develop common standards for the
community of nations as a whole.[71]

International law is inherently cosmopolitan because law is inherently general. Law purports to govern its similarly situated subjects the same, impartially,
and with "equality," even when they are states.[72] "Fundamental human rights,"
"the dignity and worth of the human person," "the equal rights of men and
women and of nations large and small," and indeed "justice" itself are all transcendent values, governing all nations, as recognized by their commitment

[64] *Ibid.*, Bederman's useful study draws examples primarily from the ancient civilizations of
Mesopotamia, Syria, and Egypt, but the same could be done of any region or period in which
politically separate societies come into contact with one another.
[65] See Stephen H. Langdon and Alan H. Gardiner, "The Treaty of Alliance between Hattusili,
King of the Hittites and the Pharaoh Ramesses II of Egypt" 6 *Journal of Egyptian Archaeology*
179 (1920).
[66] M. Tullius Cicero, *De legibus*, I. vii. 23.   [67] M. Tullius Cicero, *De officiis*, III. v. 23.
[68] Diogenes Laertius, VI, 63.
[69] Hugo Grotius, *De Iure Belli ac Pacis*, prolegomena §11.
[70] *Ibid.*, prolegomena §8.   [71] *Ibid.*, prolegomena §§25–26.
[72] See, e.g., Charter of the United Nations (1949) at 2(1).

to the United Nations Charter.[73] Thus the "principles of justice and international law" apply to all international disputes.[74] Early scholars of international law debated whether this made the world a single state or *civitas maxima* (as suggested by Christian Wolff),[75] or separate states subject to a common law (as proposed by Emer de Vattel),[76] but all understood that law must be general, universal, and binding.[77]

General law admits local exceptions in particular circumstances, and international law claims only limited jurisdiction in domestic affairs, so the simple fact of cosmopolitan justice does not explain the actual scope of cosmopolitan law, in the face of parochial particularities. Peace, war, and fundamental rights, both personal and political, have been the special province of international law,[78] whereas economic, social, and cultural affairs such as commerce, property, and religion have remained primarily domestic concerns.[79] Cosmopolitan justice begins with the insight that "all members of the human family" are "equal" in dignity and rights.[80] "Rights," in this sense, precede positive law and embrace all human beings, simply in virtue of their humanity.[81] The freedom and independence of nations (on this theory) derive from the freedom and independence of their citizens, as subjects of international law.[82] Global justice can only emerge when people accept their participation in this broader human society.

The "principles of justice and international law" on which the current world order purports to rest,[83] begin by assuming the "equal rights" and "self determination" of peoples.[84] The members of the United Nations, which now include almost all the nations of the world, have pledged not only to support and advance these principles themselves, but also to impose them on states that are not members of the United Nations, in the interest of international peace

---

[73] *Ibid.*, Preamble.   [74] *Ibid.*, Art. 1(1).

[75] Christian Wolff, *Jus Gentium Methodo Scientifica Pertractatum, in quo Jus Gentium Naturale ab eo, quod Voluntarii, Pactitii et Consuetudinarii est accurate distinguitur* (Frankfurt and Leipzig, 1764), prolegomena §§9–10, at 3–4.

[76] Emer de Vattel, *Le Droit des Gens: ou Principes de la Loi naturelle, appliqués à la conduite et aux affaires des Nations et des Souverains* (London, 1758), préface, p. xvii; préliminaires §8 at 4.

[77] See, e.g., Lassa Oppenheim, *International Law: A Treatise* (London, 1905), 3.

[78] As noted by the authors discussed earlier and reflected in the structure of the United Nations Charter and accompanying covenants.

[79] This may be becoming less true as the globalization of culture and communication alter local circumstances.

[80] Universal Declaration of Human Rights (December 10, 1948).

[81] Vattel, *Le Droit de Gens*, préliminaires §4 at 2.

[82] *Ibid.*, §§4–6 at 2–4.   [83] Charter of the United Nations, Article 1(1).

[84] *Ibid.*, Article 1(2).

and security.[85] This gives a good starting point from which to determine the properly universal elements in international law,[86] including some principles so fundamental that they admit no exceptions, even by treaty. The Vienna Convention on the Law of Treaties describes these fundamental principles as "peremptory norms" or "*ius cogens*" from which "no derogation" is permitted.[87] In defining this category of norms, the International Law Commission contemplated such violations as the use of force contrary to the principles of the charter, acts criminal under international law, and long-established prohibitions against slavery, piracy, and genocide.[88] Violations such as these share strong implications for peace, security, and fundamental human rights. They are offenses against every separate state in the international community, as well as the society of nations as a whole.[89]

The peremptory and cosmopolitan nature of universal international law logically precedes and ultimately justifies the whole superstructure of the modern law of nations. Emer de Vattel, who systematized and simplified the previous scholarship, began by identifying both what he called the "necessary" law of nations, always to be respected and obeyed by all nations and sovereigns everywhere,[90] and a "voluntary" law of nations, arising from common good and welfare of all.[91] The first depends on eternal truths, the second on circumstances, but both are universal and precede the will or consent of states.[92] Vattel said of states what has often been said of individuals; that the wisest and safest policy begins with justice.[93] Because the necessary law of nations is not subject to change, and the obligations it imposes are peremptory and admit no derogation, states cannot alter these fundamental principles by agreement, nor individually nor mutually release themselves from it.[94]

III. JUSTICE

The purpose of law and the international community is justice, as recognized by the Charter of the United Nations,[95] but also by human nature,

---

[85] *Ibid.*, Article 1(6).

[86] For the definition of "universal International Law," as opposed to "particular International Law," see, e.g., Lassa Oppenheim, *International Law: A Treatise* (London, 1905) at 3.

[87] Vienna Convention on the Law of Treaties (1969) Art. 53.

[88] Report of the International Law Commission 1966, Vol. II, Part II, 248.

[89] Case concerning the Barcelona Traction, Light and Power Company Ltd. (*Belgium v. Spain*), February 5, 1970, *International Court of Justice Reports* 1970, §33.

[90] Vattel, *Le Droit des Gens*, préface, p. xxi.   [91] *Ibid.*

[92] *Ibid.* Vattel identified international law created by the will or consent of nations as "arbitrary" international law.

[93] *Ibid.*, p. xxiv.   [94] *Ibid.*, préliminaires, §9 at 4.

[95] Charter of the United Nations, Preamble.

which demands justice in all communities, whenever it can.[96] Like all law, international law deserves our obedience and respect only when it is just, or more conducive to justice than other available arrangements.[97] The necessary connection between law and justice has particular prominence in the case of international law, which lacks the strong coercive mechanisms of other legal systems. Persons, peoples, and nations obey international law primarily because they perceive it to be just, or others do so, and states fear the burdens or opprobrium of lawlessness, whether internal or external – judged both in conscience and in public opinion – which dissuades us from transgression.[98] What Vattel called "necessary" international law arises directly from justice applied to the society of states, but so does the "voluntary" law of nations, although it is variable.[99] Both the "cosmopolitan" and the "parochial" in international law arise from justice, and justice draws the line between the two.

Aggression, war crimes, crimes against humanity, genocide, piracy, and slavery – the barest list of "necessary," *ius cogens*, and *erga omnes* violations of international law – all have it in common that they are also violations of fundamental justice. The same is true of those rights listed in the International Covenant of Civil and Political Rights as admitting no derogation, even in times of emergency – including the rights to life, against torture, against slavery, against ex post facto laws; the right to legal personality; and freedom of thought, conscience, and religion.[100] Rights such as these, which derive from the inherent dignity of the human person and extend to "all members of the human family," are "the foundation of freedom, justice and peace in the world," according to the Rights Covenants[101] and the Universal Declaration.[102] When the governments of states violate these rights, contrary to international law, they become subject to "rebellion" and other appropriate sanctions against "tyranny and oppression."[103]

The recognition and stronger institutional embodiment of global justice in international law has pursued a constant and still unfinished process of globalization, through which universal truths became universal standards, giving

---

[96] See, e.g., M. Tullius Cicero, *De re publica*, I, 39.

[97] This is self-evident but elaborated a little in M. N. S. Sellers, "Regents Lecture: The Value and Purpose of Law" in 33 *University of Baltimore Law Review* 146 (2004).

[98] See Allen Buchanan, *Justice, Legitimacy, and Self-Determination: Moral Foundations for International Law* (Oxford, 2004).

[99] Vattel, *Droit des Gens*, préliminaires, §21 at 11–12.

[100] International Covenant on Civil and Political Rights (1966), Art. 4.

[101] *Ibid.*, Preamble. *Cf.* Preamble to the International Covenant on Economic, Social and Cultural Rights (1966).

[102] Universal Declaration of Human Rights (December 10, 1948), Preamble.

[103] *Ibid.*

way to ever more specific restatements of the law, and finally to transnational enforcement against persistent violators. Universal human rights, for example, were well known and their content comprehensively established as early as 1789, when the Déclaration des droits de l'homme et du citoyen restated universal principles of justice to justify the French Revolution to the world.[104] The North American states separately and collectively recognized these universal rights in their own constitutions and also in the Federal Constitution, as amended in 1791.[105] However, each state claimed jurisdiction to interpret these fundamental and universal rights as applied to their own citizens, so it took many years and a constitutional amendment to shift interpretive authority in North America from the state to the federal level.[106] European states similarly recognized and protected universal rights in their national laws but established their own transnational Court of Human Rights only in 1959, in a tentative and very attenuated form.[107]

Americans in the nineteenth century and Europeans in the twentieth were followed by Latin Americans[108] and Africans[109] in establishing regional courts to administer some of the more cosmopolitan elements of international law, although the very presence of these regional arrangements indicates the possibility of continental divergences in the interpretation of universal rules.[110] The development of regional arrangements confirmed the perception that to "establish Justice" (in one influential early formulation), states would have to cede authority in some areas to broader authorities to achieve and protect these transnational standards.[111] "Justice" within and between states implies taking the interests and well-being of others – both separately and collectively – equally into account. Grotius derived international law from the *oikeiosis* of the Stoics, defined as the desire to live in harmony with others.[112] The whole

---

[104] Déclaration des Droits de L'Homme et du Citoyen (August 26, 1789).

[105] Constitution of the United States of America, Amendments I–IX. (1791).

[106] Constitution of the United States of America, Amendment XIV (1868). See M. N. S. Sellers "Universal Human Rights in the Law of the United States," in LVIII *American Journal of Comparative Law* 533 (2010).

[107] For the emergence of the European Court, see A. H. Robertson, "The European Court of Human Rights," 9 *American Journal of Comparative Law* 1 (1960).

[108] Statute of the Inter-American Court on Human Rights (1980).

[109] A Protocol to the African Charter on Human and Peoples' Rights on the Establishment of an African Court on Human and Peoples' Rights, entered into force January 25, 2004.

[110] See Arnulf Becker Lorca, "Universal International Law: Nineteenth-Century Histories of Imposition and Appropriation," in 51 *Harvard Journal of International Law* (2010), for an interesting discussion of the process through which regional variations were set aside in the nineteenth century.

[111] Constitution of the United States of America (1787), Preamble.

[112] Hugo Grotius, *De Jure Belli ac Pacis Libri Tres*, revised edition (Amsterdam, 1646), prolegomena, §6.

secret of international law, like law generally, has been to extend the community of law and justice beyond one's closest neighbors to the fellowship of humanity as a whole.[113]

Global justice, understood as the foundation of international law, rests on a human ability to perceive common elements, in the nature of humanity, which allow us to live together in peace.[114] What harms, but also what encourages other humans, is accessible to reason, and therefore to law[115] – a common law of humanity.[116] These common elements of universal justice provide the backbone of international law, separate and apart from the locally developed justice of particular places and peoples.[117] The parochial justice of local circumstances may be expressed either by removing certain subjects entirely from the jurisdiction of international law – as in the economic, social, and cultural exclusions of the publicists – or by recognizing in unusually situated states or individuals exceptional rights or duties or exemptions.[118] Just as in national societies, the wealthy or well-educated often have special obligations and the poor or underprivileged receive special support, so too in international society some states are better situated than others to be useful, and other states and their peoples require the assistance of their neighbors.[119]

This variable nature of justice, which treats ostensibly "equal" states differently, according to their differing circumstances, introduces enormous complexity into the practical application of international law. General rules dividing the "domestic jurisdiction" of states from the universal jurisdiction of international law will be comparatively easy to apply and adjudicate, because they admit of general answers. When states or persons claim special treatment, the calculation becomes more complicated. Yet justice must make distinctions, when the nature of human society requires it. The paradoxical solution to this dilemma arises from the inescapable differences between states and real persons. While international law arises for the most part from the obvious analogy between states as "moral persons" and the real human persons who

---

[113] In this as in much else, Grotius adopted explanations and vocabulary already well developed by Cicero and the Stoics, who recognized this need for human society as the ultimate basis of law: "societatis custodia, humano intellectui conveniens, fons est ejus juris, quod proprie tali nomine appellatur." *Ibid.*, §8.

[114] Grotius expressed this well. *Ibid.*, §9.   [115] *Ibid.*, §9.

[116] *Ibid.*, §28 "inter populos jus commune."

[117] Here too the fundamental premisses of Grotius illustrate both the simplicity and the antiquity of these observations. *Ibid.*, §30.

[118] See, e.g., Gerry Simpson, *Great Powers and Outlaw States: Unequal Sovereigns in the International Legal Order* (Cambridge, 2004).

[119] See the essays collected in Ian Shapiro and Lea Brilmayer, eds. *Global Justice* (New York, 1999).

comprise them,[120] and a dwarf should be in the eyes of the law "as much a man as a giant,"[121] it does not follow that Switzerland stands in the same position as France. Because states derive their rights and privileges from the rights of the real persons who comprise them, so justice among states depends on justice among real persons: compatriots in the universal society of human beings.

IV. THE DOMESTIC JURISDICTION OF STATES

We have seen that the classic tradition of international law made a general distinction among economic, social, and cultural concerns (properly the province of national governments) and peace, security, and fundamental rights (more usually the province of international law). This well-established distinction between "the domestic jurisdiction of states"[122] and "the principles of justice and international law"[123] assumes that certain standards are best set locally in response to local conditions.[124] Such divisions of sovereignty and responsibility have a long history, as in the U.S. Constitution, which establishes federal law as "supreme,"[125] while at the same time reserving other powers "to the States" or "to the People,"[126] or in the Treaty on European Union, which seeks to establish an "ever closer Union,"[127] by giving the Union "exclusive competence" in certain areas,[128] while at the same time embracing a principle of "subsidiarity" through which decisions should be taken "as closely as possible" to the citizen.[129]

---

[120] This analogy was best and most influentially made by Christian Wolff, *Jus Gentium Methodo Scientifica Pertractatum* (Frankfurt and Leipzig, 1764).

[121] Emer de Vattel, *Le Droit des Gens: ou principes de la Loi naturelle, Appliqués à la Conduite et aux affaires des nations et des Souverains* (London, 1758), préliminaires, §18 at 11: "Un Nain est aussi bien un homme, qu'un Géant: Une petite République n'est pas moins un État Souverain que le plus puissant Roïaume."

[122] See Charter of the United Nations (1945) at Art. 2(7).

[123] *Ibid.*, at Art. 1(1).

[124] See Vattel, *Droit des Gens*, book I, chap. III, §37 at 38 on the separate jurisdiction of states over their own "affaires domestiques."

[125] See Constitution of the United States, Art. XI: "The Constitution and the Laws of the United States which shall be made in pursuance thereof; and all Treaties made, or which shall be made, under the Authority of the United States, shall be the Supreme Law of the Land; and the Judges in every State shall be bound thereby, any Thing in the Constitution or Laws of any State to the contrary notwithstanding."

[126] *Ibid.*, Amendment X.   [127] Treaty on European Union, Preamble.

[128] Treaty on the Functioning of the European Union, Art. 2(1).

[129] Treaty on European Union, Preamble; Article 5(3): "Under the principle of subsidiarity, in areas which do not fall within its exclusive competence, the Union shall act only if and in so far as the objectives of the proposed action cannot be sufficiently achieved by the Member States . . . [or is] better achieved at the Union level."

The concept of the domestic jurisdiction of states arises from a the widely shared perception that international institutions should act only to advance objectives that cannot otherwise be "sufficiently achieved" by states (or by regional or local governments)[130] and that measures taken by international authorities should be "necessary and proper"[131] or "proportional"[132] to their legitimate objectives. This makes the breadth of domestic jurisdiction dependent on the state of international relations or of international society, and therefore variable over time.[133] The United Nations General Assembly made it clear as early as 1946 that states may not shield racist human rights violations behind their "domestic" jurisdiction.[134] This raises an analogy with European and North American regional institutions, which place human rights above the domestic jurisdiction of states, to make them more secure.[135] The experience of regional associations makes clear that greater cultural and commercial integration generally lead to broader international jurisdiction, to prevent local injustice.

The legal history of the United States provides a striking example of the narrowing of domestic jurisdiction in the face of changing circumstances. The Constitution of 1789 brought traditionally domestic concerns such as commerce, currency, and war under federal jurisdiction,[136] while still seeking to relegate issues of civil rights and slavery to the "domestic" jurisdiction of the separate states.[137] However, it proved impossible to confine the supposedly "domestic" institution of slavery within state boundaries.[138] The whole

---

[130] *Ibid.*, Article 5(3).
[131] Constitution of the United States, Article I §8.
[132] Treaty on European Union, Article 5(4).
[133] See, e.g., "Nationality Decrees Issued in Tunis and Morocco on Nov. 8th, 1921," Advisory Opinion, 1923 P.C.I.J. (Ser. B) No. 4 (Feb 7), par. 40: "The question whether a certain matter is or is not solely within the jurisdiction of a State is an essentially relative question; it depends upon the development of international relations."
[134] U.N.G.A. Res. 44 (I) (December 8, 1946) on the Treatment of Indians in the Union of South Africa. *Cf.* Charter of the United Nations (1945) Articles 55 and 56; *Universal Declaration of Human Rights*, U.N.G.A. res. 217A (III) (December 10, 1948).
[135] Constitution of the United States of America, Amendment XIV (July 9, 1868); Convention for the Protection of Human Rights and Fundamental Freedoms (signed November 4, 1950) and Protocol 11 (entered into force November 1, 1998).
[136] Constitution of the United States of America (1787) Art. I §8.
[137] See, e.g., *Barron v. Baltimore*, 32 U.S. (7 Pet.) 243 (1833).
[138] See, John C. Calhoun et al., "The Southern Address" in *The Works of John C. Calhoun*, vol. VI at 290: "It is not for them, nor for the Federal Government to determine, whether our domestic institution is good or bad; or whether it should be repressed or preserved. It belongs to us, and us only, to decide such questions." Compare *The American Review* no. XV (March, 1849), 232: "'Slavery,' he says, 'is a domestic institution,' and therefore no man must meddle with it. But it is of the very essence of despotism that it *is* domestic" and see William Wells Brown, *I have no Constitution and no Country* in the *Liberator* (November 2, 1849): "They can find no apology in the fact of slavery being a domestic institution."

political and constitutional development of the United States since 1776 has been an exercise in determining the boundaries of domestic jurisdiction in "free and independent states,"[139] when states have a duty to respect the "life, liberty . . . [and] property" of their subjects.[140] Peace, security, and fundamental rights now clearly transcend "domestic" jurisdiction, but with the passage of time and greater global integration, so too do many economic, social, and commercial problems, which require (at a minimum) interstate regulation and cooperation.[141] The Supreme Court of the United States has been particularly active in extending federal jurisdiction to economic activity, construed very broadly.[142]

When the Charter of the United Nations reaffirmed and protected the domestic jurisdiction of states after the Second World War,[143] "practically the whole sphere" of international economic relations still fell within the states' "domestic" affairs.[144] However, the consequences of economic dislocation in Europe and elsewhere convinced many lawyers that the promotion of the general welfare in general, and international economic relations in particular, now belonged to international law and "international agencies established for this purpose."[145] The World Trade Organization embodies this transnational consensus on the necessity of an "integrated," "viable," and "durable" "multilateral trading system,"[146] wielding enough independent power to impose a "common institutional framework" on member states.[147] Similar extensions of international jurisdiction now encompass such previously "domestic" affairs as environmental law,[148] international criminal law,[149] and many other formerly "domestic" areas of economic, social, and cultural significance.[150]

[139] Declaration of Independence (July 4, 1776).
[140] See, Constitution of the United States of America, Amendment XIV §1 (July 28, 1868).
[141] For a variety of views on this broader question, see Ian Shapiro and Lea Brilmayer, eds., *Global Justice* (New York, 1999).
[142] See, e.g., *Wickard v. Filburn*, 317 U.S. 111 (1942).
[143] Charter of the United Nations (1945) Art. 2(7).
[144] See, e.g., D. J. L. Davies, "Domestic Jurisdiction: A Limitation on International Law," in 32 *Transactions of the Grotius Society* 60 (1946), at 65.
[145] *Ibid.*, 66, quoting the committee appointed by the American and Canadian Bar Associations during the Second World War to consider the future of international law.
[146] Marrakesh Agreement Establishing the World Trade Organization, Preamble.
[147] *Ibid.*, Article II (1).
[148] See, e.g., the United Nations Framework Convention on Climate Change (signed May 9, 1992) and its associated protocols.
[149] See, e.g., the Rome Statute of the International Criminal Court (entered in force July 1, 2002).
[150] See, e.g., the Convention on the Elimination of All Forms of Discrimination against Women (entered in force September 3, 1981); Convention Against Transnational Organized Crime (entered in force September 29, 2003); Convention on Biological Diversity (entered in force December 29, 1993); International Covenant on Economic, Social and Cultural Rights

The contraction of the "domestic" jurisdiction of states since the Second World War gives rise to the same concerns on the global level that led to war and constitutional change in nineteenth-century North America,[151] and as in earlier regional debates, the focus has shifted from the validity of transnational "norm setting" to the mechanisms for interpreting and enforcing the relevant norms.[152] Nations in the global "South" have worried that the obvious need to address international problems collectively will give powerful states the cover through which to exercise inappropriate influence over the domestic affairs of less-developed nations.[153] Global problems that require global remedies and therefore fall outside the properly "domestic" jurisdiction of states may nevertheless provide the pretext for inappropriate intervention, when the mechanisms of international enforcement themselves are unreliable.[154]

Drawing the (ever moving) line between the jurisdiction of international law and the essentially domestic jurisdiction of states requires distinguishing cosmopolitan questions from more properly parochial affairs. Understood in this way, the relative power and different material conditions of states matter less than universal human nature and the global community of humanity. The rhetoric of *affaires domestiques* from Vattel[155] to the Charter of the United Nations,[156] minimizes the significantly different circumstances of states. "Developing countries" have from time to time asserted their stark inability to meet the high costs of certain international responsibilities, making it "imperative" that "identical obligations . . . not [be] forced on unequal participants."[157] Real differences in the nature and circumstances of states require that although all states should enjoy "sovereign equality"[158] in matters that are "essentially" within their domestic jurisdiction,[159] many questions of international importance cannot be "essentially" domestic in this way, and will have to admit exceptions.

(entered into force January 3, 1976); United Nations Convention to Combat Desertification (entered into force December 26, 1996); United Nations Convention on Contracts for the International Sale of Goods (entered into force January 1, 1988.)

[151] See, e.g., the Doha Declaration, of the Second South Summit (June 12–16, 2005) G-77/SS/2005/1.

[152] *Ibid.*, par. 10; 15 (viii) recognizing the need to "promote an open, universal, equitable, rule-based, predictable and non-discriminatory multilateral trading system."

[153] *Ibid.*, par 5: "We firmly reject the imposition of laws and regulations with extraterritorial impact."

[154] See, e.g., Antony Anghie, *Imperialism, Sovereignty and the Making of International Law* (Cambridge, 2004).

[155] Emer de Vattel, *Droit des Gens*, book I, chap. III §37 at 38).

[156] Charter of the United Nations (1945) Article 2(7).

[157] Doha Declaration of the Second South Summit (June 12–16, 2005) at par. 4.

[158] Charter of the United Nations, Article 2(1).   [159] *Ibid.*, at Article 2(7).

V. PAROCHIAL EXCEPTIONS TO INTERNATIONAL LAW

Parochial exceptions to general international law may take two forms. First, states or their governments argue that special circumstances exempt them from general rules. Such claims might follow either from inability or from heightened competence. Second, states or their governments might be subject to special limitations arising from their nature or their circumstances. "Great powers," for example, may have a special duty and expanded powers to maintain world order, whereas "outlaw states" have limited capacity under international law.[160] The distinction hinges on which limitations or special powers are most conducive to global justice.[161] The Charter of the United Nations gives special status to "permanent members" of the Security Council for the "maintenance of international peace and security,"[162] while limiting the rights of non-"peace-loving" states,[163] and the Statute of the International Court of Justice perpetuates a long-standing distinction between the "civilized" and "noncivilized" nations.[164]

Many claims for special exemptions depend on the assertion that the governments of states in a "less-developed" condition of society deserve greater freedom of action to advance the material well-being of their subjects. The Doha Declaration of the Second South Summit suggested that "differences in the level of development" warrant "flexibility" and "national policy space" in fulfilling international commitments.[165] The government of China has been particularly active in arguing that the desire of the Chinese people to "eat their fill and dress warmly" makes subsistence "the foremost human right the Chinese people long fight for."[166] As subjects of a "developing country," the people's right of subsistence would be threatened by "social turmoil," and therefore the Chinese government must "maintain national stability" to "concentrate their effort on developing the productive forces along the line which has proven to be successful," so that "subsistence will no longer be threatened."[167]

---

[160] See, e.g., Gerry Simpson, *Great Powers and Outlaw States: Unequal Sovereigns in the International Legal Order* (Cambridge, 2004).

[161] See also Joseph Markus, *Grandes puissances, petites nations et le problème de l'organisation international* (Neuchatel, 1946).

[162] *Charter of the United Nations* (1945), Art. 23(1); 27(3).

[163] *Ibid.*, Article 4(1).

[164] Statute of the International Court of Justice, Article 38(1)(c).

[165] Doha Declaration, Second South Summit (June 12–16, 2005) §4; Cf. §20.

[166] *Human Rights in China*, White Paper of the Chinese Government (November, 1991) §I: "The Right to Subsistence – the Foremost Human Right the Chinese People Long Fight for".

[167] *Ibid.*

The Chinese argument for parochial exemptions from general international law follows John Stuart Mill's well-known observation that peoples in what he called more "backward" states of society may not be ready to enjoy the full liberty of those "in the maturity of their faculties."[168] When the "race itself" is in its "nonage," Mill believed that "a ruler full of the spirit of improvement is warranted in the use of any expedients that will attain an end, perhaps otherwise unattainable."[169] Put more bluntly, Mill frankly accepted that "despotism is a legitimate mode of government in dealing with barbarians, provided the end be their improvement, and the means justified by actually effecting that end."[170] This last point poses difficult problems, however, both in determining which "means" will best serve the "end" of human improvement, and in discovering when society has reached the stage of development that finally suits its people for freedom and full membership in the community of nations.[171] "Until then there is nothing for them" (Mill admitted) "but implicit obedience to an Akbar or a Charlemagne, if they are so fortunate as to find one."[172]

The view that some peoples are "civilized" or "developed" and worthy of full participation in the benefits of general international law, whereas others are "barbarian" or "less-developed" and therefore exempt from ordinary rules raises obvious problems in a world that has accepted the "inherent dignity" and "equal and inalienable rights" of *all* members of the human family as "the foundation of freedom, justice and peace in the world."[173] The Universal Declaration of Human Rights views "tyranny" itself as justifying rebellion and demands a universal "rule of law" against "oppression."[174] This doctrine of human equality that challenged so effectively the pretensions of empire[175] applies equally to the governments of independent states, which lose legitimacy as they deny the rights of their subjects.[176] This makes the line between what count as "civilized" and "uncivilized" (in the technical sense) governments dependent on their fidelity to international law. Governments that cannot meet their obligations to law and their subjects lose rights and stature in the society of nations.

As some nations claim exemption based on weakness, so others claim privilege for strength. United States public officials have suggested that the world's

---

[168] John Stuart Mill, "On Liberty" (1859) in Stefan Collini (ed.), *On Liberty and Other Writings* (Cambridge, 1989), 13.

[169] *Ibid.*   [170] *Ibid.*, 13–14.

[171] *Ibid.*, 14.   [172] *Ibid.*

[173] Universal Declaration of Human Rights (1948), Preamble.

[174] *Ibid.*

[175] See, e.g., *An Address on the Conduct of Christian and Civilized Nations toward those Less Civilized and Enlightened* (London, 1858).

[176] See, e.g., Brad R. Roth, *Governmental Illegitimacy in International Law* (Oxford, 1999).

most powerful military nation has a special responsibility to protect peace and security and lead multinational humanitarian and other interventions to enforce international law. American soldiers and public officials therefore occupy a special position and should not be subject to the same enforcement mechanisms as other nations, which might hinder "peacekeeping" and other operations.[177] States that play "exceptional" roles in the international community require "exceptional" privileges, on this theory, which places the most powerful nations outside the ordinary law of nations.[178] Here too the claim for parochial exceptions seems subject to abuse.[179] As in the case of exemptions claimed by less-developed states, the governments of the most-developed nations will be faulty and biased judges of their own special privileges and powers.

These brief examples from well-known cases illustrate the obvious difficulties that arise in allocating special exemptions from international law. The problem with parochial exceptions is not so much that they exist and can be justified, as who will be the judge. Just as the well-known and broadly established lines between cosmopolitan international law and parochial domestic affairs require specification in particular cases, so special cases and exemptions will need to be identified in practice. As a general rule, culture and commerce are parochial, and peace, security, and rights are cosmopolitan. More authoritarian governments may in fact be justified in some circumstances as necessary to meet the needs of less-developed nations, and great powers may deserve special privileges to support their heightened responsibilities. Nonetheless, drawing such lines will be difficult in practice and subject to abuse.

VI. DRAWING THE LINES

Given that many legal questions do still properly fall within the domestic jurisdiction of states, and that states both weak and powerful may sometimes deserve special privileges or exemptions from general international law, the central problem in global justice is not so much the recognition of parochial difference – or cosmopolitan unity – as it is determining in particular cases where to draw the line. The broad boundaries between more cosmopolitan security or personal rights and more parochial culture, economics, or religion

---

[177] See, e.g., the American Service-Members' Protection Act (August, 2002).
[178] On American exceptionalism, *see* Michael Ignatieff (ed.) *American Exceptionalism and Human Rights* (Princeton, 2005).
[179] See, e.g., Memorandum for Alberto R. Gonzales, Counsel to the President Re: Standards of Conduct for Interrogation under 18 U.S.C. §§2340–2340A.

have been well established for centuries, as have certain special exemptions for "great powers" and "less-developed" states, but changing circumstances move the proper placement of these lines, and ambiguity invites error. Global justice serving a global society calls out for global authorities to police the borders of international law, but no such transcendent authority exists. The mechanics of specification in particular cases must depend on more diffuse authorities to constrain the self-judgment (and self-interest) of states.

More developed legal systems have more hierarchical methods of specification, as in the United States, where the Supreme Court polices the boundaries of public powers,[180] or in the European Union, where the Court of Justice of the European Union determines whether member states are in compliance with the treaties.[181] Yet although the Charter of the United Nations gives the Security Council power to "determine" whether there has been a breach of (or threat to) the peace, and "decide" the appropriate remedy[182] and offers the International Court of Justice as an arbitrator of disputes between states,[183] no organ has decisive authority to distinguish the jurisdiction of international law from the domestic jurisdiction of states. States and others seeking to discover the limits of their powers under international law must look to the teachings of scholars, or judicial decisions in the various nations, or to treaties between states, or state practice, as in other disputes about the requirements of international law.[184] There is no constitutional court to govern world federalism.

The recent *Kadi* case in the European Court of Justice, which defied the authority of the Security Council,[185] and the *Medellin* case in the United States, in which the Supreme Court denied the authority of the International Court of Justice,[186] both illustrate the limited power of international institutions, but also hint at global standards that might govern the adjudication of boundaries between national and international jurisdiction. The European Court of Justice disallowed European Union implementation of Security Council enforcement measures that violated certain "higher" rules of law,[187] and specifically the principles of liberty, democracy, and respect for human rights and fundamental freedoms.[188] The Supreme Court of the United States

---

[180] See Constitution of the United States, Article III §2 and more recently (e.g.) *Gonzales v. Raich* 545 U.S. 1 (2005).

[181] See Treaty on European Union, Article 259.

[182] Charter of the United Nations, Article 39.   [183] *Ibid.*, Article 94.

[184] The standard list appears in the *Statute of the International Court of Justice*, Article 38.

[185] Joined Cases C-402/05 P and C-415/05 P: Yassin Abdullah Kadi and Al Barakaat International Foundation v. Council of the European Union and Commission of the European Communities.

[186] *Medellín v. Texas*, 552 U.S. 491 (2008).

[187] *Kadi*, par. 288.   [188] *Ibid.*, par. 303 and 304.

disallowed U.S. enforcement of International Court of Justice decisions that violated the democratic self-determination of individual American states.[189]

The same principles of "liberty, democracy, respect for human rights and fundamental freedoms, and the rule of law" that play such a large part in the basic structure of the European Union[190] and in the United States[191] also permeate the purposes and principles of international law, as expressed in the Charter of the United Nations,[192] the Universal Declaration of Human Rights,[193] and the human rights covenants,[194] but without enjoying as well-developed liberal and democratic structures to support them. The Security Council, the International Court of Justice, and other international institutions, as currently constituted, lack the internal constraints of liberty, democracy, and the rule of law necessary to justify decisive authority.[195] This gives liberal, democratic, and law-bound institutions, wherever they may be found, special influence in determining both the content and the boundaries of international law.[196]

The point here is not that undemocratic, illiberal, chaotic, or despotic states do not sometimes deserve to enjoy domestic jurisdiction or special exemptions from international law, depending on their circumstances, but rather that they make poor judges of their own jurisdiction. Liberty, democracy, human rights, and the rule of law all strengthen not only the individual interests of particular citizens, but also the epistemic powers of the state. Because international law and justice rest on the separate and collective dignity of all members of the human family, all humans should be as much as possible, taken into account – and consulted – in constructing the rules of society, whether international, domestic, regional, or local. Here the basic division in the international legal order between parochial and cosmopolitan affairs begins to intersect with the epistemic authority of national and international institutions. Liberty, democracy, human rights, and the rule of law are cosmopolitan concerns precisely because they are necessary preconditions for the self-determination of peoples

[189] *Medellín v. Texas*, 552 U.S. 491 (2008) at p. 35, denied the directive authority of the president of the United States or the International Court of Justice and required an act of the United States Congress to "establish binding rules of decision that preempt contrary state law."

[190] Treaty on European Union, Article 6(1).

[191] Constitution of the United States, Amendment XIV §1.

[192] Charter of the United Nations, Articles 1, 2, 55, 56.

[193] Universal Declaration of Human Rights (1948), especially articles 2 and 21.

[194] Especially common Articles 1 of the International Covenant on Economic Social and Cultural Rights (1966) and the International Covenant on Civil and Political Rights (1966).

[195] See, e.g., *Kadi*, par. 322; 323.

[196] The problem of interpretive authority has been present since the origins of modern international law. Hugo Grotius referred to the "moratiores" as worth of special respect. Hugo Grotius, *De Jure Belli, ac Pacis*, XII.1 at 6.

and the proper specification of law, whether international or domestic. People and peoples cannot "freely determine their political status and freely pursue their economic, social and cultural development"[197] unless they enjoy their international rights and freedoms,[198] including full participation in government and elections.[199]

Drawing the lines between the parochial and cosmopolitan legal orders will be difficult in the absence of liberal democratic and just judicial and political institutions to make the determination. Regional institutions such as the European Court of Justice or the Supreme Court of the United States can approximate international justice as regards their member states, but they necessarily exclude the participation of nonmembers, which weakens their broader authority. This inescapable circumstance of existing international society places great burdens on what Hugo Grotius called the *"moratiores"* among states: those states that broadly respect the fundamental requirements of international law.[200] The history and development of international law make clear in general terms both what the law requires of nations and which matters are essentially "domestic affairs." Those nations and governments that respect their international obligations and the authority of international law in the obvious cases of liberty, rights, democracy, and the rule of law deserve special authority in determining the boundaries of more difficult cases.

VII. SUMMARY AND CONCLUSION

This book and this chapter have set out to understand the relationship between parochialism and cosmopolitanism at the foundation of international law. The great publicists of the seventeenth, eighteenth, and nineteenth centuries – Grotius, Vattel, and Wheaton – and the Charter of the United Nations, which strengthened their project after the Second World War, all agreed that justice and the common good of international society stand at the basis of international law. The law sets a cosmopolitan standard ("justice") for parochial communities ("states" or "nations"), to determine what is cosmopolitan, what should be parochial, and where to draw the boundaries between the two. Speaking very broadly, states, like real persons, should be free and independent, constrained only by those rules that are necessary for their common project of justice. The

---

[197] Common Article I(1) of the International Covenant on Civil and Political Rights (1966) and the International Covenant on Economic, Social and Cultural Rights (1966).
[198] Universal Declaration of Human Rights (1948), Art. 2.
[199] *Ibid.*, Article 21.
[200] Hugo Grotius, *De Jure Belli ac Pacis*, XII.1 at 6.

laws of international society (as of any society) are legitimate only to the extent that they advance the real interests and happiness of their subjects.

Parochial concerns such as culture, commerce, and religion belong to the essentially domestic jurisdiction of states, which requires "self-determination," such that all peoples can freely pursue their economic, social, and cultural development. This pervasive parochialism limits international law to those few subjects where the common interests of all persons (and peoples) clearly benefit from transnational jurisdiction. Throughout most of human history, the basic structures of economy, society, and culture have been primarily local and properly so. Economic, social, and cultural institutions arise in particular times and places to serve the needs of particular peoples and nations. Nothing is dearer than our parochial attachments, constructed from love and experience in familiar places, memories, and lives.

Cosmopolitan justice has a less variable grain, arising from the obvious needs of human society. All this would be true, as Grotius made clear, "even if their were no God," because international law expresses our common humanity. Liberty, equality, and fundamental human rights all have cosmopolitan resonance, because they are "necessary" elements in any just society, including the society of states. This makes international law inherently cosmopolitan, viewing "all members of the human family" with equal concern and respect. Respect entails autonomy, both personal and collective, which makes the (parochial) "equal rights" and "self-determination" of peoples fundamentally cosmopolitan values. "Necessary" international laws precede the will or consent of peoples or of persons, to protect the autonomy of peoples and persons alike. Cosmopolitan justice entails parochial liberty and independence. The cosmopolitan "principles of justice and international law" serve every separate state in the international community, as well as the society of nations as a whole.

Justice alone can justify international law, which deserves our obedience and respect only when it is just, or more just than other available arrangements. The stronger institutional embodiment of global justice in international law since the Second World War has advanced international standards by making them more certain. The purpose of international law has been to extend the community of justice beyond our closest associates to the fellowship of humanity as a whole. What harms, but also what encourages, others is accessible to reason and therefore to the law. These common elements of universal humanity provide the framework of international law, separate and apart from the locally developed justice of particular places and peoples. The parochial justice of local circumstances can be expressed either by removing certain subjects entirely from the jurisdiction of international law or by recognizing the special rights or exemptions of unusually situated states or individuals. Despite these beneficial differences, universal standards of humanity and justice will continue to bind them all.

The *domestic jurisdiction* of states offers one of the best and strongest protections of parochial justice, through which particular local standards receive necessary support. Economic, social, and cultural concerns, in particular, often work best when local authorities retain exclusive competence to decide, but the properly domestic jurisdiction of free and independent states will vary, depending on the changing nature of the world. Many economic, environmental, and immigration questions have become more international as global commerce and communication become more integrated. This natural contraction of the domestic jurisdiction of states raises problems of neoimperialism and global imbalances of power. Real differences in the nature and circumstances of states justify differential treatment, but also invite abuse. Strong general norms of sovereign equality protect the salutary autonomy and self-determination of peoples.

Parochial exceptions to general international law may arise either from the particular strengths or the particular weaknesses of states. "Great powers" (such as the United States) claim special authority to maintain world order, whereas the governments of "less-developed" peoples (such as China) claim special exemptions to regulate or discipline their subjects. Some parochial differences undoubtedly justify special privileges, beyond the domestic jurisdiction protected by general international law, but specification will be very difficult in the absence of a world state. In most cases, the parochial privileges of states adhere to their governments, either in relation to their own people or to the global order of states as a whole. This makes the nature of the governments themselves a significant factor in evaluating their claims of privilege. Illiberal, undemocratic, chaotic, or despotic governments do not have the same authority as states that generally respect the rights and welfare of their citizens or subjects.

Drawing the lines between the jurisdiction of cosmopolitan unity and the power of parochial difference simply raises the same questions again at a higher level of abstraction. Who will be the judge? The principles of liberty, democracy, respect for human rights and fundamental freedoms, and the rule of law take on an even greater importance at this epistemic level than they did in addressing the basic divisions of national and international power. States and governments that respect the liberty to think, the democracy to deliberate, and the personal security and independence necessary for investigation, knowledge, and understanding will make better and more accurate determinations of the line between parochial and cosmopolitan jurisdiction than governments or states that do not. This means that although the rights and privileges of even illiberal and undemocratic powers may often deserve protection, their authority to determine the boundaries (and content) of their international obligations will differ. Universal standards of truth, humanity, and reasonable deliberation patrol the borders of parochial difference and autonomy.

Parochialism and cosmopolitanism are two faces of international law, which recognizes our common humanity by protecting us in our differences. Cosmopolitanism provides a basis for mutual respect, but parochialism precedes universalism, because we belong to local societies first. Peace, justice, and prosperity have advanced in the world as people have expanded their sense of community more widely, but we love what is local, and rightly so. Most social, cultural, and religious life takes place among friends. International law is universal and cosmopolitan with respect to those questions properly subject to its primary jurisdiction, but law exists in part to support the freedom and independence of individual citizens and states. Just as every individual deserves a zone of privacy within which to make her or his own choices (and mistakes), so too every state deserves a broad area of self-determination, within which to construct a national identity. That local affinities are important and worthy of protection has been a guiding principle of international law from the beginning, and nothing is sweeter or more beautiful (as Vattel and Cicero insisted) than when people come together in states to build more just societies among themselves.[201]

---

[201] See the title page of Emer de Vattel, *Le Droit des Gens ou Principes de la Loi Naturelle, Appliqués à la conduite et aux affaires des Nations et des Souverains* (London 1758) quoting Marcus Tullius Cicero, *Somnium Scipionis (De re publica* VI.13): "Nihil est enim . . . acceptius quam concilia coetusque hominum jure sociati, quae Civitates appellantur." *Cf.* M. Tullius Cicero, *De legibus*, II.3.

Index